FROM
Redstone
TO
Ludlow

Mining the American West

SERIES EDITORS

Duane A. Smith ▪ Robert A. Trennert ▪ Liping Zhu

FROM
Redstone
TO
Ludlow

John Cleveland Osgood's
Struggle against the United
Mine Workers of America

F. Darrell Munsell

University Press of Colorado

© 2009 by the University Press of Colorado

Published by the University Press of Colorado
5589 Arapahoe Avenue, Suite 206C
Boulder, Colorado 80303

AAUP The University Press of Colorado is a proud member of
the Association of American University Presses.

The University Press of Colorado is a cooperative publishing enterprise supported, in part, by Adams State College, Colorado State University, Fort Lewis College, Mesa State College, Metropolitan State College of Denver, Regis University, University of Colorado, University of Northern Colorado, and Western State College of Colorado.

∞ The paper used in this publication meets the minimum requirements of the American National Standard for Information Sciences—Permanence of Paper for Printed Library Materials. ANSI Z39.48-1992

Library of Congress Cataloging-in-Publication Data

Munsell, F. Darrell.
  From Redstone to Ludlow : John Cleveland Osgood's struggle against the United Mine Workers of America / F. Darrell Munsell.
    p. cm.   (Mining the American West)
  Includes bibliographical references and index.
  ISBN 978-0-87081-934-6 (alk. paper) — 978-1-60732-100-2 (pbk : alk. paper)
  1. Osgood, John Cleveland, 1851–1926. 2. United Mine Workers of America—History. 3. Coal trade—Colorado—History. 4. Coal miners—Labor unions—Colorado—History. 5. Capitalists and financiers—Colorado—Biography. I. Title.

  HD9550.O8M86 2008
  331.89'0422334092—dc22
  [B]

                                                                2008042491

Design by Daniel Pratt

To the members of the Redstone Historical Society, Colorado Preservation, Inc., Colorado Historical Society, National Trust, Advisory Council on Historic Preservation, and Pitkin County officials who worked together to preserve the Redstone Castle as a historic treasure

John Cleveland Osgood. Courtesy, Denver Public Library, Western History Collection, call no. Z-131.

Contents

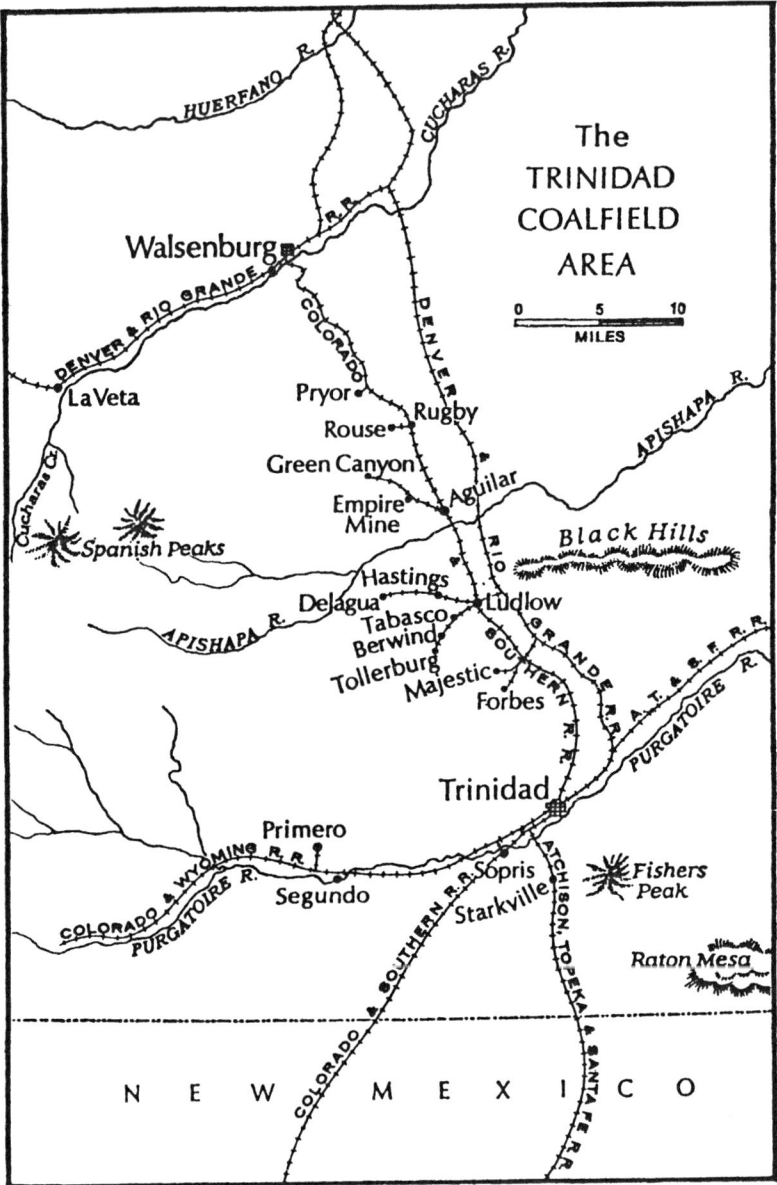

The Trinidad coalfield area. Reproduced by permission from George S. McGovern and Leonard F. Guttridge, The Great Coalfield War (Niwot: University Press of Colorado, 1996), vi.

Preface

I first became interested in John Cleveland Osgood when my wife, Jane, and I stayed at Cleveholm Manor, now more commonly referred to as the Redstone Castle, in early January 1995. Located one mile south of the village of Redstone in western Colorado, this magnificent forty-two–room Tudor Revival mansion was built by Osgood—the wealthiest and most influential of the Colorado coal barons during the late nineteenth and early twentieth centuries—and it served as his country residence until his death in 1926. Although we had visited Redstone numerous times, I had not had the opportunity to tour Cleveholm until that snowy January day. The experience was unforgettable.

We were the only overnight guests at the mansion, then operating as a bed-and-breakfast. With the caretaker's permission, we explored the main rooms of the residence, marveling at the beautiful oak and mahogany paneling, Tiffany light fixtures, and colorful marble fireplaces that reflected the opulence of the era. In the Great Hall we discovered the massive stone fireplace bearing the carved Osgood family crest. We admired the elegant formal dining room and the inviting library, with its gold-accented green leather walls. Each room, upstairs and down, revealed careful attention to detail and fine craftsmanship.

It was clear that Osgood had built the mansion to impress his many guests, including such notables as the John D. Rockefellers (Sr. and Jr.), George Gould, Lord and Lady Lennox of England, and Prince Henri de Croy of Belgium. It has also been reported that Theodore Roosevelt visited Cleveholm while hunting big game on Colorado's western slope. I had no idea that some of the most famous robber barons were part of the Redstone story. Learning that Osgood was a peer among these people prompted me to discover more about him.

After I retired from my teaching position at West Texas A&M University, Jane and I moved to our present home near the Crystal River just a few miles north of the village of Redstone. I then began my research on Osgood. It soon became apparent that his historical legacy extended far beyond Redstone and Cleveholm Manor. Until I learned that Osgood was intimately involved in the Colorado coal strike of 1913–1914 and the Coalfield War, including the Ludlow Massacre, I had intended to focus my research on his economic development of the Crystal River Valley and the founding of Redstone as a model industrial village. However, after ascertaining that Osgood was the most prominent of the Colorado coal operators and their leading spokesperson and strategist in their fight against organized labor, I decided to undertake a more comprehensive study of Osgood's labor-management policies that would transcend the "Redstone experiment" and cover all aspects of his campaign to prevent the United Mine Workers of America (UMWA) from organizing miners in the Colorado coalfields. My objective in writing this book was to mark John C. Osgood's place in U.S. labor history, first as a fierce opponent of organized labor and second as one of the men most responsible for the tragic events that occurred in the southern Colorado coalfields in 1913–1914.

<hr>

A disadvantage of living in one of the most beautiful river valleys in Colorado is that one is far from a major library. I extend my sincere thanks to the interlibrary loan staff of the Garfield County Public Library District for obtaining secondary sources for my research on this project. In particular, I thank Marilyn Murphy, manager of the Gordon Cooper Branch Library in Carbondale, and Liz Campbell, also of the Gordon Cooper Library. I made many trips to Denver to consult primary sources deposited in the Colorado State Archives, the Colorado Historical Society's Stephen H. Hart Library, and the Denver Public Library's Western History/Genealogy Collection. At each of these places, I found the staff members courteous and extremely helpful in assisting me. To all of them, I offer my gratitude.

Access to the Internet allowed me to obtain copies of documents crucial to this study from the Rockefeller Archive Center and the Library and Archives of Canada. I particularly thank Ken Rose, assistant director of the Rockefeller Archive Center, and Amy Fitch, also of the center, for directing me to pertinent documents in the archives and sending me copies. Without these documents, a comprehensive analysis of Osgood's role in the major strike of 1913–1914 and the Ludlow Massacre would have been impossible.

I extend heartfelt gratitude to everyone who encouraged me to write this book. Special thanks to Richard and James Hart and their wives, Jane and Barbara, for their hospitality in Buffalo Park, Colorado, where they shared stories about their great-grandfather, John L. Jerome; to Charlotte Blackmer, John C. Osgood's grandniece, and her family for information about "Uncle Cleve"; to Jane for editorial help in the preparation of the manuscript; and to friends in the Crystal River Valley who share an appreciation of our local treasures—Redstone and Cleveholm Manor.

FROM
Redstone
TO
Ludlow

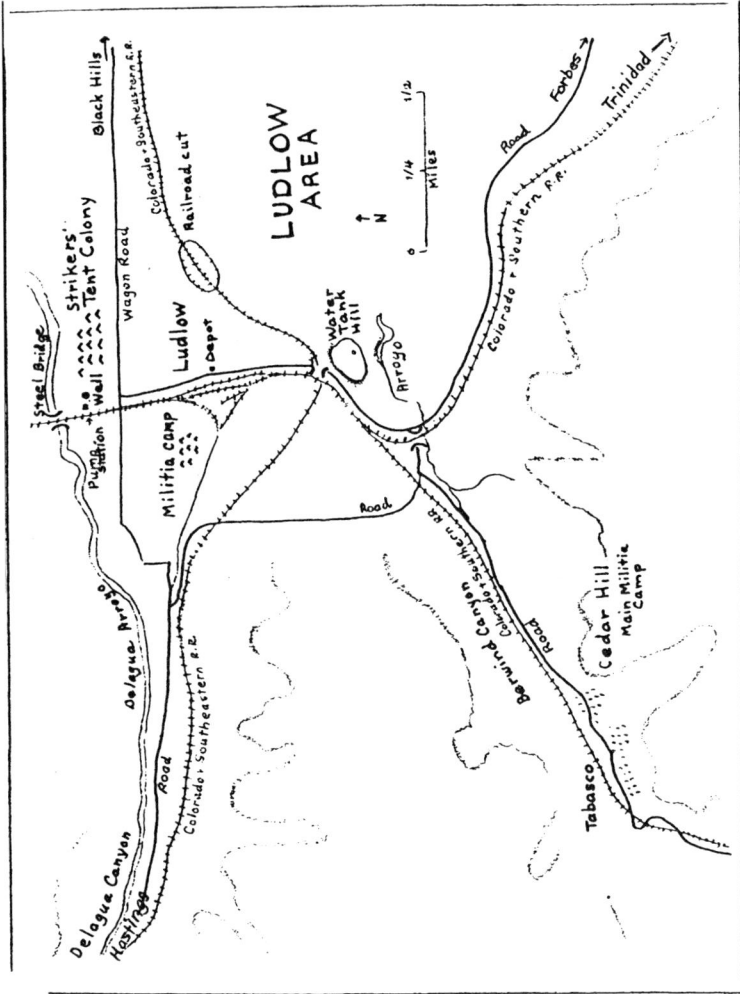

Ludlow area, 1914. Drawing by author.

Prologue

The open field a few hundred yards north of the old ghost town of Ludlow in southern Colorado is hallowed ground for the United Mine Workers of America (UMWA). It was on a few acres of this ground that the union erected a tent colony at the beginning of the 1913–1914 coal strike for hundreds of striking miners and their families who had been evicted from the nearby mining camps and towns of the Colorado Fuel and Iron (CF&I) and Victor-American Fuel companies. The Ludlow tent colony, as it was called, remained home for more than 1,000 men, women, and children from late September 1913 until it was burned to the ground by Colorado National Guard troops in a vicious attack on April 20, 1914. Today, near the "Black Hole" where two women and eleven children perished during the inferno

Ludlow tent colony, winter, 1913–1914. Black Hills are on the horizon east of the colony. Courtesy, Colorado Historical Society, Military-Strikes-Ludlow-Dold Collection, ID no. 10027993.

that day, a large granite monument commemorates the "martyrs" of the battle of Ludlow. This battle, one of several fought during the 1913–1914 coal strike between miners and their adversaries—mine guards and militiamen—is engraved on the pages of history as the "Ludlow Massacre." It is the most memorable event of a much larger battle between capital and labor in what was one of the most violent industrial struggles in American history.

It is hard to imagine that this open prairie, surrounded by deep arroyos and low-lying hills covered with piñon, now so serene, was the epicenter of that bitter strife between wealthy capitalists and industrialists like John D. Rockefeller Jr. and John C. Osgood and their laborers, the majority of whom were recent immigrants. With so few traces of the industrial past existing today, it is equally difficult to imagine that the Delagua and Berwind canyons, jutting off to the northwest and southwest from the old town site of Ludlow, were once filled with thousands of miners and their families,

mine superintendents, pit bosses, store managers, and other officials and residents of the company towns that were essentially sealed off from the outside world. The few buildings still standing at Ludlow resemble an abandoned Hollywood movie set.[1] The train depot no longer exists, and many of the old buildings are piles of rubble. An occasional stonewall or concrete foundation and a few ruined coke ovens that were once used to produce coke from coal are all that are left to mark the locations of the once busy coal camps and towns of Tabasco, Berwind, Tollerburg, Hastings, and Delagua. Near the abandoned Hastings mine, a granite marker dedicated to the memory of 121 men who died in a mine explosion on April 27, 1917, is a reminder that Colorado coalmines were among the most dangerous in the world during the early twentieth century. Little else exists to suggest that these canyons, now peaceful and quiet, were once the sites of bustling industry as well as human tragedy.

However, hundreds of photographs deposited in the Western History Collection of the Denver Public Library and in the Stephen H. Hart Library of the Colorado Historical Society help bring to life scenes of the historic struggle that occurred between the miners and their employers' agents during the 1913–1914 strike. Photographs of neat rows of the Ludlow colony's white tents provide a glimpse of a well-kept and orderly camp. Other photographs of the people of the Ludlow tent colony, posing in front of the tents for Lou Dold, the union's photographer, add a human quality to the pictures. Images of tents almost covered by huge snowdrifts from the blizzard of early December 1913 reveal some of the physical hardships the strikers had to endure. A photograph of the machine gun on top of Water Tank Hill, manned by militiamen waiting for an order to fire into the tents, depicts the cause of the horror that descended on the Ludlow colonists the morning of that terrible day in April 1914. Photographs taken shortly after the militia attack that show the smoldering ruins of the tent colony—the twisted bedsteads and coils of bed springs, broken furniture, scorched floorboards, charred clothing, and heavy cast-iron coal stoves with stove pipes still standing in place—complete the story of the Ludlow Massacre.

The photographs provide a microcosmic history of that tumultuous event. However, they do not answer the fundamental questions historians must ask. How did this tragedy occur? How did a dispute between labor and management in the southern coalfields of Colorado nearly a century ago become "one of the nearest approaches to civil war and revolution ever known in this country in connection with an industrial conflict"?[2] Who were the people most responsible for allowing the situation to escalate almost into a civil war?

Although several authors have addressed these questions in depth,[3] John Osgood's involvement in the events of the 1913–1914 strike, including the Ludlow Massacre, has not received the attention it deserves. Further, his career as a leading industrialist and coal baron has not been analyzed completely. In their classic study entitled *The Great Coalfield War*, George S. McGovern and Leonard F. Guttridge described Osgood as "an enigmatic entrepreneur" and expressed the hope that someone someday would shed more light on his character and career.[4] The present work is a response to the challenge McGovern and Guttridge posed. It is a study seen through the prism of Osgood's struggle against the UMWA. Although it is impossible to unlock all the secrets of this perplexing man, an analysis of his antiunion policies and activities in confronting the UMWA provides a major key to understanding his business philosophy and career as well as his character. Such an analysis is also important in ascertaining how and why he became one

National Guard troops manning a machine gun on Water Tank Hill, Ludlow, April 20, 1914.
Courtesy, Denver Public Library, Western History Collection, call no. X-60543.

of the most important participants in the events of 1913–1914. In a broader sense, the present study describes Osgood's role in the struggle between labor and management during this critical period of American history.

The conflict between labor and capital in the southern Colorado coalfields that resulted in the Ludlow Massacre and the Coalfield War was not an isolated incident but rather, like the earlier Homestead and Pullman strikes, was a manifestation of the nation's social instability and industrial unrest at the time. It was a time when industrial problems demanded solutions—solutions that required a major change in employers' attitudes to accept a more enlightened or progressive view of industrial relations. Few industrialists in John D. Rockefeller's generation were willing to make that change; but the bitterness, violence, and tragedy of the Colorado conflict, as Raymond Fosdick noted, "jolted" the entire nation "into a recognition of the growing industrial unrest beneath the surface of an outworn system."[5]

Osgood was a younger member of Rockefeller's generation. A self-made man, he was the very description of the coal baron depicted in Matthew

5

Ludlow tent colony after the massacre and fire that destroyed the camp, April 20, 1914. Courtesy, Denver Public Library, Western History Collection, call no. Z-199.

Josephson's *Robber Barons*.[6] Although a "lesser cousin" of the more famous robber barons—John D. Rockefeller, Cornelius Vanderbilt, Jay Gould, Andrew Carnegie, J. Pierpont Morgan, and Henry Clay Frick—Osgood nonetheless helped shape the character of the Gilded Age. It was a time when giant corporations were formed to take the place of older types of commercial and manufacturing enterprises. The corporations were formed by men who, as Dan Rottenberg noted, had an "astute understanding of the value of market domination and of the uses of credit to achieve it."[7] These captains of industry fought the unions tooth and nail. Osgood was one of these men. He was a leading participant in the transformation of the West from an area lacking capital but rich in natural resources to a place where the ascendancy to corporate capitalism was most apparent.[8]

Like his cohorts, Osgood believed in the divine right of capital, based on the concept that those who owned property and wealth were superior to other individuals and groups. Wealth was a form of entitlement. As such, those who adhered to this concept believed they should be free from interference to pursue their self-interests, which, they asserted, were for the good of society.[9] Osgood and the Colorado coal operators, state senator Helen

Ring Robinson told the U.S. Industrial Relations Commission in 1915, firmly cherished what she called "mid-Victorian ideas of the relations of capital and labor," out of which grew bitterness.[10]

Such a mind-set was a major cause of Colorado's labor troubles in 1913–1914. By focusing on Osgood and his antiunion policies, as this study does, an additional picture never completely exposed emerges to provide a clearer image of the events of that tragic episode in American history. The evidence presented in this study supports the conclusion that Osgood's tireless campaign against the UMWA was a major cause of the strike and the events, including the Ludlow Massacre, that followed. Although most coal operators in the state agreed with Osgood's antiunion views and policies, it was his dominance over them that resulted in the united front against the miners. As director of the operators' policy committee, he repeatedly voiced his conviction that it was necessary to bring about the total defeat of the union to maintain the mine owners' dominance over the Colorado coalfields. Sharing this view, the operators under Osgood's leadership carried out the strikebreaking and union-busting policies he had helped formulate over the course of his long career in the coal business.

The UMWA officials correctly regarded Osgood as their most formidable foe in the effort to organize the Colorado coalfields during the late nineteenth and early twentieth centuries. For nearly thirty years, he was the leader of the reactionary forces that opposed Colorado coalminers in their struggle for industrial democracy. Osgood adopted various strategies to defeat the union, including intimidation and racial diversification of the workforce. Intimidation was used to prevent the union from organizing the miners, and ethnic diversification prevented solidarity among the workers. He also established closed towns and camps to gain greater control over his workforce. Furthermore, he and his fellow coal operators used political power on the local and state levels to suppress unionism and break strikes. Osgood even introduced a program of welfare capitalism under the banner of industrial betterment as a way to counter the threat of unionism. The model industrial village of Redstone in western Colorado was the fulfillment of his sociological vision.

The title of this study, *From Redstone to Ludlow,* depicts the bipolarity of Osgood's approach to fighting the UMWA. Designed to improve the lives of workers and to forge their loyalty to the company through social improvement programs, Osgood's pioneer welfare work program, characterized by the establishment of the Sociological Department and the "Redstone experiment," represented the compassionate side of his antiunion policies. Ludlow—marked by armed gunmen and machine guns paid for by Osgood and other coal operators in the fight against the strikers—was the violent side. Although seemingly paradoxical, the commonality in what Redstone and Ludlow represented was Osgood's determination to defeat the UMWA and prevent unionization of the Colorado coalfields. But the miners would not be subdued by either paternalistic kindness or bare-knuckled intimidation. Therefore, his policies from Redstone to Ludlow contributed significantly to the outbreak of one of the greatest struggles for industrial freedom in American history.

Most previous accounts of the Ludlow Massacre and the Coalfield War of 1913–1914 have focused on the responsibility of John D. Rockefeller Jr. and Colorado CF&I officials for these events. Osgood was assigned a secondary role in the entire affair. This assessment of blame was established even before the end of the strike in 1914. A majority of committee and commission members investigating the causes of the strike had the preconceived view that the industrial problems of the day were caused by large corporations and their leaders. Therefore, they were far more interested in reviewing and judging the part CF&I's New York multimillionaire head had played in these matters than they were in those they judged had played a lesser role. Attacks on Rockefeller also made good press. By placing most of the blame for the Ludlow Massacre on Rockefeller, they hoped to gain more national attention that would translate into support for their reform agenda. Although not ignored completely in the nation's scrutiny of the Colorado affair, Osgood largely escaped public anger over the Ludlow Massacre by being overshadowed by Rockefeller and CF&I officials in Colorado.

The diaries of William Lyon Mackenzie King, the future prime minister of Canada, shed new light on Osgood's role in directing the Colorado coal operators' campaign against the UMWA and the striking miners. Used extensively for this study, the diaries also reveal Mackenzie King's personal assessment of Osgood's moral character and fitness as a business leader. Mackenzie King was a moralist with a mission to rehabilitate Rockefeller's reputation and to draft a new industrial plan for CF&I, but the diary entries nonetheless provide information not known publicly about the Osgood-Rockefeller rift during the aftermath of the Ludlow affair. They supplement the public accounts of Osgood's attempt to undercut Rockefeller and regain leadership of the Colorado coal operators.

The absence of private papers and records makes any study of Osgood difficult, and no attempt is made in this study to pry into his personal affairs in any depth. What little is known about his private life, however, indicates that, as with his professional career, it was embroiled in controversy. He was married three times, and the story of each of his wives is veiled in mystery. His first wife, Irene de Belot, whom he married in 1887, was a recognized writer of romantic novels, poetry, and short stories whose literary efforts appeared in various contemporary journals and magazines. Vivacious and attractive, she was described by one source as "a woman of superior culture and natural refinement."[11] Irene apparently preferred life in England and Europe to that in Colorado, and she and Osgood were divorced in 1899. Both parties soon married again.

Osgood's second wife was Alma Regina Shelgrem, a tall, beautiful young woman rumored to have had ties to Swedish royalty. The two had reportedly met in 1899 in Belgium at the court of King Leopold II while Osgood was seeking financial support for his mining operations in Colorado. Although her arrival in Colorado was surrounded by scandal, as detailed more fully in Chapter 3, she and Osgood rose to social prominence among the Denver elite when Osgood served as president of the Denver Club in 1914. At Cleveholm Manor, Osgood's Redstone estate, Alma entertained dignitaries, but she also visited the workers and their families in the nearby village of Redstone, thereby earning the beneficent title "Lady Bountiful." Information regarding the final years of their marriage is limited, but their union ended in divorce sometime around 1919. Alma, who died in 1955, outlived Osgood by nearly thirty years.

In 1920 Osgood married Lucille Reid, a capable young woman who returned with him from New York to Redstone in 1924 to reopen Cleveholm Manor as their permanent home. But Osgood's health was failing, and his plans were unfulfilled. After his death in January 1926, Lucille inherited the Redstone estate—including the village—and all of Osgood's other properties and business interests. It was reported that she burned Osgood's records, letters, documents, and personal papers. Osgood was a very private man, and the destruction of his personal papers—probably at his instruction—has largely preserved his privacy in death.

The availability of primary sources, however, provides more than enough material to analyze his labor-management policies in the context of his struggle against the UMWA. The most important primary sources for this study include published accounts of his testimony before the U.S. House Subcommittee on Mines and Mining, the U.S. Commission on Industrial Relations, and the Colorado House Committee on Mines and Mining; his presentations at various conferences; published letters and a few extant letters in the James Peabody, Elias Ammons, John Jerome, and Rockefeller collections;[12] and proceedings of a meeting between coal operators and miners in the governor's office at the state house in Denver in November 1913. The latter source has not been published previously. The Mackenzie King diaries, already mentioned, constitute another valuable primary source for this study. Osgood's numerous statements to newspapers and articles about him in the national media also provide valuable information about his labor policies and business philosophy.

The image of Osgood that emerges from these accounts is of a man who was very much the product of his age. During a period of social and political transition, he rose to prominence as one of the most influential and successful industrialists in the West. Some physical remnants of his capital investments are still visible today—the crumbling coke ovens in Redstone and Hastings, the blast furnaces and official buildings at the steel mill in Pueblo, and the quaint miners' cottages in Redstone. They are reminders of that aspect of Osgood's career. However, they do not tell the human side of the story, of which Osgood's relentless struggle against the UMWA, told in the pages that follow, is a major part. Today, the beautiful village of Redstone and the granite monument at Ludlow are manifestations of that struggle.

NOTES

1. Joanna Sampson, *Remember Ludlow* (Denver: Colorado Historical Society, 1999), 3.

2. George P. West, *Report on the Colorado Strike* (Washington, D.C.: U.S. Commission on Industrial Relations, 1915), 132.

3. For example, George S. McGovern and Leonard F. Guttridge, *The Great Coalfield War* (Boston: Houghton Mifflin, 1972); Barron B. Beshoar, *Out of the Depths: The Story of John R. Lawson, a Labor Leader* (Denver: Golden Bell, 1942); Zeese Papanikolas, *Buried Unsung: Louis Tikas and the Ludlow Massacre* (Salt Lake City: University of Utah Press, 1982); Priscilla Long, *Where the Sun Never Shines: A History of America's Bloody Coal Industry* (New York: Paragon House, 1989).

4. McGovern and Guttridge, *Coalfield War*, 353.

5. Raymond B. Fosdick, *John D. Rockefeller, Jr.: A Portrait* (New York: Harper & Row, 1956), 143.

6. Matthew Josephson, *The Robber Barons* (New York: Harcourt Brace, 1934).

7. Dan Rottenberg, *In the Kingdom of Coal: An American Family and the Rock That Changed the World* (New York: Routledge, 2003), 69.

8. William G. Robbins has argued that it was eastern U.S. and European capital that subsidized the rise of corporate capitalism in the West. He discusses the role of CF&I in this transformation at length in *Colony and Empire: The Capitalist*

Transformation of the American West (Lawrence: University of Kansas Press, 1994), 62, 94–101.

9. Marjorie Kelly, *The Divine Right of Capital: Dethroning the Corporate Aristocracy* (San Francisco: Berrett-Koehler, 2001), xi–xiii.

10. Robinson's testimony, U.S. Congress, Senate, *Industrial Relations: Final Report and Testimony Submitted to Congress by the Commission on Industrial Relations, Created by the Act of August 23, 1912,* 64th Cong., 1st sess., 1916, Doc. 415, 8: 7212 (hereafter cited as CIR/FR).

11. Elisha Hollingsworth Talbot, "Editorial Notes," *The Great West* 1, no. 3 (December 1896): 279; Jim Nelson, *Marble and Redstone: A Quick History* (Fort Collins, Colo.: FirstLight, 1968), 92–94. See Sylvia Ruland, *The Lion of Redstone* (Boulder: Johnson Books, 1981), for the most complete account of Osgood's personal life.

12. The Peabody and Ammons papers are in the Colorado State Archives, Denver; the Jerome papers are in the Stephen H. Hart Library of the Colorado Historical Society, Denver; and the Rockefeller papers are in the Rockefeller Family Archives, Rockefeller Archive Center, Pocantico Hills, New York.

Fuel King of the West

Young men migrating to the West after the Civil War took advantage of capital raised in the eastern United States and Western Europe to create industrial and transportation empires in Colorado. Among these men was John Cleveland Osgood, who became one of the wealthiest industrial capitalists of the time. His rise to industrial power and wealth is an interesting tale of western finance and industrial development, a story that includes such contemporary financial titans as J. Pierpont Morgan, Edward H. Harriman, Jay and George Gould, and the John D. Rockefellers, father and son. Described by Thomas G. Andrews as "[a] dapper dandy who cloaked a fierce temper behind impeccable attire, a handlebar mustache, and a poker face, Osgood was the quintessential self-made man." At times, according to

Perry Eberhart, he was "a reluctant dragon, a man of tempest, or a man of peace and beauty—a man of mystery."[1]

Born of humble origins in Brooklyn, New York, on March 6, 1851, Osgood lived with relatives after being orphaned as a youth. He attended public schools in Connecticut and Rhode Island. At age fourteen he went to work as an office boy for a textile manufacturing firm in Providence, Rhode Island, and two years later he was hired as a bookkeeper by the William H. Ladd Produce Commission in New York City. While employed at the firm, he attended night classes at the Peter Cooper Institute, graduating at age nineteen with a degree in accounting. Impressed by Osgood's industrious work habits, in 1870 A. D. Moss, an assistant manager for a Colorado coal company, recommended him for a job as bookkeeper and cashier for the Union Coal and Mining Company in Ottumwa, Iowa. After resigning from that position four years later, he became cashier of the First National Bank in Burlington, Iowa. With money he had saved, he purchased the financially troubled Whitebreast Coal and Mining Company, becoming the company's president in 1878.[2] The Whitebreast Coal and Mining Company became a major supplier of coal for the Chicago, Burlington and Quincy Railroad. In 1882, shortly after his thirty-first birthday, Osgood traveled to Colorado at the railroad's request to investigate the coal resources there.[3] Thus began his Colorado venture.

Colorado's vast untapped coal resources convinced Osgood to start a new business career in the West. With financial support from the executives of Burlington Railroad as well as other Burlington and Ottumwa capitalists, he and three associates from Iowa organized the Colorado Fuel Company (CFC) in 1883. The "Iowa Group," consisting of Julian Abbot Kebler, Alfred Curtis Cass, and David C. Beaman, ably assisted Osgood in his remarkable rise to fortune. They were talented and experienced men who had been associated with Osgood in the Whitebreast Coal and Mining Company. Each brought special expertise to the management table: Kebler, mining technology; Cass, marketing; Beaman, legal counsel. Two Denver lawyers—Charles H. Toll and John Lathrop Jerome—later joined them to round out the top tier of Osgood's closest associates who were instrumental in the development of his expanding coal empire.[4]

Richard Charles Hills, one of the era's most eminent geologists, also contributed significantly to Osgood's coal enterprise. Osgood employed him as a consultant to evaluate the coal lands in Colorado and adjoining states. A fellow of the Royal Geological Society of London and a founding member of the Colorado Scientific Society, Hills, over a sixteen-year period, helped Osgood locate some of the best coal deposits in the four-state area of Colorado, Wyoming, Utah, and New Mexico. He was still associated with Osgood's Victor-American Fuel Company at the time of his death in 1923.[5]

Osgood and the company officials created a tightly run operation with a strong business orientation. Unlike eastern investors who were only interested in profit from their investments in Colorado, they developed the CFC as residents of the state with the intent of making the company a lasting success. They were not plungers but cautious men who made studied decisions. Osgood focused on the coal business and limited the operation to a comparatively small number of people who held the majority of the company's stocks and bonds.[6]

In addition to his business acumen, Osgood's tremendous ability to obtain financial support was critical to the success of his various endeavors. The capital raised by the creation of the CFC enabled him to lease the Anthracite mine near Crested Butte in west-central Colorado and to purchase the Mitchell mine north of Denver. From these mines, the company supplied coal to the Chicago, Burlington and Quincy Railroad and to consumers along the rail line in eastern Colorado and western Nebraska. In 1887 he formed the Denver Fuel Company and opened a mine and erected coke ovens at Sopris, near Trinidad. The following year he established the Elk Mountain Fuel Company and began to open large coal deposits in Garfield and Pitkin counties in western Colorado.

With the financial backing of several prominent Denver businessmen recently enriched from precious metal mining and smelting interests, Osgood reorganized the CFC in 1888, enlarging its authorized capital from $500,000 to $5 million. Over the next four years the issue of the new shares enabled the reorganized company to bring the Denver Fuel and Elk Mountain companies, along with several other land and coal auxiliaries, under the umbrella of a single firm. With this expansion, by 1892 the CFC owned almost 34,000 acres of coal land, seven mines, and two coke oven plants. The company had become a formidable competitor of the Colorado Coal and Iron Company (CC&I), organized in 1880 by William Jackson Palmer, the principal builder of the Denver and Rio Grande Railroad. Prominent among CC&I's holdings was the Bessemer steelworks in Pueblo, the only integrated iron and steel plant in the West.[7]

While Osgood's company prospered through superb management, wise investments, and aggressive salesmanship, CC&I faltered as a business enterprise. It continued to record significant losses in both revenue and contracts. Disgruntled by the company's poor performance, Wall Street investors who dominated the company toppled Palmer when he defaulted on interest payments in 1884. Even under new management, the company's problems persisted. With the slowdown of railroad construction in the West, the Bessemer steelworks in Pueblo became an even greater drag on CC&I. Competition from new coal companies, particularly Osgood's CFC, prevented CC&I from expanding its share of the coal business. In 1891 the company lost large contracts with the Missouri Pacific and Union Pacific railroads that amounted to more than $1 million in fuel business to CFC. With Osgood making plans for a steelworks in Denver, CC&I was ripe for a merger, which Osgood—flush with new capital from his company's successful performance—arranged on his own terms. He "out-generaled" Edward J. Berwind, chairman of the board of CC&I, to garner a sweetheart deal.[8] Unhappy with their subordinate officials, the CC&I directors agreed to turn management of their company over to Osgood and the CFC officials even before a final agreement had been reached. Osgood was the sort of cunning and capable leader they longed for after years of suffering financial losses.[9]

The new company, Colorado Fuel and Iron (CF&I), was formally organized in October 1892. Osgood and the Iowa Group were now in control of a vast industrial empire that included $13 million in authorized capital, 71,837 acres of coal land containing an estimated 400 million tons of domestic and coking coals, fourteen mines with a capacity of 12,000 tons daily, four coking plants comprising 800 ovens that could produce 1,000 tons of coke daily, and iron lands in excess of 2,000 acres. The company also assumed ownership of the Bessemer steelworks. The formation of CF&I made Osgood the dominant coal entrepreneur in Colorado and the West. From its creation, the corporation and its subsidiaries comprised the largest enterprise in the western mountain region.[10]

With the establishment of CF&I, Osgood and company officials restored order to the Colorado coal industry, where competition for the expanding market had launched a battle for the survival of the fittest. Osgood and his associates emerged the victors in this struggle; thus, Osgood's plan to dominate the western fuel trade seemed a certainty. But the albatross around the neck of the former CC&I, the Bessemer steelworks, remained a potential problem. Unable to dispose of the steel plant legally, which was his original intent, Osgood decided that an investment in modernizing the plant and improving the company's mines and camps would make the steelworks profitable. Through expansion, he envisaged transforming the small, inefficient plant into a modern, mass-producing giant. Osgood raised over $2 million in company bonds on a European trip in 1892–1893 and borrowed additional sums for operations and improvements from Denver and New York banks. However, the modernization project was quickly halted by a decline in metallurgical sales and the depression caused by the Panic of 1893, and the Pueblo steel plant was idle for several months.[11]

The Panic of 1893, caused in part by railroad failures and the repeal of the Sherman Silver Purchase Act—which contributed to the collapse of silver—dealt devastating blows to the Colorado economy. CF&I suffered along with the other coal and rail industries in the state. Demand for coal, coke, and rails plummeted during the period June 1893–June 1894, leaving the company hard-pressed to meet its financial obligations. Like other coal companies during the depression, CF&I closed mines or worked them half-time, laid off miners, and cut the wages and hours of those who remained employed in the mines that remained open to reduce costs and lower the price of coal. The irregular work and reduced pay drove many miners into debt, forcing them to depend on the company for credit. As the depression deepened, several companies that no longer had the cash to meet their payrolls began to pay their workers in scrip. Scrip, or company money, was redeemable only at the company store, where excessively high prices were often charged. Scrip was greatly discounted when converted to cash in saloons and other establishments. All these issues—irregular work, reduced wages, and the scrip system—angered coalminers in Colorado and became a point of contention among miners throughout the nation's coal mining communities. Believing that a nationwide strike was the only way to address these grievances, the nascent United Mine Workers of America (UMWA) called a national work stoppage for late April 1894.[12]

With few union members in the state, the strike spread slowly and unevenly in the southern Colorado coalfields. Miners in the older camps, such as Engleville and Coal Creek, where union activity was strongest, were the first to respond to the strike call. Strikers from these camps began a campaign in late May to persuade miners from the newer camps to join the strike. Marching en masse from camp to camp with American flags and a brass band leading the way, the strikers managed to get hundreds of miners from Pictou, Rouse, and other newer CF&I camps to join their ranks. It was estimated that eventually between 4,000 and 5,000 miners, about three-fourths of Colorado's coalmine workers, laid down their tools during the strike. Through either persuasion or coercion, the union succeeded in shutting down most of the larger mines in Colorado, including all but three of CF&I's properties.[13]

The strike lasted until early August 1894. Although a moderate success for the union in other parts of the country, the strike was a complete failure in Colorado. Neither of the union's basic grievances—the abolition of scrip and the institution of semimonthly pay periods in legal money—was granted. The depressed economic situation doomed the strike from the beginning, for companies had no trouble hiring strikebreakers. Striking union men and their families soon began to suffer from want. As the mines reopened, many of the striking miners went back to work. Those who found employment with CF&I, however, discovered that the company had cut their wages to punish them for their insolence. Further, the company did not hire all of its former employees. Those found to have been actively involved in threatening or intimidating miners who wanted to work were refused employment.[14]

CF&I had weathered the first major labor disturbance it had faced, at a cost of $40,000. Part of the cost was for hiring mine guards to protect strikebreakers and mine property. The cost was largely offset by the company's strike fund, which Osgood had created by charging miners a small fee for every ton of coal mined. The company's aggressive action against the strikers, Osgood assured CF&I stockholders, would prevent further strikes for years to come.[15]

Osgood would later downplay the significance of the 1894 strike. In 1914, when he was called to testify before the Commission on Industrial Relations, his recollection of the 1894 strike differed greatly—whether intentionally or because of a lapse of memory—from historical fact. In the 1914 testimony he stated that the first strike in the Colorado coalfields of "anything more than of local importance or that lasted more than a few days or a week" was the "so-called Debs strike" of 1893. [The year was actually 1894, and the strike was more commonly known as the Pullman strike.][16] The Colorado strike, Osgood stated, was a sympathetic strike that grew out of the nationwide labor disturbances that year. In making this point, he observed that Colorado coalminers made no particular demands but struck out of sympathy for the men on strike in other parts of the country. It was not a complete strike, he emphasized, as many of the mines continued to operate throughout its entirety. He also stated that no labor organization had attempted to organize labor.[17]

In reality, the 1894 strike was a far more serious affair than Osgood described in his testimony. He was incorrect on several points. The strike in Colorado was not part of the Pullman railroad strike, as Osgood asserted, even though the miners probably lengthened the strike in the coalfields by expressing support for the railroad workers. Contrary to Osgood's assertion that no labor organization was involved in an attempt to organize the miners, the strike occurred as a result of the first major campaign by the UMWA to organize the Colorado coalfields. As to Osgood's statement that the miners presented no grievances, the union in Colorado issued a manifesto that made two demands: the abolition of scrip and payment of wages in legal money on a semimonthly basis. In addition, local union officials had requested a conference with the operators. The operators rejected these demands, stating that they would not participate in a conference unless the miners first returned to work.[18]

Although Osgood professed to believe that the 1894 strike was not important in Colorado, it was undoubtedly a major event in shaping his antiunion policies. He realized that the UMWA was becoming a formidable force on the national political and economic scene. Union success, Osgood and his allies believed, raised the specter of organized labor gaining control of the nation's political institutions, thus stripping away powers and property that rightfully belonged to corporations. He vowed never to allow this to happen in Colorado. Under his leadership, CF&I became the most unyielding foe of organized labor in the state, if not in the entire West. The 1894 strike convinced Osgood that he needed to initiate additional measures to defeat the UMWA. Included in his plans was the development of a new closed town system, discussed in detail in Chapter 5, that would give CF&I more control over workers and isolate them from the union. To accomplish this, he would have to wait for better economic times.

Economic conditions improved quickly. As the depression receded, the company's fuel sales increased during the second half of the 1890s. CF&I enhanced its position in the regional market by absorbing rival firms, opening new mines, and building new coking plants. Osgood's success in leasing or purchasing mining properties was astonishing. In 1901 the Rocky Mountain Coal and Iron Company, an Osgood subsidiary company, purchased 258,000 acres of the Maxwell Land Grant between the Purgatoire River in southern Colorado and the New Mexico border for $750,000. This transaction, one of Osgood's most important achievements, precluded competition for coking coal and provided the additional fuel necessary for the expansion of the Bessemer steel mill. With these acquisitions, including properties in New Mexico, CF&I's share of Colorado's coal output jumped from 45 percent to 73 percent between 1893 and 1902. The corporation now had twenty-two mines and nine coking facilities, the latter of which produced three-quarters of the coke produced in Colorado.[19]

The recovery of the steel industry throughout the nation and the increased share of the rail market for the Pueblo firm enabled Osgood and company executives to resume the program of modernization and expansion of the steelworks in September 1899. Earlier in the year, Osgood had attempted to organize a new corporation by purchasing the Victor Coal and Coke Company and consolidating it with CF&I to form the Colorado Steel Company, with authorized capital of $50 million. Although he completed the purchase of the Victor Company, which with several large mines and coke ovens in Las Animas County in southern Colorado had been a major competitor for many years, his plan to create a new corporation was scuttled in July. New York brokers withdrew their support when they learned that Osgood had suffered heavy losses from speculations in the stock and commodity markets that had temporarily endangered his personal finances. After the collapse of his plans to create the Colorado Steel Company, Osgood transferred the Victor Coal and Coke Company (reorganized as the Victor Fuel Company) to the Colorado Finance and Construction Company (CF&CC), recently established to finance and control a variety of business ventures.[20]

John Jerome, who had assumed the position of CF&I treasurer, devised the CF&CC to market CF&I's common shares as well as to acquire, control, and sell the securities of other enterprises. These financial arrangements enabled the company to purchase and develop land, mines, coke ovens, plants, and other facilities required in the fuel and steel trades. The CF&CC thus served as a conduit through which funds flowed to finance CF&I's improvements and expansion beginning in the fall of 1899.

Jerome characterized the CF&CC as Osgood's personal fief, owned and run to suit his interests. The company was designed as a "holding" company through which profits could be gained for Osgood and Jerome in enterprises conducted for the benefit of themselves and others who invested. It was modeled after the construction firms used to build and equip railroads with the proceeds of their own stock. Existing only on paper, the company's capital stock was never subscribed, and the directors met only once to organize the corporation. Jerome drafted minutes, filed by Osgood, of meetings that never occurred. Osgood kept the records in New York and refused to show them to anyone or to make any accounting of the company's finances to other officers and directors. He conducted all of the company's business ventures, most of which were related to the fuel trade, and received promoter's profits from all transactions in addition to a large percentage of the company's earnings. Ultimately, he dominated all of the auxiliaries organized under the umbrella of the CF&CC, including Victor Fuel. Jerome later speculated that the company netted between $3 and $4 million in profit from CF&I shares.[21]

In October 1899 the CF&CC entered into a contract with CF&I to finance expansion and major improvements at the Bessemer steel mill and the corporation's mining camps. Between July 1, 1899, and June 30, 1903, CF&I spent $24 million, much of it raised by the CF&CC, to expand the manufacturing capacity of the steelworks and to acquire properties and develop mines, coke ovens, and quarries to supply the Pueblo plant with the additional resources needed for increased production. With the expanded and modernized plant, CF&I became a major competitor in the western steel market and the dominant force in the fuel trade. It was the largest Colorado corporation and one of the 100 largest firms in the country.[22] Notwithstanding this remarkable success, unrest among the thousands of employees remained an undercurrent that threatened the corporation's stability and future prosperity.

The prosperity in the fuel trade at the turn of the twentieth century that facilitated the expansion of CF&I brought no concomitant reward for the coalminers. Their earning power essentially remained stagnant while their working and living conditions deteriorated. As conditions worsened, labor officials took notice. In a report of his tour of several CF&I and Northern Coal and Coke Company mining camps in southern Colorado, published in the *Rocky Mountain News* under the banner headline "Cheapest Labor in the Country," President Edward Boyce of the Western Federation of Miners (WFM) stated that he had never in his experience of visiting mining camps "seen such abject misery as I saw there." The miners, he reported, were paid less than those in any other camp in the country, and what pay they received was mostly in the form of company scrip that forever put them in their employers' debt. Boyce noted other issues, including poor housing and the company's use of spies to prevent the miners from organizing. The situation was hopeless, he conceded, unless the state intervened: "We [WFM] might organize, but every man would lose his job, and then the federation must support them. If the state of Colorado will take no care of them, it is not our fault, and it is its place first." Boyce ended his report with a prophetic observation: "I do not in the least doubt that at the end of this perpetual grinding down of the miners there will be a revolt and bloodshed, which will be an agitation for more than the one state only."[23]

An editorial in the *Rocky Mountain News*, a sympathetic voice for miners at the time, stated that Boyce's account of conditions in the mining camps was "probably not overdrawn." Despite a denial by Julian Kebler, CF&I's

general manager, the editor agreed with Boyce that the miners were "living in poverty and squalor" and that their children were "growing up in ignorance and discontent." Furthermore, the editor wrote, "Mr. Boyce is right in the assertion that this condition of affairs, if continued, will breed future trouble for the commonwealth." The editor recognized that the state was limited in what it could do to remedy the problem. For example, it could not by law determine workers' wages or bring about a more equitable division of coal mining profits between employers and employees. He suggested, however, that the state could pass a law against the issuance of scrip and that the nation could restrict immigration to prevent overcrowding of the labor market. By restricting immigration, he reasoned, the coal operators could no longer "crowd wages down to their present starvation point" by being able "to draw unlimited numbers [of miners] from Europe."[24]

Colorado's General Assembly responded to the editor's plea for action by enacting legislation allowing miners to hire check-weighmen to verify the weight of coal in the cars coming out of the mines and establishing an eight-hour workday for mine, mill, and smelter workers. The legislature had previously created the office of State Inspector of Coal Mines as well as the Bureau of Labor Statistics to collect data on the coal mining industry. In 1897 the legislature created the State Board of Arbitration. These measures, although well intended, failed to improve conditions for the miners, primarily because the operators effectively countered them. The failure of the implementation of the eight-hour legislation, which the Colorado Supreme Court declared unconstitutional, incited the miners to greater militancy. They increasingly turned to the UMWA for support in their efforts to gain greater control over their lives.

As their anguish over their conditions increased, the miners began to think of themselves as an oppressed class of workers rather than maligned individuals. The growing solidarity among experienced miners and new immigrants benefited the union at the expense of the coal operators. As a result, in late 1900 the UMWA returned to organize the western coalfields. In Colorado the miners particularly welcomed union organizers in the Cañon City coalfields—Brookside, Chandler, Coal Creek, and Rockvale—where union activity had historically been strongest and where miners saw the union as a means to attack Osgood and CF&I.[25]

The union also met with success in New Mexico, where miners at the American Fuel Company's Gallup mines, owned by Osgood, organized a local chapter of the UMWA in early 1901. Osgood refused to recognize the union, and the company's policy of discharging union men increased the miners' animosity toward the company. Membership in the local grew to encompass almost all of the workforce, and the miners struck when the company refused the union's demand to reinstate the discharged workers. The men remained resolved in their action, even though company officials tried a variety of tactics ranging from bribing them with beer to importing "thugs" to get them back to work.[26]

In mid-January 1901, around 1,000 miners from the CF&I camps of Rockvale, Brookside, and Coal Creek struck in support of their colleagues in New Mexico and the Denver Basin. Although the strikers had local grievances, the strike started as a protest against Osgood and his antiunion policies, with the main purpose of preserving the union movement within his CF&I and American Fuel Company operations. "This strike would not have occurred as soon as it did," a Rockvale miner said, "if the Colorado Fuel and Iron company had not discharged employes [sic] at Gallup, N.M., for no other cause than because the men had joined the United Mine Workers." The strikers hoped not only to force Osgood to address their grievances but also to make him give at least de facto recognition to the union.[27]

Although eight CF&I mines were closed at one time or another during the strike, the company managed to prevent the union from having any real success in the Walsenburg and Trinidad fields. John L. Gehr, UMWA president of District 15, which included Colorado, Utah, and New Mexico, claimed a pervasive system of intimidation had prevented union leaders from organizing the miners. "The men in the southern part of the state are so intimidated by the Colorado Fuel and Iron Company," Gehr observed, "that it is almost impossible to go among them or get an expression of opinion, much less an organization." He also noted that union members were systematically discharged and escorted out of the CF&I and Victor camps. The situation at Hastings, one of the Victor Fuel Company's most important mines, was the worst in the southern field, Gehr stated. Numerous deputies living there were ready to break up any meeting, and the men were reluctant to testify for fear they would lose their positions. At Pictou, a reporter noted, the miners—mostly Italians, Slavs, Mexicans, and African Americans—"frankly stated that should they appear on the stand and tell the truth they, to use a miners' vernacular, would be compelled to 'hit the road.'"[28]

There was no denying that the CF&I and Victor Fuel companies controlled the sheriffs and judges in the southern Colorado counties of Las Animas and Huerfano. Company officials blatantly and brutally violated the law to carry out the companies' will. In the words of James Smith, commissioner of labor statistics, "[p]robably at no time or place in the history of Colorado, and indeed but seldom in the history of the labor movement anywhere, has the civil authority been so shamelessly prostituted to subserve the selfish interest of corporate greed, and to crush by any and every means at its command every attempt at organization among the workers, as was seen in Huerfano county at this time." The coal company officials had "inaugurated and maintained a reign of terror." They had subjugated "the miners in these fields with fear of arrest, imprisonment and discharge." Smith added: "A condition of white slavery almost incredible of belief had been well known to exist in Huerfano county for a number of years, but never before had the outrages upon the rights of citizens been perpetrated so unblushingly and with scarcely an attempt at concealment as they were at this time."[29]

Sheriff Jefferson Farr of Huerfano County and his deputies were particularly notorious for breaking up union meetings. On one occasion in January 1901, Farr and his deputies dispersed a gathering by driving the miners into an arroyo where they beat them with revolvers. "I am the chief of this county," he told the workers, "and if you don't believe it I will blow some of you to hell, you sons of bitches."[30] The *Rocky Mountain News*, quoting President Gehr, noted that there was no free government in Huerfano County once CF&I gained control: "Men have been assaulted, beaten over the heads with revolvers and thrown into jail for no other offense than an attempt to asemble [sic] in peaceful meetings to consider the condition of the coal miners."[31] Countless other incidents of violence against union members and their leaders were recorded in affidavits and newspaper accounts during the years of bitter contention between the coal companies and the UMWA in the early twentieth century.

The story of violence and intimidation against union members and organizers was one of John Osgood's most important legacies in his struggle against the UMWA. However, other policies were also employed to prevent unionization. CF&I officials, along with most other major coal operators, used racial and ethnic diversity as a way to prevent labor solidarity in the mines by making sure no racial or ethnic group predominated at any location. They employed Hispanics, African Americans, Chinese, Japanese, and European groups, especially Italians, as a means to reduce labor costs and purge union members from their employment ranks. Unskilled laborers who had neither experience with nor knowledge of unions replaced experienced miners, usually Anglo-Americans with a long history of union membership. The tactic worked well for Osgood in 1901 when the American Fuel Company in New Mexico locked the strikers out and employed Japanese workers to take their place. In Sopris and Walsenburg, union organizers disbanded the locals when newly arrived immigrant workers refused to join the union or go out on strike for fear of losing their jobs and company homes.[32]

Osgood could not use the tactic of racial and ethnic diversity or bring in unskilled replacement workers everywhere within his coal empire, however. Where mining was difficult, as in the central Colorado coalfield, he needed experienced miners to extract what was considered the finest domestic coal in the state. For this reason, Osgood was willing to settle with these men on terms more favorable to them than he was with miners elsewhere in the state or in New Mexico. He agreed to modify the coal weighing system to benefit the miners, reduce the cost of blasting powder, and allow employment of a check-weighman paid for by the miners through a checkoff system. In making these concessions, the company made it clear that it had no intention of recognizing the union. Although the miners accepted these terms, they returned to work in early April only after the company removed the blacklist against union members and strike leaders. The miners in the Walsenburg, Trinidad, and Gallup areas were less fortunate. Those who still remained in the area eventually went back to work unconditionally with no semblance of a union to support them.[33]

Although CF&I was forced to make few substantial concessions to the miners, the adverse publicity about Osgood and the coal companies generated by the strike combined with the public's general feeling that the coal companies were responsible for the labor disturbances resulted in the appointment in January 1901 of a state legislative committee to investigate the Colorado coalfields. The committee's hearings and findings focused public attention on living and working conditions in the mining camps. Reports in the *Rocky Mountain News* under the banner headlines "Struggle for Bread in Coal Miners' Homes" and "Coal Miners Tell Story of Their Hardships,"[34] which described poor housing, inadequate water supplies, and unsanitary conditions in the camps occupied by miners who were paid starvation wages, crystallized public opinion against the coal companies, particularly CF&I and the Northern Coal and Coke Company. The *Pueblo Courier* called the committee's investigation of the coal mining industry the most thorough and sweeping ever undertaken in Colorado. The paper, an advocate of labor, stated that the committee was "open, fair and impartial," with representatives from the major companies and organized labor allowed to present their cases.[35]

In some instances the committee could not gain access to the miners, as the *Courier* noted in the case of those at Pictou, related above, who were intimidated by CF&I officials to prevent them from testifying. On this occasion, however, the committee found a way to circumvent the company's obstruction of its investigation. Recognizing that the presence of company officials at the official hearing made it "impossible to get any expression of the real feeling of the miners," the committee privately interviewed some miners who had refused to testify publicly for fear of losing their jobs.[36] The tale of woe of those who testified was the same as the stories told in other mining camps. Among the grievances were poor living conditions, high rents and fees, exorbitant prices at the company store exacerbated by the company's use of scrip, and poor ventilation in the mines.

Many miners were most aggrieved by the screening system used extensively in weighing coal. They demanded the "run of mine" method, in which the coal was weighed in pit cars before it was screened. But in most of their mines, CF&I and Northern Coal and Coke ran the coal over screens before they weighed it. The miners were not paid for the "slack" coal that fell through the screens, which the companies later sold at a reduced price. The miners claimed the companies' method of weighing coal reduced their wages by 30 percent.[37]

The screening system of weighing coal was a universal complaint of miners throughout the state, as it was nationwide. John Lavierz of the Chandler mine revealed another aspect of that grievance. He testified that the Victor Coal and Coke Company always employed a "dock boss" whenever miners succeeded in obtaining a check-weighman to check the weights of coal. "Well," he explained to the investigative committee, "a dock boss is [there] to rob us of half our coal. If a miner gets a lump so big of dirt [measuring about twelve inches] the dock boss takes off 500 pounds." The Chandler and Rockvale miners added that an eight-hour workday and a biweekly payday would help them the most. In camp after camp, the miners also expressed anger over being prevented from joining the union.[38]

After visiting several mining camps and interviewing dozens of miners, the legislative investigating committee moved to Denver in late January to take testimony from Osgood and James Cannon, president of the Northern Coal and Coke Company. The *Rocky Mountain News* described Osgood's testimony as a "bitter denunciation" of the UMWA, which, he believed, was "a kind of multiple Satan going about seeking what it may devour."[39] Osgood began his testimony by reading a statement, a "little essay" as he called it, in which he made it clear that he regarded the growth of unionism as a monstrous threat not only to businessmen but also to the entire country. He proclaimed that unions were "a curse to the men as well as to the employers" and that the UMWA was the most objectionable organization of all. John Mitchell, its president, was "a greater tyrant and autocrat than the czar of Russia. No selfish and coldblooded employer ever exacted the blind obedience, absolute surrender of independence or contribution of hard won earnings that he and his organization exacts from his dupes. No slavery can be worse than the slavery which his organization imposes on its members." Ending his tirade, Osgood emphasized that he and his company officials were "unalterably opposed" to the UMWA and would never recognize it or knowingly hire any men belonging to it. He would rather close all his company's mines "and let them remain idle for all time to come" than operate them with workers "allied with" the union.[40]

In his testimony, Osgood manifested a paternalistic attitude toward his employees. By opposing the UMWA, he believed he was protecting them from a corrupt illegal organization whose leaders were only interested in their own financial and political well-being. Not everyone accepted his benevolent stance, however. An editorial in the *Denver News* mocked his assertion that his chief objection to the UMWA was that it was harmful to laborers. "The truth is," the writer argued, "the heads of the big concerns are not a bit worried over the possibility of their employes [sic] injuring themselves by joining labor unions. If the union did not occasionally try to get higher wages, shorter hours or some other betterment for its members, the president of great iron or coal companies scarcely would know or care that it existed. It is because the union is organized labor that organized capital doesn't like it."[41] Yet Osgood's perception of himself as the protector of his employees formed the foundation for his belief that by opposing the union he was upholding a fundamental principle—the right of workers to work where and under what circumstances they chose. The right-to-work principle became the major refrain in Osgood's opposition to the UMWA.

In response to the miners' demands, Osgood told the legislative committee that he was willing to meet with those employed by his company, but only if they were not members of the union. He also indicated that most of the workers' grievances could be resolved, except those related to the wage scale and a checkoff system by which the company would deduct any dues, fees, or fines imposed by the union from the miners' payroll. Accepting the latter was tantamount to recognizing the union, he believed, something he stressed repeatedly he would never do. As for other specific issues, Osgood said he was in favor of a check-weighman in each mine but added that the miners themselves had discontinued the practice when disputes arose over whether the company or the workers, as the company insisted, should collect the money to pay them. He argued that company stores were a great advantage as long as they did not compel miners and their families to trade with them, something, he stressed, his company did not do. He also argued that the company's use of scrip was legal and beneficial to the miners as a form of credit. "I think I can explain the scrip system satisfactorily," he commented, "for I believe I was the father of the system in this country. We were obliged to open a store at a mine I was connected with years ago in order to accommodate the miners. We tried to use pass books, which proved unsatisfactory, and after investigation we introduced the use of scrip, redeemable in merchandise, but not in cash. If scrip were redeemable in cash it would be a violation of the laws of the United States, which are very strict in prohibiting the use of anything made in imitation of money and used as such."[42] Years later Osgood claimed the workers themselves had caused the problems with the system by using scrip to get cash in saloons or somewhere else rather than strictly using it for credit at the company store.

Osgood admitted that his company used the screen method in weighing coal at several of its larger mines. He believed that paying on lump coal after screening was a premium for good work that was beneficial to both miner and employer. He insisted that the screens at his company's mines were one and a half inches wide and were not sprung wider, as reported in the newspapers. Although he contended that the miners' insistence on weighing coal by "run of mine" was just another ploy for raising the pay scale, he was willing to accede to their demand as long as a method could be worked out that would not increase the wage scale or the price of coal.[43] Yet it was only at Brookside, Coal Creek, Rockvale, and Chandler in the central district—where the company needed experienced miners and the union was strongest—that CF&I actually conceded to the demand. The company maintained screening at all the rest of its mines, as did Osgood at his Victor Fuel mines, even after the state legislature passed an anti-screening law.[44]

Osgood was far less conciliatory on many of the other issues the miners had raised. He was opposed to biweekly paydays, for example. "Every additional pay day would be a gain to the saloonkeepers and a loss to the men," he said. There was no justification for an increase in wages because the Colorado miners were the highest paid in any state except Montana. He further stated that CF&I was willing to work with the miners to make community improvements and to improve their housing; but the Mexicans and Italians preferred to live in shacks, and he feared they would "quit if they had to live in a house."[45]

Quizzed about the reports of alleged unlawful activities by Sheriff Jefferson Farr and his deputies in Huerfano County and the connection between them and CF&I, Osgood denied that he knew Farr or anything about the sheriff's campaign against union members and organizers. Although he argued that CF&I was not involved in politics, he conceded that some mine superintendents and pit bosses might have influence with

27

foreigners. He was confident, however, that no officers of the company had ever coerced workers to vote in a certain way or discharged them if they refused to do so. But, he added, "I do not believe that any miner should be disfranchised because he works for this company. Neither do I believe that because a man is an officer of this company he should refrain from taking an active interest in politics. I am a citizen of Colorado and vote in this state and feel that as a large employer of labor I should have a larger influence than otherwise."[46] He categorically denied that CF&I took an active part in politics, a claim congressional investigators in 1914 found to be a complete fabrication.

Osgood's demeanor before the committee—that of an arrogant man insensitive to his miners' condition—strengthened the conviction of those who believed the coal companies were responsible for the labor disturbances. The testimony of the miners and union leaders concerning working conditions in the mines increased public support for legislative measures to address such matters as the weighing of coal, use of scrip, mine safety, and the eight-hour workday. At the completion of the hearings, the committee endorsed measures to address these matters, including recommending amendments to the state constitution that would implement the eight-hour day and biweekly paydays.[47]

Although Osgood had largely withstood UMWA's attack on CF&I in 1901, he now faced another threat to his independence and freedom of action—that of the state. He realized that he would have to take aggressive action to head off or limit the adverse effects of legislation on his business activities. He also realized that he had to do something about conditions in the mining camps to improve the public's image of the company and gain greater control over his workers. By building new company towns and introducing a program of industrial paternalism, Osgood hoped to win over both workers and the public while at the same time placing yet another obstacle in the way of the UMWA in its effort to unionize the Colorado coalfields.

NOTES

1. Thomas G. Andrews, "The Road to Ludlow: Work, Environment, and Industrialization in Southern Colorado, 1870–1915" (Ph.D. diss., University of Wisconsin–Madison, 2003), 462, note 72; Perry Eberhart, *Guide to the Colorado Ghost Towns and Mining Camps* (Chicago: Sage Books, 4th revised ed., 1974), 312.

2. Osgood told members of the U.S. House Subcommittee on Mines and Mining in 1914 that his first coal mining business venture started with $6,000 (Osgood's testimony, U.S. Congress, House, *Conditions in the Coal Mines of Colorado, Hearings before*

a Subcommittee of the Committee on Mines and Mining, 63rd Cong., 2nd sess., 1914, p. 482; hereafter cited as SMM).

3. This biographical material is taken from H. Lee Scamehorn, "John C. Osgood and the Western Steel Industry," *Arizona and the West* 15 (Summer 1973): 133–134; Ruland, *Lion of Redstone*, 9–11; *New York Times*, September 7, 1902; *Trinidad Daily News*, January 5, 1926.

4. Milo Lee Whittaker attributed the company's success to Osgood's business acumen and his ability to surround himself with "business and political advisors of unusual merit" (*Pathbreakers and Pioneers of the Pueblo Region* [Pueblo, Colo.: Franklin Press, 1917], 125).

5. *Rocky Mountain News*, August 15, 1923.

6. David Wolff, *Industrializing the Rockies: Growth, Competition, and Turmoil in the Coalfields of Colorado and Wyoming, 1868–1914* (Boulder: University Press of Colorado, 2003), 125.

7. Information for this and the preceding paragraph is from Scamehorn, "Osgood and the Western Steel Industry," 136–137, and Scamehorn, *Pioneer Steelmaker in the West: The Colorado Fuel and Iron Company, 1872–1903* (Boulder: Pruett, 1976), 81–90.

8. John L. Jerome, "Statement of Business and Personal Relations—John C. Osgood and John L. Jerome August 1882 to August 1903," Jerome Papers, Colorado Historical Society, FF 1, 7.

9. Andrews, "Road to Ludlow," 425; Scamehorn, *Pioneer Steelmaker*, 71, 91–92; Wolff, *Industrializing the Rockies*, 124–125.

10. Scamehorn, "Osgood and the Western Steel Industry," 138, 140; Andrews, "Road to Ludlow," 426; Wolff, *Industrializing the Rockies*, 121.

11. Wolff, *Industrializing the Rockies*, 139; Andrews, "Road to Ludlow," 426; Howard K. Wilson, "A Study of Paternalism in the Colorado Fuel and Iron Company under John C. Osgood: 1892–1903" (M.A. thesis, University of Denver, 1967), 57; Scamehorn, "Osgood and the Western Steel Industry," 139.

12. Wolff, *Industrializing the Rockies*, 149–151.

13. Ibid., 151; Andrews, "Road to Ludlow," 423, citing *Second Annual Report of the Colorado Fuel and Iron Company for the Year Ending June 30, 1894* (Denver: n.p., 1894), 10–11.

14. Wolff, *Industrializing the Rockies*, 152; Andrews, "Road to Ludlow," 423.

15. Ruland, *Lion of Redstone*, 46; Wolff, *Industrializing the Rockies*, 152–153.

16. On May 11, 1894, a strike occurred at the Pullman Company plant in Pullman, Illinois, near Chicago. The American Railway Union, formed by Eugene V. Debs in 1893, participated in the strike, which resulted in the obstruction of the mail and destruction of property. President Grover Cleveland sent federal troops to Chicago and issued an injunction ordering the union to desist in its activities. When the union refused to obey the injunction, President Cleveland, with the sanction of the United States circuit court, applied the Sherman Anti-Trust Act against labor unions judged to be engaged in a "conspiracy to hinder and obstruct interstate commerce." In 1895 the United States Supreme Court upheld the lower court in the use

of the act, which subsequently gave capital a formidable weapon against labor. Debs was sentenced to six months in prison for defying the first injunction (William L. Langer, ed., *An Encyclopedia of World History* [Boston: Houghton Mifflin, 1968], 825).

17. Osgood's testimony, CIR/FR 7: 6423–6424.

18. Wolff, *Industrializing the Rockies,* 151.

19. Scamehorn, "Osgood and the Western Steel Industry," 140. Thomas Andrews observed: "The coking-coal seams underlying much of this vast country [Maxwell Land Grant] promised to sate the fuel needs of the steel mills for decades to come, while the lands above seemed to Osgood ripe to become, despite a tendentious history of settler–grant company conflict, a domain fit for a feudal lord" ("Road to Ludlow," 427).

20. "Minutes of Colo. Finance and Construction Company," Jerome Papers, FF 8; "Bill of Complaint, John L. Jerome vs. John C. Osgood and the Colorado Finance and Construction Company," Jerome Papers, FF 26; Scamehorn, *Pioneer Steelmaker,* 97–99.

21. Scamehorn, *Pioneer Steelmaker,* 98–99; "Bill of Complaint," Jerome Papers, FF 26.

22. Scamehorn, "Osgood and the Western Steel Industry," 143–144; Scamehorn, *Pioneer Steelmaker,* 101–102; *Denver Times,* May 18, 1901; Long, *Where the Sun Never Shines,* 212. "Incredible as it may seem to Pitsburghers [sic]," Herbert Casson observed in *The Romance of Steel* (1907), "the fact is that the Colorado Fuel and Iron is the most self-sufficient and elaborate of all steel-making companies. It is more than a business: it is a civilization" (quoted in Andrews, "Road to Ludlow," 146).

23. *Rocky Mountain News,* January 26, 1899.

24. Ibid., January 27, 29, 1899.

25. Wolff, *Industrializing the Rockies,* 182–183; Colorado Bureau of Labor Statistics, *Eighth Biennial Report of the Bureau of Labor Statistics of the State of Colorado, 1901–1902* (Denver: Smith-Brooks, 1902), 130 (hereafter cited as CBLS, *Eighth Biennial Report*).

26. Wolff, *Industrializing the Rockies,* 184, citing the *United Mine Workers' Journal,* January 10, 24, 31, 1901.

27. Quote in *Rocky Mountain News,* January 23, 1901; Wolff, *Industrializing the Rockies,* 184–185. Osgood's American Fuel Company, not CF&I, owned the mines in Gallup, but the miners in Colorado made no distinction among companies with which Osgood was associated.

28. "Among the Coal Miners," *Pueblo Courier,* January 25, 1901; last quote in paragraph in "The Coal Miners of Colorado," *Pueblo Courier,* February 8, 1901; Gehr quote in *Rocky Mountain News,* January 31, 1901; CBLS, *Eighth Biennial Report,* 130.

29. Smith quote in CBLS, *Eighth Biennial Report,* 155–156.

30. "Among the Coal Miners," *Pueblo Courier,* January 25, 1901.

31. *Rocky Mountain News,* January 30, 1901.

32. Ibid., January 20, 22, 1901; Wolff, *Industrializing the Rockies,* 136–137, 186–187; CBLS, *Eighth Biennial Report,* 156.

33. CBLS, *Eighth Biennial Report*, 155; Wolff, *Industrializing the Rockies*, 187; Scamehorn, *Pioneer Steelmaker*, 125–126; "Abstracts of Official Reports: Colorado Fuel and Iron Company," *Engineering and Mining Journal* 72, no. 14 (October 5, 1901): 430.

34. *Rocky Mountain News*, January 20, 23, 1901.

35. *Pueblo Courier*, February 8, 1901.

36. *Rocky Mountain News*, January 24, 1901.

37. Ibid., January 23, 24, 1901. The *News* reporter observed that the steel bars that made up the screen were "sprung four or five inches" apart instead of the customary inch and a half.

38. Quote in ibid., January 23, 1901; Maier B. Fox, *United We Stand: The United Mine Workers of America 1890–1990* (Washington, D.C.: United Mine Workers of America, 1990), 24.

39. *Rocky Mountain News*, January, 31, 1901.

40. Osgood quoted in the *Denver Times*, January 31, 1901.

41. Editorial in the *Denver News*, reprinted in the *Pueblo Courier*, February 8, 1901.

42. Osgood quoted in the *Denver Times*, January 31, 1901. Osgood's claim to be the "father of the scrip system in this country," presumably the United States, is dubious. Henry Clay Frick issued scrip, known as "Frick dollars," for goods workers purchased at his stores as early as 1873 (Rottenberg, *In the Kingdom of Coal*, 70).

43. *Rocky Mountain News*, January 31, 1901.

44. The price paid to miners for a ton of screened coal before the strike was ninety cents. After the strike, the price was seventy-five cents for a "run of the mine" ton of coal. Although they received fifteen cents a ton less for coal, miners considered that the changed system of weighing coal resulted in a 15 percent increase in their wages (CBLS, *Eighth Biennial Report*, 155).

45. Osgood quoted in ibid.

46. Ibid.; quote in *Denver Times*, January 31, 1901.

47. CBLS, *Eighth Biennial Report*, 154; Wolff, *Industrializing the Rockies*, 189; Fox, *United We Stand*, 71.

Industrial Betterment and the Redstone Experiment

John C. Osgood faced critical problems in the immediate aftermath of the
1901 strike. Public opinion in Colorado had shifted in favor of the working class, in part as a result of the negative publicity generated by the
legislative committee's investigation of coalfield conditions. Pressed by an
outraged public, the state legislature seemed poised to pass legislation that
Osgood and other coal operators considered ruinous to the coal industry.
Waiting in the wings was the United Mine Workers of America (UMWA),
which, although largely checked in its strike against Osgood's Colorado Fuel
and Iron (CF&I) and Victor Fuel mines in 1901, was ready to use the miners' discontent to continue its effort to unionize the Colorado coalfields. In
addition, the prospect of renewed labor disturbances threatened Osgood's

plans to resume expansion of CF&I operations. For these reasons, Osgood turned to a program of welfare capitalism promoted nationally under the banner of industrial or social betterment. Such a program, Osgood hoped, would create a stable and productive workforce loyal to CF&I rather than to the UMWA. Furthermore, Osgood calculated that a program designed to enhance the workers' moral character and physical quality of life would improve his corporation's public image.

Industrial betterment was a labor-management strategy inspired by the settlement house movement and advocated by leading professional social scientists and reformers during the late nineteenth and early twentieth centuries as a way to address the problems of modern industrialism. As a national movement, it played a significant role in the transition from the old paternalistic practices of the nineteenth century to a new industrial strategy that would extend management "to every level of the worker's life, from the factory to the school to the home." The focus of industrial betterment was on improving employees' living and working conditions by establishing welfare or sociological departments that would promote their social and physical welfare.[1]

Osgood was the first coal baron in the West and one of the earliest of the country's prominent industrialists to adopt a program of industrial bet-terment as a strategy to improve labor-management relations. Furthermore, at a time when few industrialists built model company towns or planned communities, Osgood applied the sociological concept of industrial bet-terment to the development of a new town system.[2] Both industrial bet-terment and the new town system were integral parts of his campaign to defeat the UMWA.

CF&I launched its program of industrial betterment on July 25, 1901, when Julian Kebler, the company's general manager, announced the creation of the Sociological Department. He defined its function in a letter to super-visory personnel: "This department will have general charge of all matters pertaining to education and sanitary conditions and any other matters which should assist in bettering the conditions under which our men live. It is not the object to exercise a paternal control over the men, but to put them in the way of information that will arouse their ambition and make them desirous of doing the best they can for themselves, as well as for their employer."[3]

Osgood and Kebler established the Sociological Department to pro-vide CF&I with a managerial model for initiating programs, with the goals of reducing labor turnover, preventing union organization, improving the company's image, and creating a new generation of contented and productive workers.[4] The appointed head of the new department was Dr. Richard Corwin, chief surgeon and director of CF&I's Medical Department. In his 1902 annual report, Corwin observed that Osgood and Kebler had established the department because of an appreciation of the importance of sociological work, "not only that it would be an aid to the company, but [also] a benefit to the employees and their families, a means of educating the younger generation, of improving the home relations and furthering the interests of the men, making them better citizens and more contented with their work." Much of the responsibility for providing "a healthy social and intellectual life for . . . adults," Corwin stressed, "must be [borne] by the great corporations controlling the coal fields, for they have the means and control the situation." Thus, Osgood and Kebler's program of industrial welfare, under Corwin's direction, was designed to make the company a social as well as an economic force in the lives of employees and their families.[5]

Corwin was an advanced social thinker who believed business should be conducted with scrupulous regard for moral principles. In forming his views, he was greatly influenced by the League for Social Service, which William H. Tolman and Josiah Strong formed in 1898 to espouse the philosophy of industrial betterment, a term Tolman coined to describe this early variant of welfare capitalism. CF&I had a commercial membership in the league and received *Social Service*, its monthly publication, as well as weekly bulletins and reports of sociological conditions, experiments, and reform movements from all over the world. Corwin shared the philosophy expressed in an article in *Social Service* that "education and improved environment may be the means of bringing about brotherly love and the application of the Golden Rule—the foundation of all Sociological thought and Social Betterment in the Rockies as well as elsewhere."[6] Through a program of social betterment, he believed it was possible to create communities free from strife and want.

Other leading social reformers and social movements influenced Corwin. While completing his medical training in Chicago, he had become acquainted with Jane Addams and the settlement house movement at Hull House. From this movement, Corwin derived a conceptual model based on the settlement philosophy that he used to guide the Sociological Department's program of industrial welfare work. Corwin also shared many of the ideals of progressive reformers, particularly with respect to the belief that the social evolutionary process would produce persons shaped

Dr. Richard Corwin. Courtesy, Colorado Fuel and Iron Archives, Bessemer Historical Society, Pueblo.

by the principles of hard work, self-discipline, personal responsibility, and sobriety. The optimistic belief that education could change people for the better and that American society had always manifested constant improvement permeated all of Corwin's thoughts and endeavors.[7]

Although they shared many of the same goals, Osgood's businesslike approach to industrial welfare differed from Corwin's humanitarian view of the movement. Osgood's view of labor-management relations was straightforward: employers and employees must be bound together by mutual respect and common allegiance to the company. The relationship, however, would be established on the basis of the employer's "parental solicitude and the employee's filial subservience." The worker's loyalty to the company, Osgood conceded, could only be won by assuring his physical health and mental tranquility. Neglecting this tranquility not only threatened declining production as a result of worker dissatisfaction but also increased the chances that workers would listen to socialists and union organizers. Thus, Osgood stressed, an improved working environment was absolutely necessary to negate union activity in the camps. Businessmen, Osgood added, had the duty to conduct their business in a Christian manner. They should create corporations "with a soul," not for benevolent or altruistic reasons but for business reasons. "We do not ask credit as philanthropists," he proclaimed. "We are aiming to carry out commonsense business ideals in the conduct of the business."[8]

Although he remained paternalistic toward his employees, Osgood, with Corwin's influence, adopted a form of welfare capitalism that not only provided opportunities for improvement but also stressed the need to educate workers to take advantage of those opportunities. Permanent success in social betterment, Corwin believed, depended upon teaching employees how to improve their quality of life on their own. By teaching self-help, Corwin stressed, the Sociological Department's program of industrial betterment was not paternalistic. According to a staff member, Corwin "discarded purely paternal methods for those of suggestion . . . and cooperation." He made no effort "to force improvements upon indifferent communities." In sum, Corwin believed a good living environment would improve the workers' well-being and morality, which in turn would promote hard work and efficiency.[9] Corwin's social idealism combined with Osgood's business acumen produced a program of industrial welfare that was important in the development of twentieth-century welfare capitalism.

One of the most important contributions of the League for Social Service was the idea of a professional social secretary to act as a personal link between a company and its employees. William Tolman defined the social secretary as "one who can devote his whole time to become acquainted with the employees and promoting their general welfare; one who looks after sanitary conditions, seeks to increase the general intelligence, fosters a healthful social life and strives to improve the general morale."[10] As superintendent of the Sociological Department, Corwin perfectly fit Tolman's job description of a social secretary in his role of developing and administrating CF&I's industrial betterment policies. Tolman and Josiah Strong noted that Corwin was one of the first social secretaries appointed by a large industrial firm. "The Colorado Fuel and Iron Company, which employs seventeen thousand people in mines extending over three states," Strong observed in 1906, "depends largely upon a Social Secretary to Americanize its men and to see that the conditions under which they live and work are as favorable as it is possible to make them."[11]

Under Corwin's leadership, the department, with a staff of two dozen people, took responsibility over five areas: education, social training, industrial training, housing, and communications. With an ambitious program during the first year, the department built employee housing and established public schools, night schools, and kindergartens. Also initiated were a variety of other activities, including cooking classes, traveling libraries, lecture series, and clubs for boys and girls. The communications staff published a biweekly company magazine entitled *Camp and Plant* to promote the work of the Sociological Department and draw workers at the thirty-eight CF&I camps, rolling mills, and steelworks closer together.[12]

Throughout its brief three-year history, *Camp and Plant* faithfully espoused the Sociological Department's philosophy of social betterment while reporting its accomplishments. The publication featured prose, poetry, travel articles, anecdotes, and reports written in a folksy manner from all the camps and mills. Informational articles on such subjects as sociology, hygiene and sanitation, domestic science, and education were often published in three languages besides English—German, Italian, and Spanish—and stressed the virtues of education, self-help, patriotism, domestic improvement, and appreciation for labor. Politics and religion were not discussed, although it was stated that Christianity would be "taught in its truest and broadest sense," with the "moral tone . . . always uplifting."[13] Many photographs were included to depict the company's progress in plant expansion and camp improvement. The articles that accompanied the photographs were often overly flattering and clearly propagandistic to counter the criticisms of muckraking journalists. One article, for instance, noted that the company cottages are "neat and comfortable. . . . One who has gleaned his ideas of a coal camp from the yellow journals would look in vain for the hovels and squalor so often depicted."[14]

Camp and Plant was a major disseminator of information about the company throughout the country. Corwin noted in the second *Annual Report* that a number of stockholders and people involved in business and finance nationwide subscribed to the publication to keep informed about the Sociological Department's programs or to use it as a model for establishing similar publications. Many of the articles originally published in *Camp and Plant* were reprinted with favorable comments in such trade journals as *The Iron Trade Review, The Iron and Machinery World, Popular Mechanics,* and *The Mining and Engineering Journal.* Leading national newspapers also published stories about CF&I's program of social betterment. *"Camp and Plant,"* Corwin wrote, "measures its success not as a money maker nor even as a project that is financially self-supporting, but as a means of disproving the current though false notion that great corporations wish to avoid publicity in their methods of operation, and as a maker of good will, of contentment, of healthful rivalry among camps and employes [sic], and of general social and industrial betterment."[15]

Officials of the League for Social Service praised CF&I's program of industrial betterment in frequent articles in *Social Service* detailing the company's sociological work. Much of the information for these articles was taken from the Sociological Department's annual reports, which Corwin prepared for the company. Other publications also praised the program. In *Social Engineering,* William Tolman described CF&I's industrial betterment program at length, with particular emphasis on its hospital and medical facilities, sanitary and hygienic conditions, education, recreation, and housing. Tolman believed the company's welfare work was innovative in several ways. He noted, for example, that in a number of the camps the company erected houses for teachers in the public schools and kindergartens that would also serve as centers for sociological work. At Redstone, Osgood's model village, a "show" cottage was furnished in an inexpensive but artistic style to demonstrate ways of making a home attractive with a small outlay of time and money.[16]

Additional features of CF&I's program of industrial betterment were brought to the nation's attention. The company's experiment with restricted saloons—first tried at Coalbasin and Redstone—was nationally recognized as a "peculiarly instructive" attempt to deal with the "liquor problem." "Billiards, pool and poker may be played there [in the clubhouse] for strictly limited stakes," an article in the *Inter Ocean of Chicago* observed. "Liquors are sold, of the best quality, and at the lowest prices, but no man is encouraged to drink, no man is permitted to get drunk, and no treating is allowed." *The Echo*, a monthly publication of the Filene Co-operative Association of

Boston, opined that "[t]he effort of this great corporation to improve the moral, mental and physical welfare of its employes [sic] is a move which will be followed closely by those who are interested in the development of a higher type of American citizen." The *Outlook,* one of the most respected social reform periodicals, stated that "[t]he sense of responsibility thus shown by this Western mining company [CF&I] in seeking to ameliorate the condition of its employees and to beautify their surroundings furnishes an example which Eastern operators might well emulate." In response to the complaints of "some stockholders [who] might criticize the using of company funds for humanizing purposes," Osgood stated that he was "simply carrying out good business principles in promoting the welfare of his employees."[17]

Most authors of these articles and editorials found CF&I's program of industrial betterment praiseworthy for emphasizing self-help. They endorsed the concept of employers promoting their employees' social and moral welfare through a program based on education. "Like an increasing number of great corporations," *Camp and Plant* stated, "the Colorado Fuel and Iron Company finds it good business policy not only to see that its employes [sic] do their work well, but also to look after the manner in which they spend their leisure hours, and to endeavor to have them spent profitably, or at least harmlessly." In even more paternalistic terms, the *Daily Republican* of Springfield, Massachusetts, observed, "Colorado," in contrast to the reactionary policies of Pennsylvania coalfields, "has treated the toilers as friendly allies, if not as brethren; rather, we might say, as younger brothers who were to be humored and taught by their elders."[18]

Yet to some reformers, the "social-uplift" aspect of industrial betterment carried the negative connotation of philanthropic work that offended the workers' pride and independence. The terms "industrial betterment" and "social uplift" suggested that the workers' character flaws, rather than their conditions of employment, were the primary objects of the reforms.[19] As events in the southern Colorado coalfields would prove, this criticism was valid, for the miners were far more concerned with improving their working conditions than they were with improving their moral character.

Although industrial unrest and adverse public opinion toward CF&I in 1901 were the factors most instrumental in prompting Osgood and Kebler to create the Sociological Department, company officials had begun to look at the poor condition of the camps as early as 1899 during the expansion of the steelworks in Pueblo. John Jerome, for instance, had found many of the employee houses in Bessemer adjacent to the steel plant, as well as the town itself, to be "dirty, in poor repair, and repulsive." But, he added, with a relatively small investment in the construction of houses and other improvements, the town could be made "comparatively attractive."[20] Osgood agreed, and these improvements as well as other major projects in the town and at the steel mill were commenced in the fall of 1899.

At about the same time, Corwin's personal inspection of El Moro convinced him that the high incidence of disease and illness among coke workers at that camp was caused by poor living conditions. Most of the Italian workers lived in shacks, dugouts, or poorly constructed adobe structures they had built on company land. Corwin found in one instance that thirty-eight men slept in two shifts in the "midst of unspeakable filth and vermin" in one fifteen- by forty-foot adobe bunkhouse. After hearing Corwin's report on this and similar situations, Osgood and Kebler ordered the worst of the places on company property to be torn down and new company houses constructed. They also decreed, with limited success, that employees could no longer put up their own houses on company land.[21]

El Moro was just the beginning of the company's campaign to improve sanitary and living conditions in all the mining and coking camps, a campaign put in full swing with the official commencement of the industrial betterment program. The Medical Department sent staff members to inspect conditions in the camps and to ensure that the camps had adequate and safe water supplies. Water systems were constructed in communities that needed them, and wells and cisterns were cleaned and inspected periodically. Medical staff supervised the cleanup of the camps by, among other things, removing unsanitary outbuildings and cleaning cesspools. In keeping with the concept that all betterment work was educational in the broadest sense, officials from the Sociological Department traveled to the camps to give lectures on physiology and hygiene and the dangers of alcohol use. Bulletins printed in English, German, Italian, and Spanish were circulated, explaining the causes of diseases and how to prevent them. Adult education classes were also conducted to teach employees how to improve themselves and their families.[22]

Corwin and CF&I officials also realized that large companies had to provide medical services to employees in order to attract and maintain a workforce. As the company expanded, Corwin extended medical services in each of the camps. Most camps had well-equipped doctors' offices with resident physicians on fixed salaries who provided "gratuitous services for all cases except venereal diseases, injuries resulting from violations of state laws or municipal ordinances, and confinement cases." Physicians could treat these ailments for an additional charge beyond the one dollar per month all employees paid for the basic health care service.[23]

Medical services for CF&I employees also included access to a new company hospital in Pueblo known as the Minnequa Hospital. Opened in August 1902, the new facility consisted of thirteen Spanish mission–style buildings erected on a twenty-acre tract of land. It was a state-of-the-art medical center that Corwin designed in his capacity as director of the company's Medical Department. The new facility included modern laboratories, convalescent lodging, teaching facilities, and a School of Nursing. The medical center served the steel mill workers and severely ill and injured employees from CF&I camps. All employees of the company who could not be treated locally were admitted to the hospital free of charge.[24] The Minnequa Hospital was Corwin's crowning achievement in the area of health care. He made CF&I a leader in industrial medicine, and his work in the Sociological Department also made the company a leader in industrial sociology.

––––––––––

Although conditions in the older, established coal camps were improved through the work of the Sociological Department after 1901, it was the development of eight new camps during the corporation's expansion program that enabled Osgood to pursue social betterment and company town planning according to his own ideas. In establishing the Sociological Department objectives, CF&I determined that all new camps would be carefully planned, with houses built to company specifications. Between 1901 and 1903, the company built 895 new houses, ranging in size from three to five rooms. A few basic architectural designs and simple building techniques were used to provide the quickest and cheapest methods of construction. A simple four-room house cost between $700 and $800 to build. Building materials for these structures ranged from concrete block in the Purgatoire Valley near Trinidad to clapboard over wooden frame in the rest of the camps. The company rented the houses to its employees for $2 a room per month. Indoor water and toilets were seldom provided, although water was available from hydrants for domestic use and fire protection. Renters paid a monthly charge of 35 cents per electrical outlet in houses where electricity was supplied and $1.50 to $2.00 per ton of coal for heating and cooking.[25]

Better housing and sanitary conditions constituted only part of the Sociological Department's endeavor to improve the quality of life in company camps. Even more important was the department's emphasis on education, domestic and industrial training, and leisure activities. Education, Corwin stated, "is the master-key to the whole social betterment situation." It places "every class and nationality on an equal standing, and while recognizing differences . . . it attempts to inculcate the true democratic spirit." Although educational programs were established for all ages of both sexes, the department made kindergartens one of its top priorities. Kindergartens, Corwin believed, were the incubators of the next generation of miners and miners' wives who would be assimilated into American society far better than their parents had been or ever could be. "It is difficult to change the way and manners of adults; their habits have been formed and are not easily altered," he explained. "With age come indifference, a desire to be let alone and a loss of ambition; but not so is it with the young. Children are tractable, easily managed and molded, have no set ways to correct and recast; hence the importance of kindergarten."[26]

CF&I established free kindergartens in every camp large enough to warrant them. Besides a regimen of the "three Rs" in the classroom, there were games and other activities to help mold the total child and to draw parents into their children's social world. The experience of Christmas was another way to bring American values to immigrant families. The Sociological Department arranged for each child in the kindergartens to receive candy and fruit, as well as dolls for girls and drums for boys. By making little gifts for their parents in return, the children, Corwin observed, learned to look at Christmas "as a time of giving rather than receiving, of good will and generosity rather than of selfishness." The teaching of English was a paramount function of these activities. The success of this aspect of social betterment rested squarely on the teachers, especially the "kindergartners," recognized by Corwin as "social settlement workers" devoted to creating responsible adult citizens.[27]

The Sociological Department was also extensively involved in primary school education. Between 1901 and 1903, CF&I built ten public school buildings at a total cost of a little over $24 million.[28] In most cases, local school boards administered the schools; however, since many of the school buildings were built with company money on company property, CF&I insisted on and was granted dominant influence over the districts. In most camps the school board consisted of company superintendents and managers. CF&I also supplied free textbooks and selected teachers, many trained at company expense. At Corwin's insistence, the state imposed a uniform curriculum throughout the mining districts that included reading, math, science, writing, and art. With a uniform curriculum, a child's education would not be interrupted if the father moved to another camp within company jurisdiction.[29]

Education to Corwin meant more than kindergarten and primary education. It also included courses in domestic science for girls and vocational training for boys, as well as night school for adults.[30] Clubs for boys and girls were established in the camps to channel boys into more useful activities and to keep girls from being "turned out on the streets to amuse and care for themselves." Like the schools, the clubs were formed to teach "American" values and "proper" gender roles. The Sociological Department had little faith in immigrant parents' ability to raise their children adequately, particularly boys. "The typical boy of the coal camps is an interesting personage," Corwin noted. "His horizon has been naturally limited; his whole training and environment has cultivated in him a narrow spirit, a selfishness which fails to see any good in a movement which does not benefit him personally. He is stoical and ambitious to be thought 'grownup,' and sometimes even 'tough.' It is his delight to hang around the saloons, listening to the ever present accordion, learning to drink—he is already a veteran tobacco user—and taking fascinating lessons in profane and vile language." Corwin added that the coal camp boy was "good hearted" and "by no means wholly bad." To correct any "moral deficiency," Corwin believed it was necessary to change the social habits, especially the drinking culture, of European immigrants.[31]

Girls fared better than boys in the department's evaluation because "girls are more refined and subject to fewer temptations, and their problems, therefore, are much easier to solve." Corwin was determined to solve those problems by establishing sewing and cooking classes. An itinerant teacher traveled from camp to camp teaching girls and their mothers how to prepare wholesome food. Other girls' and mothers' clubs were formed, including a child study club for mothers at Rockvale.[32]

The Sociological Department's efforts to teach camp residents American values and the American way of life also included the establishment of libraries, reading rooms, recreation halls, and clubhouses. Libraries and circulating art collections were placed in school buildings, where students and adults shared books, and in reading rooms. Osgood made certain the Redstone library was particularly well stocked; it held 422 volumes, including valuable reference books and full sets of works by such authors as Irving, Cooper, Scott, Kipling, and Dickens. Reading rooms in the camps contained newspapers in several languages and periodicals that reflected "mainstream" American values, such as *Success, Harper's Weekly, Scribner's Magazine, Cosmopolitan, McClure's, Youth's Companion, Ladies Home Journal, Craftsman,* and the *Denver Republican*. Strict censorship was practiced. Charles Darwin's *Origin of Species,* for example, was banned, as was all socialist literature and material critical of the company. *Harper's Weekly* was no longer allowed in the libraries after a series of articles appeared in 1914 that were sympathetic to the strikers and critical of the coal operators and John D. Rockefeller Jr. Company officials reasoned that anything detrimental to the country or to the company was also detrimental to the workers.[33]

Recreation halls, auditoriums, and clubhouses were built in some of the larger and newer camps to promote educational and social programs. Harmony Hall in Starkville and the Redstone auditorium were especially grand in scale and decor. *Camp and Plant* noted in January 1902 that "[t]he Redstone Auditorium will be completed within three months. While Denver brags about what it is going to do, Redstone, thanks to its 'first citizen' [Osgood], does things." All kinds of activities, including lectures, lantern shows, plays, concerts, dances, and local talent shows, were held in the halls. Saturday night dances with musicians from Trinidad and Walsenburg were particularly popular in the southern Colorado coal camps. Realizing that "there is little in the way of diversion," the Sociological Department experimented in 1902 and 1903 with an "entertainment course," featuring touring regional entertainers. Corwin was a frequent lecturer on a variety of subjects, including "The Ruins of the Nile" and "Art in the Decoration of Schools and Homes."[34]

A serious concern for the Sociological Department was the miners' social behavior. Corwin and company officials were alarmed at the widespread abuse of alcohol in the camps. Drunkenness was a major problem that adversely affected job performance and created safety problems. It also cost the company in terms of lost production and frequently resulted in a disgruntled workforce more susceptible to union organizers. Therefore, the Sociological Department attempted to control the flow of alcohol into the camps, particularly those established after 1901, by strictly regulating the conditions under which alcohol could be sold in saloons and clubs and by attempting to entice the men away from drink by providing "soft drink clubs," libraries, and reading rooms. Osgood accepted saloons as "a necessity of camp life" and concluded, along with Corwin, that outright prohibition led to bootlegging. Although neither man was satisfied with the results of their efforts to mitigate the effects of alcohol consumption in the camps, the Sociological Department was praised for leading the company's thousands of workers and their families "from conditions of drunkenness and dirt to well-ordered living" and for "doing everything possible to make the men and their families contented and happy."[35]

Budgett Meakin, a British social reformer and journalist, was greatly impressed with CF&I's industrial betterment program. Although he did not list the company's "model" towns individually, Meakin grouped them collectively under the heading "Colorado Mining Camps" in his 1905 survey titled *Model Factories and Villages*. "The rough-and-tumble mining shanties of the early camps of the Colorado Fuel and Iron Company out on the bleak foot-hills of the Rockies," he wrote, "have given way under praiseworthy management to what for that part of the world are model industrial villages."[36]

Meakin was probably describing such towns as Primero, Rugby, Segundo, Tabasco, and Tercio—all new company towns in the southern Colorado coalfield around Trinidad. The two other towns built during CF&I's period of expansion from 1899 to 1903 were Coalbasin and Redstone, both in the Crystal River Valley in western Colorado. Redstone was the jewel among them—"The Ruby of the Rockies," the *New York Times* dubbed the village in 1902. It was Osgood's showplace for his sociological experiment and the model for the new CF&I towns. "Redstone," the *Denver Republican* noted, "is to be the model village of the Fuel and Iron company. There . . . Mr. Osgood will construct a village after his own ideas." Although Redstone was the "grand" model village, Osgood believed it was necessary to initiate a similar innovative program of industrial paternalism throughout the CF&I empire "to safeguard the worker, and his output, from boredom, indignity, drink, and disgust."[37]

Unlike the other new towns created during the 1899–1903 period of CF&I expansion, Redstone was never a company town in the true sense of the term. Osgood transferred money, which he considered his own private funds, from the Colorado Finance and Construction Company (CF&CC) into the Redstone Improvement Company to develop the village as part of his private estate that included Cleveholm Manor, his palatial country residence. For this reason the village, unlike the coke ovens built nearby with company funds, was never part of the CF&I corporation and remained a part of Osgood's estate after the Rockefeller-Gould takeover of the company in 1903.[38]

Osgood began development of the Redstone industrial enterprise in 1899 by building 100 coke ovens on the west bank of the Crystal River near the junction of the Crystal River Railroad and the narrow-gauge railroad (the "High Line") that climbed the steep grade to the Coal Basin mine eight miles to the west. During the next two years another 150 ovens were constructed to complete the coking plant. Osgood brought in 100 stonemasons and bricklayers from Denver to construct what was planned to be the largest coking plant in the state.[39] However, his decision to establish coking operations there was not based on a realistic appraisal of market conditions. The weak condition of the smelter industry in western Colorado in the late 1890s did not justify building more coking plants in the region, and it was not economical to haul coke from the western mountain district to the Pueblo steel mill hundreds of miles away.[40] His determination to create a model industrial community near the site he had selected for Cleveholm Manor overrode the negative business considerations for constructing a coking enterprise at that location.

Even before launching his industrial enterprise at Redstone, Osgood had established a ranch—the Crystal River Ranch—and a summer home on a vast estate of over 4,200 acres that would encompass the planned village and his new country mansion. For the site of Cleveholm Manor, Osgood chose a prime location on a gentle slope at the widest part of a clearing about a mile south of the village of Redstone. He began construction of the mansion in 1899, the same year he began to build the coke ovens and develop Redstone as an industrial facility. He retained the prominent Denver architectural firm Boal & Harnois to design the mansion and, eventually, all the buildings on the estate, as well as those planned for the new model community of Redstone. Cleveholm Manor, the estate buildings, and the village of Redstone were all completed within a remarkably short construction period, between 1899 and 1902.

With an expenditure of over $300,000 through the Redstone Improvement Company, Osgood personally supervised the construction of his self-contained model town of well-built homes for workers and managers and its substantial public facilities. Although still not completed, the *Denver Times* described the marvel of the emerging new town:

> The great reservoir of the Colorado Iron and Fuel [sic] company at
> Redstone was finished this week and the electric lights were turned on
> Wednesday. Redstone is now assuming metropolitan airs. When one
> comes to think of it all, it seems simply wonderful—the transformation.
> On this spot but a few short years ago the wolf howled and the coyote
> skulked; the elk, the deer, the bear, the mountain lion and other wild
> animals roamed undisturbed by the presence of man. It was a solitude.
> Now it is a hive of industry, a thrifty mountain town emerging from its
> swaddling clothes with a future. All is activity, and the modern electric
> light turns night into day.[41]

Cleveholm Manor (Redstone Castle). Courtesy, Lane Stewart.

Influenced by the traditions of English country living, Osgood built Cleveholm Manor in the Tudor Revival architectural style in conformity with his interpretation of an English country house; the layout of the village, with the larger managerial houses on a hill above the workers' cottages, reflected the social hierarchy Osgood envisaged for an English company town.[42] The setting gave the appearance of a baronial fiefdom, an impression Osgood intended to convey. In terms more contemporary to his time, Cleveholm Manor was a monument to Osgood's wealth and power and a showplace to impress his many wealthy, world-famous guests, such as the John D. Rockefellers (Sr. and Jr.), J. Pierpont Morgan, George Gould, Theodore Roosevelt, and Prince Henri de Croy of Belgium.[43]

The majority of the workers' cottages in the village that lined either side of River Road, now called Redstone Boulevard, were square four-room structures with hip roofs and lap siding. Whitewashed board fences ran along the road in front of all the cottages, and fences also divided the yards of individual houses. All the cottages and houses had electricity, running water, and plaster and lath interiors with wall covering. In its first issue, *Camp and Plant*, touting Redstone as one of the Sociological Department's achievements, proudly announced that

[a] group of fifty houses in the lower part of the town will shortly be finished and ready for occupation. These cottages, or a greater number of them, will be occupied by the Italians, who are coke and stone workers. They believe that their health will thus be greatly improved. Beauty has been the guiding principle in building up our little town. We do not have monotonous rows of box-car houses with battened walls, painted a dreary mineral red, but tasteful little cottages in different styles, prettily ornamented, comfortably arranged internally and painted in every variety of restful color.

The article also noted that houses of different sizes were grouped to give a pleasant and diversified appearance and to avoid the monotony of the stereotyped form of a company town.[44]

The managerial houses located on the hill overlooking the cottages were far more spacious, with most having at least six rooms. They had more ornate architectural details, although they were still mainly in the Queen Anne or Swiss Chalet style. Unlike the workers' cottages, they had indoor baths. The school building and the Redstone club were also located on the hill above the workers' cottages and the village's commercial buildings. The school was an imposing building with a stone entrance tower and massive Tudor arch. It was considered the finest school building in the CF&I camps. The Redstone club, built at a cost of $25,000, was the pride of the village. It was the most pretentious clubhouse in the CF&I system, and, according to the *New York Times*, "for completeness" it rivaled "many a city club."[45] Located on the first floor of the clubhouse was a large lounging area that included a billiard and pool room, library and reading room, and a bar. Furniture from the Gustav Stickley firm furnished the room. On the second floor was a large auditorium with a stage where community entertainment and meetings were held. In the basement were showers, baths, and dressing rooms. The village's firehouse was located across from the clubhouse.

Another large public building, the Big Horn Lodge, was located across the river west of the coke ovens. Built in 1902 in Swiss Chalet style, the lodge had luxurious appointments and included a bowling alley. It was built to hold banquets and business meetings as well as to accommodate important visitors. The Redstone Inn, a hostelry for single men, and the Colorado Supply Company Store—with a soda fountain and a complete array of household goods, tools, clothing, and groceries—were located at the southern end of River Road closest to the coke ovens.

"Redstone . . . is a town to rave over from the standpoint of both beauty and philanthropy," the *New York Times* effusively declared. "Fifteen months ago Redstone consisted of little outside of some rude huts or 'dug-outs,' to use the more expressive Western vernacular. Today it is the most beautiful town in Colorado." With all its beauty and amenities, "[c]ould any coal camp ask [for] more?"[46] Redstone "certainly is a most beautiful camp!" Lawrence Lewis of the *Engineering and Mining Journal* exclaimed to Superintendent T. M. Gibb, who replied: "This isn't a *camp*—it's a mountain village!"[47]

Redstone served Osgood well in generating positive press for his sociological experiment. The glowing reports portrayed Osgood and Kebler as benevolent executives whose social betterment work had produced grateful and contented employees.[48] The *Denver Times* added its praise: "Quietly, but withal thoroughly, the Colorado Fuel and Iron company has perfected a fine system of beneficiences [sic] for its employes [sic] such as stamps it indelibly as one of the greatest philanthropic corporations of civilization." Osgood's philanthropic work, the writer added, would not eliminate the "possibility of strikes or disputes. . . . But it will unquestionably raise the morals of the employes [sic] to such a height that they will reason out their differences with their employers and they will certainly not be so easily misled by agitators."[49] Osgood was undoubtedly pleased with such glowing accounts of his company's sociological work.

From all indications, workers in Redstone seemed satisfied with their working and living conditions up to the time the coke ovens were shut down in 1909. Unlike many of their fellow workers in the southern coalfields, neither they nor the miners at Coalbasin went on strike in 1903–1904. The complaints of abusive paternalistic control heard in the towns and camps in southern Colorado were absent in Redstone and Coalbasin, and the workers in these two "model" villages continued to enjoy the positive aspects of industrial betterment—better-quality housing, a more sanitary environment, more extensive entertainment offerings, and better educational opportunities than the old company towns provided.

In addition, the workers and their families enjoyed a close relationship with their benefactors—Osgood and his wife, Alma Regina, "Lady Bountiful" as Redstone residents fondly called her. She received the honorary title for her generosity and her compassion. She was remembered for the lavish Christmas parties and the gifts the Osgoods gave to the children of the village, for her rides through the village in her horse and buggy or her 1904 Pope Winton electric car inquiring about people's welfare, and for her expressed determination to provide amenities to enhance the quality of life for residents of her husband's "workers' paradise."[50] These are the qualities for which the Osgoods are still remembered today by many of those acquainted with the Redstone story.

The glory of Osgood's Redstone, however, was short-lived. The decline of the precious metal mining and smelting industries in western Colorado created a downward spiral in the demand for coke. As a consequence, CF&I, the largest producer and distributor of coke in Colorado, was forced to abandon several of its coking plants. Although the Coal Basin mine produced some of the finest coking coal in the West, the distance from the Pueblo steel mill sealed Redstone's fate. CF&I closed both the Redstone coking plant and the Coal Basin mine in 1909. The village of Redstone gradually shut down, with only a small caretaker and railroad staff remaining. Between 1910 and 1924 the larger buildings were literally packed away in mothballs. Maintenance workers prevented the major buildings and the underground water system from deteriorating completely. Even the village's founder and patron left his beloved Cleveholm in 1911, not to return permanently until the fall of 1924. He resided there with his third wife, Lucille, until his death in January 1926.[51] After his death, Redstone again fell into decay. The school building, clubhouse, Big Horn Lodge, and Colorado Supply store were demolished in the 1930s and 1940s. Some of the workers' cottages were torn down or moved. Yet in the 1950s Redstone began to come to life again as a historic and tourist attraction. Today, Cleveholm Manor, the Redstone Inn, and the Osgood-era workers' cottages and managerial houses are included in the Redstone National Register Historic District.

For all practical purposes, Osgood's experiment with industrial betterment came to an end after he and his close associates lost control of CF&I to John D. Rockefeller and George Gould, an event discussed in Chapter 3. Like the majority of the nation's industrialists, the new CF&I administration did not believe welfare capitalism was justified on a cost basis. Therefore, the company allowed the sociological program to dissipate over the next few years. *Camp and Plant* was discontinued at the end of April 1904, and Sociological Department activities diminished as funds were cut. Night schooling was curtailed, and construction of new family homes was halted in favor of dwellings for single men. The emphasis on social and cultural well-being shifted to the workers' physical health. By the end of the decade, the company had abandoned almost all aspects of Osgood's industrial betterment program.

Osgood later claimed that CF&I's abandonment of his policy of industrial welfare was a major cause of worker dissatisfaction that led to the strike in 1913 and the Ludlow Massacre on April 20, 1914.[52] Evidence casts considerable doubt on his claim. In the first place, the Sociological Department's programs to assimilate immigrant miners and steelworkers into American society and to improve their lives by encouraging them to accept middle-class values created a clash of cultures. Many immigrant miners clung tenaciously to their traditional customs and lifestyle and resented the "paternalistic" meddling of company officials in their private lives. Some of the programs Corwin patterned after the settlement house movement—such as domestic improvement courses for women, adult night school classes, and reading rooms—proved ineffective with the miners and their wives, although the educational programs designed for children were more successful. The assimilation of the young into American society, Corwin's principal goal, occurred too late to prevent the strike of 1913–1914.

Other aspects of CF&I's industrial welfare program, such as housing, increased the company's control over the miners; still others, such as the company-controlled saloons that were profitable for the mine superintendents and the company, were viewed by the miners as exploitive—much like the company stores. Many of CF&I's welfare programs, as Frank Weed observed, "became symbols of the stifling company control and exploitation in the coal camps."[53] The mine superintendents made certain of that. Their utilization of an old managerial model calculated to maximize profit for themselves and the company trumped Corwin's idealistic approach to the resolution of labor troubles. They controlled the mines and camps, and it was against their policies and methods—condoned by company officials—as well as the closed town system that the miners protested in 1913.

Osgood's failure to pursue a comprehensive program of industrial welfare in his Victor-American camps and towns after 1903 further weakened his argument that the abandonment of welfare work was a major cause of the 1913–1914 strike. Nevertheless, there was some merit to his contention that the poor condition of the camps spread discontentment among workers. Recognizing the deplorable condition of the camps, CF&I adopted a multiple program of camp improvements and welfare work in 1915 that incorporated much of Osgood's earlier pioneer efforts in industrial betterment and model town planning. Eventually, these programs would become the standard in the West.[54]

NOTES

1. Quote in Gwendolyn Wright, *Building the Dream: A Social History of Housing in America* (New York: Pantheon Books, 1981), 177; Stuart Brandes, *American Welfare Capitalism, 1880–1940* (Chicago: University of Chicago Press, 1976), 8–9. Brandes defined welfare capitalism as "anything for the comfort and improvement, intellectual or social, of the employees, over and above wages paid, which is not a necessity of the industry nor required by law" (ibid., 5–6).

2. Daniel Nelson, *Managers and Workers: Origins of the New Factory System in the United States 1880–1920* (Madison: University of Wisconsin Press, 1975), 116; Brandes, *American Welfare Capitalism,* 61; Wright, *Building the Dream,* 177.

3. "Plans to Better Condition," *Pueblo Chieftain,* August 25, 1901.

4. Frank J. Weed, "The Sociological Department at the Colorado Fuel and Iron Company, 1901–1907: Scientific Paternalism and Industrial Control," *Journal of the History of the Behavioral Sciences* 41, no. 3 (Summer 2005): 271.

5. Colorado Fuel and Iron, *Annual Report of the Sociological Department of the CF&I for 1901–1902* (Denver, 1902), 5; ibid., *1904–1905* (Denver, 1905), 12 ; *Camp and Plant* 2, no. 8 (August 23, 1902): 178.

6. "Social Betterment in the Rocky Mountains," *Social Service* (December 1901), reprinted in *Camp and Plant* 1, no. 12 (March 1, 1902): 182.

7. Weed, "Sociological Department," 275; Wilson, "Study of Paternalism," 80; Vaughn Mechau, *Redstone on the Crystal* (Denver: Westerners Brand Book, 1948), 42.

8. First quote in McGovern and Guttridge, *Coalfield War,* 9; second quote in *Camp and Plant* 2, no. 12 (September 20, 1902): 318; Wilson, "Study of Paternalism," 55; Andrews, "Road to Ludlow," 428.

9. Quotes in Lawrence Lewis, "How One Corporation Helped Its Employees," *The Engineering and Mining Journal* 83, no. 26 (June 29, 1907): 1234; Weed, "Sociological Department," 270.

10. William H. Tolman, *Social Engineering: A Record of Things Done by American Industrialists Employing Upwards of One and One-Half Million People* (New York: McGraw, 1909), 54–55.

11. Josiah Strong, "What Social Service Means: A Clearing House of Experience in Social and Industrial Betterment," *Craftsman* 9 (February 1906): 620.

12. *Camp and Plant* 1, no. 1 (December 14, 1901): 3. The publication sold for ten cents a copy or a dollar for a one-year subscription.

13. Ibid., 1, no. 12 (March 2, 1902): 182.

14. Quoted in McGovern and Guttridge, *Coalfield War,* 11.

15. CF&I, *Annual Report, 1902–1903,* 29–30.

16. Tolman, *Social Engineering,* 247, 306.

17. "Social Betterment in Mining Camps," *Boston Transcript* (April 22, 1903), reprinted in *Camp and Plant* 4, no. 8 (September 5, 1903): 188–189; "A Great Corporation's Social Work," *Inter Ocean of Chicago* (November 12, 1902), reprinted in ibid., 2, no. 22 (November 29, 1902): 528–529; editorial in *The Echo,* January 1903, reprinted in ibid., 3, no. 5 (February 4, 1903): 112; Osgood quote in "A Western Mining Company's Sociological Work," *Outlook* 72 (September 20, 1902): 149–150.

18. "A Great Corporation's Social Work," 528–529; "Sociology in Mining Camps," *Daily Republican,* September 27, 1902, reprinted in *Camp and Plant* 2, no. 24 (December 13, 1902): 574.

19. Andrea Tone, *The Business of Benevolence: Industrial Paternalism in Progressive America* (Ithaca, N.Y.: Cornell University Press, 1997), 71.

20. Jerome to Osgood, August 28, 1899, Jerome Papers, FF 33.

21. Lewis, "How One Corporation Helped Its Employees," 1235.

22. *Camp and Plant* 1, no. 8 (February 1, 1902): 113; ibid., 1, no. 12 (March 2, 1902): 181.

23. Quote in ibid., 1, no. 8 (February 1, 1902): 108; Rick Clyne, *Coal People: Life in Southern Colorado's Company Towns, 1890–1930* (Denver: Colorado Historical Society, 1999), 53.

24. Scamehorn, *Pioneer Steelmaker*, 142; Clyne, *Coal People*, 54.

25. H. Lee Scamehorn, *Mill and Mine: The CF&I in the Twentieth Century* (Lincoln: University of Nebraska Press, 1992), 84; Clyne, *Coal People*, 26.

26. CF&I, *Annual Report, 1901–1902*, 5–6, 16.

27. Quote in ibid., 18; Weed, "Sociological Department," 278–279.

28. Lewis, "How One Corporation Helped Its Employees," 1234.

29. Scamehorn, *Pioneer Steelmaker*, 151; Clyne, *Coal People*, 90. The company not only dictated the selection of teachers but also demanded the dismissal of those it found objectionable.

30. *Camp and Plant* 1, no. 6 (January 18, 1902): 86; Scamehorn, *Pioneer Steelmaker*, 152.

31. CF&I, *Annual Report, 1901–1902*, 21–22, 24.

32. *Camp and Plant* 1, no. 6 (January 18, 1902): 75.

33. Ibid., 1, no. 2 (December 20, 1901): 18; ibid., 1, no. 6 (January 18, 1902): 75; Brandes, *American Welfare Capitalism*, 62. The articles included Henry A. Atkinson, "Why the Miners Struck," *Harper's Weekly* 58 (May 23, 1914): 9–11; McGregor, "The Way Rockefeller Looks at It," ibid., 12–13; George Creel, "Poisoners of Public Opinion," ibid., 59 (November 14, 1914): 465–466.

34. *Camp and Plant* 1, no. 7 (January 25, 1902): 98; quotes in Clyne, *Coal People*, 58.

35. Quotes in James Whiteside, *Regulating Danger: The Struggle for Mine Safety in the Rocky Mountain Coal Industry* (Lincoln: University of Nebraska Press, 1990), 24; Osgood's testimony, SMM, 424.

36. Budgett Meakin, *Model Factories and Villages: Ideal Conditions of Labour and Housing* (London: T. F. Unwin, 1905), 389.

37. *New York Times*, September 7, 1902; *Denver Republican*, July 19, 1901; Osgood quote in McGovern and Guttridge, *Coalfield War*, 9–10.

38. "Bill of Complaint," Jerome Papers, Box 2, FF 26; Scamehorn, *Pioneer Steelmaker*, 98–99.

39. *Denver Times*, October 1, 1899.

40. Scamehorn, *Pioneer Steelmaker*, 125.

41. *Denver Times*, February 2, 1901.

42. When visiting England, Osgood frequently stayed at the estate of Edward Bulwer-Lytton, British diplomat and poet. It was reported that he eventually bought the estate (Michael William Mulnix, "The Story of Cleveholm Manor" [Redstone, Colo.: Morrison's Nostalgia Shop Antiques, n.d.], n.p.). Also, on at least one occasion

while staying in England, Osgood rented Knebwerth Castle (William Lyon Mackenzie King Diary, William Lyon Mackenzie King Papers, Library and Archives Canada, Series J13, G2539, 473, Ottawa, Ontario, Canada; hereafter cited as King Diary).

43. Ruland, *Lion of Redstone,* 42.

44. *Camp and Plant* 1, no. 1 (December 14, 1901): 8; Lewis, "How One Corporation Helped Its Employees," 1230.

45. *New York Times,* September 7, 1902.

46. Ibid.

47. Lewis, "How One Corporation Helped Its Employees," 1230 (original emphasis).

48. See, for example, "Helping Mine Workers," *Boston Evening Transcript,* August 24, 1904, newspaper cutting in Jerome Papers, MSS. 346, Scrapbook, FF-G.

49. *Denver Times,* October 21, 1901.

50. Ruland, *Lion of Redstone,* 43; Nelson, *Marble and Redstone,* 116–118.

51. Norma Kenney, *The Hidden Place Redstone* (Carbondale, Colo.: Redstone Press, 1992), 87–91.

52. McGovern and Guttridge, *Coalfield War,* 18.

53. Weed, "Sociological Department," 280–282, quotation on 282.

54. Wolff, *Industrializing the Rockies,* 192. For a description of CF&I's social and industrial betterment policies included in the Industrial Representation Plan of 1915, see "The Rockefeller Plan," *The Survey* 35, no. 3 (October 16, 1915): 75.

Rockefeller-Gould Takeover of Colorado Fuel and Iron

The village of Redstone served John Osgood in two specific ways: as his private model village to showcase Colorado Fuel and Iron's (CF&I's) program of industrial betterment and as the prototype and standard for the construction of new company towns for his corporation and also for other mining communities in the western United States. Redstone represented Osgood's dream of achieving harmony between labor and capital. He, Julian Kebler, and Richard Corwin believed they could end labor strife in the Colorado coalfields by changing "the allegiances of mine workers and their families from ethnicity, class, and union onto country, company, and home." They would do this by creating new, more tightly controlled town environments that provided welfare opportunities for social improvement.[1]

These attempts to pacify the workers and transform them into loyal company employees through a program of welfare capitalism came at a price. To fund this program and CF&I's expansion, which included building new towns, opening new mines, and making improvements at the Pueblo steelworks, Osgood issued more stocks and bonds to cover the company's greatly increased debt. Company officials had no choice than to accept his scheme, even though it made CF&I a tempting target for a takeover bid.[2] Through his financial dealings associated with the corporate expansion, Osgood whetted the appetites of eastern capitalists and gave them an opportunity to feast on CF&I. This suited Osgood well, for, among other things, it led to an appreciation of company stock. Although in Colorado during the period 1901–1903 he was regarded as a local hero who fought tenaciously to retain control of the company and maintain it as an independent steel manufacturer under western management, in actuality he willingly participated with Chicago and New York financiers to bring about a reorganization of the company so he could garner a handsome profit for himself and perhaps a few friends who remained loyal. John Jerome's detailed record of transactions during this period clearly reveals that Osgood was more interested in creating the best terms for selling CF&I than he was in saving the company from outside interests.[3] After failing to reach a deal with John W. Gates, a Chicago financier and former American Steel and Wire Company magnate, in 1903 Osgood delivered the heavily indebted company and most of its profitable auxiliaries to George Gould and John D. Rockefeller on terms favorable to himself but not to three of his closest friends and associates—Cass, Kebler, and Jerome—who had been with him from the very start of the company. These transactions and events are the subject of this chapter.

Osgood could not match the financial resources of the most formidable industrial and financial giants during a time when trusts and holding companies, particularly in the steel industry, were being formed and individuals were realizing tremendous financial gains from the resulting combinations. Nonetheless, he played the game of stock manipulation, which allowed him to enter the corporate sweepstakes. He did not always play the game according to the established rules of the corporate world, however. For example, some adversaries accused Osgood of operating CF&I through control of a galaxy of subsidiaries for the benefit of himself and his friends, leaving stockholders out in the cold.[4] The charge was only partially true. While Osgood and a few others reaped financial rewards from the subsidiary or auxiliary operations, the relatively small number of stockholders in the parent company also shared in CF&I's prosperity. However, by increasing the number of shares from 130,000 in 1892 to 400,000 in mid-1901, Osgood and company officials were compelled to heed the wishes of those who demanded changes in operation of the corporation that would bring about greater financial gain for shareholders.

As developers rather than speculators, Osgood and his partners had created a successful business in Colorado; the new investors, mainly interested in profit, now insisted that the proceeds of the enterprise flow eastward. Osgood was caught in this trap, for he realized that the company could not continue without an infusion of new capital. After a costly fight to retain control of the company in 1902, he came to realize that new capital meant new leadership. He struck a deal with Gould and Rockefeller that not only brought in the necessary capital to save CF&I from receivership but also completely turned the corporation over to the new investors. The new majority owners asked Osgood to resign from leadership of the company. He decided to take his winnings and turn his attention once again to developing a fuel company over which he had nearly absolute control. That company became the Victor-American Fuel Company in 1909.

The story began in the spring of 1901 when Osgood went shopping for a buyer for CF&I. John W. Gates and John J. Mitchell of the Illinois Trust and Savings Bank were the first speculators to take advantage of the opening Osgood presented. Osgood wrote to Jerome on April 20 to tell him he had talked with Gates, who told him United States Steel wanted to buy CF&I "and would pay a high price for it" if, Osgood noted, "I wanted to do so [sell the company]." It was clear from the rest of the letter that Osgood was interested in pursuing the matter and that he felt no restraints on his actions from long-standing friendships. "All of my old friends," he wrote somewhat defensively, "who have been with the company so long have sold out. I think they might have been a little more decent, as they must have known that they were simply selfishly taking their profits and letting me hold the bag. This has some compensations, however, as I do not feel under any further obligations to them."[5]

Osgood continued negotiations with Gates concerning CF&I's financial needs. The *Denver Times* noted that two banking firms—one in New York and the other in Chicago—had agreed to underwrite the entire issue of debenture bonds offered by CF&I, with the important proviso that Gates and a representative of the house of J. P. Morgan "be associated with the active direction of the big western company." In May 1901 Osgood, desperately in need of financial support to complete the expansion of the Pueblo steel mill and the construction of new mining camps and coking plants, made an oral agreement with Mitchell and Gates—the latter of whom through stock purchases had become the company's second largest stockholder—to allow them to name a majority of CF&I directors. In return, the two men promised Osgood that management of the company would remain the same, that is, that it would remain in the hands of Osgood and the Colorado officials.[6]

Gates's sole objective in gaining a majority on the directorate, other than making money through stock appreciation, was to bring about the sale of the company to United States Steel, a proposition Osgood totally supported. The U.S. Steel interests "are seriously considering buying our property," Osgood informed Jerome. "Whether or not they will come to our terms is an open question."[7] During the summer, Gates discussed the possibility of the sale with J. P. Morgan, while Osgood talked with Charles Schwab, president of the giant steel trust. But the negotiations stalled when Osgood demanded too high a price. Osgood then decided to fight for independent control of CF&I. After making sure the issue of debenture bonds for financing the additional modernization and expansion of the steel and fuel departments was secure, he repudiated his May oral agreement with Gates and Mitchell and set out to round up the proxies he needed to retain control of the corporation's board of directors. Perhaps in anticipation of an offer from United States Steel to purchase the company, Gates supported Osgood and accepted a minority position of four seats on the board for himself and his associates, leaving the Iowa Group of Osgood, Kebler, Cass, and Jerome in control. But when he learned that Osgood had turned down United States Steel's offer in October, Gates vowed to take over CF&I.[8] Thereupon, the struggle between Osgood and Gates for control of CF&I began in earnest.

The struggle resumed in 1902 when both Gates and Osgood maneuvered to gain or retain control of the board of directors through stock purchases and court actions. By the end of July 1902, Gates and his associates had strengthened their position and now claimed they owned or controlled a majority of the company's shares. With the annual meeting fast approaching, Osgood scrambled to devise a strategy to retain control of the company's directorate. He either had to find a way to invalidate approximately 100,000 proxy shares claimed by Gates or seek an injunction enjoining the annual meeting until the confusion over shareholders was settled. Jerome objected to both courses of action on the grounds that they were highhanded and bound to fail. By prolonging the struggle, he believed, the company's financial difficulties would deepen. Convinced that Osgood would lose the company, he arranged a meeting with Gates and Mitchell on the eve of the annual stockholders meeting to discuss disposal of the auxiliary corporations in which Osgood, Jerome, and a few others had large interests.[9]

Osgood was aware of Jerome's endeavor, and he agreed to meet with Edward O. Wolcott, Gates's representative, to continue the discussion of the subordinate corporations. Neither man, however, was willing to make the necessary concessions for a compromise. Osgood accused Wolcott of overbearing arrogance in demanding "humiliating concessions" as a condition for purchase of the properties, while Wolcott charged Osgood with wanting either to retain some power in the fuel company to "sustain his dignity" or to place Gates and "the other parties in a beaten position."[10] Certainly, the observation that Osgood wanted to retain at least some control over the company was valid.

Although Osgood was disadvantaged in terms of stock holdings and proxies, the final battle was waged in Denver where he—a masterful technician on his home ground—had overwhelming public support and superior knowledge of Colorado law, which he used to his advantage. Gates indeed suffered a setback in federal court on the eve of the stockholders meeting scheduled for August 20. The judge in the ruling refused to grant Gates an injunction that would make his proxy votes legal. Furthermore, the court ruled that the stockholders meeting had to be conducted in accordance with Colorado law. Greatly strengthened by the ruling, Osgood, on the morning of the scheduled meeting, filed a petition in state district court for an injunction to prevent the stockholders from conducting a regular annual meeting later that day. Agreeing that a meeting held under the existing circumstances would be illegal, the judge granted a temporary injunction postponing the annual meeting until December 10. A few hours later, the writ of injunction was read to the stockholders at the opening of the enjoined meeting. Osgood then announced that "there can be nothing done but to adjourn this meeting subject to further order of the court."[11] Gates, defeated, had no option but to take his leave.

Following further setbacks in court and on the New York Stock Exchange, Gates and his friends abandoned the fight to overthrow Osgood. They sold their stock in the company to recover some of their losses. In what the Denver press heralded as the biggest battle of financial giants the West had ever seen, Gates and his associates suffered an aggregate loss of nearly $7 million.[12] Gates's plight was not lost on one New York writer:

Plunger Gates went away
With much ado; a great display
Of banners floating and trumpets sounding

And triumph on his bosom bounding.
Plunger Gates in coming back,
And sighs and tears to mark his track.
In sweeping down on Eldorado
He was trapped and skinned in Colorado.[13]

The final victory over Gates was assured by railroad money. The autumn 1902 phase of the struggle was billed as the first round between warring railroad interests for possession of CF&I. During this time, Osgood sought a railroad alliance with Edwin Hawley, Edward H. Harriman, George J. Gould, and E. P. Ripley. With the support of these railroad giants, Osgood hoped to nominate a majority of the directors at the substitute stockholders meeting. If he succeeded, he would be able to dominate the management of CF&I for at least the next year. However, the proposed railroad syndicate did not materialize, and Osgood was forced to form a pact with George Gould alone. Gould had purchased Gates's shares in the company prior to the meeting.[14]

The pact with Gould had far more significance for the company's fate than anyone, including the press, realized at the time. Gould, in fact, was a stalking horse for his banker, John D. Rockefeller, who had become interested in Colorado's natural resources and CF&I's potential. In turning to Gould, Osgood had actually opened the door for the one man who had the resources to purchase the company outright if he so desired. In the fall of 1902 Rockefeller sent his son, John D. Rockefeller Jr., and agent Frederick T. Gates (no relation to John Gates) on an unpublicized inspection trip to Pueblo and the Trinidad coalfields. A few weeks later Rockefeller himself visited the region. He liked what he saw and decided to invest $6 million in CF&I stock. Rockefeller's stock purchase ultimately sealed Osgood's fate with respect to ownership and control of the corporation.[15]

For the moment, however, the pact with Gould assured Osgood's election as chair of the board and the reelection of his Iowa Group friends as officers. Gould became a member of the board, as did Hawley and Harriman. Rounding out the board were J. M. Herbert, president of the Denver and Rio Grande Railroad, and Frank Trumbull, president of the Colorado and Southern and the Colorado Midland railroads. With all these railroad executives on the board, it was no wonder that Osgood, in his victory speech, stated that the corporation "will go forward in developing the fuel and iron interest of the Rocky Mountain region . . . in harmony with the railway and other interests of the West as in the past." Osgood was confident that all members of the board would "pull together" to assure the company's progress.[16]

There was jubilation throughout Colorado when it was learned that Osgood and the other members of the Iowa Group had retained their seats as company directors. The outcome of the struggle over control of the company was seen as a personal triumph for Osgood. *Camp and Plant* reported victory celebrations in Pueblo and the Trinidad coalfield that demonstrated a "spontaneous outburst of approval participated in by all the foreign and native population, showing they are a happy people, proud to continue their labors under the Osgood management." In Engle a "celebration of considerable magnitude" ended with a large bonfire that lit up the hill overlooking Trinidad and the igniting of 200 pounds of dynamite that "awoke the echoes of the surrounding canons." The *Pueblo Daily Chieftain* noted that most of the mines remained closed the next day because of the intensity of the celebrations.[17] Osgood's village of Redstone was shaken by an act of nature rather than a charge of dynamite preceding a celebration for the local hero, as reported in *Camp and Plant:* "J. C. Osgood, Mrs. Osgood and J. A. Kebler arrived here on Saturday, and simultaneously with their arrival here was an earthquake that shattered some of the large window panes in the village. On Saturday evening a large concourse of people assembled at the opera house [clubhouse] to welcome our victorious chief."[18]

In Denver and many other parts of Colorado, there was also strong support for Osgood against the "buccaneers of Wall Street." The Panic of 1893 and the collapse of silver had produced a strong populist sentiment in the state that was directed against eastern and foreign investment. It was widely believed that the state had been virtually "colonized" by outside capital. As a *Denver News* commentator noted, "Colorado in proportion to its population . . . is more largely dominated by corporation influences than any other state."[19] It was feared that frontier enterprise and individualism had given way to absentee corporatism bent on creating "commercial feudalism" in the state.

Although Osgood depended on eastern and foreign capital, the people of Colorado still regarded him as one of their own. The press in Colorado, regardless of politics, saluted him for saving CF&I from the grasp of the United States Steel Corporation, leading Osgood to remark, "[i]n ordinary times, gentlemen, almost every newspaper in the state is attacking us. Let an outsider venture to attack us, and every paper in Colorado joins in repelling the invasion."[20] As noted in the *New York Times*, the adulation for Osgood resounded beyond Main Street: "Never was an employer more stanchly [sic] upheld than is John C. Osgood by the employees of the Colorado Fuel and Iron Company. He has not yet left them millions a la Carnegie, but he has done more, he has improved their condition of living, even in the coal camps high up in the mountains, at the coking plants and the iron works, and privileges are accorded them that few, if any, mining camps of the Pennsylvania region boast."[21]

The defeat of Gates in 1902 also brought Osgood admiration on Wall Street, where his entrepreneurial skills and business acumen were recognized. The author of the *New York Times* article just quoted observed: "The personality of the Colorado millionaire is striking; it personifies business sagacity. The shrewd eyes, the firm mouth, the neatly trimmed mustache, the high forehead, and the concise manner of speaking, all denote the leader." But to others, the shrewd eyes connoted avarice and ruthlessness. In 1902 there could be no doubt that Osgood was the most influential among the coal operators in Colorado who were, according to George McGovern and Leonard Guttridge, "circumspect and sure-footed, intensely ambitious but planners rather than plungers, given to realistic assessment before investment, and once committed, merciless in the management and growth of their business."[22] Within a year, Osgood's business sagacity and sure-footedness would be sorely tested.

The struggle with Gates and the costs of the modernization and expansion programs left CF&I on the edge of bankruptcy. Although Jerome warned him of an impending financial crisis in the spring of 1902, Osgood remained confident that the worst was over. With the completion of the plant improvements, he anticipated earnings for the year to be more than $3 million. This, he argued, along with the $5 million in debentures yet to be issued, would be enough to authorize another blast furnace at the mill and other improvements. As the year progressed, Osgood's calculations proved to be badly wrong. The expansion program fell behind schedule, resulting in a loss of production. The delays also drove up the cost of the expansion program to the extent that when the new furnaces, mills, and mines began production in 1903, the corporation's obligations far exceeded its financial resources. In December 1902 Jerome told Osgood that the company would need at least $3 million more to stay solvent. The financial situation had become so desperate by late February 1903 that Jerome urged Osgood to go to New York immediately to describe in frank terms the impending crisis to the Gould-Rockefeller interests. Although reluctant to reveal how bad the situation was, Osgood finally realized that he had no choice but to ask the financial titans for help.[23]

While in New York, Osgood was unable to secure additional funds for the company by selling its railroad bonds, a maneuver he had counted on to get CF&I through the short-term financial difficulties. However, he was able to secure enough money in the form of loans to keep the company going for a short time. Over the next three months, he borrowed nearly $3 million from Rockefeller and Gould, but it was not enough to meet the company's long-term financial obligations. In early June Jerome again informed Osgood of the desperate condition of CF&I's finances and advised him to give up trying to hold on to the company. Osgood, still optimistic that he could devise means that would enable the company to pull through its difficulties, criticized Jerome for not keeping him informed and for giving him insufficient financial estimates. Of course they were insufficient, Jerome told Kebler, but Osgood knew the situation, adding that Osgood was "desperate and depending upon his streak of fatalism." Kebler agreed.[24]

Reality soon set in, and Osgood admitted that he was at the end of his resources and could not prevent the company from financial collapse. The *Denver Times* stated that for the first time in his career, Osgood faced an "impregnable wall."[25] With a sense of desperation, Osgood explained the situation to George P. Butler, George Gould's New York broker. "The Company is in a most deplorable condition," he wrote, "and unless it can get immediate relief there is nothing but a receivership and reorganization before it." He took full responsibility for the situation, which he blamed on equipment estimates connected with the auxiliary plants inaugurated by Gates and his associates in the spring of 1901 that "were unreliable and inadequate." He did not want to "shirk any responsibility" for this matter, he added, but he professed that "I accepted their plans more with a desire to maintain peaceable relations than because I considered them well matured or the best under all the circumstances." In addition, CF&I's engineers and management at the steelworks "were not sufficiently foresighted" in planning for necessary additions and changes, which "finally exhausted and exceeded the financial provision originally made." The changes to the original plans included an additional furnace at the steelworks, housing for employees, railroad terminals and equipment, and new mines and coke ovens to meet a growing commercial demand for iron and steel. "The foregoing is by way of explanation and not as an excuse," he concluded. "I fully realize that the management can only be judged by its success or failure."[26]

Admitting that he could not raise the money necessary to cover the deficiency, which he estimated as being $3,798,173.40, Osgood urged Gould and his partners to devise a financial plan to save the company from receivership. He pledged to do all he could to facilitate such an arrangement and to promote the Gould interests in connection with CF&I. However, he added, "as the new interests in the Company are so strong and can dominate the situation as they see fit, and as I am unwilling to serve simply as an employe [sic] of the Company, I shall resign as soon as I properly can, but that will not alter my desire to be of service to you in connection with C. F. & I. Co. matters."[27]

Osgood's appeal to the Gould interests paid off, but only after he acceded to their demand that he step down immediately as head of the company. With Osgood's agreement to reorganization of the company's directorate, Gould, who had become the largest shareholder in the Denver and Rio Grande Railroad, persuaded John D. Rockefeller Sr. to take over CF&I. At the stockholders meeting in August, it was divulged that the previous month, Osgood had disposed of enough stock holdings in the company to secure $5 million from Gould and Rockefeller, thus putting control of CF&I in their hands.[28]

On June 24 Osgood resigned as an officer and director of the company, as did the three other members of the Iowa Group. Their places on the board were quickly filled by men representing the Rockefeller interest, the most conspicuous of whom was John D. Rockefeller Jr. However, Osgood and Kebler were elected to the directorate, and the former was appointed to the executive at the annual meeting in August. Osgood, who held that position until September 1904, thus participated in the financial reorganization of the company.[29] The *Denver Times* observed that the appointment of Osgood and Kebler "was largely in the nature of a concession to public sentiment in Colorado, which is hostile to the Rockefeller control." But the "concession" did little to mollify public opinion in the state. Denver newspapers lamented the betrayal that had allowed the state to be annexed by eastern capitalists. Although Osgood's reputation suffered as a result of the takeover, the papers placed the blame on Rockefeller and Gould. "OSGOOD WALKED INTO ROCKEFELLER'S TRAP" declared a headline in the *Denver Times* on August 25. The *Denver Post* concurred. "The ruthless hand of fate," an editorial exclaimed, "has been laid with an iron weight upon the 'Big Four of CF&I.'" To the people of Colorado, Rockefeller, "forbidding and terrible," was the "Genghis Khan" of the twentieth century.[30]

Osgood publicly denied any betrayal. In fact, he noted truthfully that the recent changes were made at his suggestion and that he was perfectly satisfied with them. He issued a signed statement following the annual meeting in an attempt to silence critics and answer questions about the reorganization of the company:

> The strong financial interests which have acquired control of the stock of the company and have assumed its management, and who will give

it the financial backing which is necessary to the full development of its properties, have treated me with the utmost consideration and fairness and at no time has there been the slightest friction or antagonism between myself and the new interests. I can state positively that it is not the desire of these [interests] to change the character of the corporation as a distinctively Colorado enterprise, and that the business will be managed by residents of Colorado.[31]

He also stated that he would give the new leadership all the assistance he could in building up the company and that he had no intention of becoming involved with any business enterprise antagonistic to CF&I. It soon became evident, however, that Osgood had no intention of excluding the fuel trade from business competition with CF&I.

Some of what Osgood stated would prove to be true. Between 1903 and 1907 the new directors paid little attention to CF&I's operations, leaving management of the company largely in the hands of Osgood's former subordinates. Jesse Floyd Welborn, who became president in 1907, was a good example. Welborn had started as a bookkeeper in 1893 and had risen to vice president in 1903, and he was one of Osgood's most dedicated company officials. He as well as the others loyal to Osgood who remained in managerial roles carried on operations in much the same way as they had under Osgood's leadership. This was particularly true with regard to Osgood's antiunion policies, as events of the 1903–1904 strike made clear. Even after the Rockefellers sent LaMont Montgomery Bowers to Denver in 1907 to assume more control over CF&I, the company still remained a Colorado operation with absentee owners.

Although Denver newspapers generally regarded Osgood as a victim of a malicious scheme, a *Wall Street Journal* reporter was far more realistic in his analysis. Osgood was a victim of his own mistakes, the reporter suggested. The Pueblo steelworks "are very much what they may be expected to be when constructed in boom times by men who just lacked the supreme knowledge of the industry displayed by the iron masters at Pittsburgh." The Osgood team's fundamental mistake, he added, "was the attempt of the management to do too much at one time . . . and to do it with borrowed money. Adding to this the accident of delivery of material, it is not difficult to see where the Osgood management was weak. It was a case for a long purse: nothing else would do, and Mr. Rockefeller had the long purse. Consequently the company is his." Thus, the writer intimated with considerable insight, Rockefeller had freed Osgood from a business he did not understand. Now the men from Colorado, he concluded, could concentrate on the coal business, which they understood thoroughly.[32]

The reporter was absolutely correct. Lacking the necessary financial resources, Osgood had been forced to rely on borrowed money in his attempt to pull the company through the crisis and save his leadership over it. CF&I was the collateral for the loans. This was the trap, for it was only a matter of time before Gould and Rockefeller demanded repayment. The only way Osgood could repay the loans was to surrender the company on their terms. Despite the public outrage in Colorado over the Rockefeller-Gould takeover, Osgood was pleased with a "deal" that extricated him from a difficult financial situation. Although he had suffered the only serious business reversal of his career, which spanned over half a century, for the rest of his life he remained proud that he had created the "Pittsburgh of the West," with properties worth more than $50 million. Because of the burden of the steelworks, he had not been able to accomplish his major goal of dominating the western fuel trade.[33] Freed from that burden, he was able to concentrate on that trade by developing his Victor and American fuel companies. He was still a wealthy man, and his influence among coal operators remained paramount.

The Rockefeller-Gould takeover of CF&I left Osgood, Jerome, Cass, and Kebler with only a small portion of the large industrial empire they had created. Of the many auxiliary companies they had formed, only the Crystal River Land and Improvement Company, Redstone Improvement Company, and Steel Wheel and Wagon Company remained in their possession.[34] Continued ownership of the two improvement companies enabled Osgood to pursue his vast land and commercial interests in the Crystal River Valley and to keep Redstone, his model industrial village, as part of his personal estate. More important, Osgood retained ownership of the Victor and American fuel companies, which he had kept separate from CF&I when he organized them in 1900.

The Victor Fuel Company was organized through consolidation of the Victor Coal and Coke, Colorado Coke, Gray Creek Coal and Coking, and Gray Creek Coke companies, with assets that consisted of 14,000 acres of coal land, seven mines, and 200 coke ovens in Huerfano and Las Animas counties. Annual production of 1.5 million tons of coal in Colorado made Victor the second ranking producer of coal and coke in the state. The largest of the Victor mines—Hastings, Delagua, and Gray Creek—were in the Trinidad district along with the smaller Cass and Bowen mines, while the company's Maitland and Ravenwood mines were in Huerfano County near

Walsenburg. The Victor Chandler and Radiant mines in Fremont County near Cañon City produced coal on land the Santa Fe Railway leased to the company. The American Fuel Company operated mines in New Mexico in the Gallup area and was a major supplier of fuel to railroads, especially the Santa Fe, and commercial consumers in the Southwest and along the Pacific Coast. It supplied the largest share of the coal used in Los Angeles and surrounding cities until Osgood sold the Gallup properties in 1917.[35]

The two fuel companies gave Osgood a powerful base from which to challenge CF&I in the western fuel trade. What form that competition would take became a matter of public interest even before CF&I had been officially transferred to Rockefeller and Gould. Reports in the *Denver Post* and the *Denver Times* speculated that Osgood planned to ally himself with eastern interests to create a CF&I replica in the form of a new Utah Iron and Steel Company. Although Osgood later denied the report, speculation persisted about a possible consolidation of coal and iron properties under his control. On August 6, 1903, the *Denver Times* noted that even though the American Fuel Company owned no iron ore lands, sufficient iron properties held by other interests could easily pass into Osgood's hands. The paper reported on reliable authority that Osgood had received "flattering" offers to join with other corporations. Perhaps one such offer, the newspaper indirectly intimated, came from John Gates, who still represented the United States Steel Corporation.[36]

No evidence suggests that Osgood seriously considered any of these offers or courses of action. It was soon apparent that he had no interest in joining others in developing an iron and steel competitor to CF&I. In fact, he was no longer interested in joining others in any business pursuit. He intended instead to pursue his interest in the western fuel trade as an individual rather than as the head of a large corporation. As a person of independent wealth, most of which he had gained by developing CF&I as a successful corporation, he no longer needed the capital investments of others or financial dealings on Wall Street to pursue his business interests. In 1909 he again became a major coal operator by combining the Victor and American enterprises to form the Victor-American Fuel Company. As chair of the board of directors and owner of 90 percent of Victor-American's stock, Osgood subsequently enjoyed considerable financial success by gaining a greater share of the fuel market in Colorado at the expense of CF&I.[37]

While Osgood continued to benefit financially after the Rockefeller-Gould takeover, his former Iowa Group associates were less fortunate. Kebler, Cass, and Jerome, all of whom had been an integral part of his previous business ventures, would not share in his post-1903 success because they were dead by the end of the year. Even had they lived, they would have played only a small part, if any, in Osgood's business ventures after 1903. The three men had perceived a change in Osgood's attitude toward them during the period leading up to the loss of the company to Rockefeller and Gould. Jerome in particular felt Osgood had betrayed them by placing his own interests above theirs, and he suspected that Osgood intended to defraud them by refusing to settle the accounts of the companies—mainly the Colorado Finance and Construction Company (CF&CC) and the Victor Fuel Company—in which they, or at least Jerome, still had a financial interest. Unable to get a financial accounting of the two companies from Osgood, in the summer of 1903 Jerome began to draft a Bill of Complaint in preparation for a lawsuit against him. Basing his argument on the claim that Osgood's denial of his rights in the two companies was wrongful and fraudulent, Jerome demanded access to the financial records and papers relating to each company's business operations. He also requested the appointment of a receiver to supervise the dissolution of the CF&CC.[38]

The ensuing controversy between Jerome and Osgood over the two companies brought to a head a growing estrangement that Jerome perceived had begun much earlier. In his meticulously recorded personal statements of events, Jerome recounted a number of incidents he believed had stirred Osgood's ire and formed a wedge between them. One concern was the delicate subject of social status, particularly involving Alma, Osgood's second wife. Scandal had accompanied Alma and a friend, a Mrs. McKibbon, on a visit to Redstone with Osgood in September 1899. Shortly before their arrival in Colorado, newspapers had reported that Alma Regina Shelgrem had been involved in a situation in New York in which an acquaintance, Arthur Cobb, had committed suicide. In a note written "for the public," Cobb placed responsibility for his death on Alma, whom he accused of enticing his friend (Mrs. McKibbon) away from him. This information, along with speculation that Osgood had been seeing Alma while still married to his first wife, Irene, was doubtlessly received with interest among Denver's social elite. In a period when propriety and background largely determined social standing, Alma's sketchy past was open to gossip. Evidence supports the claim that she was not readily received into Denver society after her marriage to Osgood and was not recognized by the "smart set," the "Sacred Thirty-Six"—Denver's most prominent social families—until years later.[39]

Jerome, in fact, believed his and his wife's failure to recognize Alma was a point of contention with Osgood and that this factor, along with their disagreements over the fate of CF&I, fueled his estrangement from Osgood.

Left to right: J. M. Herbert, president of the Denver and Rio Grande Railroad; Dr. Richard Corwin, head of CF&I's Sociological Department; Eugene Grubb, Carbondale, Colorado, rancher and renowned potato grower; Governor James Peabody; John C. Osgood; C. E. Carson; and W. E. McGraw. Courtesy, Denver Public Library, Western History Collection, call no. Osgood Biography, F-20602.

As a consequence, he believed Osgood sought to discredit him by rejecting his business decisions, misrepresenting his actions to others, and withholding relevant information from him. Some of these fears were recorded on a visit to Redstone in August 1901, during which he met Alma Osgood:

> On the thirteenth I went to Redstone, and . . . got my first acquaintance with Mrs. Osgood, and on the 15th I made up my mind that I must count on her enmity. This was not due to any lack of courtesy in our relations, but . . . there had been no social recognition by my family, and my attention was aroused to the fact that this was probably resented. I became very nervous over my interest with Osgood. I had two or three talks with him about the Finance and Construction Co. deal and he seemed more reluctant to give me any information, and finally was a little short about talking on the subject.[40]

Jerome explained that he wanted a settlement of CF&CC funds to reimburse CF&I for an overdraft of $25,000 he had made to cover speculation in the cotton market. "My personal affairs were in a condition to make me particularly restless of the delay in the settlement of this business," he

John L. Jerome. Courtesy, Colorado Historical Society, ID no. 10038338.

Alfred C. Cass. Courtesy, Colorado Fuel and Iron Archives, Bessemer Historical Society, Pueblo.

recorded. "I had had no relief from my debts," even though Osgood "had, during the Finance and Construction Co. operations, relieved himself of debt, settled money on his wife and sister and was engaged in very extensive private speculations, and in the construction of his Redstone improvements, which were carried on at large cost."[41]

Jerome continued to press Osgood for a settlement of CF&CC funds after the two men returned to Denver for meetings of CF&I directors and stockholders on August 21. Angered at being excluded from business affairs and by being treated, he felt, as a paid employee in a minor position rather than a partner, Jerome expressed his desire to Osgood to leave the company and return to private law practice. Showing some temper, Osgood acknowledged that Jerome "was of very little use [to him] under present conditions." Defending his position, Jerome responded that he realized he had been remiss in permitting the business of the Finance and Construction and Victor companies to be transacted without knowing all the details. Jerome recorded: "I told him I doubted whether he realized what position he placed me in; that if sudden death came to him I would have the utmost difficulty in establishing any interest; that my mouth would be sealed as to all conversations with him and that the stock or money which was due me would pass to his heirs, and that it was extremely doubtful whether I would realize anything and that Kebler and Cass were in the same position."[42]

Osgood strongly defended his right to conduct CF&CC business as he saw fit. He also stated that dividing the funds with Jerome at that time would leave him with fewer resources, "which," he stressed, "might be necessary in preserving the control in the Fuel Co. [CF&I]." The fight to save the company was still on, Osgood exclaimed, with obvious irritation. "He also said," Jerome noted, "that I expected more consideration than my services would entitle me to and gave me such a lecture that I felt very much disturbed."

Julian A. Kebler. Courtesy, Denver Public Library, Western History Collection, call no. H-55.

After further heated discussion, Osgood wrote a telegram directing C. E. Phelps in New York to hold 3,000 shares of CF&I stock subject to Jerome's order as the final settlement of the CF&CC deal. "He said," Jerome continued, "that he wanted it understood that there was to be no further accounting in that matter, but that the Victor Fuel Co. was still unsettled, and that I should have my share of that when it had been brought to such a point that a distribution could be made." Osgood implied that Jerome should realize from $100,000 to $200,000 when the Victor account was settled.[43]

Jerome was "taken back" by a settlement he had not expected because, he explained, there was no statement of accounts and he felt Osgood "held a string" on the 3,000 shares of CF&I stock. Furthermore, the amount of the stock was far less than he expected. As long as Osgood felt the way he did about their relationship, Jerome concluded, the only thing he could do was renew the discussion, insist on an accounting of all business transactions, and then withdraw from his association with Osgood.[44]

During another lengthy and acrimonious meeting in Osgood's office the next morning, Jerome demanded a general statement of accounting for the CF&CC that would show exactly what he was owed. According to his calculations, Jerome believed he should have at least 5,000 shares of CF&I stock or $200,000 as a settlement for everything, including the Victor Fuel Company. He indicated that he was willing to settle for less if a general statement of the two companies proved his calculations wrong. In response, Osgood finally admitted that through his "hazardous speculations" in an attempt to acquire the Colorado and Southern Railroad, he had lost over $1 million. It "humiliated him" to admit this, Jerome noted.[45]

Osgood's admission softened Jerome's position. When Osgood came to his office later that day Jerome told Osgood that he regretted saying things he should not have said. He explained that his anger stemmed more from Osgood's refusal to consider him a partner in the Victor Fuel venture than from disappointment over the results of his investment in the CF&CC. After studying the matter over the next few days, Jerome, "sore and bruised of mind," finally accepted Osgood's offer. He used the 3,000 shares of CF&I stock as collateral for borrowing money to pay off a large portion of his older debts.[46]

Relations between the two men remained strained even after the settlement. Osgood continued to criticize Jerome for his inattention to CF&I business. But more than anything, Jerome's constant opposition to Osgood's decision to carry on the fight for control of CF&I well beyond a time when, in Jerome's judgment, an advantageous settlement could have been reached led Osgood to criticize Jerome bitterly. Henry R. Wolcott, acting somewhat as an intermediary, confirmed to Jerome that there was "a good deal of bitterness in Osgood's feeling" and that Osgood was a very difficult man to get along with.[47] Jerome shied away from talking to Osgood about their business dealings again until shortly after Alfred Cass's death from a stroke on July 4, 1903. On July 10, Osgood apprised Jerome that he had made a settlement with Mrs. Cass and that he would loan Jerome funds to "fix up" his overdraft with CF&I. Jerome reluctantly accepted the loan, but then he asked Osgood for a statement of the Victor Fuel account. "He spoke sharply,"

Jerome noted, "saying, 'There is nothing to say about the Victor; there is no statement coming.'" Jerome disagreed. "There is certainly something coming to me," he countered. "No," Osgood shot back, "you have already had more than your share and I have all that I can do to take care of Mrs. Cass and Kebler." Jerome left Osgood's office without saying anything further.[48]

That evening Jerome dined with Osgood at the Denver Club. "We had a conversation before and during dinner," Jerome recorded, "in which he said that he was certain he had been fair in all his dealings with me, and that if the matter had been as I always insisted and wanted it, a regular partnership, that I would not have come out as well as I did." Osgood continued to insist that he had done everything he was legally and honorably obliged to do. Then, Jerome noted, Osgood "went on to talk about the future that was before us, and the fact that we were to be interested in other schemes together, and that we ought to be in a position to make a great deal of money." Jerome left the club convinced that further personal conversations with Osgood would be fruitless.[49]

Yet, in Osgood's office on the afternoon of July 21, Jerome spent what seemed to him the "most exasperating hour" of his entire experience with Osgood. Jerome was again disappointed that Osgood refused to recognize his financial interests in Victor Fuel or to present the matter to a disinterested party as a way to reach a mutual understanding. "There is nothing to talk about," Osgood said, according to Jerome's account of the meeting. He then asked Jerome: "Do you claim that you have an interest in my house at Redstone, or in the Redstone Improvement Co. or in the Sullivan Machinery Co.?" Such a suggestion was absurd, Jerome responded. "Well," Osgood retorted, "the Victor Fuel Company was the same. I purchased that with my own funds; you took no risk and are entitled to no consideration." Jerome refused to "accept such a dismissal" from Osgood, who reacted angrily when Jerome told him he was prepared to take the matter to court. "Osgood, you are impossible and it is no use for me to talk longer with you," Jerome exclaimed as he left the room. The two men never met again.[50]

Jerome appreciated "the peculiar reasons" why he should not pursue litigation with regard to the Victor Fuel Company. One of the reasons that "embarrassed" him most about potential litigation against Osgood was that the actual ownership of the Victor Fuel Company might be questioned if the facts concerning that property were revealed. CF&I officials, Jerome feared, could make a good case that they were the sole owners, since most of the funds for the purchase of the company had come from CF&I and CF&CC sources rather than from Osgood's own pocket. He turned to Cass Herrington, one of Osgood's lawyers, in a final effort to persuade Osgood to reach a settlement with him concerning his Victor Fuel claim. Herrington agreed to take up the matter, although in doing so he realized he was jeopardizing his relationship with Osgood, who, Herrington noted, was "very angry and bitter" and would not "listen to any talk" that gave merit to Jerome's claims. Nonetheless, after consulting with Kebler and David Beaman, who strongly felt Osgood should reach a settlement with Jerome, Herrington continued to pursue the matter. Osgood remained obstinate, however, and vowed to publish letters that would make Jerome "an object of scorn" to everyone who knew him if he brought the matter to court.[51]

Osgood softened his stand when Herrington advised him that Jerome was sincere in his determination to file suit if a settlement could not be reached. "Osgood was a very difficult man to handle," Herrington reported to Jerome, but from his talks with him and with others familiar with the situation, Herrington thought a settlement could be reached if Jerome was reasonable in his demands and "could put the matter in some way whereby Osgood's pride would not be injured." The plan Herrington suggested was for Osgood to buy out Jerome's interests in the auxiliary companies.[52] Herrington knew Osgood well, for when approached, Osgood agreed to the plan and indicated his readiness to set a price to purchase Jerome's interests in the auxiliary companies. He stipulated, however, that Jerome must issue a statement repudiating his alleged charges that there were "matters in connection with his [Osgood's] management of the Fuel Company [CF&I] which would injure him if they came to light." Although Jerome considered Osgood's position "childish," he reluctantly submitted such a statement in a letter to Herrington. Contrary to speculation, Jerome wrote, "[n]o proposition has ever been hinted at that Mr. Osgood should 'purchase my silence.'" The fact that such a suggestion could arise was "degrading and utterly impossible between honorable men." In conclusion, Jerome stated that he hoped the matter could be kept quiet, for "it would be detrimental for our private business relations to be made the subject of gossip."[53]

Following CF&I's annual meeting on August 20, 1903, Osgood offered to purchase Jerome's stock in the auxiliary companies for $92,875. Jerome considered the proposition absurd, for he believed that valuation was far below the fair value of the stocks. Furthermore, the proposition included no compensation for Jerome's interest in Victor Fuel, which Jerome considered the most vital issue of all. Herrington despaired of being able to do anything more. Osgood, he confided to Jerome, was the most difficult man he had ever dealt with "because he would see only one side of a question and had such infinite ingenuity in presenting his arguments that he was difficult to answer." Nevertheless, he would work with Kebler, Beaman, and his brother, Fred Herrington, to get a reasonable settlement and "lay down" on Osgood to make him submit.[54]

Jerome made it clear to Herrington that he would receive no proposition from Osgood unless it was "preceded by a withdrawal of his repeated allegations to them [the Herringtons, Kebler, Beaman, and others] that this was a holdup or anything in the nature of blackmail." He reassured Herrington that he was ready to take the matter to court if that was the only way to demonstrate to Osgood that his claim was not a form of blackmail. Herrington's response was emphatic: "You need have no expectation of ever being friends with Osgood again." It was not a question of friendship, Jerome responded, but a matter of "sealing" Osgood's mouth to prevent him from further impugning Jerome's reputation. In despair, Jerome agonized over the probability that the whole truth about the Victor Fuel affair would never be told and that his reputation would never be restored.[55]

To console Jerome, Herrington promised to try to get Osgood to add another $25,000 to the existing offer, making the total $117,875 for the purchase of Jerome's interest in the auxiliary companies—an amount Jerome still considered inadequate. Before he could counter with his own proposition, Jerome learned that Osgood had sailed for Europe and was not expected back until early December.[56]

Although Jerome prepared the legal brief against Osgood, it was never filed; nor did the details ever become public knowledge. However, an article in the *Denver Times* alluded to the dispute between Osgood and his three former associates. According to a knowledgeable source, the article stated, Cass, Kebler, and Jerome had experienced unexpected losses as a result of the Rockefeller-Gould takeover of CF&I. The article continued: "They had stood loyally by Osgood, relying on his ability to steer the company through the dangerous places, as he had done once before. After control passed to Gould and Rockefeller the three . . . made an inventory, and with information which they possessed they came to the conclusion that they had been betrayed by Osgood."[57] As far as public information was concerned, the speculation ended there. Whether the three had justification for their complaint was never determined, for their attempt to recover their financial losses by legal means ended abruptly with their untimely deaths. Cass's death on July 4 was a surprise to many, but the news of Kebler's death from a cerebral hemorrhage on November 20 was even more shocking. To Jerome, the news was devastating. The death of his two friends "shattered Jerome's hope of recovering his fortune from Osgood by legal process."[58] Thirty hours after Kebler died, Jerome was found dead at his country estate.

"John L. Jerome Joins His Old C.F. & I. Business Associates in Death," the *Rocky Mountain News* headline proclaimed on November 23. The detailed account, and a similar one in the *Denver Post*, attributed the death to an accidental overdose of a drug used to induce sleep. Local gossip, however, implied deeper motives, and family accounts confirm that Jerome, distraught over his personal finances and events, died from a self-inflicted gunshot wound.[59] Certainly, the preceding weeks had been agonizing. In addition to the dispute with Osgood, Jerome's financial difficulties had been compounded by his ownership of the Overland Cotton Mills, near Denver. The *Denver Post*, in a series of scathing articles, had dubbed Jerome's firm "Misery Hollow" during its campaign against child labor. He had depleted his personal resources in an effort to keep the plant open, but the prolonged labor troubles and failure to obtain coal during the strike finally forced him to shut it down. Even after the plant's closure, Jerome allowed his 500 idle employees to live rent-free in company houses. He promised to supply them with food and coal for domestic use during the shutdown and was reported to be devising other plans to help the workers' families at the time of his death. Those worries, combined with the loss of his two close friends and associates and his dispute with Osgood, had left him deeply distraught.[60]

The untimely deaths of Osgood's three top business associates within a five-month period raised questions. An article in the *Denver Post* blamed John D. Rockefeller for the "annihilation of the 'Iowa Crowd.'" Cass, Kebler, and Jerome, the headline stated, were "Victims of Rockefeller Rapacity."[61] Had the three been financially ruined by the Rockefeller-Gould takeover? Were they hounded to death by Rockefeller and his agents' relentless pursuit for control of CF&I?

The last question was taken seriously enough by the company's new management to elicit a response. Denying that Rockefeller and his agents had anything to do with the deaths of the three associates, Cass Herrington commented in a public statement that the health of "each of the deceased gentlemen was undermined by unceasing labor in the interests of the company long before Gould and Rockefeller had any interest there." In fact, Herrington stated, the three "were pleased to be relieved of the arduous duties required of them" and were happy to see the company come under the control of "substantial men who could operate it for the best interests of the stockholders and the state at large."[62]

Herrington's statement probably convinced few people in Colorado, where Cass, Kebler, and Jerome, along with Osgood, were considered heroes. No one doubted that the stress of the preceding months had taken its toll on the three men most financially vulnerable to the loss of the enterprise they had played pivotal roles in establishing. Herrington's statement, however, hid the extent of the pain and suffering the three endured as a result of the loss of CF&I. Herrington also kept secret the circumstances surrounding the acrimonious dispute between Jerome and Osgood. In one of their last conversations, Jerome had told Herrington that Osgood would never show him or anyone else "the papers about any of this business, either his own correspondence or mine."[63] Perhaps these papers, including the CF&CC files, were among those put to the match shortly after Osgood's death.

The loss of his most important associates did not prevent Osgood from quickly regaining a substantial portion of the western fuel trade. By 1910 the competition between Victor-American and CF&I for markets shares had reached the point that John D. Rockefeller Jr. asked LaMont Bowers, chair of the CF&I board, to explain why sought-after business contracts were going to Osgood's company. Bowers responded with a vilification of Victor-American and Rocky Mountain Fuel, which had purchased the Northern Coal and Coke properties, his company's principal rivals. "We have positive proof," he wrote, "that these two coal companies have been systematically robbing their miners by underweight." He was astonished that men like Osgood were able to "hoodwink and swindle" the public.[64]

The divisive force of economic competition, however, was trumped by powerful factors that brought the coal companies together. The most powerful of these factors was the resurgence of the United Mine Workers of America and the renewal of its campaign to organize coalminers in Colorado. Coal operators described the union's challenge as a threat to the American way of life, indeed, to civilization itself. In the face of this threat, the coal operators united in 1903 and again in 1913 to defend their business ethics, industrial philosophy, and societal virtue.

NOTES

1. Andrews, "Road to Ludlow," 430 (quote), 439.

2. Scamehorn, "Osgood and the Western Steel Industry," 143–144; Scamehorn, *Pioneer Steelmaker*, 101–102; *Denver Times*, May 18, 1901; Long, *Where the Sun Never Shines*, 212. Scott Martelle noted that although Osgood was a pioneer in the development of Colorado industry, business and financial problems "dogged him." "Given capitalism's cannibalistic nature," Martelle continued, "Osgood's problems were a

blood scent" (*Blood Passion: The Ludlow Massacre and Class War in the American West* [New Brunswick, N.J.: Rutgers University Press, 2007], 36).

3. "Statement of Business and Personal Relations," Jerome Papers, FF 1–FF 26.

4. Long, *Where the Sun Never Shines*, 213. Osgood's suspension of stock dividends in 1902 prompted Union Pacific's Edward Harriman and other eastern investors to join John Gates in an attempt to force Osgood out and take over CF&I's coalfields (Martelle, *Blood Passion,* 36, citing "To Oust J. C. Osgood," *New York Times,* June 28, 1902).

5. Osgood to Jerome, April 20, 1901, Jerome Papers, Correspondence, FF 40.

6. *Denver Times,* May 18, 1901; Scamehorn, *Pioneer Steelmaker,* 159. Actually, two firms in Chicago marketed the first installment of the debenture bonds—Illinois Trust and Savings Bank and Blair and Company.

7. Osgood to Jerome, June 15, 1901, Jerome Papers, Correspondence, FF 41.

8. Scamehorn, *Pioneer Steelmaker,* 157; McGovern and Guttridge, *Coalfield War,* 12–13.

9. Included were the Crystal River Railroad, the Colorado and Wyoming Railroad, Rocky Mountain Coal and Iron Company, Pueblo Realty Trust Company, Colorado Supply Company, Mountain Telegraph Company, Laramie Iron and Steel Company, Minnequa Cooperage Company, Rocky Mountain Timber Company, Minnequa Town Company, Redstone Improvement Company, and Steel Wheel and Wagon Company. List from Scamehorn, *Pioneer Steelmaker,* 167.

10. "Statement of Business and Personal Relations," Jerome Papers, FF 21.

11. Scamehorn, *Pioneer Steelmaker,* 162, quoting Colorado Fuel and Iron Company, Minute Book of Stockholders, 78.

12. Scamehorn, *Pioneer Steelmaker,* 163; McGovern and Guttridge, *Coalfield War,* 14.

13. *New York Sunday World,* reprinted in the *Denver Republican,* August 28, 1902.

14. "Statement of Business and Personal Relations," Jerome Papers, FF 22; McGovern and Guttridge, *Coalfield War,* 15; Scamehorn, *Pioneer Steelmaker,* 164.

15. *Denver Times,* June 25, 1903, describing Rockefeller and Gould visit; McGovern and Guttridge, *Coalfield War,* 13–14.

16. *Denver Times,* December 11, 1902.

17. *Camp and Plant* 2, no. 25 (December 20, 1902): 601–602; *Pueblo Chieftain,* December 12, 1902.

18. *Camp and Plant* 2, no. 25 (December 20, 1902): 603. Other celebrations were reported. In Rouse, for example, "The people of this place had quite a jollification on the evening of December 10 over the fact that the present management of the Colorado Fuel and Iron Company is to be retained in control" (ibid., 604).

19. *Denver News,* November 6, 1891, cited in Leon W. Fuller, "Colorado's Revolt against Capitalism," *Mississippi Valley Historical Review* 21, issue 3 (December 1934): 345.

20. *Denver Times*, September 12, 1902.

21. "Newest Figure in Finance," *New York Times*, September 7, 1902.

22. Ibid.; McGovern and Guttridge, *Coalfield War*, 6.

23. "Statement of Business and Personal Relations," Jerome Papers, FF 22; Scamehorn, *Pioneer Steelmaker*, 165.

24. "Statement of Business and Personal Relations," Jerome Papers, FF 22.

25. *Denver Times*, June 25, 1903.

26. John C. Osgood to George P. Butler, June 12, 1903, folder 204, box 22, Business Interests series, Record Group 2, Office of the Messrs. Rockefeller (OMR), Rockefeller Family Archives, Rockefeller Archive Center, Pocantinco Hills, N.Y.

27. Ibid.

28. *Denver Times*, August 20, 1903; Andrews, "Road to Ludlow," 169, note 82.

29. It was reported that when he resigned as chair of the CF&I board, Osgood exclaimed that he would not be "a hired man, no matter who his employer might be" (quoted in Whittaker, *Pathbreakers and Pioneers*, 125).

30. *Denver Times*, August 25, 1903; *Denver Post*, November 23, 1903. The "Big Four" were Osgood, Kebler, Cass, and Jerome. Cass had died on July 4, 1903, at his home in Redstone. Jerome, who had long expressed his desire to resign from the directorate and had fallen out of favor with Osgood, was excluded from the deliberations establishing the corporation's new leadership.

31. Quote in *Denver Times*, August 20, 1903; *Denver Post*, June 30, 1903.

32. "Osgood Walked into Rockefeller's Trap," *Denver Times*, August 25, 1903; *Wall Street Journal* article reprinted in the *Denver Times*, August 17, 1903.

33. *Denver Times*, August 6, 1903; Scamehorn, "Osgood and the Western Steel Industry," 146; McGovern and Guttridge, *Coalfield War*, 16.

34. Scamehorn, *Pioneer Steelmaker*, 167.

35. Ibid., 99, 167–168; Osgood's testimony, SMM, 395; *Denver Times*, August 6, 1903; Whiteside, *Regulating Danger*, 14–15.

36. *Denver Times*, June 25, August 6, 1903; *Denver Post*, June 26, 1903.

37. Scamehorn, *Pioneer Steelmaker*, 168; Osgood's testimony, SMM, 465–466. Osgood noted that in 1914, Victor-American's capital stock was worth $5.4 million and that the company owned about 35,000 acres of coal land, compared to CF&I's 300,000 acres (ibid., 463).

38. "Bill of Complaint," Jerome Papers, FF 26. The suit was not instituted because of Jerome's death in 1903.

39. Ruland, *Lion of Redstone*, 33; Nelson, *Marble and Redstone*, 96; King Diary, March 29, 1915, G2539, 474.

40. "Statement of Business and Personal Relations," Jerome Papers, FF 19.

41. Ibid.

42. Ibid.

43. Ibid.

44. Ibid.

45. Ibid.

46. Ibid.

47. Ibid., November 11, 1901, FF 20.

48. Ibid., July 10, 1903, FF 22.

49. Ibid.

50. July 21, 1903, FF 24.

51. Ibid., July 28, 29 (quote), August 3, 1903, FF 24.

52. The auxiliary companies were American Fuel, Minnequa Town Company, Steel Wheel and Wagon Company, and Colorado Supply Company. Victor Fuel was not included in the list.

53. "Statement of Business and Personal Relations," FF 24. From what Jerome implied, one can conclude that the "matters in connection with Osgood's management of CF&I" pertained directly to the establishment and operation of the Colorado Finance and Construction Company. Osgood also seemed very sensitive about the source of the funds sent to the Redstone Improvement Company for development of the village of Redstone.

54. Ibid., August 24 (first quote), 28 (second quote), 1903, FF 24.

55. Ibid., August 28, 1903, FF 24.

56. Ibid.

57. *Denver Times,* November 23, 1903.

58. Ibid.

59. *Rocky Mountain News,* November 23, 1903; *Denver Post,* November 23, 1903; Ruland, *Lion of Redstone,* 61; Nelson, *Marble and Redstone,* 121.

60. *Camp and Plant* 5, no. 15 (April 23, 1904): 353–355 (Kebler obituary); ibid., 4, no. 8 (September 5, 1903): 186–187 (Cass obituary); ibid., 5, no. 15 (April 23, 1904): 353–355 (Kebler obituary); ibid., 5, no. 16 (April 30, 1904): 398–399 (Jerome obituary).

61. *Denver Post,* November 23, 1903.

62. Herrington quoted in *Rocky Mountain News,* November 24, 1903.

63. "Statement of Business and Personal Relations," August 1903, FF 24.

64. Quoted in McGovern and Guttridge, *Coalfield War,* 59.

The 1903–1904 Strike

Shortly after the reorganization of the CF&I board of directors in August 1903, John Osgood left on a three-month trip to Europe. When he returned in December, he found the southern and central Colorado coalfields plunged into another major strike. In calling the strike, the United Mine Workers of America (UMWA) wanted to challenge Colorado Fuel and Iron's (CF&I's) new ownership, with the hope that the departure of Osgood and some of the most antiunion officials of the company's old guard would make the new management more amenable to unionization. As in 1901, the union targeted Osgood, this time in an effort to divide CF&I and the Victor Fuel Company, the latter now under Osgood's ownership. Success with CF&I, the union believed, would put tremendous pressure on Osgood to abandon or at least modify his strident opposition to unionization.[1]

Rumors of a pending strike were in the air even before Osgood left for Europe. After a two-year hiatus, the national UMWA again began an organizational effort in Colorado in early 1903. The union organizers met with a modicum of success, as many miners in southern and central Colorado were eager to confront the companies with long-held grievances. In particular, John Gehr, UMWA national organizer and former president of District 15, noted that the miners were determined to obtain enforcement of the anti-screen and biweekly payday laws and the enactment of legislation for an eight-hour workday. In addition, miners at the Victor camps registered protests against Victor Fuel for prohibiting organization and discharging union members. By late summer, an increasing number of miners demanded that the union call a strike against CF&I and Victor Fuel.[2]

William Howells and District 15 officials were also eager to test the new ownership of CF&I. On August 13 Howells addressed an open letter, a "manifesto," to the public and to Governor James Peabody that listed the miners' grievances and warned of a strike if action was not taken. The long list of complaints against coalmine owners and the state included the denial of miners' rights, violation of laws, and the loss of craft traditions in coal mining. Specifically, the manifesto charged that the companies employed renegade deputy sheriffs to prevent union organization, fired workers who were union members, collected excessively high rents for shoddy housing, refused to give miners a voice in determining wages and working conditions, forced workers to shop at company stores where prices were exorbitantly high, and hired cheap foreign labor to intimidate native workers. Howells also asserted that the state had failed to enforce state laws governing health and safety in the mines. Coal company policies, he concluded, were "strongly tinctured with the old time feudal slavery." In an accompanying letter, Howells urged Peabody to use his powerful influence to redress these grievances in order to avert a strike.[3]

Peabody was extremely hesitant to intervene, but faced with the spread of strikes by the Western Federation of Miners (WFM) in the hard-rock mining districts and growing criticism from pro-labor newspapers, he agreed to confer with a union committee in an effort to persuade coalmine operators to grant concessions to their miners. At his behest, the state deputy commissioner of labor, W. H. Montgomery, sent letters to the operators asking them to meet with union officers in Denver on September 11 "for the purpose of devising means to more fully comply with the present laws relating to the operation of mines, and to consider measures to avoid possible friction between employees and operators."[4]

Although the union officials appeared for the meeting, only three coal companies from the northern field sent representatives. Neither CF&I nor the Victor Fuel Company sent a representative to that meeting or to one scheduled the following week. Officials of the two companies remained steadfast in rejecting third-party arbitration of the miners' grievances and in refusing to extend any recognition of the union as a bargaining agent for the miners. Although operators in the northern Colorado coalfields, including the Northern Coal and Coke Company, came to terms with the UMWA, operators in the south remained inflexible in their terms, especially on the matter of union recognition. The position of CF&I and Victor Fuel officials forced union leaders to choose either to strike or to accept existing conditions in the southern coalfields.[5]

Several signs augured badly for a strike at this time. The union's hope of receiving a more conciliatory response from CF&I that would drive a wedge between that company and Victor Fuel seemed illusionary. Although Osgood and W. J. Murray, former general superintendent, were no longer associated with CF&I, men still loyal to Osgood remained in leadership positions in the reorganized company. They were determined to follow the old policy relative to the UMWA that had been successful in the past under Osgood's leadership. Therefore, in all likelihood, in the event of a strike the union would face the united force of the two most powerful coal companies in southern Colorado. The result of a strike, cautious union leaders predicted, would be the same as that of the 1901 strike.[6]

Another reason to doubt that a strike would be successful was the strength of antiunion forces in the state. One such organization, the Citizens' Alliance of Denver, had increased class-consciousness among capitalists and their supporters and mobilized them against organized labor. The alliance described the struggle between employers and labor as one between American individualism, freedom, justice, and progress on one side and the forces of despotism, tyranny, and slavery bent on ruining civilization on the other. Organized as a law-and-order movement opposing the eight-hour workday and promoting the open-shop principle, the alliance's major objective was to protect the "inalienable rights" of its members "to manage their business in such lawful manner as they may deem proper, without domination or coercion by any organized movement against such right."[7] By the end of 1903, the alliance had enrolled nearly 3,000 individual and corporate members, gained the support of the influential *Denver Republican*, and established a war chest of nearly $20,000 to use in the fight against labor.[8]

With its praise for the coal companies and condemnation of the UMWA, the alliance easily won the support of Governor Peabody and the major coal operators.

Faced with this concentration of capital and power as represented in the Citizens' Alliance of Denver, the UMWA seemed extremely weak. Although successful in rousing the miners' anger over working and living conditions, union organizers were less successful in getting them to join the union. Those who did faced considerable intimidation. Company spies "dogged" union organizers and their recruits. "Whenever we organized any men they were discharged the next morning," an organizer stated. Hundreds of miners were beaten and fired at Primero, Hastings, and other large camps on suspicion that they were union men. From 1900 to 1903, according to union estimates, Colorado coal companies discharged and blacklisted 6,000 of 8,000 new recruits. Some union estimates put the number of members still working in the mines at fewer than 300 at the time of the strike.[9]

John Gehr read the signs correctly. At a meeting of UMWA delegates in Pueblo on September 24, 1903, he argued that the time for a successful strike had not yet arrived. Besides the weakness of the union, he noted that the governor, the Citizens' Alliance, and the National Guard all supported the operators. He conjectured that the operators wanted the strike in order to crush the union. He also worried that a strike in the coalfields would be lumped together with the WFM strike in the silver and gold mines and that the state troops at Cripple Creek would be sent to the coalfields to end the strike quickly and destroy the union. "I believe it would be little less than a sacrifice of my friends should I counsel them to strike at this time," he was quoted as having said in the *Rocky Mountain News*. "I was outspoken in my denunciation of the plan [to strike] all along," Gehr continued, "and I have prepared a report to present to the national executive board when they convene in Indianapolis, October 5."[10]

Other voices were heard and other reports prepared at the Pueblo convention. Mary Harris Jones, known as Mother Jones, already recognized as the union's most famous organizer and flamboyant agitator, was one of those voices. The union's executive board had sent her to Colorado to look into conditions there and report back on the miners' sentiments. She traveled from camp to camp, "eating in the homes of the miners, staying all night with their families." She described the conditions under which they lived as "deplorable." The miners, she reported, were practically company slaves. "I felt, after listening to their stories, after witnessing their long patience that the time was ripe for revolt against such brutal conditions," she later wrote in her autobiography. As for the sentiments of the miners, she reported to the officials in Indianapolis, "the fever was there and at fever heat. The men were almost wild to come out."[11]

After reporting directly to John Mitchell and other UMWA officials in Indianapolis, Mother Jones returned to Colorado in time to take part in the delegate convention in Pueblo. She sided with Howells, who pressed for a strike call, and WFM president Charles Moyer, who preached solidarity among all miners and advocated a combined WFM and UMWA effort to bring justice to workers throughout the state. The *Pueblo Labor Advocate* gave Mother Jones credit for organizing the miners and bringing them out on strike.[12]

After hearing the official reports, the delegates expressed strong displeasure with Gehr by passing a resolution censuring him for his opposition to a strike call. The next day, the delegates drew up a list of demands that went little beyond existing state law: bimonthly paydays, abolition of the scrip system, defining a ton as 2,000 rather than 2,400 pounds, better ventilation in the mines, an eight-hour day, and a 20 percent increase in contract and tonnage prices. The last two demands were the only ones not covered by existing state statutes. Conspicuously absent from the list was a demand for union recognition.[13]

Of these grievances, the primary issue for the miners was the Colorado Assembly's refusal to pass legislation earlier in the year for an eight-hour workday despite overwhelming public support for such a measure. A writer for *McClures* was scathing in his comment on the measure's defeat: "Rarely, indeed, has there been in this country a more brazen, conscienceless defeat of the will of the people, plainly expressed, not only at the ballot box, but by the pledges of both parties."[14] The failure of the eight-hour measure was the principal catalyst for the strike in 1903, and Osgood's role in defeating the legislation raised the ire of the miners and made him once again the UMWA's prime target.

Osgood, in fact, had been the leader of the opposition to the eight-hour proposal. He was instrumental in forging an alliance among CF&I, Victor Fuel, the American Smelting and Refining Company, and the Citizens' Alliance of Denver to oppose the legislation, and he took full credit for introducing amendments that ultimately killed the measure. He told the Colorado House Committee on Mines and Mining in February 1903 that limiting the workday to eight hours was arbitrary and a serious menace to both industry and labor. Since the miners were contract rather than wage workers, they would be hurt the most by the proposed legislation, he stressed. Indeed, in his testimony Osgood presented himself as a defender of the rights of labor: "The company with which I am connected [CF&I]

employs upwards of 17,000 men. I consider myself their representative, although I have not been delegated as such, but I have not in all the years I have been connected with the company lost sight of their welfare."[15]

The miners regarded Osgood's statement as self-serving. They wanted the union to represent them, not a millionaire coal operator who only professed to have their interests at heart. Osgood's opposition to the eight-hour workday brought other issues to a boiling point. "We have grievous wrongs," one miner exclaimed in late October. "We are American!" The miners companied that they were "often robbed of 50 per cent of the coal mined" and that the company store cheated them "disgracefully." As one miner lamented, "A man . . . dare not call his soul his own. If two men are talking together, a deputy sheriff or paid tool of the company will edge up alongside of him to find out if he is talking about his work or labor unions."[16]

Although it realized that the miners were restive, the UMWA's national executive board requested further negotiations before it sanctioned the strike. The board authorized John Mitchell, the union's president, to inform officers of the leading coal companies that the union desired a negotiated settlement. Mitchell corresponded with Jesse Welborn, president of CF&I, and George W. Bartlett, general manager of the Victor Fuel Company, but both refused to negotiate on the grounds that the union did not represent their employees and that the men they employed had no desire to strike. In his response, Welborn added a warning. "If you understand the situation as it really is," he wrote, "you no doubt regard the inciting of any further industrial disturbance in Colorado as ill-advised and criminal."[17]

With this snub, the executive board authorized the national officers to call a strike in Colorado on November 9 if a conference with the operators could not be arranged or the situation there settled in some other way. Mitchell continued his efforts to reach an agreement with CF&I and Victor Fuel, but in a letter to Howells on October 26 he expressed regret because he had been unsuccessful. He also recognized that District 15 officials were convinced that the time for a confrontation with Colorado's coal operators was now or never. Information from some of the camps indicated "a growing restlessness and impatience upon the part of the miners and mine workers, whose conditions of employment, especially under the two companies [CF&I and Victor Fuel] referred to, have grown to be intolerable." In view of the circumstances, he authorized Howells to announce a strike on November 9 unless an agreement was reached or negotiations entered into by the two principal companies before that date.[18]

With the state's financial and military resources dangerously extended (hundreds of troops were deployed in the Cripple Creek district and hundreds more pledged for use in the Telluride district), Governor Peabody summoned the general managers of CF&I and Victor Fuel to a meeting in Denver on November 4. The governor urged them to meet with union leaders in an effort to reach a settlement. Again, the company officials refused, although they expressed a willingness to confer with a committee of their own employees who were not union members. They made it absolutely clear that anything that might give the impression of union recognition was unacceptable. Thus, the southern operators' intransigence in refusing to meet with union officials, even though recognition of the union was not one of the UMWA's demands, destroyed any chance of preventing the strike.[19]

Both company officials and union leaders were surprised when over 10,000 miners—95 percent of the coalminers employed in Colorado—answered the strike call on November 9. It was the "biggest surprise party in the history of the West," declared the *Pueblo Labor Advocate*. "Union and non-union, white and Mexican, all obeyed the strike order of President Mitchell and the tie-up is complete." With the miners' overwhelming support for the strike, which certainly contradicted the operators' claim that working conditions were satisfactory, union leaders were hopeful that the operators would grant their call for a conference. Although John T. Kebler, general manager of CF&I's Fuel Department, stressed that the company would follow its past policy with regard to conferences, strike leaders believed a conference could not be refused. "The chief bone of contention in the strike is the Victor Fuel Company," the article concluded. The union claimed the company's oppressive policies toward labor had precipitated the strike.[20]

The union's optimism was badly misplaced. There would be no conference, and the hope of dividing CF&I and Victor Fuel was shattered when Kebler and Bartlett, vowing never to negotiate with the union, announced they would work together to break the strike. "The strike will be fought out to a finish, whether it takes ten days, six months or ten years," Kebler proclaimed.[21] He might have added "at whatever cost," for all the companies in the region were prepared to spend whatever was necessary for guns, mine guards, and the importation of strikebreakers to crush the union. During the first week of the strike, Victor Fuel had purchased the entire stock of rifles and revolvers at a Trinidad hardware store and ordered more. At CF&I and Victor Fuel's expense, Sheriff O. T. Clark of Las Animas County appointed 115 deputy sheriffs to help guard the mines and fight the strikers.[22]

Although still in Europe at the outbreak of the strike, Osgood kept in close touch with his company's officials and advised them throughout the strike.[23] With his old friend and former associate Jesse Welborn at the helm of CF&I, Osgood was assured that the close alliance between the two com-

panies would continue. Without missing a beat, Victor Fuel and CF&I officials proceeded to implement a plan of attack against the union borrowed
largely from the one devised by eastern corporate interests during earlier
struggles against organized labor. The companies first evicted strikers from
company housing and demolished houses built by workers on leased company ground. The evictions embittered many strikers against the companies, especially Victor Fuel, which, it was reported, acted more aggressively
against the strikers. Claiming that the camps of Hastings and Delagua were
located entirely on property owned by the company, Victor Fuel closed
them to all strikers and union members. Deputy sheriffs employed by the
company arrested unauthorized personnel who attempted to enter the
towns and held them in jail for a brief period before escorting them out of
town with instructions never to return. As another means of harassment, in
early December Victor Fuel filed a suit for damages amounting to $85,000
against national and district officials of the UMWA. The defendants were
charged with interfering with the conduct of the company's business and
intimidating its employees. The suit forced the union to spend strike funds
already in short supply to defend itself.[24]

In response to the companies' actions, the UMWA provided winter shelter for evicted strikers in the form of tents erected on leased ground. The
union also provided food, clothing, medicines, and strike benefits (five dollars per week for single men and eight dollars a week for married men) for
workers who stayed in the strike district. At the beginning of the strike, the
union provided transportation for miners who wanted to leave Colorado.
John Mitchell told Governor Peabody that the union had furnished transportation for 1,300 or 1,400 strikers to other fields where union jobs were
waiting. Another 1,000 strikers paid for their own transportation to other
places of employment. Many Italian workers returned to Italy, while others
left their wives and children behind in the union's care while they looked for
work elsewhere. The union, Mitchell assured the governor, was prepared to
continue these benefits as long as the strike lasted or until the men could be
transported to other fields.[25]

The evictions and closing of the Victor Fuel towns of Hastings and
Delagua provoked sporadic outbreaks of protest and violence. One of the
first protests occurred in Hastings when a group of Italian women attempted
to prevent the demolition of shanties workers had previously occupied. On
another occasion at Hastings, violence erupted when a group of miners
attempted to blow up the Victor Fuel Company's powerhouse.

In mid-November Major Zeph T. Hill of the Colorado National Guard
assessed the situation in southern Colorado for the governor. Although he

warned that potential for trouble clearly existed, he believed the mine operators had enough deputies to protect their property without guard troops. However, he added, if the union attempted a complete shutdown of the mines or the companies resumed large-scale production with strikebreakers, the situation could change. Both factors existed by the time Hill submitted his report to Governor Peabody.[26]

Despite the warnings about impending violence, the companies increased the importation of strikebreakers—especially African American, Chinese, and Japanese workers—in late November. CF&I transferred Italian workers from the Pueblo steel plant to work the mines. By the end of the strike, strikebreakers, mainly from southern and southeastern Europe, had replaced the departed British and Welsh strikers. Governor Peabody gave his approval to this procedure when he promised Welborn that he would use the "entire military force of this state" to preserve order and protect the rights of non-union workers. With an increase in violence resulting from the importation of strikebreakers, it was only a matter of time before Peabody would have to make good on his promise.[27]

As the strike spread to encompass most of the central and southern coalfields, UMWA president John Mitchell arrived in Trinidad on December 2, 1903, to investigate conditions and review the conduct of the strike. Addressing a public meeting of 3,000 people the following day, he encouraged the miners to continue the strike. "I recognize that the lands and mines belong to the coal companies," he told the crowd. "I deny that the men belong to the companies. I deny that the company shall say that you shall not belong to the union; that you shall not trade where you wish to; that you shall be paid in any other than American money." It was futile for coal company managers to think the UMWA could be driven out of Colorado, he continued. "We propose to live within the law, to obey every law of the country. If you feel as I do, you will mine no more coal until you receive reasonable wages and better conditions and until the companies obey the law, just as they ask you to do. Stand together, fight together, fight peacefully, be good union men, for when you are good union men you are good citizens."[28]

The following day Mitchell traveled to Denver, where he addressed the Chamber of Commerce. He told the members that the miners in southern Colorado worked under conditions that were "un-American." They were not allowed to spend their earnings where they pleased and were shorted in the weighing of the coal they dug. By continuing to pay workers on a monthly basis, the coal companies were violating state law that required them to pay the miners twice a month. As a consequence, many miners had to draw credit in the form of scrip, which forced them to shop at the company store or cash the scrip at a 20 percent discount. Lastly, Mitchell observed that most of the American-born miners had been driven from the field and replaced by immigrant workers who were paid a lower wage. "If the conditions were fair, if the conditions were American, it would not be so," he concluded.[29]

Mitchell's words fell on unsympathetic ears. The Denver Chamber of Commerce urged Governor Peabody to intervene in the strike on the side of the operators. Pressure on Peabody to intervene came from several other quarters as well. The recently formed Trinidad Citizens' Alliance carried on a campaign in the local *Chronicle-News,* a rabidly pro-operator paper, against union leaders. State senators Casimiro Barela and Frank R. Wood urged the governor to give coal companies state militia protection to end the strike, which was causing the state great financial loss. On December 2 a group of operators met with Peabody in Denver to request troops. Among them was Delos Chappell, president of the Victor Fuel Company, who told the governor that 1,400 of his striking employees were ready to return to work if they were protected from union violence. He also stressed the importance of the state assuming the cost of protecting lives and property to allow the companies to resume profitable mining operations. Notwithstanding these entreaties, Peabody demurred. Perhaps it was a combination of poor state finances and the controversy over his dispatch of state troops to the metal-lurgical camps that caused him to hesitate.[30]

Peabody had another reason to hold off on sending troops. Mitchell was in town, and he wanted to talk with him to see if a resolution of the strike was possible. While he had made no attempt to meet with major mine operators, who had declared once again that they would not confer with him or any other union official, Mitchell readily accepted Peabody's request for a meeting. The meeting proved fruitless, however, as Mitchell found the governor unyielding on every issue. In spite of his desire to end the strike, Peabody remained firmly convinced that he should not inter-fere except to assure coal production and maintain law and order. He also refused to attempt arbitration, as he believed the strike was a private rather than a public matter. He told Mitchell he would protect the operators' right to hire strikebreakers and warned him that he would send troops to the area to suppress any violence the use of strikebreakers might provoke. Mitchell left the conference convinced that there was no immediate probability that the strike would be settled. Officials at CF&I and Victor Fuel were simi-larly convinced, for following his meeting with Mitchell, Peabody told a confidant that he would support the operators "solely for the well-being of the business interests of this State." Assured of the governor's support, the operators continued their course of action to defeat the union.[31]

Besides continuing to pressure Governor Peabody to dispatch troops to the strike zone, the operators employed other means to break the strike and destroy the union. Both the CF&I and Victor Fuel companies had strike funds with which they hired mine guards and paid extra deputies to harass and bully union organizers and strikers, guard mine property, and protect strikebreakers imported to work the mines. The *Rocky Mountain News* observed that CF&I's strike fund, which Osgood had started in the 1890s by charging miners between one and three cents per ton of coal they mined, had grown to "become a large amount" of money by 1903.[32] The actions of the mine guards and the importation of strikebreakers heightened tensions and significantly increased incidents of violence during the late winter and early spring of 1904. Most victims of the violence were strikers and union organizers, and many strikers acquired weapons to defend themselves.

Alarmed by the prospect of an armed conflict between strikers and mine guards and deputies, a delegation from Trinidad and Las Animas County, including Sheriff Clark, met with Peabody in Denver on March 21, 1904, to plead for help. In a letter of the same date, Clark informed the governor that incidents of discontent were becoming alarming and that many unemployed miners were arming themselves in preparation for an anticipated "open and violent conflict." The acquisition of arms by 1,500 "idle" men, he stressed, made it impossible for him to maintain law and order. Therefore, he urged the governor to send troops immediately to the southern coalfields "to enforce the law, maintain peace, suppress any violence, tumult or riot, and to protect the lives and property of the citizens of this community." Peabody needed no further prodding. On March 22 he dispatched 400 state troops to Las Animas County, which he proclaimed was in a "state of insurrection and rebellion." It was better, he said in response to praise from Wall Street, "to suppress wrong-doing . . . than to wait until the damage is accomplished and then attempt to punish the offenders."[33]

Peabody did not make the decision to send troops to the troubled area until he had guarantees that the expense of their employment would be covered. He had arranged for the principal beneficiaries of the intervention to share the cost of the campaign, estimated at $200,000. Of this amount, CF&I contributed $80,000, Victor Fuel $70,000, and the Trinidad Citizens' Alliance $30,000. The balance of $20,000 was contributed by railroads. Funded by the mine companies and their allies, the military campaign's impartiality was undermined from the beginning, even though the state was obligated to repay the funds.[34]

Peabody's order to send troops into southern Colorado assured victory for the coal operators, but it prolonged rather than hastened the end of the strike. The order came precisely at the time the UMWA's national executive board had decided to call a special convention of District 15 for the purpose of ending the strike. Peabody's proclamation establishing martial law, however, forced the national leaders to support District 15 in continuing the strike. As Vice President T. L. Lewis later stated, "We could not afford to declare that strike off in the face of the declaration of the Governor." They had to continue the strike, he added, "notwithstanding the fact that we knew it was lost." The UMWA's prestige had been put on the line, John Mitchell recounted in 1905, and to resume work while civil laws had been suspended "would be regarded . . . as a cowardly surrender to Peabody, who was then suspected of being . . . and who has since demonstrated himself to have been . . . simply a tool of the mining corporations."[35]

Major Zeph Hill, commander of the military campaign, promptly promulgated Peabody's proclamation of martial law throughout the Trinidad field. Although the purpose of the campaign was to defuse an explosive situation, Hill's actions from the beginning manifested a provocative anti-labor bias. His disarmament policy was selective rather than general, taking guns from the strikers, for example, while leaving them in the hands of "good and law-abiding" people. Members of his signal corps listened to all incoming telephone calls and prohibited those that were not in English. Only approved telegraph messages were allowed to pass over the wires. Major Hill also suppressed the Italian newspaper, *Il Lavatore Italiano,* because he believed its articles might provoke the Italians into "riot or disturbance." His action was also punitive, for the paper had disclosed the report that CF&I, the Victor Fuel Company, and the Citizens' Alliance of Denver had contributed most of the $200,000 necessary to keep state troops in the strike zone. The paper reported that the alliance had justified the suppression of insurgent labor by stating: "The socialists and anarchists of the United States have selected Colorado as the best field in which to exploit their peculiar ideas." Therefore, all efforts should be made to "resist their political encroachments."[36]

Following Major Hill's orders, military authorities arrested at least 160 men and incarcerated them in the Las Animas County jail, where they were kept as long as possible to prevent them from undermining the strikebreaking campaign. Offenses that might lead to an arrest included criticizing the governor or his military officers, selling whiskey to the troops, intimidating strikebreakers, displaying union posters in store windows, committing vagrancy, purchasing and hiding weapons, and agitating. Furthermore, after consulting with the coal company officials, Governor Peabody ordered

Hill to deport all nonresident strike leaders from Las Animas County. Claiming they were a "menace to the peace," Hill extended the order by deporting dozens of local residents as well. Before the strike ended, Hill's troops had escorted around 97 individuals—including labor leaders, miners, saloon keepers, and newspaper editors—from the district to eastern Colorado, Kansas, or New Mexico. Hill's actions left the strikers leaderless and weaponless.[37]

Mother Jones was one of the labor leaders arrested and sent to La Junta in southeastern Colorado for deportation out of the state. True to her nature, she had other ideas, and she boarded a Denver-bound train. The conductor agreed to take her to Denver, despite the letter she carried from Governor Peabody ordering her out of the state. Soon after she arrived in Denver she wrote the governor a letter, stating:

> Mr. Governor, you notified your dogs of war to put me out of the state. They complied with your instructions. I hold in my hand a letter that was handed to me by one of them, which says "under no circumstances return to this state." I wish to notify you, governor, that you don't own the state. When it was admitted to the sisterhood of states, my fathers gave me a share of stock in it; and that is all they gave to you. The civil courts are open. If I break a law of state or nation it is the duty of the civil courts to deal with me. That is why my forefathers established those courts to keep dictators and tyrants such as you from interfering with civilians. I am right here in the capital . . . four or five blocks from your office. I want to ask you, governor, what in Hell are you going to do about it?

The governor did nothing, and Mother Jones went to the Western Slope to "encourage those toiling and disinherited miners who were fighting against such monstrous odds."[38]

Governor Peabody had more to worry about than the fiery Mother Jones. The strike went on, even though the deployment of troops to the largest mines and camps kept violence and destruction of property to a minimum. The strikers were not responsible for all the incidents. The burning of the Victor Fuel Company's machine shop at Hastings, to single out one case, was later attributed to mine guards who wanted to demonstrate the continued need for private guards around company property. Although the strikers were accused of many acts of violence, few arrests were made. Major Hill, however, went beyond strictly maintaining law and order to assure the strikers' defeat. The National Guard's general harassment of the strikers while protecting strikebreakers the companies brought in was what most angered the workers. By the summer of 1904, the employment of strikebreakers, which the miners were powerless to prevent, had brought coal production up to 80 percent of the pre-strike level. With production on the increase, the operators were in no mood to make even minimal concessions to the union and strikers.[39]

The coal companies and their allies had alienated the strikers further with an extensive public relations campaign. While Major Hill threatened to expel reporters from the strike district if they printed unflattering articles about the militia, company officials gave sympathetic reporters from such publications as Denver's *Polly Pry,* the *Denver Republican,* and the *Trinidad Chronicle-News* access to the camps to encourage favorable coverage of the strike situation. They also arranged for the publication of extensive statements to the press and placed spurious articles in "friendly" publications designed to counter the UMWA's assertions about conditions in the camps and the attitudes of the miners. These publications also contained arguments or "talking points" that presented the coal operators' views of union leaders and the striking miners. Similar arguments and strategy would serve the same purpose a decade later during the 1913–1914 strike.[40]

The argument exonerating the companies from any responsibility for the strike was foremost among the talking points. Miners in the southern coalfields, the argument purported, had been content with their conditions and wages before the outside union agitators arrived. The union organizers, interested in advancing their own careers, "took advantage of the ignorance of the foreign miners and incited their savage proclivities" by promising impossible changes and improvements in the workplace.[41] Union organizers then intimidated the miners into striking. The labor officials, CF&I counsel David C. Beaman stated in the *Denver News,* had "failed to educate their unions to make better men or better workmen." Instead, they had "educated the lawless and brutal instinct until the lawless element" had gone beyond their control.[42]

The refrain was voiced so often that it became indisputable truth to the coal operators and their allies. In the eyes of John Osgood and most of the other coal operators, the outside agitators were "anarchists" or "revolutionaries" bent upon destroying the "American way of life." By believing this, the coal operators and their allies justified their stand against the UMWA in 1903–1904 as well as a decade later. Their self-delusional faith that they were defending the basic principles of American democracy, indeed, of civilization, prevented them from seeing the reasons for the labor militancy and periodic rebellion in the southern Colorado coalfields.[43]

Governor Peabody's order to send National Guard troops to Colorado City, Telluride, and Cripple Creek against the WFM in defense of the metallurgical mine owners and, subsequently, to Colorado's central and southern coalfields in support of the coal operators won him the great admiration of antiunion interests in the state. Among those who congratulated him for his bold action in intervening in the WFM strike and for opposing the eight-hour legislation were John Osgood and Julian Kebler, both still with CF&I. In answering Osgood's congratulatory note, Peabody observed that he had "attempted simply to do my duty, and to preserve the commercial and industrial enterprises of Colorado from assault or annihilation."[44] The struggle over the eight-hour issue forged a close alliance between Osgood and Peabody and drew the two men into closer association with the Law and Order campaign of the Colorado alliance movement.[45]

The Citizens' Alliance of Denver scheduled a testimonial banquet on February 23, 1904, to honor Governor Peabody for his policies against the WFM and the eight-hour workday proposal. Attended by business, industrial, academic, and religious leaders from across the state, the "Law and Order Banquet" was one of the most memorable events of its kind in Colorado history. The list of donors supporting the event included some of the state's most powerful business and financial leaders and their firms. John Osgood, Jesse Welborn, and Delos Chappell, president of the Victor Fuel Company, were among the prominent sponsors.[46]

David Beaman, legal counsel for CF&I and one of Osgood's closest former associates, delivered the principal address, a blunt attack on organized labor. Beaman blamed labor leaders for the current unstable industrial conditions, asserting that they were responsible for the widespread dissatisfaction with the status quo and the introduction of dangerous measures designed "to regulate nearly every phase of industry by so-called constitutional amendment and statutory laws." The union leaders' greatest offenses, however, were their resort to violence and their doctrine purporting that a union member had a "vested right to his job equal to his right to life," both of which he vowed to defend to the death. The actions taken by Governor Peabody, the employers, and the citizens' alliances against the strikers, Beaman argued, were completely justified in that the strikes by the WFM and the UMWA were equivalent to war or insurrection against laws that assured the protection of liberty and property. He upheld the use of the injunction against striking workers, defended military intervention as necessary and constitutional, and supported the deportation of striking workers by the state as a humane policy intended to avoid bloodshed.[47]

The Law and Order Banquet was more than just a testimonial to Governor Peabody; it was also a celebration of the defeat of the WFM. The antiunion forces had reason to celebrate. The Citizens' Alliance of Denver had awakened the Colorado business community to the union threat and successfully enlisted Governor Peabody's support of its pro-business, antiunion position. The alliance had convinced the governor to use military force to end the strike in the metalliferous camps. The declaration of martial law also allowed the governor to suspend the writ of habeas corpus. The antiunion forces now had all the power of the state at their disposal in their effort to combat organized labor. Within a month, those forces were unleashed against strikers in the central and southern Colorado coalfields. As a result, the strike was broken and the UMWA was defeated.

With the strike "irretrievably lost," on April 27, 1904, the UMWA's national executive board voted "to close up affairs in Colorado." John Mitchell explained the decision to District 15 officials in a letter on June 2, in which he stated that the union had exhausted every means in its attempts to settle the strike. The coal companies' refusal to meet with union representatives doomed any prospect of concessions, and their employment of strikebreakers to keep the mines open made further efforts to continue the strike impossible. For those reasons, the board determined that the strike must be brought to a close "at the earliest possible date."[48]

Mitchell directed the officers of District 15 to call a convention for the purpose of ending the strike. Following this direction, local officials met in Pueblo on June 20. The majority of the delegates to the convention, however, responded negatively to the call to end the strike. With mixed emotions, district president William Howells reported that the delegates had rejected the national position and unanimously declared in favor of continuing the strike. "From one standpoint," Howells wrote, "I feel sorry that such action has been taken, but from another I do not. The operators absolutely refuse to treat with us in any way and leave us no alternative than to continue the strike."[49]

The attempt to carry on the strike was futile. With the steady employment of strikebreakers and the return of strikers who had not been blacklisted, operators were able to operate their mines at full capacity by June. Relative peace in the area allowed Governor Peabody to withdraw the troops by June 11. Still, local union officials refused to call off the strike. In yet another attempt to achieve their goals, those officials issued a call for a walkout in September, a call answered by fewer than 100 miners. Nonetheless, delegates to the District 15 annual convention voted to continue the strike. By October, however, even local union officials could no longer support continuation. On October 12, the men still on strike were given cards that allowed them to return to work if they could find employment in the mines.[50]

The strike had devastated the UMWA in Colorado, and the workers gained absolutely nothing from the bitter struggle. Conditions in the mines and camps remained the same, as the coal operators returned to business as usual. The miners were forced either to accept these conditions or, as Osgood said, to leave and seek employment elsewhere. Consequently, a decade later, the same grievances that had driven the miners to strike in 1903 compelled them to strike again. Nothing had been done about their demands: bimonthly paydays, check-weighmen, an eight-hour workday, and better housing. As they had before the strike, operators continued to violate state laws with impunity. The miners still protested the use of scrip, the companies' refusal to allow employees to trade where they wanted, the dismissal of union workers, and the employment of armed mine guards. The failure to resolve these issues during the strike of 1903–1904 left a festering bitterness among returning strikers that "spread contagion-like through the years." The coal companies and their allies had developed a strategy to defeat the union, one they would employ again in 1913 when the UMWA again attempted to organize Colorado's southern coalfields. Thus, by defying the miners and perfecting the means to defeat the union, the 1903–1904 strike was a prelude to the strike of 1913–1914, which resulted in the infamous Ludlow Massacre and the Coalfield War.[51]

NOTES

1. Wolff, *Industrializing the Rockies*, 205, citing *United Mine Workers' Journal*, March 26, June 18, 1903.

2. *Rocky Mountain News*, September 18, 1903.

3. William Howells to James Peabody, August 13, 1903, cited in George G. Suggs Jr., *Colorado's War on Militant Unionism: James H. Peabody and the Western Federation of Miners* (Detroit: Wayne State University Press, 1972), 38 (source of the manifesto); Long, *Where the Sun Never Shines*, 217; Carroll D. Wright, *A Report on Labor Disturbances in the State of Colorado, from 1880 to 1904, Inclusive, with Correspondence Relating Thereto* (Washington, D.C.: Government Printing Office, 1905), 330–332; Wolff, *Industrializing the Rockies*, 208.

4. Montgomery to J. A. Kebler, September 8, 1903, in CBLS, *Ninth Biennial Report*, 183.

5. Ibid., 183–184; George G. Suggs Jr., "The Colorado Coal Miners' Strike, 1903–1904: A Prelude to Ludlow?" *Journal of the West* 12 (January 1973): 39.

6. CBLS, *Ninth Biennial Report*, 185; *Rocky Mountain News*, September 18, 1903; Wolff, *Industrializing the Rockies*, 210.

7. James C. Craig, *The History of the Strike That Brought the Citizens' Alliance of Denver, Colorado into Existence*, reprinted from *George's Weekly* (Denver, July 4, 1903).

8. Suggs, *Colorado's War*, 68, 146. In October 1903 the various local alliances in Colorado were organized into a statewide organization called the State Citizens' Alliance of Colorado, the first of its kind in the nation.

9. Quotations in Long, *Where the Sun Never Shines*, 212–214; CBLS, *Ninth Biennial Report*, 194.

10. *Rocky Mountain News*, September 27, 1903; Gehr report in CBLS, *Ninth Biennial Report*, 185.

11. Mary Field Parton, ed., *The Autobiography of Mother Jones* (Chicago: Charles H. Kerr, 1972), 95–97; last quote in Fred Thompson, "Introduction," in ibid., vii.

12. *Pueblo Labor Advocate*, November 13, 1903.

13. *Rocky Mountain News*, September 26, 1903; Suggs, "Prelude to Ludlow," 40.

14. Ray Stannard Baker, "The Reign of Lawlessness: Anarchy and Despotism in Colorado," *McClures* 23 (May 1904): 52, cited in George S. McGovern, "The Colorado Coal Strike, 1913–1914" (Ph.D. diss., Northwestern University, 1953), 102.

15. Osgood's Testimony, SMM, 401–402; Suggs, *Colorado's War*, 75; Wright, *Labor Disturbances in Colorado*, 65; David L. Lonsdale, "The Movement for an Eight-Hour Law in Colorado, 1893–1913" (unpublished Ph.D. diss., University of Colorado, Boulder, 1963), 289–290; John C. Osgood, *Statement before the House Committee on Mines and Mining* (Denver, February 16, 1903), 1–8 (quote on 1–2).

16. *Rocky Mountain News*, October 31, 1903.

17. Mitchell to Welborn and Bartlett, October 6, 1903; Welborn to Mitchell and Bartlett to Mitchell, October 7, 1903, in Wright, *Labor Disturbances in Colorado*, 332–333.

18. Mitchell to Howells, October 26, 1903, in ibid., 333–334; CBLS, *Ninth Biennial Report*, 186–187.

19. Suggs, "Prelude to Ludlow," 41. The northern Colorado operators were more flexible, and the miners gained enough concessions, including an eight-hour day, to end the strike on November 30. The end of the strike in the north greatly undermined the strike in the southern field.

20. Ibid.; *Pueblo Labor Advocate*, November 13, 1903; *Rocky Mountain News*, November 10, 12, 1903; Wolff, *Industrializing the Rockies*, 212. John T. Kebler was the brother of Julian A. Kebler, former general manager of CF&I and an Iowa Group associate of Osgood's.

21. "Getting Ready for the Strike," *Rocky Mountain News*, November 6, 1903.

22. Suggs, "Prelude to Ludlow," 41; Long, *Where the Sun Never Shines*, 224.

23. Osgood's testimony, CIR/FR 7: 6425.

24. *Rocky Mountain* News, November 12, 18, 1913; Wright, *Labor Disturbances in Colorado*, 338–339; Suggs, "Prelude to Ludlow," 42. The state district court in Trinidad dismissed the suit on July 20, 1906.

25. Long, *Where the Sun Never Shines*, 221; Wright, *Labor Disturbances in Colorado*, 340; *Rocky Mountain News*, November 15, 18, 1913.

26. Suggs, "Prelude to Ludlow," 42–43.

27. Quote in ibid., 43; McGovern and Guttridge, *Coalfield War*, 50; *Rocky Mountain News*, November 18, 1903.

28. Mitchell quoted in Wright, *Labor Disturbances in Colorado*, 338.

29. Ibid., 339.

30. Suggs, "Prelude to Ludlow," 43–44.

31. Ibid., 44; Wright, *Labor Disturbances in Colorado*, 340–341; quote in Fox, *United We Stand*, 73.

32. *Rocky Mountain News*, November 10, 1903; Wolff, *Industrializing the Rockies*, 215.

33. Clark to Peabody, March 21, 1904, in Wright, *Labor Disturbances in Colorado*, 345; Governor Peabody's Proclamation, March 22, 1904, in ibid., 346; Peabody quoted in Fox, *United We Stand*, 72.

34. Suggs, "Prelude to Ludlow," 46.

35. Fox, *United We Stand*, 72–73; quotations in ibid., 45, 50.

36. Suggs, "Prelude to Ludlow," 47; quotes in McGovern and Guttridge, *Coalfield War*, 49.

37. Suggs, "Prelude to Ludlow," 46–49; Andrews, "Road to Ludlow," 489–490; Wright, *Labor Disturbances in Colorado*, 350–355; Donald Joseph McClurg, "Labor Organization in the Coal Mines of Colorado, 1878–1933" (unpublished Ph.D. diss., University of California at Los Angeles, 1959), 137–138.

38. Parton, *Autobiography of Mother Jones*, 103–104.

39. Suggs, "Prelude to Ludlow," 49; Andrews, "Road to Ludlow," 491.

40. The bulletins with the title *Facts Concerning the Struggle in Colorado for Industrial Freedom*, edited by Ivy Ledbetter Lee for John D. Rockefeller Jr. and the Colorado operators in 1914, represent a prime example of "friendly" publications.

41. Andrews, "Road to Ludlow," 490, citing the *Denver Republican*, December 10, 1903.

42. Ibid., 491, citing the *Denver News*, November 29, 1903.

43. For comparison, see ibid.

44. James H. Peabody (copy) to J. A. Kebler, March 4, 1903, and Peabody to Osgood (copy), July 16, 1903, James H. Peabody Papers, Colorado State Archives, Denver, Letterpress 37, 39.

45. Lonsdale, "Movement for an Eight-Hour Law," 289.

46. Suggs, *Colorado's War*, 214; "Banquet in Honor of Peabody," *Denver Republican*, February 24, 1904.

47. David C. Beaman, *Address at the Testimonial Banquet to Governor James H. Peabody at Denver, Colorado, February 23, 1904* (Denver: Citizens' Alliance of Denver,

n.d.), 1–7, cited in Suggs, *Colorado's War,* 155–156; *Rocky Mountain News,* February 24, 1904.

48. Mitchell to Harry Bousfield, June 2, 1904, in Wright, *Labor Disturbances in Colorado,* 356.

49. Howells quoted in ibid., 356.

50. Ibid., 358–359.

51. Quote in Suggs, "Prelude to Ludlow," 52; Andrews, "Road to Ludlow," 493.

Company Coal Towns and Camps in Southern Colorado

The close cooperation between Colorado Fuel and Iron (CF&I) and Victor Fuel during the 1903–1904 strike assured the defeat of the United Mine Workers of America (UMWA). The union had failed to divide the two major fuel companies in Colorado. As a consequence, the companies' officials refused to make any major concessions to their employees and became even more imperious in their conduct toward their miners in southern and central Colorado. With a worsening economic situation, the companies made little effort to improve the miners' living and working conditions. After the Rockefeller-Gould takeover in 1903, CF&I largely abandoned the program of industrial betterment John Osgood and Julian Kebler had introduced in 1901. Osgood, for economic reasons, did not introduce a betterment program for the towns and camps of his Victor Fuel Company, over which he presided as chair of the board and principal owner. As a result of this retrenchment in expenditures for social welfare, conditions in most company towns and camps deteriorated. Based on their failure to prevent many of their miners from striking in 1903, CF&I officials concluded that industrial paternalism did not guarantee a happy and loyal workforce insulated from the UMWA. Consequently, they, along with Osgood, were less interested in their workers' social welfare than they were in gaining greater control over them by creating a closed town system. Closing company-owned towns and camps to keep all strangers and unauthorized personnel out and the miners in, therefore, became the coal operators' first line of defense against the union.[1]

Although not the first corporation to build company towns, for over half a century CF&I became the most prolific developer and manager of such towns in Colorado and the West. At one time or another it had partial or complete control over sixty-two towns in the western region. The corporation established thirty-seven company-owned towns in Colorado, most of which were coal mining or coking camps. In 1915 CF&I owned all land and buildings and provided all services in fourteen of the twenty-four towns in which it conducted mining operations. These were the "closed" camps and towns, enclosed by fences and gates across public roads that blocked access to them. The company provided all available services, including water, sewers, and police and fire protection for the community. In these closed camps, the company dominated economic life by controlling all business activity. "Open" camps, where the mine operators did not own all the property and did not have to supply all the necessities of life for employees living there, were located near established hub towns like Trinidad and Walsenburg, which provided additional social and commercial opportunities for workers.[2]

Company ownership of towns, John Fitch wrote in *The Survey*, gave the coal operators more power over their employees than they could have dreamed of possessing had they been conducting business in an open environment.[3] Certainly, the complete ownership of all property provided an effective way for coal companies to suppress the economic and political freedom of miners and their families. As George P. West wrote in his *Report on the Colorado Strike* (1915),

> This domination was maintained by the companies in order that they might be free to obey or disregard state laws governing coal mining as they pleased; arbitrarily determine wages and working conditions; and retain arbitrary power to discharge without stated cause. The power

to discharge was in turn used as a club to force employees and their families to submit to company control of every activity in the mining communities, from the selling of liquor and groceries to the choice of teachers, ministers of the gospel, election judges, and town and county officials.[4]

The company town also provided another means for owners to reduce labor turnover by tightening the bonds that tied workers to the town. "This arrangement," historian Dan Rottenberg has argued, "essentially reduced the relationship between operators and miners to that of feudal lords and serfs. The rights and protections granted to other Americans under the U. S. Constitution were largely nonexistent in company towns."[5]

Besides gaining dominance over his employees, Osgood's primary objective in creating a system of closed towns was to obliterate the conditions that fostered independence among the miners and fed labor militancy and unionism. After 1894, Osgood and CF&I officials took aim at the open camps, individual ownership of property and houses, and anything the company believed fostered independence and solidarity among the workers. In short, the company strove to achieve as much dominance over its workers as possible, primarily to prevent them from having any contact or association with the UMWA. Instead of quelling militancy, however, closed towns intensified the miners' determination to achieve industrial democracy.[6]

Although CF&I was at first reluctant to expend the money necessary to provide housing for its workers, after the 1894 strike Osgood and CF&I officials found employee-owned housing intolerable. The "open," or non-company-controlled, camps and towns in which many miners owned their own homes were centers for union activity and played a central role in initiating strikes.[7] In the closed camps the employees, forbidden from building or owning their own homes, were forced to live in company houses or in dwellings built on company-owned land. The companies calculated that the threat of losing company housing would be a strong deterrent to strikes and union organization. Workers who joined the union or went on strike were forced to vacate company housing. Even miners in the older camps who built their own houses on land rented from the company were evicted and their ramshackle dwellings destroyed if they joined the strike. Therefore, company housing became an excellent method of social control that helped the operators keep unions out of their towns and camps, break strikes, maintain low wages, enforce segregation, and control local government.[8]

It was much easier for CF&I to achieve its objectives in the new towns and camps the company built after 1901 than it was in the older, established ones that contained many privately owned houses and businesses, especially those close to hub towns. Sopris and Starkville, both near Trinidad, were two such camps. "In Sopris the houses in the new part of the town are owned by the C. F. & I. Company, and are of exceedingly good construction, and they can control that part of the town," Colorado National Guard officer Zeph T. Hill wrote to Governor James Peabody in 1903. "However," he continued, "on the road from Sopris to Starkville, and immediately outside of the new part of Sopris, there is a part of the town which is more or less controlled by a disturbing element." That part of the town was a hotbed of militancy. The same situation existed in Starkville, where, Hill reported, the houses "are owned largely by the people living in them, and the C. F. & I. Company can not control the situation." Norman Samo, a former miner, painted a similar picture of Starkville during the 1913–1914 strike: "There were a lot of people that owned their own homes here and they didn't care if they went to work or not while the strike was on. But the people who lived in company houses didn't have anywhere else to go and they were forced to work against their own brothers."[9]

Through either purchase or eviction, CF&I and other coal companies, including the Victor Fuel Company, leveled hundreds of "shacks" and "shanties" in the southern Colorado coalfields during the early twentieth century. While some were destroyed as part of improvement programs, others were destroyed in retaliation against strikers. Rows of new company houses appeared in their place. *Camp and Plant* published photographs in issue after issue that contrasted the company's clean model homes with the filthy, unsanitary shacks built by immigrant and non-white workers. The companies, however, were not always successful in forcing workers to give up their houses, as Osgood revealed in his testimony before the Commission on Industrial Relations in 1914. There was a class of houses at the Victor-American mines, he admitted, that the company had nothing to do with and which it had tried to eliminate, without success. Osgood stated: "There are certain of the foreigners who want to build their own shacks. We have absolutely refused to give them ground for them; and then we found we could not retain their services, for they felt they were being deprived of their liberty. . . . We found we had to let them have the ground, and they built these shacks . . . made of bits of waste material and usually with dirt floors, and [they] are often occupied by the sheep or the goats that go in with the family. They say this is the way they live at home, and they are going to live that way here."[10]

Osgood further noted in his testimony that the company charged a dollar a month for rental of the land on which these vernacular houses were built. When asked about the sanitary and health conditions under which workers lived, Osgood responded: "We have a comparatively small percentage of illness there. The men are healthy and well, and I should imagine that the people living in these shacks probably get a little more air than the people living in the [company] houses, maybe more—[because of] crevices."[11]

Although Osgood's intent in making this statement was to explain to the commissioners why some substandard housing existed on his mine properties, his testimony confirmed that some miners cherished their liberty far more than they did the comforts of good housing and the benefits of living in a town or camp under conditions imposed by the company. Living in their own "shacks" on company property, however, did not protect them from eviction if they went out on strike. But as the strikers in 1913 made abundantly clear, they preferred living in tents in open fields to living in company houses when conditions in the mines became too unbearable. Thus, the companies' attempt to gain greater control over their employees through an imposed housing policy failed in the long run.

In addition to corporate control, there were economic reasons for building company houses for the miners. By retaining ownership of the houses, the companies were able to recoup some of the wages they paid to miners in the form of rent. By keeping the rent low, two dollars per room per month, companies could justify paying their employees lower wages. Four-room houses, Osgood told the commission, cost between $700 and $800 to build, and the income from them if they were occupied the entire year was about $96. "But the houses are pretty badly used," he added, "and with the repairs, and the painting of them frequently, and the supplying of water, why, the investment of houses yields us not over 6 per cent as interest on the investment."[12]

Company stores also played an important role in the coal companies' economic scheme. As with housing, they enabled the companies to recover a portion of the wages paid to miners. For this reason, the miners regarded the stores as another means of coercive exploitation rather than a necessary service rendered by the company. The "gyp-me" or "pluck-me" stores, as workers commonly called them, were almost always a central issue in coalminers' strikes for more than half a century. The workers complained that mine officials forced them to trade exclusively with the company stores, which, they contended, charged substantially higher prices for goods than independent merchants did.[13]

Company stores existed in mining communities throughout the country, but the stores operated by CF&I were the most strongly criticized in Colorado. Founded in 1888 by Osgood and a few partners, the Colorado Supply Company established stores in every CF&I mining camp as well as in Pueblo and Trinidad. The company, operating as a subsidiary of CF&I, recorded substantial profits throughout Osgood's tenure at the parent company. The Colorado Supply Company's large profits constituted proof to the union that the company was exploitative, a charge it emphatically denied. Store officials explained that the large profits were the result of a large volume of sales and large-scale purchases that reduced wholesale costs rather than of high prices. Although store management argued that the prices were competitive with and in some cases even lower than those in private stores in nearby towns, workers continued to view the company store as part of a system that kept them in virtual economic slavery.

The most serious complaint, however, was about the companies' use of scrip. Employees and union officials accused the coal companies of using wage deductions and credit in the form of scrip as a deliberate means of keeping cash away from employees prior to payday. Few miners received cash that even closely equaled the amount of their earnings. Employees who needed advances between paychecks were compelled to trade at company stores. Those who wished to receive cash were further disadvantaged by brokers who discounted scrip at rates up to 25 percent. They, in turn, received face value for the scrip at the company store. Therefore, union officials alleged, most miners were kept perpetually in debt, creating a state of peonage that made it necessary for them to continue to work for the company for cheap wages.[14]

Both the U.S. House Subcommittee on Mines and Mining (the Foster Congressional Committee) and the Commission on Industrial Relations took the issue of scrip seriously in their investigations of conditions in the Colorado coalfields. As with other coal mining communities and camps that had company stores, the issue of scrip in the towns of Hastings and Delagua was linked to the charge that the miners were pressured to trade at the Western Stores Company, a subsidiary of Osgood's Victor-American Fuel Company. Osgood denied the charge. "As . . . evidence that we don't coerce our men, and that we give them absolute freedom," he testified in 1914, "I wish to say that most of our mines are near enough to some town so that once a week or so the men can go into town and trade, and that the maximum amount of our sales at any time has not exceeded 25 per cent of the pay roll, so that it does not look like we are forcing our men to make all their purchases at our stores." Even with this competition, Osgood noted, the Western Stores Company earned at least 20 percent on its capital investment.[15]

The superintendents at Hastings and Delagua confirmed before the Foster Congressional Committee that the company stores in their towns used scrip as a form of credit, and Superintendent W. B. Snodgrass of Delagua admitted that the company regarded those holding scrip as being under a contract to spend it in the company store. He and James Cameron, superintendent of the Hastings mine, agreed that scrip could not be converted to cash in either town. Reminded that a state law forbade the issue of scrip as payment for miners, Cameron responded that the Western Stores Company rather than Victor-American issued scrip to workers who needed store credit. Congressman Howard Sutherland challenged Cameron to explain why it was legal for the Western Stores Company, which was owned by Victor-American, to issue scrip when it was illegal for the mining company to do so. "[I]s this not, then, rather in the light of a subterfuge," the congressman asked, "letting the store company issue the scrip rather than the mining company itself? It accomplishes the same purpose; the men are paid partly in scrip." Cameron affirmed that the store company had always issued scrip.[16] Neither the Foster Congressional Committee nor the Commission on Industrial Relations determined whether the practice of companies issuing scrip through their company stores was a violation or merely an evasion of state law.

The members of both investigative bodies were skeptical of the operators' claim that their employees were not compelled to trade at company stores. The miners who testified before both bodies asserted that there was an understanding that an employee would be dismissed if he did not purchase a reasonable amount of goods at these stores. The testimony showed, George West determined, that "mine employees, particularly in closed camps, risked the displeasure of the local officials, and the possibility of discharge, if they did not trade at the company stores." In its investigation, the Colorado Bureau of Labor Statistics found that any attempt to purchase supplies from sources other than the company store meant "instant dismissal to the purchaser."[17]

Evidence also supports the charge that company executives pressured mine superintendents to encourage their employees to trade at company stores and that many local officials regarded this encouragement as an order to fire any man or the husband of any woman who traded with town merchants, peddlers, or small rural producers.[18] LaMont Bowers, chair of the CF&I board of directors after 1907, provided a prime example of this encouragement in a letter in which he noted that CF&I had two interests in operating the Colorado Supply Store. The first was to supply its thousands of employees "with good goods and at reasonable prices" and to protect employees from being "swindled by unscrupulous Jews, Italians and other cut-throat dealers who would control the business if we should withdraw and leave the field open." The second was to "make for the company a reasonable profit in consideration of our investment and management. It needs no argument to convince any reasonable employe [sic] that the above is a fair and honorable proposition. This being true, the company is entitled to the cordial support of our employees [sic]."[19] Bowers's remarks linked a sense of paternalism with business opportunity, a linkage that mirrored Osgood's attitude toward industrial paternalism. Bowers also reflected the belief of the coal operators, including Osgood, that their employees owed them loyalty.

Short of firing the workers, superintendents and pit bosses had other means to pressure them to trade at the company store. These included docking a worker on his weights, placing him in a "bad" room or area in the mine where his earnings were much less, or putting him at the top of the list of those to be laid off if the company had to cut back on its workforce during slack periods.[20] The absence of competition in the closed company towns, George West wrote, "can only be ascribed to the refusal of the companies to sell land for homes or other purposes, and this refusal in turn appears to have been actuated by a desire to monopolize the merchandising as well as every other activity of the community." Store managers, West added, "were closely associated with the mine superintendents in the control of the political and social life of the camps, and it seems reasonable to infer that ambitious local managers enlisted the superintendents' influence to swell their business and improve their showing."[21]

Although little substantive evidence supports the union charges that the companies pursued a deliberate policy of industrial bondage in operating company stores, there is little doubt that they used the stores in an exploitive way to gain greater control over employees in closed company towns and camps. George West called the company stores another part of the coal companies' system of monopolistic feudalism. Even though only a minority of employees found themselves bound to a company by perpetual debt, the company store was an effective way of enforcing corporate control.[22]

Company stores were also business ventures. The Colorado Supply stores were a lucrative source of revenue for CF&I in financing the construction and operation of company towns. Capital invested in stores, housing, saloons, and services was expected to produce a return the same way capital invested in tipples, railroads, and mining machinery did. Revenue from these sources substantially reduced the company's cash flow and, consequently, the need to borrow, which allowed the company to accumulate capital more rapidly without reliance on outside investors. Thus, the entire system of company towns was designed to accumulate profit as well as to maximize control over the workers.[23]

The Victor-American Fuel Company towns of Hastings and Delagua, both within a short distance of Ludlow—the epicenter of the violence and strike agitation of 1914—were typical of most mining camps, except that they were incorporated towns. Established in 1889 by the Victor Fuel Company, Hastings was the first coal operation opened in Delagua Canyon, twenty miles northwest of Trinidad. Delagua, the largest of the Victor-American mines—reported as the largest coalmine west of the Mississippi—was founded in 1903 during the expansion of operations in Delagua and Berwind canyons. Just before the strike in 1913, the Delagua mine employed about 650 workers and had a capacity of 3,000 tons of coal a day. The town of Hastings at the time of the strike had a population of around 300.[24] Almost all inhabitants of the two towns were employed by Victor-American, the Western States Company, or the Colorado and Southeastern Railroad—the company's branch railroad that connected the mines to the main lines of the Colorado and Southern, the Denver and Rio Grande, and the Santa Fe.

Delos A. Chappell, founder and operator of Victor Fuel, had been an important ally of CF&I against the UMWA during the 1890s and the early twentieth century. After Osgood purchased the company, Chappell remained as president, forming an even closer antiunion association with Osgood. Undoubtedly with Osgood's approval, Chappell relied on workforce diversity and absolute control of the Victor camps to prevent union activities and the establishment of union locals. In 1902 the company hired mine guards at Hastings to prevent union organizational efforts and, using the Hastings precedent, incorporated the Chandler camp near Cañon City. As a result of the incorporation, Victor Fuel gained greater control over Chandler by assuring that all the town's elective officials were company officials. As with Hastings and Delagua, incorporation provided the company with a more effective way of disrupting union activity.[25]

Incorporated towns, in which the company owned all the property and dominated all aspects of town governance, made it far easier for companies to control their employees. This was particularly true with Osgood's Victor-American Fuel Company. Both Hastings and Delagua had elected city councils, mayors, and school boards. With few exceptions, the elected officials were employees from the company's managerial ranks, with mine superintendents serving as mayors. Without exception, company policy became town policy. Revenue for the towns was derived mainly from three principal sources: saloon licenses, poll taxes, and school levies. Since neither town had a property tax, the Victor-American Fuel Company paid absolutely nothing to defray the expenses of the towns and schools. The burden fell entirely on the inhabitants, the majority of whom were company employees.

With six saloons in Hastings and two in Delagua, the saloon license fee was the most important source of income for both towns. According to the testimony of the superintendents before the congressional hearing in 1914, Hastings collected about $2,200 and Delagua $1,000 a year from this source. A poll tax of $2 a year on all residents was another important source of revenue for the towns. The tax produced between $500 and $600 a year for Hastings and double that amount for Delagua. The tax was collected either by the town marshal or by a checkoff system whereby the company deducted the amount from the workers' wages. A similar procedure was followed for collecting a school tax of 25 cents a month or $3 a year from each employee, married or single. Although the company-owned boardinghouses were privately operated, the proprietors could, and often did, ask the company to deduct the rent from their tenants' wages. Additionally, the company deducted $1 a month for a hospital and medical fund from each employee's wages.[26]

Without its own hospital, Victor-American sent employees who needed care beyond what could be provided in the towns and camps to Mount San Rafael Hospital in Trinidad. The *Rocky Mountain News* reported that the cost of maintaining the Victor Medical Department in 1903 was $800 a month on average, with about $2,000 a month offset. The hospital fund by the end of 1902, the paper observed, amounted to more than $60,000 for the company.[27] In 1903, miners in Hastings and Delagua objected to deductions from their wages for the medical and hospital fund and demanded the right to consult a private physician of their choice rather than having to see the company doctor, whom many considered incompetent. They also protested deductions from their wages for the school fund, which, they argued, was at variance with the state's special school tax on property levied in cities and incorporated towns.[28]

The salaries of the town marshals and other town officials at Delagua and Hastings were paid from the general fund generated by the towns' revenue sources. John Fitch of *The Survey* learned by quizzing several coal company officials that one of the main functions of the camp marshals was to ascertain the business of all strangers seeking entrance to the camps. They had specific orders to prevent any union organizers from entering the camps and to eject those who had entered. This was particularly true at Delagua and Hastings. This practice seemed to be an invasion of the miners' rights, Fitch told Osgood. "If as a matter of right he could keep out men to whom he did not wish his employes [sic] to talk, there seemed to be no good reason why he should not also prevent his men from taking from the post office papers which he thought they should not read," Fitch asserted. " 'Well,' said Mr. Osgood, 'you may be sure of this, when this strike is over we shall try a damn sight harder to keep the organizers out of our camps than we ever have before.' "[29]

The two towns were also required to maintain the streets and alleys within their boundaries, as well as the road that ran from Ludlow station through the middle of each town. The road had been a public road before the county vacated it after the opening of the Hastings mine. Thereafter, the company considered the road private property and closed it during strikes to keep strikers, union leaders, and unauthorized personnel out of the towns. The company used mine guards at the gates on the road leading into Hastings and Delagua at the commencement of the strikes in both 1903 and 1913 to control traffic into the towns and to prevent workers, most of whom were newly employed strikebreakers, from leaving the towns without a pass. In addition, the post offices were located in the Western States Company stores within town boundaries, and individuals without a pass were prevented from entering the towns to collect their mail.

Victor-American practices at Hastings and Delagua in 1913–1914, particularly the closing of the road, led to charges that the company had interfered with or obstructed mail facilities and created a condition of peonage. The basis for the latter charge was the report that company officials forcibly kept men in camp until their debts were paid. After considerable testimony, the Foster Committee concluded that there was no clear evidence that a condition of peonage existed at Hastings and Delagua or anywhere else in the Colorado coalfields. However, the majority members stated in their report that the operators had "endeavored to hold in camp those who were already in the camp before the strike and to prevent those who had been taken in as strike breakers from going outside." The mine guards and militia "did everything they could to . . . keep these men in the camp, where they might be used for the purpose of mining coal and thus help break the strike." The committee members were also unable to determine if Victor-American's refusal to allow strikers to enter Hastings and Delagua to collect their mail was a violation of federal law. They simply stated that the company had "exercised the right, whether lawfully or unlawfully, to put guards at the entrances of these towns . . . so that if anyone desired to receive mail at the post office he must first secure a pass in order to get past the guards and go to the post office."[30]

Another matter raised by members of both the Foster Committee and the Commission on Industrial Relations concerning company towns, particularly those belonging to Victor-American, involved saloons. George West noted that saloons, besides producing considerable revenue for the companies, formed part of the "feudal system" of camp and town structure. "The policy of the Company," West declared, "has been to farm out their privilege for these joints to human ghouls, who operate them, by the Camp Marshal's consent, without regard to the restrictive statutes of the state, that would interfere with their business." Despite Osgood's claim that Victor-American strictly regulated the hours of its company saloons and prohibited the "selling of liquor to men who are already intoxicated and to minors," the Commission on Industrial Relations found evidence to the contrary. In one instance, West noted that the proprietor of a saloon in Delagua kept his establishment open on Sundays, in violation of state law. When questioned by an officer of the National Guard about the violation, the proprietor replied: "I am justice of the peace in this town and we don't pay much attention to such things as State laws." It was also noted that the selling of liquor to minors and to those already intoxicated was condoned without protest.[31]

The majority of the members of the Foster Committee were particularly critical of other conditions that existed in Delagua and Hastings. At Hastings, it was noted, many church services and social functions were relegated to a meeting room connected to a saloon. There were few, if any, other places of recreation or amusement for workers. These conditions, the committee members argued in their report, showed "an utter disregard for all things that have to do with the upbuilding of character and making men's condition better. It is to be regretted that a man employed in these mines could find nothing more elevating than a saloon for a social place where he can go to meet his friends and enjoy the evening." The lack of emphasis on social improvement in the closed camps of southern Colorado, the report concluded, was a major failure of the large industrial corporations.[32]

Although conditions in the coal district of southern Colorado varied from camp to camp, for the most part they were dirty and unsightly, with inadequate housing, poor sanitary conditions, bad water supplies, and few opportunities for constructive social activity. Many of them were, in the view of a reporter from the *Outlook*, "as nearly a moral and social desert as is possible to imagine in a civilized country." The camps were often under the control of oppressive superintendents who placed the mines' production and profitability over camp improvement. The Reverend Eugene S. Gaddis, Richard Corwin's successor as head of CF&I's Sociological Department, testified in 1915 that the superintendents were "blasphemous bullies" who often ruled the camps as personal fiefdoms. In his view, they were uncouth, ignorant, immoral, and brutal men.[33]

Although these comments were based on observations of CF&I camps, Osgood's Victor-American mining communities were little better. Osgood took scant interest in the condition of the company's towns and camps after 1903. Indeed, for most of the period between 1903 and 1913, he was largely an absentee owner who spent much of his time in New York City and Europe. The company's executive officials and officials of the other leading companies maintained offices in Denver but seldom visited their coalmines and communities in the southern part of the state. "The record . . . shows," George West wrote, "that responsible executive officials in Denver lacked personal knowledge of living and working conditions in the coal camps, and personal touch with the miners, in almost the same degree as did the controlling directors and stockholders."[34]

The coal camps and company towns in southern Colorado were subjected to intense public scrutiny following the coalminer's strike in 1913–1914. A parade of witnesses testified before the Commission on Industrial Relations about the dismal conditions in the camps, but Eugene Gaddis's testimony was the most critical. He stated that housing in the camps was largely substandard. Many of the miners and their families lived in "hovels, box-car shacks, and adobe sheds" unfit for the habitation of human beings, he proclaimed. According to the camp physician at Sopris, Gaddis reported, CF&I owned and rented "shacks" in the Italian quarter that were uninhabitable, where people lived "on the very level of a pigsty."[35] Among the "outrageous conditions" in the camps, Gaddis continued, was poor sanitation that was causing the spread of typhus. Camp physicians were not given the authority or the funds to improve sanitary facilities and medical care. He also told the commission that the public schools were inadequate and frequently staffed by unqualified teachers, that local officials dictated the outcome of elections, and that saloons, gambling halls, and brothels robbed employees of their earnings. Employees and their families could not appeal to state officials for redress of conditions because company men were charged with enforcing local and state laws. Gaddis asserted that the company had the necessary resources to improve conditions in the towns but chose not to do so. Concluding, he said: "I have never seen a situation to my mind more despicable and damnable, as I believe it, to the best interests of the American Commonwealth. It is an oligarchy that is controlling everything."[36]

Dr. Peter Roberts, who surveyed the mining towns in Huerfano and Las Animas counties in the summer of 1915 for the YMCA, confirmed much of what Gaddis reported. Like Gaddis, he described the towns as unattractive, devoid of trees and landscaping. Substandard housing consisted of row houses of the same design painted in a monotonous mineral red. The close proximity to the mines and coke ovens, Roberts noted, with the latter spewing smoke and noxious gases, made the air unpleasant to breathe and unhealthy for residents. Roberts agreed with Gaddis that the consumption of liquor was a major problem and that the absence of sanitation systems and the lack of good supplies of water posed health problems for residents of the towns.

Although Roberts gave the schools in the camps a higher grade than Gaddis had, he observed that the lack of strict enforcement of compulsory attendance laws contributed to the fact that 95 percent of students failed to complete eighth grade. Additionally, he noted, there were no organized activities for young people. Unlike Gaddis, Roberts concluded that the mining camps were prosperous and that residents enjoyed a high standard of living when the mines and coking ovens operated at or near capacity.[37] Roberts failed to say that they rarely did so.

Captain Philip Van Cise, commander of Company K of the Colorado National Guard, gave the Commission on Industrial Relations a valuable snapshot of conditions in the coal camps and towns around Ludlow at the time of the 1913–1914 strike. His company was stationed at Ludlow immediately across from the tent colony during the state militia's occupancy of the strike zone. He frequently observed the coal camps and towns in his jurisdiction while he and his troops were on patrol. These communities included the Victor-American towns of Hastings and Delagua; the CF&I mines and camps up Berwind Canyon; and Aguilar, Forbes, and Rameyville. Of these camps, he found the Victor-American towns of Hastings and Delagua by far the best. The houses there were better, and the towns seemed much cleaner than the others. In all the camps and towns he visited he found that the companies had provided houses that were generally in good condition and stores that were stocked better than those of independent traders outside the camps. He described the school facilities as at least average, with the school building doubling as the place for such entertainment as motion-

Mining families, Las Animas County, Colorado. Courtesy, Colorado Historical Society, ID no. X4867.

picture shows and dances. But even with these advantages, Van Cise discovered that before the strike the inhabitants of these towns and camps had been consumed with anger. Living conditions in the towns, he concluded, were not the source of the miners' discontent but rather "the un-American conduct of the closed camps," where there was "very little freedom of action. . . . I always thought that the strikers had a very just grievance in the un-American operation of the coal camps."[38]

Van Cise knew the Ludlow tent colony residents well. As commander of Company K, he fostered good relations between his men and the strikers. Frequently, militiamen and strikers shared meals and played baseball games together. All the while, Van Cise held conferences with the colonists. His thorough knowledge of their views undoubtedly led him to conclude that they found the closed company towns oppressive, whatever the conditions within them. This conclusion is borne out by the coalminers' oral history. Life in the closed company towns and camps of southern Colorado was a story of men, women, and children totally dependent on the mining corporations for all their basic needs.[39]

Ethnic diversity was, as Rick Clyne noted in his study of the coal people, "the most conspicuous social characteristic of the coal communities."[40] The demographic and ethnic makeup of the camps had changed considerably between 1890 and 1910. Before 1890, most of the miners were single and came from the British Isles, particularly England and Wales. These experienced miners had developed the techniques of mining coal and adapted to the social organization of coal camps in the West. Eventually, those who remained in the camps became managers, foremen, or superintendents.[41] Their places in the mines and around the coke ovens were taken by Hispanics from southern Colorado and northern New Mexico, a small contingency of African Americans, and a large number of men from southern, southeastern, and eastern Europe. By 1900, two-thirds of CF&I's miners were immigrants from Italy and the Slavic areas of Austria (Slovaks, Slovenes, Croats, and Serbs). Other nationalities—Russians, Spaniards, Germans, Japanese, Irish, and Greeks, the last to arrive in significant numbers—joined the other immigrants during the early twentieth century. There were thirty-two nationalities represented on CF&I's payroll and twenty-seven languages spoken in the camps.[42]

With the almost complete depletion of the workforce during the labor struggles of 1903–1904, operators were forced to recruit increasing numbers of immigrants. Osgood considered sending a recruiting agent to Europe with enticing pictures of coal camps and pamphlets listing wage scales. He made at least one trip to Europe himself to investigate the possibility of foreign recruitment, even though the commissioner of immigration proclaimed that such recruitment was a violation of U.S. labor laws. Evidently, the commissioner's announcement did not entirely deter the major operators, for Upton Sinclair claimed in 1914 to have seen "lying advertisements with bright colored pictures" printed by CF&I posted at railroad stations in southern Europe.[43]

The coal operators stressed that the ethnic diversity in the coalfields was a result of the nature of Colorado's labor market rather than a deliberate hiring strategy to prevent solidarity among the miners. Although this argument had some validity by the early twentieth century, it had not always been the case. During the 1880s and 1890s, as discussed before, the major coal companies had adopted a policy of racial and ethnic mixing as a way to quell labor activism. Companies gained advantages from pitting one ethnic group against another, and operators frequently used the practice as a conscious strategy to keep the men divided. The multitude of languages prevented miners from discussing grievances. Ethelbert Stewart, labor mediator for the U.S. Department of Labor, observed that the purpose of having so many languages in a single camp "was, of course, to produce in advance a condition of confusion of tongues, so that no tower upon which they might ascend into the heavens, could be erected."[44]

Stewart's statement might have been fair had he expressed it a decade or so earlier. By 1914, however, the coal companies' policy of hiring the cheapest nonunion labor possible had transformed what originally had been a deliberate strategy to combat unionization into an economic necessity. Unwilling to pay the price to hire skilled miners, usually Anglo-Americans and northern Europeans, the operators filled their employment ranks with an ethnically and racially diverse workforce out of necessity. Nevertheless, most of the camps remained segregated communities divided along ethnic, cultural, and racial lines—more by the workers' choice than by company policy. Immigrants usually chose to settle in neighborhoods with others from their ethnic group. African Americans and Hispanics lived in their own areas, as did southern and eastern Europeans. In Delagua, for example, African Americans lived in "Uptown," Slavs in "Bricktown," Italians in "Cast Town," and Japanese in "Japtown." Superintendents and managers lived in the largest and best houses located in a section separate from the workers.[45]

For a time, ethnic animosity and racial prejudice in the mines and camps worked against the development of a sense of community. A class hierarchy existed in most camps. Each group of newcomers started at the bottom in the competition for housing, jobs, good locations in the mines, and cars to load. Last to arrive, the Greeks suffered the greatest abuse on the eve of the 1913–1914 strike, while the Italians enjoyed a hard-won position at or near the top of the ethnic hierarchy, below only the Anglo-Americans. Gradually, a greater sense of community developed among the miners. The influx of European immigrants, who brought their wives and families with them or who sent for them and encouraged relatives to join them once they became established, began to create more cohesion in the coal camps. By 1914, the ratio of family members to miners was three to one. Furthermore, as Osgood noted, the majority of the immigrant miners came to Colorado to stay. Coal mining's dangerous nature also helped to create a strong bond of mutual aid and interdependence among miners who worked together to forge a better life for themselves and their families. They resented the oppressive town system that exerted control over them. But the unsafe working conditions in the mines constituted the most important factor that drove the miners to another strike.[46]

The miners themselves rebelled against the system imposed on them. The UMWA did not create the miners' anger and militancy; the union only helped to organize and channel that anger once the miners had reached the point where they could no longer tolerate the system under which they were forced to live and work. Unlike previous years, in 1913 the miners were more united than ever when they turned to the union for support in their struggle against coalmine operators. Most of the remaining ethnic and racial animosity melted away in the tent colonies during the long strike of 1913–1914.

NOTES

1. The distinction made in this study between towns and camps is a legal one. Hastings, Delagua, and Chandler—all Victor-American Fuel Company communities—were incorporated towns. The mining camps were unincorporated. Both incorporated mining towns and unincorporated mining camps could be "closed" communities.

2. Clyne, *Coal People*, 16; Scamehorn, *Mill and Mine*, 82–83; James B. Allen, "The Company-Owned Mining Town in the West: Exploitation or Benevolent Paternalism?" in John A. Carroll, ed., *Reflections of Western Historians* (Tucson, Ariz.: University of Arizona Press, 1976), 178.

3. John A. Fitch, "Law and Order: The Issue in Colorado," *The Survey* 33 (December 5, 1914): 246.

4. West, *Report on the Colorado Strike*, 15.

5. Rottenberg, *In the Kingdom of Coal*, 51.

6. Andrews, "Road to Ludlow," 404–405; Eric Margolis, "Western Coal Mining as a Way of Life: An Oral History of the Colorado Coal Miners to 1914," *Journal of the West* 24, no. 3 (July 1985): 66–67.

7. Andrews, "Road to Ludlow," 410. The UMWA found it easier to organize miners in the northern (Denver Basin) coalfields because of the open towns in which many miners owned their own homes. In addition, there were far more Anglo-American miners in the district who had a long association with union membership than was the case in the southern Colorado coalfields.

8. Brandes, *American Welfare Capitalism*, 48.

9. Hill to Peabody, November 18, 1903, and Norman Samo quoted in Andrews, "Road to Ludlow," 454, note 22.

10. Osgood's testimony, CIR/FR 7: 6436.

11. Ibid., 6437.

12. Ibid., 6436.

13. The *Rocky Mountain News*, November 12, 1903, reported that the Western Stores in the Victor town of Hastings had a profit of $39,300 in 1902. The prices for some of the items in the store were as follows: $2.00 per 100 pounds for potatoes; $1.50 for a sack of flour; 15 cents each or two for 25 cents for canned goods in Hastings, whereas the price in Trinidad was three for 25 cents; five half-size bars of

laundry soap for 25 cents in Hastings, whereas the price in Trinidad was 25 cents for seven full-size bars; $3.25 a gallon for maple syrup in Hastings, whereas in Trinidad the price was $1.25.

14. Scamehorn, *Mill and Mine*, 104–111; Allen, "Company-Owned Mining Town," 190–194.

15. Osgood testimony, SMM, 403–404; West, *Report on the Colorado Strike*, 68. Trinidad and Walsenburg were the nearest hub towns to Hastings and Delagua. Ludlow was over twelve miles from Trinidad and over fifteen miles from Walsenburg. Without automobiles, it would have been very difficult for the miners and their families to shop in these hub towns on a regular basis. The Delagua and Hastings miners and their families had limited opportunity for independent shopping in Ludlow, three to five miles away.

16. Cameron testimony, SMM, 1531.

17. CBLS, *Twelfth Biennial Report,* 27; West, *Report on the Colorado Strike,* 68.

18. Andrews, "Road to Ludlow," 436.

19. Ibid., 469, note 117.

20. Ibid., 436.

21. West, *Report on the Colorado Strike*, 70.

22. Ibid., 69; Allen, "Company-Owned Mining Town," 190–191, 194; Clyne, *Coal People,* 22–24.

23. Margolis, "Western Coal Mining," 67.

24. Snodgrass testimony, SMM, 1194; Cameron testimony, SMM, 1521.

25. Wolff, *Industrializing the Rockies*, 193–194. The Chandler miners, with the support of their local union, unsuccessfully fought incorporation of the town. They gained the support of the Colorado Federation of Labor, which declared Victor Fuel Company unfair to labor and issued a boycott of the company in May 1902 (CBLS, *Eighth Biennial Report,* 235).

26. Information on Hastings and Delagua is from Cameron testimony, SMM, 1510–1533, 2126–2135; Snodgrass testimony, SMM, 1182–1221.

27. *Rocky Mountain News,* November 12, 1903.

28. Wright, *Labor Disturbances in Colorado*, 332.

29. Fitch, "Law and Order," 247.

30. U.S. Congress, House, *Report on the Colorado Strike Investigation,* in Leon Stein and Philip Taft, eds., *Massacre at Ludlow: Four Reports* (New York: Arno and the *New York Times,* 1971), 32; hereafter cited as Stein and Taft, *Massacre at Ludlow.*

31. West, *Report on the Colorado Strike,* 71–72; Osgood's testimony, SMM, 424.

32. Stein and Taft, *Massacre at Ludlow,* 38–39.

33. W. T. Davis, "The Conditions in the Strike Region," *Outlook* 107 (May 9, 1914): 70; Gaddis testimony, CIR/FR 9: 8486–8487.

34. West, *Report on the Colorado Strike,* 35–36.

35. Gaddis testimony, CIR/FR 9: 8492.

36. Ibid., 8516.

37. Roberts cited in Scamehorn, *Mill and Mine*, 86–91.

38. Van Cise testimony, CIR/FR 7: 6821–6822.

39. McGovern, "Colorado Coal Strike," 22; Margolis, "Western Coal Mining," 66.

40. Clyne, *Coal People,* 42.

41. A good example was James Cameron, superintendent of the Hastings mine. Scotland, where he learned the art of mining, was his native country.

42. Margolis, "Western Coal Mining," 27; Clyne, *Coal People,* 44–46.

43. Sinclair quoted in McGovern and Guttridge, *Coalfield War,* 50–51.

44. Stewart quoted in ibid., 51; Wolff, *Industrializing the Rockies,* 136–137; Margolis, "Western Coal Mining," 44.

45. Clyne, *Coal People,* 46–47; Scamehorn, *Mill and Mine,* 87.

46. Osgood's testimony, SMM, 406; McGovern and Guttridge, *Coalfield War,* 51. One of the objectives of the new town system was to curtail the workers' mobility. "Despite company efforts to limit their mobility," Andrews wrote, "mine workers continued to move around; in 1906–1907, so many left the coal fields for agricultural work that mining companies faced a severe labor shortage" ("Road to Ludlow," 449).

Conditions in Southern Colorado Coalmines

For over two decades, from the 1880s to the early twentieth century, Colorado coalminers sought legislation that would enhance their quality of life, provide better safety in the mines, and protect them from coal companies' capricious actions. With the support of organized labor—first the Knights of Labor and then the United Mine Workers of America (UMWA)—and after strikes in 1884–1885, 1894, and 1901, they had gained legislation that provided them with greater protection and addressed some of their grievances. As discussed in Chapter 1, the state legislature created the office of State Inspector of Coal Mines, the Bureau of Labor Statistics, and the State Board of Arbitration. The legislature also passed laws that allowed miners to hire check-weighmen, banned the use of scrip, eliminated screens when weighing coal, and instituted biweekly paydays; in 1899, the legislature rewarded workers with a law establishing an eight-hour workday for mine, mill, and smelter workers.[1]

These gains were more illusionary than real, however. The Colorado Supreme Court declared the eight-hour workday law unconstitutional before it was even enacted. After another protracted struggle between coal and smelter operators and their allies on one side and the public and workers on the other, an eight-hour law was finally passed in 1913. Believing they were superior to state lawmakers, or at least more knowledgeable about how to operate a coal business, coal operators simply violated or found ways to circumvent these state laws, including the eight-hour law. They refused to pay their miners twice a month or to discontinue the use of screens in weighing coal. They no longer paid wages in scrip, but, as discussed in Chapter 5, they created a system of credit based on scrip that still served their purposes of keeping cash out of the hands of miners and forcing them to trade at the company stores.[2]

But to the miners, the most serious of the violations was the operators' refusal to obey mining laws, which put the miners in grave danger. The coal executives' blatant violation of these laws was the major reason the miners struck in 1913. Had the coal operators obeyed the mining laws, Edward P. Costigan, attorney for the UMWA, told the Commission on Industrial Relations, they "would have averted the distressing strike which occurred [in Colorado], with or without the recognition of organized labor and with or without [a] conference with its people."[3] Considering that the striking miners' brief made lawlessness the most essential part of the indictment against the mining companies, it is difficult to disagree with Costigan's argument.

The combination of an inadequate coal mining law and its ineffectual enforcement by inspectors, operators, and miners, along with natural geological features, made Colorado's coalmines the most dangerous in the nation—perhaps in the world—during the early twentieth century. Statistics for the state during the years 1886 to 1913 recorded an average of 7.14 deaths per 1,000 employed miners, twice the national figure and four times that of Illinois, Iowa, and Missouri, where the mines were operated under an UMWA contract.[4] Issues related to conditions in the coalmines formed the mainspring that drove the miners to strike in 1913.

Considering the natural and geological conditions in southern Colorado, it is not surprising that death rates for miners in the state from either explosions or rock falls were on average comparable to the national rate of coalmine deaths from all causes.[5] The geological upheaval of the Rocky Mountains in southern Colorado thousands of years ago fractured the strata of coal and rock, causing the sandstone rock overlaying the coal seam to slip and sag along hidden faults as the coal was removed. Consequently, mine cave-ins were frequent. Inadequate timbering to support the roofs of the mines magnified the danger. According to James Dalrymple, the state mine inspector, not a single mine in the state was properly timbered at the time. More than half of the fatalities from rock falls could have been avoided, he believed, had the coal companies seen to proper timbering of the mines.[6]

However, the miners themselves were partially responsible for the lack of adequate timbering, a task that was part of dead work for which they were not paid directly. Dead work became one of the most contentious issues between operators and miners. The operators insisted that this form of work was necessary for the production of coal and was taken into consideration in setting the tonnage rates of miners' pay. John Osgood considered the coalminer a contractor who was paid for the amount of coal he mined rather than for the hours he spent in the mine or the specific tasks he performed. The miner, he said, "agrees to lay track in his run, timber his run, drill holes for the shot firer and when the coal is broken down, to load and send it out. If through his carelessness there is a fall in the roof, he has to clean that up. He has also to make his break through from one room to the other." All this work, Osgood insisted, was part of the miner's contract. Thus, he asserted, it was "simply a quibble to say that he [the miner] does a lot of work that isn't paid for." The miners' insistence on being paid for dead work, he added, was merely a guise for an increase in wages.[7]

The miners, of course, strongly disagreed with Osgood's viewpoint and continued to demand extra pay for such work as timbering, laying rails, and clearing rock in the mines. Without the extra pay, miners frequently endangered their own safety by devoting as little time as possible to timbering so they could maximize their coal production. For the miners, safety usually meant more dead work, resulting in less pay; greater production meant skimping on timbering, inspection, and gas and dust abatement, resulting all too often in more mine accidents. According to Thomas Andrews, it was a devil's bargain of mine economics: miners seeking extra earnings sometimes paid for the chances they took with their own lives, while more careful miners paid for their safety by foregoing wages they could have earned by mining coal instead of timbering their workplaces.[8]

Some miners unwilling to risk working in unsafe mines blamed management for not providing timbers and other needed supplies. This failure by management resulted in idleness and lost wages, they charged. Dave Hammond, a miner who worked for Victor-American sometime around 1910, stated that "time and again" miners lost hours when props stored far from the mine did not arrive when needed because the foreman "could not stop hauling coal to haul these props over to the mine." With no props to secure the roofs of their rooms in the mine, the men left work and lost pay. "It was not safe for them in the mine in their working place to stay in there," Hammond said; "they had to go home." F. W. Whiteside, chief engineer for Victor-American, disagreed with the miners' claim. He contended that the company furnished everything the miners needed to provide for safety. When an accident occurred, he stated, "it is usually possible to trace the fault to the carelessness of the injured man or his partner."[9]

Regardless of whether Hammond's assertion was true, the UMWA blamed the superintendents and mine bosses for the lack of safety in the mines. The *United Mine Workers Journal* in 1914 asserted that mine bosses and superintendents, "hard driven by the knowledge that their jobs depend on their ability to produce coal cheaply" and realizing the miners' powerlessness to protest, "take chances with human life that result in the deplorable percentages of casualties the statistics reveal." Concurring with this assessment, the U.S. Coal Commission judged that the disregard for safety caused by the continual pressure on mine superintendents to increase production was a "moral hazard" of coal mining.[10]

Coal company safety policies depended primarily on the ability and willingness of superintendents and mine bosses to enforce them. As with the miners over whom they exercised authority, their livelihood depended on quantity of production. Just as miners sometimes had to choose between timbering rooms or loading coal, superintendents and mine bosses sometimes had to determine whether their best interests lay in implementing safety policies or encouraging men to get as much coal out as quickly as possible. Instructions from the top were seldom helpful, as indicated by W. J. Murray's 1912 circular letter to Victor-American superintendents. Murray instructed them to do everything possible to increase production, but under no circumstances, Murray implored, were the superintendents to let their "anxiety to get out coal" cause them to "forget to watch the safety of the men" they employed.[11] Notwithstanding such instructions, far too often the superintendents and other mine officials chose production over safety. They forced the miners to make the decision as to whether to work in unsafe mines. Those who refused were quickly replaced by those who were willing to do so.

Even the most careful timbering could not prevent all rock falls, which killed more Colorado miners—usually one or two at a time—than any other cause. However, mine explosions, which killed dozens and even hundreds of miners at a time, were what captured the headlines. Coal dust, which is highly combustible in southern Colorado's dry atmosphere, and methane gas made the mines extremely susceptible to explosions. There were 46 deaths from explosions in Colorado Fuel and Iron (CF&I) mines between April 1906 and May 1907. In 1909, 89 men were killed and 116 injured from gas or dust explosions in the state. Violent explosions occurred in three major mines in the Trinidad field in 1910: the Primero mine in January, killing 76; the Starkville mine in October, killing 56; and the Victor-American mine at Delagua in November, killing 79. By 1913, 449 miners had been killed in thirteen major explosions in Colorado's coalmines.[12]

The explosions were caused primarily by the coal companies' failure to provide fresh air to clear the mines of "bad" air that contained highly flammable methane gas or coal dust. The miners referred to bad air as "damps." "Stink damp," with its rotten-egg smell, was caused by the presence of hydrogen sulfide. Although a nuisance, it rarely caused death. "Black damp," a mixture of nitrogen and carbon dioxide, also rarely caused death. However, it could render miners depressed, fatigued, or even unconscious. It was a common mixture of gases in Colorado mines produced by exhaling miners and mules, burning lamps, exploding powder, oxidizing coal, decaying timbers, and smoldering mine fires. More dangerous was "after damp." Most of the miners killed in mine explosions died from carbon monoxide poisoning caused by this condition rather than from the explosion itself. A fourth air mixture, "fire damp," was the one most dreaded by coalminers. Fire damp was a highly flammable mixture of methane gas and carbon monoxide. Any number of sources—a spark, a flickering wick, a match—could easily ignite it. The explosion caused by ignition of the gas mixture spread with devastating force until all available fuel was consumed. The highly explosive, dry, coal dust–laden air suspended in the mine could also catch fire directly and explode with horrendous force. Although the presence of highly flammable gases in the mines provoked greater alarm, coal dust probably caused more harm. This fact was made clear by coal dust explosions in 1910 that killed over 150 men.[13]

Many in the coal industry were slow to acknowledge that coal dust could ignite under the right conditions. However, as a precautionary measure, CF&I began to "sprinkle" the most arid of its mines in Las Animas County in the 1890s, but the company discontinued or limited the practice when it became too expensive to ship water to the mines. The Primero mine explosion in 1910 was most assuredly caused by coal dust, even though a Las Animas County coroner's jury—five of whose six members were CF&I employees—exonerated the company of any blame when it could not determine the cause of the explosion. Inspectors in the office of the Bureau of Labor Statistics were less generous toward the company; they charged CF&I with willful neglect for failing to have the mine sprinkled or to apply other safety measures since the accidents in 1907. By compelling men to work under those conditions, Deputy Labor Commissioner Edwin Brake told Governor John Shafroth, the company was guilty of "cold-blooded barbarism."[14]

Osgood's mines fell under scrutiny as well. The massive explosion in the Victor-American mine at Delagua in 1910 was caused by the ignition of methane gas. Despite numerous reports indicating the mine's gaseous nature and the company's failure to remedy the problem, Osgood denied before the Foster Congressional Committee in 1914 that his company was in any way at fault. The coroner's jury, he stressed, had acquitted the company of blame for the explosion, which he had good reason to believe was caused by the intentional burning of a wooden door in the mine; he added, "while we were never able to prove the connection of any individual with it, we had good grounds for serious suspicions that it was not caused accidentally." Like his fellow operators, Osgood blamed almost all mine accidents on careless miners or on those who violated the laws or company rules. He noted in the same testimony that European experts on mine safety had suggested to him the advantage of their system of law, which imposed heavy fines and prison sentences on miners who endangered the lives of others by violating laws.[15]

Although Osgood's claim that careless miners caused most mine accidents was clearly wide of the mark, miners sometimes did ignore safety precautions. In addition, the incompetence of some miners and the failure of coal operators to supervise or train new miners in proper mining techniques and to enforce the state's mining laws increased the number of mine accidents.[16] James Dalrymple and others believed the presence of incompetent miners who knew neither the art of mining nor the laws pertaining to the industry was the result of operators' antiunion activities and their desire to hire the cheapest labor possible. In a 1902 article in the *Engineering and Mining Journal,* F. L. Hoffman argued that "the introduction of inexperienced, non-English speaking common labor, represented by emigrants from southern Europe," was the main cause of the growing accident and death rates in the United States. Mine inspector John D. Jones reported that the coal companies' policy of bringing in thousands of untrained immigrant laborers as strikebreakers in 1904 resulted in increased accidents, especially those caused by rock falls. In 1913 the *Boulder County Miner* accused operators of having "driven from the state thousands of competent miners" and replacing them with "an incompetent class of labor," resulting in "an appalling death rate among those engaged in the industry." It was "unfair" to all miners, Edwin Brake proclaimed, "to allow inexperienced workers in dangerous occupations to endanger their own and fellow employes' [sic] lives." It was, he strongly felt, "inhuman and un-American to operate coal mines with inexperienced men."[17]

Osgood, in contrast, turned the argument over inexperienced versus experienced miners on its head. He blamed most mine accidents on the recklessness of experienced miners rather than the carelessness or incompetence of less experienced miners. The difficulty operators faced, he said, was that experienced men will frequently "take a chance . . . and run the risk of receiving injury that is entirely unnecessary." New and inexperienced miners, on the other hand, "will take every precaution." The old, seasoned miner would say, "I will load this car out and take a chance." Such foolhardiness, Osgood added, was like that of a small boy who "runs out in front of an automobile . . . to see how close he can come to it without being run down."[18]

Not only did experienced miners dispute Osgood's contention, shared by most coal operators, that negligence or recklessness by miners was the main cause of mine accidents, but mine inspector James Dalrymple rejected it as well. "I do not agree with this," he told the Commission on Industrial Relations, "because I believe incompetence, and not negligence, is the cause, and the person who is so incompetent that he knows practically nothing about the business in which he is engaged, and is able to understand practically nothing of what is said to him by those in charge, should not be held responsible for accidents to himself or others through his actions." Dalrymple asserted that coal mining would be much safer if "a more intelligent class of men could be secured to work in the mines."[19]

In a 1910 report, Colorado secretary of state James B. Pearce chastised mine owners who, for fear of having "to spend some of their wealth in making it reasonably safe for men to dig coal," preferred inexperienced foreign-born miners who, presumably, were less restive and more plentiful than native-born miners. If the inexperienced miners came to a full understanding of their rights, coalmines might cease to be "human slaughterhouses." A story Mother Jones repeated a few years later about a CF&I mine manager's response to a reporter about why his mine was not adequately timbered added validity to Pearce's report. "[D]amn it," the manager shouted, "Dagoes are cheaper than props."[20]

Skilled practical miners agreed with the contention that inexperienced miners caused many mine accidents. The presence of young boys, some as young as ten, and inexperienced men in the mines caused constant consternation. Fearful of catastrophic accidents caused by these men's and boys' carelessness and ignorance, the practical miners were motivated to instruct less experienced workers in the art of mining. Although they recommended certification of all miners by a board of examiners as well as teaming inexperienced with experienced miners, measures the UMWA sponsored, experienced miners believed only the union could assist them in achieving these practices and that mine safety could be attained only by unionization of all workers.[21]

Osgood scoffed at the notion that inexperienced foreign-born workers increased the likelihood of accidents in the mines. He also rejected reports that unionized mines were safer than nonunion ones. He told the Foster Congressional Committee in 1914 that many "green" miners had relatives or friends in the camps who looked out for them and taught them to be good miners. They did not need a union for that purpose. "The majority of these men come out here to stay," he said, "and I don't believe there is an iota of difference between these men and the union men. I don't believe that a man is a bit better [a] miner the day after he gets his red [union] card than he is the day before."[22] In his statements before both the Foster Congressional Committee and the Commission on Industrial Relations, Osgood rebutted the charge made against coal operators in southern Colorado that they preferred inexperienced immigrant labor to experienced native miners to deter union activity and cheapen production costs. Instead, he asserted, it was a matter of the available supply of labor.

The debate over who was responsible for the majority of mine accidents was decided by local authorities almost invariably against the miners and in favor of the owners. CF&I and Victor-American dominated the southern Colorado counties of Huerfano and Las Animas both politically and industrially and exercised tremendous political power throughout the state as well. The *Rocky Mountain News* observed in 1903 that "as the Colorado Fuel and Iron Company goes, so goes the [Republican] Party. It has always been the dominating influence in party affairs, for it controls enough votes in the various counties in which it operates to hold the balance of power."[23] Coal operators in the southern coalfield did everything in their power to gain control over all local public officials, from county clerks to sheriffs and their deputies on up to judges. As allies of the coal operators, the sheriffs of the two counties in the southern field determined the jury lists for district courts. The same was true for coroners' juries, which, under the direction of coroners who had long played cheap politics, were part of the companies' political machine.[24] As a result, the coal companies were almost always exonerated from blame for deaths in their mines. The accidents, according to most coroners' verdicts, were either unavoidable or caused by the victims' negligence.

Such verdicts relieved the companies of any legal or moral obligation to compensate surviving family members beyond providing a cheap casket and a meager burial fee for those killed in mine accidents. In many cases, widows with children suffered the most. Between 1907 and 1912, 200 married coalminers were killed in Las Animas County alone, leaving widows responsible for the care of nearly 700 children. Most of the widows were destitute, with no means of support. Although state law required coal companies to compensate widows if the accident that killed their husbands was the companies' fault, coroners' juries made sure no coal company was ever found liable. As a consequence, 70 to 80 children each year were sent to various state institutions and put up for adoption.[25]

Injured workers received only short-term medical assistance, if any. Until workers' compensation programs were introduced after 1915, injured miners and their family members relied on the generosity of friends, unions, burial societies, and ethnic associations for financial help. The only way workers and their families could seek long-term compensation for injury or death was to sue for damages. Such an action was almost certain to fail during the late nineteenth and early twentieth centuries because plaintiffs confronted a body of common-law doctrine that strongly favored industry. Personal injury law at that time held miners liable for their own injuries and deaths even if their employers had disobeyed state mining laws, hired incompetent co-workers, or placed them in the charge of incompetent supervisors. The miners assumed the risk of injury or death if they knowingly entered an extremely dangerous area, even if ordered to do so by superintendents or mine bosses. Even when there was evidence of negligence by operators, the doctrine of contributory negligence could absolve operators of liability. It was virtually impossible for an injured worker or his survivors to prove not only negligence on the part of the company but also that there had been no contributory negligence by the worker in causing the accident.[26]

In his *Report on the Colorado Strike*, George West asserted that the operators' "use of political control to deny justice to injured workmen and the families of employees killed or maimed in accidents must be regarded as the most dastardly of all the unsocial and criminal practices that caused the strike" of 1913–1914.[27] The strike drew public attention to the injustices of the system, and in the 1914 election Colorado voters approved a measure that abolished assumption of risk as a defense in suits involving employees injured or killed as a result of their employer's negligence. The statute further stipulated that an injured worker was not barred from compensation even if he had knowledge of a hazard in the workplace.[28]

Colorado was not the only state to effect changes that helped put workers in a more secure position with regard to personal injury law. Gradually, courts and legislatures across the country weakened the doctrines of assumption of risk, fellow servant negligence, and contributory negligence. Even with these changes, however, the concept of worker responsibility remained basic legal doctrine. Courts in Colorado continued to rule that miners assumed the risk of injury or death in their normal workplaces and that only the operator's failure to provide such basic things as adequate ventilation mitigated the miner's liability.[29]

In the immediate post–1913–1914 strike period, Colorado adopted a new workers' compensation program that mandated employers of more than four persons to participate either by contributing to the state's compensation fund or by providing insurance through private providers, self-insurance, or mutual insurance groups. The program had the blessing of the major coal operators, Osgood among them. Osgood, who had served for four years on a commission appointed by the legislature to study the issue, supported the principle of workers' compensation. For him as well as the other major operators, the advantages outweighed the disadvantages. The program raised the cost of doing business, but it freed companies from the expense of defending against lawsuits. It also limited the amounts paid for compensating injury and death on the job to the amounts paid in insurance premiums. In many cases, however, coal operators across the nation apparently recovered the expense of workers' compensation by reducing miners' wages.[30]

Coalminers also liked the workers' compensation program, which assured them at least some benefits for injury or death on the job. More important, the new legislation had a positive impact on conditions in the mines. Companies belonging to mutual insurance programs adopted uniform rules to improve mine safety, with the anticipated benefit of reducing accidents and lowering insurance rates. As a result, some miners detected a new company attitude toward their safety with the passage of the legislation. As one miner observed, men became more important than mules after workers' compensation was enacted.[31]

Although records indicate that accident rates increased rather than fell nationally after the shift from negligence liability to workers' compensation, the Seth Low Commission found in 1916 that workers' compensation had a positive effect on conditions in Colorado's coalmines, particularly with respect to rock falls. There was "undoubtedly very much more timbering being done since the enactment of the workmen's compensation act to protect the lives and health of the miners than was ever done before," the commission reported. "This is one of the indirect benefits which in part, at least, offset the losses caused by the great strike." The commission also proclaimed that the success of Colorado's workers' compensation program was assured by linking it to a mutual insurance program that spread compensation costs statewide across the industry. The new legislation helped produce more than a decade of relative calm in the Colorado coalfields following the strike of 1913–1914.[32]

Labor's main contention concerning mine safety was the inadequacy of the 1883 mining law, compounded by the operators' refusal to obey it. Following the deadly mine explosion at Victor-American's Delagua mine in November, the third major mine explosion of 1910, labor leaders and editorialists joined forces to demand investigations and reform of the 1883 law. John Lawson of the UMWA stated that because of the three disasters, "a change has come over the people of this state, and they are finally demanding that the reckless slaughter of our people shall cease."[33] A thorough investigation of the disasters, the *Rocky Mountain News* argued, should be conducted by state authorities and not left in the hands of Las Animas County officials, who had no "very close acquaintance with facts." George Creel of the *Denver Post* observed that the state's mining law was inadequate and that the underfunded and understaffed state inspector's office could not do its job. An editorial in the paper was even more emphatic in its call for reform after the Delagua disaster: "Colorado wants laws to protect its miners—not reports telling how they came to their death." The paper urged Colorado lawmakers to "forget the corporations, overlook the mine owners . . . and legislate for the protection of the husband, the father, the provider—and in so doing help the men with the pick and shovel."[34]

Responding to the call for action, Governor John Shafroth appointed a special commission to investigate the mine explosions and recommend measures for preventing such disasters in the future. In announcing the appointment of the commission, Shafroth acknowledged the inadequacy of the 1883 mine law and declared his intention to "use every possible means to have an effective law placed on the statute books."[35] Victor C. Alderson, president of the Colorado School of Mines, headed the commission, which also included

Russell D. George, state geologist and professor of geology at the University of Colorado; John B. Ekeley, professor of chemistry at the University of Colorado; and James Dalrymple, state inspector of coalmines.

After investigating such matters as ventilation, gas and dust problems, mining methods, explosives, mine drainage, surface operations, inspection procedures, rescue equipment and procedures, and training of mine officials, the commission concluded, in the words of the chair, that mining conditions were bad throughout the state and that the operators and their employees as a rule were guilty of "gross carelessness." Based on the information it had gathered, the commission drafted a new coal mining bill, the Alderson bill, which was introduced in the legislature in February 1911. The bill provided for an expanded coalmine inspection department that would be paid for by a tax on coal production of one cent per ton. It also empowered mine inspectors to order miners out of critically dangerous areas, required sprinkling in dusty mines, raised the minimum ventilation standards, and established a standard for timbering at seven-foot intervals. Only explosives tested and approved by the Federal Bureau of Mines could be used in the mines. Operators were also required to provide rescue and resuscitation equipment and construct separate man ways to allow miners to get out of the way of coal cars.[36]

Acting quickly to preserve their position, the operators made their stand against the Alderson bill in the Colorado Senate after it passed the House. The major operators, Osgood among them, pressured the Senate to adopt several amendments designed to weaken the measure. One amendment crippled the coalmine inspection department by reducing the mine inspection force from seven to five deputies without changing the sixty-day inspection cycle. Other amendments cut the coal tax from one cent to one-third of a cent per ton and weakened the ventilation standards. Still others were purely punitive or anti-labor provisions, such as requiring miners to pay the salaries of shot firers out of their own wages and allowing operators to weigh coal after screening. The latter measure, as discussed before, had been one of the most contentious issues contributing to the strikes of 1901 and 1903–1904. The greatly amended measure was sent back to the House, where it was approved with little debate on May 6, 1911. However, Governor Shafroth, agreeing with labor leaders that the measure was largely the work of the operators and that workers would shoulder most of the costs of mine safety, vetoed the bill.[37]

The governor's veto played into the operators' hands. For the time being, Osgood and the major operators had stalled mine-law reform. Osgood told the Foster Congressional Committee in 1914 that he and his colleagues and allies had opposed the Alderson bill because of its many unworkable provisions as well as the way it was prepared and submitted. He noted that the Alderson Commission was made up of individuals who, with the exception of Dalrymple, had no experience in practical mining and that the operators had no representation in preparing the measure. They were not willing to let a group of scholars appointed by a progressive Democratic governor determine law for the mines and were unwilling to make concessions to organized labor at a time of increased labor militancy. Without input from the operators, Osgood asserted, many of the provisions of the legislation "were of such a nature that they could not practically be carried out."[38] Although the operators realized that public opinion demanded a new law, they had put themselves in a determined position to dictate its terms.

The coal operators took careful notice of the mounting criticism against them in the wake of the recent mine disasters. They were well aware that news of the recurrence of fatalities in the mines provided ammunition for unionists, radicals, and muckraking journalists. An article about the 1910 Starkville mine disaster in *Pearson's Magazine* entitled "How Coal Owners Sacrifice Workers" was a good example of the "yellow" journalism of the time.[39] To counter this negative publicity, coal officials in the mountain West formed the Rocky Mountain Coal Mining Institute in November 1912 to educate the public about practical and scientific mining and to promote the study of and research on mining problems. The institute's main objective was twofold: to advance the interests of the mining industry and to gain public acceptance of a new mining law that would be acceptable to coal operators.

The group elected E. H. Weitzel, CF&I's fuel manager, president and F. W. Whiteside, Victor-American's chief engineer, secretary-treasurer. Speaking on behalf of the organization, CF&I mine superintendent David Griffiths, former state mine inspector, stated that it was time to enact a "clear, explicit, practical mining law that will not hamper or impede industry," one that would define the duty of "every man connected with coal mining" and one "with a main motive in view of protecting the life and limb of our workmen."[40] Griffiths was calling for a new law tailored to suit the views and needs of the major operators, a law that would impose few new costs and leave most of the burden of safety with individual mine workers.

The leading coal operators used the institute to signal their readiness to accept a new mining law as long as it encompassed their principal views. Such a law, they believed, would work to their advantage for several reasons. Many in the mining industry had concluded that unsafe mines were costly not only in terms of property and life but also in terms of production. The operators, coalmine inspector John Jones had observed in 1908, were "realizing that a mine conducted on the safest and most sanitary basis is also the most economical to operate." Since most operators stood to profit from improved mine safety in terms of both economic return and a more positive public image, they began to promote mine efficiency and safety as a way to forestall a larger government regulatory role in the industry.[41] Osgood told the Foster Congressional Committee that his company had begun conducting experiments to further mine safety and had hired special inspectors to review safety conditions in the mines. These experiments included the use of electric lamps and steam to mitigate the danger from dust explosions. "We have spent large sums of money in our time to improve the safety of our mines regardless of any provisions of the laws in that regard," he proclaimed.[42]

Encouraged by the operators' apparent willingness to entertain a new proposal, in early 1913 Governor Shafroth instructed the incoming legislature to pass a new coal mining law. The House quickly approved a measure drafted primarily by James Dalrymple and John Lawson of the UMWA and sent it to the Senate, where it met the same fate as the 1911 Alderson bill. Unhappy with the measure, the Senate sent it to a newly appointed commission for revision. The interests of labor and capital were equally divided on the commission, with Dalrymple and Lawson representing the miners and Weitzel and George Peart of the Rocky Mountain Fuel Company representing the coal industry. State senator John F. Pearson was the fifth member, presumably appointed to represent the public interest. Following the commission's recommendations, both the Senate and House approved the revised bill in March 1913, and Governor Elias Ammons, Shafroth's successor, signed it into law.[43]

The new mining law was a compromise between the Alderson Commission's bill and the Senate version Governor Shafroth had vetoed. It reorganized the coalmine inspection department and did away with the cumbersome enforcement procedures of the 1883 law. The ventilation requirements recommended by the 1911 Alderson bill were restored, and operators were required to institute dust-control measures. Fire bosses were to inspect mines daily for the presence of explosive gas. The new legislation also required mines to use a systematic method of timbering approved by the chief inspector. Foremen, assistant foremen, shot firers, and company inspectors were all to be examined and certified by a board composed of working miners, company officials, and a mining engineer. The foremen were to inspect the mines daily to make sure they were safe and that operations were conducted according to the law. They were also to see that employees obeyed the law. Additionally, the legislation regulated mine procedures, such as the use of explosives, electricity, and electrical appliances, and required the provision of rescue and resuscitation equipment. Of great importance to the miners, the law provided for the appointment of checkweighmen and forbade superintendents and other officials from using their positions to extort money or favors from miners in exchange for employment, job security, or favorable work assignments. Lastly, violations of the law, including willful negligence by miners, were misdemeanors punishable by fines or imprisonment.[44]

With the enlarged coalmine inspection department and increased powers of inspectors; higher ventilation, equipment, and plant standards; and a more rigid system of supervision, the 1913 act was an improvement over the 1883 law. Both labor and industry expressed satisfaction with the new measure. Lawson believed it would provide "the best and safest working conditions for miners in the world," while Weitzel, the most important industry representative on the Senate commission, noted that he and CF&I officials were "perfectly satisfied" with the measure. Certainly, this was the case with Osgood, who was pleased that the operators had played the leading role in drafting it.[45] Despite Lawson's praise, there was little doubt that the new law mainly reflected the operators' interests rather than those of the miners.

There were other reasons the major operators accepted the new mining law after resisting reform two years earlier. Public opinion in favor of reform had certainly influenced their decision. In addition, increased labor militancy and the UMWA's campaign to organize miners throughout the state had put them on the defensive. With union organizers in full swing in the southern Colorado district in early 1913, the operators endorsed the new law as a way to placate miners and deny the union an issue concerning a lack of safety in the mines. Governor Ammons, recently elected, shared the operators' hope that the newly enacted legislation might help quiet labor unrest and thus head off a strike.[46]

Although it was an improvement over the 1883 law, the 1913 Colorado coal mining law failed for several reasons. Enacted within the recent memory of the 1910 mine tragedies, its main purpose was to prevent future disasters as a result of mine explosions. This it failed to do, as witnessed by the massive explosions in the Victor-American mine at Hastings in 1917 and 1921. It also failed because it did not depart substantially from previous laws or alter basic relations and attitudes regarding safety. It did not forbid the hiring of illiterate or incompetent workers or require companies to train them before sending them into the mines, as the UMWA had continually advocated. Nor did it address the problem of the miners' willingness to take chances by avoiding dead work because they were paid according to production. Furthermore, it did not remove the pressure on mine officials to get the coal out as fast as possible. For all these reasons, it failed to prevent those accidents that caused the majority of deaths in the mines. Rock falls remained the primary cause of deaths and injuries, and there was little significant improvement in casualty rates for many years to come. Worst of all, however, was the failure to change the prevailing view that held miners responsible for their own injuries and deaths through carelessness, greed, or inexperience.[47]

By treating the miners as independent contract workers rather than as members of a collective workforce, Osgood and most of the coal operators, whether motivated by sincere belief or cold calculation, clung to the old-fashioned notion that miners had the right to bargain individually with their employers as equals. With this concept of labor-management relations prevailing, the miners had little authority to help shape the workplace. They were dependent on the good faith of the companies that employed them; but after the bitter experiences of the past several years, the miners believed the companies would never conduct business in a way that would safeguard their interests. Instead, they looked to the union to protect them and advance their cause either through direct bargaining or through lobbying with the state legislature to compel companies to obey laws and adopt better safety practices and technologies. Despite their significant ethnic and cultural divisions, coalminers united behind the UMWA banner.[48] After launching another organizational campaign in the West, by 1913 the union was once again ready to take up the miners' cause in Colorado.

NOTES

1. Wolff, *Industrializing the Rockies*, 189.

2. Ibid., 195.

3. McGovern, "Colorado Coal Strike," 75, citing Costigan's testimony, CIR/FR 9: 8123.

4. Whiteside, *Regulating Danger*, 74–75.

5. Ibid., 75. Whiteside noted that between 1884 and 1912 the national death rate for miners was 3.12 per 1,000 employed; during the same period, Colorado's average death rate from explosions was 2.68 per 1,000 and from rock and coal falls 3.00 per 1,000 employed. Thus, Colorado's death rate from explosions and rock and coal falls was 5.68 per 1,000 employed, compared with the national rate of 3.12 per 1,000 employed for all causes.

6. CBLS, *Thirteenth Biennial Report,* 264; McGovern and Guttridge, *Coalfield War,* 66.

7. Whiteside, *Regulating Danger*, 52; Osgood's statement at the editors' conference in *Pueblo Star-Journal*, November 16, 1913; Osgood's testimony, SMM, 401.

8. Whiteside, *Regulating Danger*, 80; Fox, *United We Stand*, 198; Andrews, "Road to Ludlow," 261.

9. Hammond quoted in Whiteside, *Regulating Danger*, 50; F. W. Whiteside quoted in ibid., 78.

10. Quotes in ibid., 53.

11. Murray to all superintendents, October 2, 1912, in CIR/FR 8: 7351.

12. John A. Fitch, "The Steel Industry and the People in Colorado," *The Survey* 27, no. 18 (February 3, 1912): 1709; Whiteside, *Regulating Danger*, 76.

13. The information in this paragraph is from Andrews, "Road to Ludlow," 269–272. The Primero and Starkville mine explosions were attributed to dust, whereas the Delagua mine explosion that killed seventy-nine men was a gas explosion (Fitch, "The Steel Industry and the People in Colorado," 1709).

14. "Report of State Mining Inspector John D. Jones on Primero Mine Explosion," in CBLS, *Fourteenth Biennial Report*, 145; Edwin V. Brake, "Report of the Bureau of Labor Statistics on the Primero Mine Disasters of January 23, 1907, and January 31, 1910," in CBLS, *Twelfth Biennial Report*, 26, cited in Fitch, "The Steel Industry and the People in Colorado," 1709, n. 2.

15. Osgood's testimony, SMM, 438, 470.

16. Price V. Fishback, "The Miner's Work Environment: Safety and Company Towns in the Early 1900s," in John H.M. Laslett, ed., *The United Mine Workers of America: A Model of Industrial Solidarity?* (University Park: Pennsylvania State University Press, 1996), 204; McGovern and Guttridge, *Coalfield War*, 66.

17. F. L. Hoffman, "Problems of Labor and Life in Anthracite Coal Mining," *Engineering and Mining Journal* 74 (December 20, 1902): 811; Colorado State Inspector of Mines, *Eleventh Biennial Report*, 6, cited in Whiteside, *Regulating Danger*, 81; *Boulder County Miner* quoted in Margolis, "Western Coal Mining," 42; CBLS, *Twelfth Biennial Report*, 13 (Brake quote), 22.

18. Osgood's testimony, CIR/FR 7: 6454–6455.

19. Dalrymple quoted in West, *Report on the Colorado Strike*, 79; CBLS, *Thirteenth Biennial Report*, 264.

20. Mother Jones's story related in Papanikolas, *Buried Unsung*, 38; Pearce quoted in Whiteside, *Regulating Danger*, 83–84.

21. Deputy Inspector Coray, "Report on Primero Disaster," in CBLS, *Twelfth Biennial Report*, 30; Andrews, "Road to Ludlow," 305.

22. Osgood's testimony, SMM, 406.

23. *Rocky Mountain News*, August 14, 1903.

24. Fitch, "The Steel Industry and the People in Colorado," 1714.

25. Long, *Where the Sun Never Shines*, 247.

26. The information for this paragraph is from Whiteside, *Regulating Danger*, 86–89; Fishback, "Miner's Work Environment," 207.

27. West, *Report on the Colorado Strike*, 82–83.

28. Ibid., 82; Whiteside, *Regulating Danger*, 91.

29. Whiteside, *Regulating Danger*, 92.

30. Ibid., 128; Osgood's testimony, CIR/*FR* 7: 6455; Fishback, "Miner's Work Environment," 208.

31. Whiteside, *Regulating Danger*, 127–129.

32. Fishback, "Miner's Work Environment," 208–209; "Report of the Colorado Coal Commission on the Labor Difficulties in the Coal Fields of Colorado during the Years 1914 and 1915," *Labor Difficulties in the Coal Fields of Colorado*, House of Representatives, 64th Congress, 1st Session, 1916, Document 859 (Washington, D.C., 1916), 14–15; hereafter cited as *Labor Difficulties in the Coal Fields of Colorado*. The shift to workers' compensation, Fishback argued, did not result in fewer accidents in the nation's coalmines; in fact, nationally, he noted, the rate of accidents increased by approximately 28 percent. Perhaps the explanation for this increase, Fishback stated, is that miners, knowing they would be compensated for an injury, were willing to take greater risks to increase their earnings ("Miner's Work Environment," 208–209).

33. Lawson quoted in *United Mine Workers Journal*, December 15, 1910, 3, cited in Whiteside, *Regulating Danger*, 100.

34. *Rocky Mountain News*, February 1, 1910; *Denver Post*, February 3 (Creel quote), November 19 (editorial), 1910, cited in Whiteside, *Regulating Danger*, 99–100.

35. Shafroth quoted in Whiteside, *Regulating Danger*, 102.

36. Ibid., 102–103.

37. Ibid., 103.

38. Osgood's testimony, SMM, 405.

39. McGovern and Guttridge, *Coalfield War*, 63.

40. Griffiths quoted in Whiteside, *Regulating Danger*, 105.

41. Ibid., 98–99, Jones quote on 98.

42. Osgood's testimony, SMM, 405.

43. Whiteside, *Regulating Danger*, 106.

44. Ibid., 106–107.

45. Lawson and Weitzel quoted in ibid., 107; Osgood's testimony, SMM, 405.

46. Whiteside, *Regulating Danger*, 108–109; McGovern and Guttridge, *Coalfield War*, 83.

47. Whiteside, *Regulating Danger*, 110, 114.

48. Ibid., 50–54; Margolis, "Western Coal Mining," 26–27; Andrews, "Road to Ludlow," 293–294, 302–305.

The 1913–1914 Strike

The coalminers of southern Colorado began the second decade of the twentieth century with growing resentment over coal companies' treatment of them and with increased determination to organize under the United Mine Workers of America (UMWA) banner. Since the 1903–1904 strike, the Colorado Fuel and Iron (CF&I) and Victor-American Fuel companies had tightened control over their employees by creating a closed town system and had continued to violate state laws. They still denied the miners' legal right to have a check-weighman at each mine. For economic reasons, mine safety was sacrificed and social welfare programs were curtailed, resulting in mine accidents and deteriorating living conditions for the miners. According to the Foster Congressional Committee, the miners "worked under conditions that were in existence in scarcely any state except Colorado."[1] For all these reasons, the miners demanded a union to advance their rights and protect them from their employers' abuses. By the spring of 1912, the cry for a union was so great that many miners were ready to go on strike. The national union, however, believing a strike was premature, refused to support their effort at that time.

With the bitter experience of the failed 1903–1904 strike in mind and the union in disarray, officials of the national UMWA were even reluctant to sanction the resumption of a full-scale organizational campaign. With officials of CF&I and Victor-American and their allies—the sheriffs of Huerfano and Las Animas counties—in complete control of the coalfields, only surreptitious union activity had been possible during most of the decade following the 1903–1904 debacle. For union efforts to succeed, strong local leadership was needed. That opportunity came through the efforts of John Lawson, one of the most important union organizers who worked to organize miners in the Colorado coalfields during this period of extreme corporate repression.

A superb organizer who was well acquainted with the state's coalfields, Lawson took advantage of the festering bitterness to keep the union cause alive among the miners. He had worked briefly as a miner for CF&I before taking on the role of union organizer. Unionism was his passion, and, to the alarm of coal operators, he soon gained a large following among the miners. Disdainful of compromise, he sometimes pursued a course of action that risked violence. The failure of the 1903–1904 strike only strengthened his determination to organize the southern Colorado coalfield. Not even the national executive board's refusal to sanction such a campaign deterred him from carrying on his work, much of it done in secrecy.[2]

Lawson was well aware of the dangers of being a union organizer. A dynamite explosion, which almost killed his wife and infant daughter, had destroyed his home in New Castle in western Colorado in 1903. The suspected dynamiter, Perry C. Coryell, was an owner of a small mining company in Garfield County. Shot and wounded by Coryell on a New Castle street five months later, Lawson was crippled for months by the shotgun blast, but the incident raised him to prominence as a union leader.[3] In the spring of 1907, at age thirty, Lawson began an organizing operation in the Walsenburg area. There he encountered Huerfano County sheriff Jefferson Farr, who ran county politics from his string of whorehouses and saloons and referred to himself as king of the "kingdom of Huerfano County."[4] Farr's unrelenting harassment of Lawson, including jailing him on a trumped-up charge of carrying a concealed weapon, forced the union organizer to transfer his office to Trinidad.

Shortly thereafter, Lawson shifted his activity to the northern coal district northwest of Denver, where circumstances made his task much easier. Most miners in this area were English speaking, and many owned their own homes in nearby Lafayette, Louisville, and Frederick. Although their demands were the same as those of their colleagues to the south, they did not suffer the harsh and oppressive conditions that existed in the camps and mines of the southern field. Consequently, Lawson and his associates quickly achieved victory. On July 14, 1908, the UMWA won its first major contract in Colorado, affecting seventeen companies in the northern field.[5]

Largely through Lawson's efforts, miners in the northern field gained an eight-hour workday, semimonthly paydays, payment for dead work, improved safety measures, and settlement of disputes through grievance committees. State law already covered some of the concessions. Recognition of the union, with a checkoff system for union dues and fees, was the most important achievement. There were political and psychological benefits as well. With union support, John Shafroth, the Democratic candidate, won the gubernatorial election. The election of a progressive Democrat augured well for the passage of legislation that would benefit miners as well as workers in general throughout the state. Psychologically, the establishment of a foothold in Colorado raised the spirits of union organizers and energized them for the greater battle in the south.

The southern coal operators realized too late that they had done too little to aid their northern comrades in resisting the UMWA's demands. Convinced by labor spies and newspaper accounts that the national union was on the verge of foundering and confident that it would take the union in Colorado many years, if ever, to recover from the crushing defeat it had suffered in 1904, the operators were unprepared for union success of this magnitude. The union's victory prompted the major southern operators to offer various inducements, such as price agreements and improved markets, to northern mine owners as a way of encouraging them to end their contracts with the union. In the spring of 1910, the CF&I and Victor-American companies applied intense pressure on the northern operators to reject renewal of the contracts. When the union demanded a five-and-a-half cent wage boost and a half-holiday on Saturdays, the northern operators were more than willing to accede to the wishes of their southern neighbors. The outright rejection of the union's demands precipitated a prolonged strike in the northern field that began on April 4, 1910.[6]

The northern companies quickly instituted the standard procedure for breaking strikes, but their tactics failed. They hired Baldwin-Felts agents and other armed guards and imported strikebreakers from the East, but the sheriff of Boulder County, MP Capp, refused to deputize the guards or appeal to the governor for state troops. Governor Shafroth and his secretary of state, well aware of the "habit" of "certain interests" to break strikes by using the militia, denied all requests for military intervention. The decision of a federal district judge to uphold the strikers' rights to picket and assemble was yet another blow to the operators. With these developments, it seemed that neither side in the labor conflict in the northern coalfield had an advantage. With the expenditure of large sums of money, both sides soon exhausted themselves financially.[7]

These setbacks affected all of Colorado's major coal operators. The methods used so successfully to break the strike and crush the union in 1903–1904 were now challenged by local and state authorities as well as a federal court. As the strike continued, even more ominous developments alarmed the operators, both north and south. Public opinion in Colorado and the rest of the nation was clearly shifting in favor of labor against corporate power. In winning the White House in 1912, Woodrow Wilson carried Colorado by a large majority, and the Democratic candidate for governor, Elias Ammons, won by a comfortable margin. The stage was set for a redress in the balance of power between labor and big business on both the local and national levels.[8]

The changed political climate and increased union organizational activity in the southern region prompted coal operators to adjust their policies to improve their public image and forestall further union organization. In April 1912, in a calculated move to undercut the union, CF&I announced a 10 percent wage increase for all of its 10,000 miners. Victor-American Fuel and Rocky Mountain Fuel quickly followed suit. In early 1913, CF&I abolished the scrip system, adopted a semimonthly payday, and implemented the eight-hour workday. Although Jesse Welborn, the company's president, claimed these changes in policy were not influenced by the activities of union organizers, LaMont Bowers indicated otherwise in private correspondence with Starr Murphy, a legal adviser to John D. Rockefeller Jr. "We have spent a great deal of time," he wrote, "and studied with a good deal of care, all the questions in connection with labor unions among miners and men employed by industrial corporations during the past two or three years, anticipating in time having to meet the demands of union labor." These changes, he stressed, were made as a matter of policy in anticipation that they would "arise sooner or later."[9] Also realizing that they were on the wrong side of these issues, Victor-American and many of the other coal companies again followed CF&I's lead in making similar policy changes, although Victor-American refused to abolish the scrip system.

The passage of the new coal mining law in 1913, which addressed some of the miners' concerns about safety in the mines, cast further doubt on the claim that the union was necessary to gain rights for miners and protection of their interests. Although the miners gave the UMWA credit for the 10 percent wage hike, which resulted in a large increase in the union's secret membership, the other "concessions" made by operators worried union officials. Even if these measures were tactical ones designed to meet the exigency of the moment, union leaders feared that in granting them, the coal companies had undermined justification for the union's presence in the coalfields in Colorado. How these actions would affect the achievement of the fundamental goal of union recognition was uppermost in their minds. Doubts about support of the union among miners and the public at large, as well as the stalemated situation in the northern district, caused the national executive officials to be cautious about further activity. With the national organization plagued by dissension and a depleted treasury, John Philip White, the newly elected president of the UMWA, had determined that the union was in no position to conduct an intensified organizational campaign in Colorado.[10]

Undeterred by the executive's hesitancy, Lawson continued to plead with White and the other national officers to sanction and fund an organizational campaign in southern Colorado. As a member of the international executive board, his pleading carried considerable weight. He was convinced that the struggle for union recognition in the state had to be fought in the south. Victory for the miners in the northern field, he believed, could only be achieved by stopping the flow of money and arms from CF&I and Victor-American that sustained the intransigence of northern operators. This could be accomplished only by confronting the southern operators with an all-out organizational campaign of miners in their area. Furthermore, Lawson argued that the union could not remain passive and let the operators undermine the union's cause by offering the miners wage increases and agreeing to obey state laws, especially since these concessions would be withdrawn as soon as the threat of unionization passed.

President White had learned enough about Colorado's coal operators to know that they were a formidable group. "These operators of yours are tough babies," he told Lawson. "I thought I had run across some bad ones in the East, but they are wishy-washy compared to the kind you breed around here." Lawson agreed that the operators were bad, "but," he added, "we can beat them if we can have a little money for more organization work. The south has to be organized completely before we can do anything worthwhile." Concurring, White accepted the notion that Colorado "should be a good proving ground for the entire nation" and promised to aid Lawson in organizing the state "as fast as we can muster our strength for the effort."[11]

The prospect of the northern miners being defeated in a costly strike prolonged by aid from southern operators finally convinced White to sanction the southern Colorado organizational campaign. "Financial assistance will be yours," he told Lawson. "We are in shape now to take those Colorado operators into camp once and for all."[12] By threatening the southern operators with an all-out effort to organize their area, White hoped to convince them to support a settlement of the costly northern strike, thereby preserving and strengthening the union's presence in Colorado. Although Lawson warned the members of the executive committee that the campaign would be extremely costly, they agreed with White that the gamble was worth taking. Thus, they granted Lawson authority to conduct a full-scale campaign beginning in early 1913 to organize the southern Colorado coalminers.[13]

Although Lawson did not publicly announce the campaign until July 24, 1913, teams of trained union organizers had moved into the Trinidad coalfield during the spring. The organizers, very aware that they were putting themselves in great danger, had to work secretly in the camps. They frequently worked in pairs, one the active organizer operating in the open and the other an undercover man who feigned antiunion bias to gain the confidence of pit bosses and superintendents. Once this confidence was gained, the undercover organizer could identify potential candidates for union membership and report ardent antiunion miners to mine authorities as union members. If the scheme succeeded, the places of antiunion miners who were "run down the canyon" would be filled with carefully coached men with union affiliation.[14]

The experiences of two married couples at the Victor-American camp of Delagua illustrate the lengths to which organizers went in their "whispering campaign" to recruit miners. In their role as organizers, Charles and Cedi Costa and Tony and Margo Gorci used Saturday night dances to bring miners together. While the camp's dance band—which included Tony Gorci, an expert fiddler—played, organizers milled among the crowd, recruiting for the union in full sight of the company's detectives. The couples later added Mary Thomas to their entertainment ticket. A miner's wife from Wales, Mary had a beautiful voice, and her singing attracted even more miners to the dances. Although not at first aware that she was being used to recruit new members, she soon became an avid supporter of the union cause. All these people would eventually make their way to the Ludlow tent colony after the beginning of the strike in September 1913. Gorci had to be carried there on a mattress, having been severely beaten by mine guards after his union sympathies were revealed.[15]

The career of another famous union organizer, Michael Livoda, also illustrates the dangers organizers faced and the conviction to the union that led them to continue their activities. In 1912, John Lawson hired Livoda, a Croat who could speak all the Slavic languages, to recruit Slavic miners in the Walsenburg and Trinidad areas. Shortly after he arrived in Walsenburg, deputy sheriffs hauled him before Sheriff Farr, who ordered him out of town. Even though he was followed for several weeks, Livoda was able to sign up miners on company property under the cover of darkness. His luck ran out one night in June 1912. Around midnight, five men burst into his room and dragged him from the bachelors' quarters at the Victor-American mine of Ravenwood. Besides the deputy sheriffs, the group also included the mine superintendent and a boss of the mule drivers. They beat him severely. When he started to yell for help, one of the men put his hand over Livoda's mouth and said, "Shut up, you son of a bitch, or we'll kill you." While he was on the ground, they kicked him so hard that for two months he could not stand or sit without assistance. Eventually, the men escorted him out of the camp and told him to get out of Colorado. He managed to walk the five miles to Walsenburg, where he lay on a mattress in a Jewish tailor's coal shed for two days before a doctor was able to attend to him. Despite the severe beating, Livoda went back to recruiting as soon as he was able to do so.[16]

Well aware of the increased union activity, the operators of CF&I, Victor-American, and Rocky Mountain Fuel hired elite men from the Baldwin-Felts Agency and other $3-a-day gunmen to guard their mine properties and harass union organizers. They commissioned Albert Felts, director of the agency, to import gunmen as well as arms—including machine guns—into southern Colorado. Felts and his agency comrade, Walter Belk, brought in as many as seventy-five Baldwin-Felts men, many of them veterans of the bloody strike in West Virginia.[17] The sheriffs of Huerfano and Las Animas counties, contrary to state law in most cases, immediately deputized the agency men and other gunmen upon their arrival. More than a few of these men were among the worst elements of society; they were, as George West described them in his report on the Colorado strike, of the lowest and most vicious character. Sheriff Farr rarely checked the backgrounds of the men he deputized, some of whom, he confessed, might have been "red-handed murderers."[18] The large operators quickly availed themselves of this army of deputies by furnishing them with guns and paying them $3.50 a day to guard their mines and property and keep union organizers out of the camps.

Union organizers were not the only targets of the mine officials' repressive activities. Union members as well as state officials, including a labor commissioner, were followed and spied on. "One does not need to be a sleuth," the official commented, "to become acquainted with the elaborate and complete system of surveillance that is maintained by the fuel corporations of this district."[19] Mine guards intimidated men they suspected of being union members, escorting many of them out of the camps. The UMWA estimated that in 1912, Colorado coal companies fired 1,200 mine workers suspected of having union sympathies. In a well-publicized case, a Methodist minister testified before the Foster Congressional Committee that he had observed two deputy sheriffs "herding" three miners out of the Victor-American Hastings camp. The minister "thought that there must be a terrible charge to have them herded out of town in this way, that they must have been guilty of murder or some other terrible crime." Upon inquiry, however, he "found that the trouble was that they were suspected of being union men."[20]

Such incidents raised the miners' passion to fever pitch, and the collective voice in the coal camps called for a strike in the southern Colorado coalfield. In response, Frank J. Hayes, UMWA's vice president, took command of the Colorado campaign. He appointed a committee composed of himself; Lawson; Ed Doyle, secretary-treasurer of District 15; and John McLennan, president of District 15, to formulate policy. The national executive board gave the committee absolute authority "to call out on strike any part or all of the district" if in its judgment doing so became necessary for the success of the strike in northern Colorado.[21]

Hayes, however, hoped for a peaceful settlement. He honestly but naively believed that if the operators were sensible businessmen, they would agree to talk with him and his union colleagues to avoid a costly strike. In a call for common sense and conciliation, the policy committee informed the public that the union was determined "to exhaust all honorable means in an endeavor to bring about a settlement" before a strike was ordered. The committee continued: "We are for Colorado; we are for good citizenship; we are for enforcement of the law; we stand for justice. We hope the situation may be cleared up without a strike and that the disgraceful scenes of years gone by that have placed a blot upon the fair name of Colorado will never be enacted in this state again." Hayes warned the mine owners of the consequences of failure. The men, he stated, "have been clamoring for a strike and I am empowered to call them out if their efforts to unionize are resisted."[22]

Meanwhile, the policy committee sent a circular letter to miners in all camps in District 15, which read: "This is the day of your emancipation. This is the day when liberty and progress come to abide in your midst. We call upon you this day to enroll as a member of the greatest and most powerful labor organization in the world, the United Mine Workers of America."[23] The miners responded enthusiastically. With an onrush of men eager to join the union, organizers opened branch offices in Aguilar, Walsenburg, and Florence to supplement the Trinidad headquarters. In every camp there were predictions of a strike that would be bigger and more important than any that had occurred before.

The operators regarded the circular letter as a declaration of war. Jesse Welborn of CF&I and David Brown of Rocky Mountain Fuel met with John Osgood to plan measures to counter the union activities. Almost immediately, they began to implement the strategy that had served them well in the strike of 1903–1904 and that had become doctrine among coal operators. They established a defense fund to purchase huge quantities of arms and ammunition, including eight machine guns purchased from the Coal Operators' Association of West Virginia, and to employ spies. The companies hired William Hiram ("Billy") Reno, director of CF&I's detective department, to supervise company spies; recruit professional gunmen from Salt Lake City, Kansas City, and Chicago; and bring in experienced union busters from Cripple Creek, Colorado. In addition, they made preparations to protect their mines by doubling the number of guards, stringing barbed wire around closed camps, and placing more gates across public roads to control traffic. They hired spotters (detectives) to spy on union activities and foment dissension and distrust among the miners, and they instructed guards and sheriffs to assault union organizers and expel hundreds of miners suspected of belonging to the UMWA from the camps.[24]

Also anticipating trouble, union agents purchased arms and ammunition and paid informants for information about the coal executives' plans and operations. During the summer, Ed Doyle quietly leased large tracts of land from landowners to use as sites for tent colonies in the event of a strike. With the sites secured, Doyle procured tents from a Pueblo dealer and from the union's stockpile of surplus tents used by miners in West Virginia in their recent mine wars. Doyle also arranged to supply the camps with drinking water from wells or barrels, as well as with stoves, coal for heating and cooking, and lumber for walls and floors. By September 23, the day the strike began, the union had established tent colonies on all eight of the tracts Doyle had leased.[25]

With the organizational activities in full swing, on August 6 members of the union's policy committee asked Governor Ammons to arrange a conference between themselves and the leading operators. Ammons's attempts to do so failed. Osgood, Welborn, and Brown refused to meet with the union representatives on the ground that such a meeting would constitute recognition of the union. "We told Governor Ammons," Osgood later stated before the Foster Congressional Committee, "that we did not want to make any contract with the United Mine Workers of America, that consequently no interview with Mr. Hayes would be fruitful—and we therefore declined to see him." In a subsequent conversation, the owners informed the governor that as far as they knew, their "men were satisfied with their wages and conditions" and had not expressed any complaints. Therefore, Osgood and the other operators had concluded, there was no need "for any change in the conditions that existed . . . for a number of years preceding." To underscore the operators' private comments to the governor, Welborn released a public statement from his Denver office: "We will never accede to union recognition. That is the absolute, determined and certain ultimatum of the operators—strike or no strike."[26]

Osgood's confidence in the correctness of the operators' decision to refuse to meet with union leaders was based not only on his righteous belief in the open-shop philosophy but also on his perception of the weakness of the union position. He had learned from a fellow operator, probably Welborn, that during a meeting between Hayes and Ammons, the union leader in effect admitted that "the mine operators of Colorado had taken the wind out of their [the union's] sails by granting a good many things to the miners" that they intended to demand, and that the only thing he wanted in meeting with the operators was recognition of the union.[27] Even after the strike was under way, Osgood scoffed at Hayes's claim that the union rather than the mine owners represented the miners. The union's published records, Osgood stated, showed that of 23,000 men in District 15, only 2,000 were union members. He asserted that most of the 2,000 union men were located in northern Colorado, with only "a mere handful, a few hundred, settled throughout the mines in the south and that was after ten years' effort to organize the men." Based on these facts, Osgood argued, Hayes had no right to claim that the union represented the miners and that the operators were obligated to "treat" with him. Furthermore, he asserted that the "actual" mine workers did not want to strike and that the UMWA leaders were intruders determined to engage in a power struggle with the coal executives for their own benefit, not that of the miners.[28]

Osgood and the other major operators successfully convinced Governor Ammons to support their stand against meeting with union leaders. Furthermore, the governor rejected the advice of Deputy Labor Commissioner Edwin Brake to instruct the sheriffs of Huerfano and Las

Animas counties to disarm every man in the district, discharge some of their unsuitable deputy sheriffs, and deputize only reputable citizens. By late August, with the streets filled with armed guards, detectives, and union organizers, the atmosphere in Trinidad was explosive. Brake warned Ammons that something had to be done quickly "or there would be an outbreak there that would be disastrous." But the governor "did nothing to allay the trouble," Brake lamented, conceding that "other advisers were stronger evidently with him than myself." Instead, Ammons proposed a three-point compromise plan drafted by Brake that offered all miners—union as well as nonunion—the right to use a check-weighman, to trade where they pleased, and to work in the mines. Frank Hayes immediately rejected the proposal. "Nothing less than full recognition of the union will satisfy us," he told the governor.[29]

Although the clamor for a strike intensified among the miners, the union's policy committee was not ready to give up on its efforts to reach an agreement with the operators. On August 26 the committee sent a letter to every coal operator in District 15:

> While we know your past policy has been one of keen opposition to our union, we are hopeful at this time that you will look at this matter in a different way, and will meet with us in joint conference for the purpose of amicably adjusting all points at issue in the present controversy. We are no more desirous of a strike than you are, and it seems to us that we owe it to our respective interests, as well as the general public, to make every honest endeavor to adjust our differences in an enlightened manner.

The union leaders noted that the operators who had signed union contracts were satisfied "and much pleased over the security and stability given to the industry through the medium of the trade agreement." It was evident that Colorado could not stand alone in opposition to the union, they argued. "Why oppose us here, spending millions of dollars in an industrial conflict for no good purpose? Why is it not possible and practical for you to do in this state what the operators in all the neighboring states have already done?" In closing, the union leaders added: "Let us meet now as friends and proceed to settle this entire controversy with honor to ourselves, with credit to our people, and with faith in each other."[30]

As the union leaders expected, the operators did not reply to their request for a conference. When it became apparent that the operators would not meet with them, they scheduled a convention of delegates representing Colorado coalminers for September 15–16 in Trinidad. They then publicly appealed to the miners of the district to join the UMWA, "which has advanced the interests of its members in a hundred different ways and has brought sunshine and happiness into thousands of homes."[31] On September 8, in "a final effort for peace," union officials addressed another letter inviting the mine owners to meet with them at the Trinidad convention to resolve their differences amicably. UMWA president John White, still clinging to a faint hope of gaining recognition for the union without a costly strike, warned the operators that they would face a union determined to launch a strike that would be fought "to the limit of its resources" if they failed to attend.[32]

Few in the labor camp expected the owners to accept the invitation or, perhaps more correctly, the ultimatum. Most union leaders and the vast majority of mine workers knew the coal operators of southern Colorado had no interest in negotiating a settlement with the union. The final appeal was offered primarily as a way to enhance the union's image in the arena of public opinion, which labor leaders feared favored the operators. Indeed, the operators, believing their own propaganda, were certain that public opinion was on their side and that the strike would be of little consequence. "There is no good of talking now, anybody can see for himself on Tuesday what the strike will amount to and how many men will go out," Osgood stated publicly.[33] Convinced of the righteousness of their cause and of their ability to outlast the union in terms of both the money they could spend and the political support they expected to receive, the operators vowed to fight to the finish. Thus, the positions of the two sides on the eve of the miners' convention were cast in stone.

On the morning the convention opened, an Irish brass band and a Welsh choir led a parade of 253 delegates followed by 3,000 men, women, and children from across the Colorado coalfields through the streets of Trinidad toward Castle Hall, the site of the meeting. According to the *Denver Express*, the marchers "took up the swelling chorus" of "The Colorado Strike Song" as they approached the hall.[34] The chorus was heard throughout Trinidad's business district:

> We will win the fight today, boys,
> We'll win the fight today,
> Shouting the battle cry of union;
> We will rally from the coal mines,
> We'll battle to the end,
> Shouting the battle cry of union.

> *Chorus:*
> The union forever, Hurrah! Boys, hurrah!
> Down with the Baldwins, up with the law;

For we're coming, Colorado, we're coming all the way,
Shouting the battle cry of union.

We have fought them here for years, boys,
We'll fight them in the end,
Shouting the battle cry of union.
We have fought them in the North, now we'll fight them in the South,
Shouting the battle cry of union.

Chorus:
We are fighting for our rights, boys,
We're fighting for our homes,
Shouting the battle cry of union.
Men have died to win the struggle, they've died to set us free,
Shouting the battle cry of union.[35]

The lyrics reinforced the faith of those who sang them that the fight ahead was a historic struggle for justice and freedom. The fervor displayed by miners and their family members in singing the "Strike Song" indicated their readiness to do what was necessary to free themselves from their "historic servitude to the mine owners."[36]

Inside the convention hall, John McLennan told the delegates that "the welfare, the hopes, and aspirations of thousands of coal miners and their families" were in their hands. If a strike were called, he declared, it would be the fault of the operators, who had spurned every offer to meet with union officials to address the miners' issues. "If the strike is called," he assured the delegates, "the strike will be carried on with all the characteristic vigor of the organization and every coal miner in America will be in back of us."[37]

That evening, a crowd of 2,000 filled every available space in the West Opera House to hear Frank Hayes and Mother Jones speak. For over two hours, Mother Jones held the audience spellbound. According to the *Rocky Mountain News*, she "mercilessly" scored the operators and the Baldwin-Felts guards, "who she declared had joined in a conspiracy to keep the working class in subjection." She pleaded for arbitration and urged the governor to use his official authority to compel the operators to meet with union officials. The miners' rights must be recognized, she exclaimed, or a strike was inevitable. With clenched fists she shouted: "If it is strike or submit . . . why for God's sake, strike—strike until you win!" With this utterance, the men sprang from their seats and shouted their approval "until they dropped back exhausted."[38]

Inside the convention hall the next morning, the delegates heard miner after miner from all areas of the state recount a plethora of griev-

Mother Jones with John Lawson (left) and Horace Hawkins (right). Courtesy, West Virginia and Regional History Collection, West Virginia University Libraries, Morgantown.

ances concerning working and living conditions in the mines and camps. In "recitals of alleged wrongs dating back many years," the *Trinidad Chronicle-News* reported, for two days delegates told their version of the history of the southern Colorado coalfields. Some complained of the lack of mine safety, with several miners recounting the great colliery explosions in 1910 and many other mining disasters. Others told of being short-changed on payments for coal they had dug; of salaries paid in company scrip honored only at the rapacious company store or the saloon; of incompetent super-intendents, corrupt pit bosses, and bullying mine guards. There were com-plaints of forced voting for company-approved candidates and of chasing "down the canyon" and blacklisting miners who had joined the union or had dared to ask for a check-weighman. Still others complained of being compelled to live in unsanitary shacks. "The complaints were many and various and embraced about everything in the catalogue," the zealously antiunion *Trinidad Chronicle-News* characterized the speeches. "Humorous and pathetic were these narratives," the paper added.[39]

No delegates were wavering after this emotional recital of perceived injustice. The speeches of the miners, many of them the oldest and most experienced among their cohorts, convinced everyone that they would have to fight to get what they wanted from the dogmatic and obstinate operators and that a fight was not only necessary but just. They were absolutely convinced that only through the union could they free themselves from servitude and achieve the future they had come to Colorado to find.[40] After hearing John Lawson's report of the Policy and Scale Committee, which included the strike resolution, the delegates voted unanimously to accept the report. In a fiery speech following the vote, Mother Jones again implored the miners to strike. "If it is to be slavery or strike," she exclaimed, "then I say strike—strike—until the last one of you drop into your graves." The miners' cause was that of industrial freedom, she shouted. "The operators must be given to understand that human life is to be regarded above property rights."[41]

Frank Hayes was the last to speak. He observed that the union had taken "every honorable means to bring about an adjustment" but had failed to obtain a conference with the operators, leaving them no other option but to strike: "I know we cannot lose in this great industrial struggle because our demands are just." He pledged to support the miners with "all the wealth and all the power of our great union. We will never leave this field until we have stricken the shackles from every mine worker." Their victory, which would not be long in coming, he concluded, would be "the greatest victory in the history of the organization."[42]

The official call for the strike was sent out the following day, September 17, notifying all mineworkers that the strike for improved conditions, better wages, and union recognition would begin on Tuesday, September 23, 1913. The policy committee also published the strike resolution the delegates had approved unanimously the previous evening. It contained seven demands: recognition of the union; a 10 percent wage increase for miners, coke oven workers, and all other classes of labor in and around the mines; an eight-hour workday for all classes of labor in and around the mines; pay for dead work; the appointment of a check-weighman at every mine; workers' right to trade at any store and to choose their own boarding places and doctors; and enforcement of Colorado's mining laws and the abolition of the guard system in the mining camps.[43]

Union leaders knew from the beginning that the demand for recognition of the union would not only be the hardest demand to achieve but also the rationale on which the operators would frame their refusal to meet with them. The public, they feared, would view the demand as arbitrary and unreasonable, thus siding with the operators. However, both union leaders and miners knew there would be no victory without recognition of the union as the bargaining agent between operators and miners, for, as they had in the past, companies would simply wait for the opportune moment to retract any concessions granted. Both miners and operators understood that union recognition was the only way to assure that the collective work-force had any real power.[44]

Despite the critical importance of this issue, on the eve of the strike call Frank Hayes tried to correct the impression left by the operators and their allies, particularly the Denver Chamber of Commerce, that union recognition was the only reason for the strike. Union recognition, he stressed, was only a minor issue. Contrary to what the operators were saying in "trying to deceive themselves and the public," the strike situation was largely about the improvement of conditions. "The miners are fighting for improved conditions, for rights granted them by the state law, and they are eager for a strike," he stated. "The fact [that] the men are willing and anxious to strike shows they are not getting their rights."[45]

Indeed, union leaders were having trouble preventing workers from leaving the mines and camps even before the strike call went out. The *Denver Express* reported on September 16 that the word "strike" and the miners' new strike song "are traveling like wildfire through the camps." The newspaper also recounted reports of men leaving their workplaces in anticipation of the event: "One hundred and seventy-five men laid down their tools at Valdez last night; all the miners have quit work at Tercio." Although unconfirmed, the paper observed that the report that 137 miners who walked out at the Victor-American mine at Delagua were being held prisoner in the camp by Baldwin-Felts gunmen had "aroused a storm of protest." Similar reports of miners held against their will in stockades in the northern district at Louisville and Superior reached John McLennan, president of District 15. At least they were not working, McLennan commented, "and I feel sure they will escape and join the men whose places they took three years ago."[46]

At the behest of conservatives in the union leadership, the policy committee had delayed the start of the strike until September 23 to give the union more time to prepare for the struggle ahead. The national leaders also knew that William B. Wilson, U.S. secretary of labor, had dispatched Ethelbert Stewart, chief clerk of the Bureau of Labor Statistics, to New York City for a personal conference with John D. Rockefeller Jr. to persuade the multimillionaire to intervene in the Colorado dispute in an effort to ward off a strike. Although union officials, particularly in Colorado, doubted that Stewart would be successful and had no illusions that the coal operators would change their minds and meet with them, they believed, nonetheless, that a delay in the walkout would generate even greater sympathy among the public. Both the union leaders and the coal operators were convinced that public opinion would play the decisive role in the coming conflict.[47]

The assumption that the operators would never concede to meet with union leaders was well-placed. The few days' delay between the time the strike was called and the time it went into effect gave Osgood and the leading operators more time to prepare for the strike, as he later explained to the Foster Congressional Committee: "[W]e called all of the operators that we could get together in a meeting and discussed the way we would handle the strike—the method of meeting strike conditions." The operators authorized the representatives of the state's three largest coal producers—Welborn of CF&I, Osgood of Victor-American, and David Brown of Rocky Mountain Fuel—to take the lead in all matters pertaining to the strike. Organized as the operators' policy committee, the three men reached a tacit understanding that they would meet jointly to formulate and carry out their course of action. Specifically, Osgood noted that the committee's main purposes were to create a unified message in meeting the public demand for information about the strike, prepare and put out advertisements, and coordinate testimony before public groups such as the Chamber of Commerce, newspaper editors, and the governor. As an example of their activities, Osgood revealed that he, Welborn, and Brown acted in conjunction in urging the governor to bring troops into the field to preserve law and order and protect their properties.[48]

From its inception, the three members of the policy committee met in Osgood's office almost daily during the early days of the strike. As the events of the strike unfolded, it became clear that the committee's main function was to implement the strikebreaking, union-busting strategy that had worked so well for the operators during the 1903–1904 strike. Except for the owners of two small companies in the northern district, the Colorado operators vowed to resist unionization and never to sign a contract with the UMWA. They were resolute in their determination to defeat the union, even if it meant withstanding a strike. The operators were buoyed by reports from their superintendents and spies that only 10 percent of the miners were union members and that a smaller number than that would actually go out on strike. The miners were so satisfied with their working conditions, LaMont Bowers reported to Rockefeller through Starr Murphy just four days before the strike began, that they would not join the union or heed the strike call. Those who did go on strike would, "after a few days when they find we are able to protect them, return to their work."[49] The other operators agreed that the strike would not last long.

There also were signs that the union leaders were weakening. Reports circulated that Lawson was ready to withdraw the union's demand for recognition if the operators conceded some small points, one of which was presumably to grant a conference with union leaders. This point was confirmed by Bowers, who admitted that by arranging such a meeting, the operators could have prevented the strike. The operators were unwilling to do so, he explained, for many believed the union officials, "anticipating being whipped," would have undertaken "to sneak out" if they could gain "an interview with the operators . . . thus boasting before the public that they have secured the principal point; namely, recognition of the union."[50]

"The operators' refusal to grant such a conference," George West wrote in 1915, "must be regarded as making them responsible for all the disasters that followed."[51] Commissioner Brake shared that opinion on the eve of the strike. The operators' intransigence in refusing to allow genuine collective bargaining and their outmoded antiunion policies and tactics contradicted the modern concept of industrial relations, he concluded.[52] Unfazed by criticism, the three operators on the policy committee remained adamantly opposed to granting any concessions, especially one that might give the impression of even token recognition of the union. Not one of the major operators expressed any interest in avoiding the strike. Instead, they were content to blame the strike on the union leaders. With $5 million in their treasury dedicated to fight the union, they were confident that complete victory would be theirs in the end. Equally defiant, the miners believed the only way they could achieve their rights and freedom was to strike.[53]

"The fight is on—a fight which as the operators have maintained may be 'to the finish,' or as head officials of the miners' organization have asserted may be a short battle crowned with a glorious victory," the *Trinidad Chronicle-News* reported the day of the strike call. With the opening of the Trinidad–Las Animas County Fair the same day, there was a strange mix of "pleasure seekers" passing in and out of the fairgrounds and hundreds of idle miners in the streets of Trinidad. With many miners already evicted from their homes, "The coal camps of the county were scenes of busy moving, families transferring their belongings to the tented cities of the unions." Knowing that a long winter of hardship and privation probably awaited them, the miners faced "the crisis like determined men, secure in the knowledge that behind them is a national organization with 150,000 members and untold wealth and that the power and wealth of this organization will see them through if the strike lasts ten years."[54] Thousands of other miners and their families joined these early strikers the next day when the real exodus from the coal mining camps began.

NOTES

1. Quoted in Stein and Taft, *Massacre at Ludlow,* 5.

2. McGovern and Guttridge, *Coalfield War,* 72; Fox, *United We Stand,* 152–153.

3. Beshoar, *Out of the Depths,* 6. Coryell was forced to leave the state after the shooting.

4. Papanikolas, *Buried Unsung,* 39, 66.

5. Ibid., 18–20; McGovern and Guttridge, *Coalfield War,* 74.

6. McGovern and Guttridge, *Coalfield War,* 75; Beshoar, *Out of the Depths,* 21–22; Fox, *United We Stand,* 153–154.

7. Beshoar, *Out of the Depths,* 38–41; McGovern and Guttridge, *Coalfield War,* 76–77.

8. McGovern and Guttridge, *Coalfield War,* 78.

9. Bowers to Starr Murphy, September 19, 1913, in CIR/FR 9: 8414–8415.

10. Information for this and the next paragraph is from McGovern and Guttridge, *Coalfield War,* 82–85; Beshoar, *Out of the Depths,* 43–47.

11. Quotations in Beshoar, *Out of the Depths,* 43–44.

12. Ibid., 44.

13. McGovern and Guttridge, *Coalfield War,* 84–85; Long, *Where the Sun Never Shines,* 266–267.

14. McGovern and Guttridge, *Coalfield War,* 85; Papanikolas, *Buried Unsung,* 68–69; Fox, *United We Stand,* 154.

15. Long, *Where the Sun Never Shines,* 268, 274.

16. Ibid., 265, based on interview with Livoda conducted by Eric Margolis, director of the Coal Project at the Institute of Behavioral Science, University of Colorado–Boulder, January 1975; Papanikolas, *Buried Unsung,* 66–67.

17. The Baldwin-Felts Agency was an accredited corporation with main offices in Roanoke, Virginia, and Bluefield, West Virginia. The agency was one of several private "detective agencies" like Pinkerton, W. J. Burns, and Waddell-Mahon that specialized in labor and industrial struggles. The Baldwin-Felts Agency came of age in the troubled coalfields of West Virginia in the early twentieth century.

18. West, *Report on the Colorado Strike,* 22. In Huerfano County alone, Sheriff Farr had deputized 326 men, many imported from other states, by September 1, 1913, three weeks before the strike was called.

19. Official quoted in CBLS, *Twelfth Biennial Report,* 32.

20. Long, *Where the Sun Never Shines,* 203; minister quoted in West, *Report on the Colorado Strike,* 78.

21. *United Mine Workers Journal* 24, no. 1 (July 24, 1913), in U.S. Congress, House, *Conditions in the Coal Mines of Colorado: Brief of the Coal Mining Operators* (Washington, D.C., 1914), 14; hereafter cited as *Brief of the Coal Mining Operators.*

22. Committee quoted in Beshoar, *Out of the Depths,* 49; Hayes quoted in McGovern and Guttridge, *Coalfield War,* 89.

23. Quoted in Beshoar, *Out of the Depths,* 48.

24. Ibid., 48–49; Andrews, "Road to Ludlow," 487, 493; *Denver Express*, September 19, 1913.

25. The tent colonies were Walsenburg, Aguilar, Rugby, Ludlow, Sopris, Piedmont, Segundo, and Tercio.

26. Osgood's testimony, SMM, 397–398; Welborn quoted in McGovern and Guttridge, *Coalfield War*, 90.

27. Osgood quoted in *Pueblo Star-Journal*, November 16, 1913.

28. Ibid.

29. Brake quoted in CBLS, *Fourteenth Biennial Report*, 165–166; Hayes quoted in McGovern and Guttridge, *Coalfield War*, 94.

30. In West, *Report on the Colorado Strike*, 29–30.

31. "An Appeal to All Mine Workers in District 15," September 5, 1913, in CIR/FR 8: 7067.

32. Quotations in West, *Report on the Colorado Strike*, 30; McGovern and Guttridge, *Coalfield War*, 97.

33. Osgood quoted in *Rocky Mountain News*, September 21, 1913.

34. *Denver Express*, September 15, 1913; *Trinidad Chronicle-News*, September 15, 1913. "The Colorado Strike Song" was supposedly penned by Frank Hayes and set to the tune of the old Civil War hymn, "The Battle Cry of Freedom," a song based on the free labor ideology of the Civil War and the liberationist promise of battle (Andrews, "Road to Ludlow," 479).

35. *Denver Express*, September 15, 1913.

36. Quotation in Andrews, "Road to Ludlow," 481.

37. McLennan quoted in *Trinidad Chronicle-News*, September 15, 1913.

38. "Hayes Predicts Strike Victory," *Rocky Mountain News*, September 15, 1913.

39. *Trinidad Chronicle-News*, September 16, 1913; Andrews, "Road to Ludlow," 481–482; McGovern and Guttridge, *Coalfield War*, 101. The *Trinidad Chronicle-News* was an antiunion paper owned by Judge Jesse Northcutt, a CF&I attorney.

40. Andrews, "Road to Ludlow," 482.

41. Mother Jones quoted in *Trinidad Chronicle-News*, September 17, 1913.

42. Hayes quoted in ibid.

43. McGovern and Guttridge, *Coalfield War*, 102.

44. Long, *Where the Sun Never Shines*, 270.

45. Hayes quoted in *Denver Express*, September 22, 1913.

46. Ibid., September 16, 23 (McLennan quote), 1913. Deputy Labor Commissioner Brake was in the Trinidad field the day the strike began. He verified some of the reports of miners being held in camp against their will: "I found practically these conditions of detaining people by force . . . prevailing in all the strike districts dominated by the coal operators" (CBLS, *Fourteenth Biennial Report*, 166).

47. McGovern and Guttridge, *Coalfield War*, 97–98.

48. Osgood's testimony, SMM, 398, 422, 446, 479.

49. Bowers to Starr Murphy, September 19, 1913, in CIR/FR 9: 8414–8416.

50. Ibid., 8416.

51. West, *Report on the Colorado Strike*, 86.

52. *Rocky Mountain News,* September 17, 1913.

53. McGovern, "Colorado Strike," 151. Both the *Rocky Mountain News*, September 23, 1913, and the *Denver Express*, September 24, 1913, refer to the operators' strike fund.

54. *Trinidad Chronicle-News*, September 23, 1913. The *Rocky Mountain News* reported that 3,000 men quit work in Las Animas County on September 22, the day before the strike officially began.

Tents, Arms, and a Tumult Threatened

Frank Hayes described September 23, 1913, as the most miserable day he had ever known. On that day, the first day of the strike, thousands of miners and their families who had been evicted from their homes made their way in a freezing rain that later turned to sleet and snow to tent colonies set up for them by the United Mine Workers of America (UMWA). They proceeded to "White City" near Ludlow, to "Union Town" at Pictou, or to one of six other tent colonies in southern Colorado. Hundreds of strikers moved slowly down the muddy roads from Berwind, Tabasco, Hastings, Delagua, and Cedar Hill toward the tent colony set up near Ludlow, a small rail junction consisting of a depot, a few saloons, and a mercantile store about twelve miles north of Trinidad.[1]

Ludlow became the largest and subsequently the most famous of the eight tent colonies established during the early days of the strike in 1913. Situated at the openings of Delagua and Berwind canyons, where some of the largest and most important Colorado Fuel and Iron (CF&I) and Victor-American Fuel Company mines were located, the tent colony was perfectly placed to allow the strikers to interfere with the traffic to and from the mines in both canyons and to establish picket lines against the trainloads of strikebreakers—"scabs," as the strikers called them—brought in by the mine companies. Containing the most militant of the strikers from the Victor-American camps of Hastings and Delagua and the CF&I Berwind and Tabasco camps, the Ludlow tent colony became the flash point in the struggle between the strikers and their families on the one side and the agents of the coal corporations—mine guards, elements of the state militia, and Baldwin-Felts gunmen—on the other.[2]

The day of misery recalled by Hayes marked the beginning of one of the greatest industrial struggles in U.S. history. Don MacGregor of the *Denver Express* described in moving detail the exodus of the striking miners and their families. "It rained all day long," his somber account of the trek began. "A driving, searching rain, in the saddle of a bitterly cold wind. Snow followed under cover of night's blackness. There never was a more pitiful sight than the exodus of those miners fortunate enough to get wagons for their household goods and families. . . . The faces of the men were set heavy with foreboding; the faces of the women stolid with the memory of suffering that had gone before and the sure knowledge of more to come; the faces of the children were twisted in misery."[3]

The wagons, MacGregor reported, were all the same. On one, a "bewildered, woebegone family" was perched atop piles of furniture.

> And the furniture! What a mockery of the state's boasted riches! What a commentary on the talk of the prosperity of the miners of Colorado! Prosperity! Little piles of rickety chairs! Little piles of miserable looking straw bedding! Little piles of kitchen utensils! . . . Prosperity! With never a single article even approaching luxury, save, once in a score of wagons, a cheap, gaily painted gramophone! With never a bookcase! With never a book! . . . And these were the contents of the homes of the miners whom the mine owners have called prosperous and contented![4]

Recounting the scene in a less dramatic way, George West wrote: "No more eloquent proof could be given of the intense discontent of the miners and their families, and of their determination to endure any hardship rather than remain at work under existing conditions."[5]

The strikers and their families who reached the Ludlow site found the camp far from complete. A shipment of 1,000 tents from West Virginia had not yet arrived, forcing the homeless refugees to spend several more days and nights in makeshift shelters or huddled beneath wagons loaded with their rain-soaked belongings. The arrival of the tents, as well as of Frank Hayes and John Lawson, on September 27 lifted the spirits of the new camp residents, who immediately set to work erecting their tent city. The work was completed in a few days. The tents were pitched on timbered floors. Heavy Excelsior stoves were installed and furniture arranged in each tent. The union provided coal for the stoves and supplied water in barrels. The colonists dug sanitary trenches and storage pits and laid out a baseball diamond. A large community tent, the "Big Tent," was set up in the center of the camp to serve numerous functions: as a school, church, local headquarters, commissary, communal workspace, and public meeting place. A speaker's platform surrounded by a large parade ground was erected near the community tent. American flags, ceremoniously raised and lowered each day, flew prominently over the Big Tent and the parade ground, symbolizing the strikers' faith in the American promise of democracy and freedom.[6]

The Ludlow tent colony soon became an elaborately organized village of 1,200–1,300 inhabitants who spoke a total of twenty-four languages. A visiting journalist was amazed at how systematically the colony was arranged. John Lawson assumed the position of camp boss and was assisted by Louis Tikas, the Greek organizer, who became resident camp leader. Lawson and Tikas appointed committees to carry out such varied tasks as cleaning, guard duty, emergency duty, and picketing. The camp had its own police officers, head musician (Tony Gorci), and official greeter-singer (Mary Thomas).[7]

Once settled, most colonists quickly adapted to their new surroundings. With the union providing the necessities of life—including strike pay of three dollars per week for each miner, a dollar a week for his wife, and fifty cents per child—life became tolerable in the colony, even preferable for many to life in the coal camps. "[W]e were kind of happy you know, we were getting $3 a week, for food, and we were making it," Victor Bazanelle, one of the miners, recalled. "Potatoes, sometimes a little meat. A fella could live on $6 a month." As the days passed, the colony became a close-knit multiethnic community, "just like a big family."[8] The hardships of the severe winter, one of the worst in recorded history, and intimidation from their adversaries brought the nationalities together. Solidarity trumped racial and ethnic divisions. The Ludlow experience during the strike taught people from many different cultural and ethnic backgrounds that, despite their differences, they possessed a common humanity and a common interest in

Louis Tikas and John Lawson (center, next to Tikas). Courtesy, Colorado Historical Society, Military-Strikes-Ludlow-Dold Collection, ID no. 10025637.

the strike's success. When visiting the colony the following spring, state senator Helen Ring Robinson stated that she "saw the true melting pot at Ludlow."[9]

According to oral history, the Ludlow colonists not only got along with one another but they actually enjoyed themselves. The women cared for the children and shared other domestic chores. The men played baseball and bolo. Music was a special pleasure enjoyed by many camp inhabitants. Union organizer Mike Livoda listened to music played on accordions, violins, mouth harps, guitars, and tambarizzas as he walked through the community at night. "I used to get out and listen [to] the songs," he recounted many years later. He heard "Asian music, Italian music, Spanish-American music, American music." From time to time, he added, "they put on a dance, they used to polka. You just begin to feel like that even though they're out on strike, they're happy, because they're singing and enjoying themselves." The regular dances in the big tent became "a wedding of the races."[10]

The outward appearances of congeniality prompted one *Denver Express* reporter to comment on the role women played in the camp. According to the reporter, "The spirit of women seems more determined than [that of] men." The miners' wives "with babies in arms" were noticeable at all camp meetings. Mother Jones, a compelling role model, implored the women "to win the fight because their lazy, hulking men had not fight enough in them."[11] The women not only took charge of entertainment in the Ludlow camp by serving coffee and cake at social occasions, among other things, but they also took up picketing. They followed the leadership of the union and of their husbands, but they also formed antagonistic feelings toward the coal companies based on their own observations and experiences.[12] Without women's strong devotion to their families and to the strikers' cause, the transition from the coal camps to the tent colonies would have been impossible.

Yet beneath the surface of daily life, the tensions of the strike were simmering, and the colonists would soon be roused to action. In the coming weeks, Ludlow, more than the other tent colonies, would not only represent a growing solidarity among previously disparate and segregated people but would also display "the outward sign of civil war, red and bloody, with its hates and its assassinations, its woes and its suffering."[13]

The mass exodus of coal people from the mining camps caught the operators by surprise. From their detectives, guards, and spies in the field, they had concluded that only an insignificant fraction of the miners, probably less than 10 percent, would obey the strike call. Shortly before the strike, the Victor-American Fuel Company published the results of a poll taken at four of its camps—Gray Creek, Bowen, Hastings, and Delagua—which showed that 79 percent of the men employed in the mines opposed calling a strike. The report stressed that the men had voluntarily recorded their vote and had not been pressured by the company. Even after the strike began, Frank E. Gove, the company's attorney and counsel for the operators' policy committee, stated that less than 30 percent of the workforce had "taken out their tools" from the mines and asserted that most of them had been forced to leave their jobs by union terrorism or intimidation.[14]

Contrary to the operators' reports, union records indicated that 11,232 of the state's 13,980 coalminers—9,000 of them from the southern district— were on strike at the end of September. Even the coal company–friendly *Trinidad Chronicle-News* put the number of striking miners at 85 percent of the workforce, an estimate much closer to the union's claim than to that of the operators. Not all the strikers went to the tent colonies. It was reported that thousands either went back to their native countries or, in the case of the best miners, left the strike zone to take jobs the UMWA procured for them in unionized fields in Pennsylvania, Wyoming, or West Virginia.[15] Still others, particularly the less skilled laborers, joined the westward labor migration. Nonetheless, more than 20,000 strikers and their families remained in Colorado, many filling the eight tent colonies in southern Colorado.[16]

Company officials were deceived about the extent of union support in their mines by their own intimidation policies and antiunion activities, which forced miners to hide their union sympathies for fear of being "sent down the canyon." Although company spokesmen continued to argue that the miners had been terrorized into joining the ranks of the union strikers, the mass departure of miners from the mines undercut the operators' portrayal of a highly paid and contented workforce.[17] Belied by the numbers of miners on strike and the strikers' statements in support of the union, coal company spokesmen had to crank up the propaganda machinery to convince the public that their view of the situation was correct. It was a monumental task, for it defied logic to assert that a relatively small number of union organizers could have forced thousands of miners to give up their homes and jobs to live with their families in tent colonies on a meager union allowance unless they were an oppressed people with long-standing grievances.[18]

Frank Gove, John Osgood's principal lawyer, was the first person assigned the propaganda task. Shortly after the strike began, the operators' policy committee appointed him to draft a public statement that presented the industry's point of view concerning the strike. The statement was first sent to the editors of newspapers in the state and later, at the suggestion of several of the editors, to a number of individuals they believed would be interested in its "indisputable facts." Gove's recital became the operators' apology, and the main arguments contained therein were repeated in every pro-industry statement and publication during the remainder of the strike and beyond.[19]

Gove began by stressing that no substantial differences had existed between the mine owners and their employees prior to the calling of the strike and that the only reason for the strike was the union's determination to compel the mine owners to recognize the union and sign a contract that required them to employ only union men in and about the coalmines. He contended that all union demands other than for recognition were nothing more than window dressing for "effect upon the public." These new demands, Gove conceded, "properly appeal, with some force, to all right-thinking men who are not definitely advised of the facts." Nonetheless, he stated emphatically, none of them were justified.

Gove recited all the arguments Osgood and the other operators had previously made: that the wage increase had already been granted in April 1912; that the demands for a semimonthly payday, an eight-hour workday, and a check-weighman had been granted; and that the rights of miners to trade and board where they pleased were not and had never been denied. The demand for better working conditions in the mines was, as Gove described it, "an indefinite and all-inclusive demand," but he believed the mine owners and the miners shared the hope that better conditions would come with time. "Coal mining," he wrote, "is universally recognized as a hazardous and dangerous business—hazardous for the mine owner and dangerous for the miner. But the owner of a coal property is neither a brute nor a fool. He will not knowingly subject his property to destruction nor his men to unnecessary danger. Selfish interests alone dictate a contrary policy." The public, he cautioned, should wait to see the effects of the new law on mine safety "before giving too much heed to careless criticism of existing operating methods affecting the welfare of the miners and the employers alike."

Finally, Gove justified the owners' employment of armed mine guards to protect their properties and the safety of miners who continued to work in the mines. The strikers' aggressive actions and acts of violence, he contended, forced the use of armed guards: "If the striking miners will keep away from the property of others, they need fear no molestation. If they insist upon trespassing upon private ground, they must expect to be halted on their way."[20]

The operators voiced their views of the strike in even more strident language in the legal brief prepared for the Foster Congressional Committee, as well as in other private and public statements. In their brief they portrayed the conflict as "an armed insurrection against the sovereign authority of the State of Colorado" rather than a strike. It was, they claimed, "conceived, planned, financed, managed, and directed by the officers and leaders of the United Mine Workers of America" and pursued by them "with a persistency and villainy" in a "most insidious and reprehensible" way.[21] It was a war waged against the institution of private property, which, Osgood and the operators argued, was the foundation of all civilized government. In their view, the struggle in Colorado was part of the larger national labor revolution, and they believed they had the moral duty to oppose violence with violence to defend their property and free their employees from the union's tyranny. In their judgment, they deserved the public's support and gratitude for fighting this battle to save Colorado from the socialists, anarchists, and officials of the UMWA.[22]

Throughout the strike, Osgood, Jesse Welborn, and David Brown adamantly held to the position that the strike should not be settled by arbitration or negotiation with the strike leaders, whom they regarded as criminals morally and legally responsible for every murder and crime committed in support of the strike. Instead, they believed state authorities should arrest and prosecute the strike leaders for these crimes. Only in this way, they stressed, could the strike be settled effectively and the labor revolution suppressed in Colorado.

With these views, the three major members of the operators' policy committee doomed any chance for mediation of the Colorado conflict. Ethelbert Stewart, chief clerk of the U.S. Bureau of Labor Statistics, learned this during his trip to Colorado in late September–early October 1913 to confer with the coal executives in an endeavor to end the strike. Although Bowers immediately rebuffed his request for a meeting, Stewart remained in Colorado for several days to collect information. He read both sides' written statements and interviewed operators, miners, state labor officials, and Governor Ammons. On the night of October 9, Ammons, at Stewart's request, invited Osgood, Welborn, and Brown to meet with Stewart in the governor's office. The operators had only one reason to come to the meeting, Osgood explained to the Foster Congressional Committee in 1914:

> We told him [Stewart] that we had come to meet him with the desire to give him all the information that he wished about the strike from our point of view. He answered that he was not an investigator, that he was a mediator, and that he didn't want any information. He had no proposition of mediation. We asked him if he felt that he was a disinterested party, and he practically declined to answer. He said that he would simply report to his superior that there should be a congressional investigation of the strike.[23]

Osgood's account did not reflect the operators' anger when Stewart informed them that he was only interested in suggestions for a settlement and asked them if they would meet with union officials informally or propose an alternative. The operators' negative response and their hostility toward him convinced Stewart that he could not resolve a matter that was in essence "a strike of the twentieth century against the tenth century mental attitude, as to the industrial relations that should obtain between employers and employees." Stewart told Secretary William B. Wilson in a letter that the "situation here is very tense, and unyielding. Governor Ammons says he could have got the miners everything they asked for except recognition of the union. This is the essence of the struggle, I fear, and you know what an ugly problem it presents."[24] Frustrated, he returned to Washington without attempting further mediation between the mine owners and the unionists.

LaMont Bowers assured John D. Rockefeller Jr. that the operators, "working in perfect harmony," had done the right thing in rebuffing Stewart, who, Bowers commented, "came here under false colors" and had listened only to those who were "at the bottom of this strike." CF&I officials, he proclaimed, would stand by their decision to combat the union "until our bones were bleached as white as [the] chalk in these Rocky Mountains. We are right from every standpoint, and . . . we shall never recede an inch from the stand we have taken." Bowers happily reported that the other leading operators, buoyed by the knowledge that Rockefeller was unflinching in his support of their stand against the union, were committed to fight "this unjust, uncalled-for, and iniquitous strike."[25]

Although Bowers painted an optimistic picture of the strike situation to Rockefeller, he cautioned that it would take resolute action to drive the "agitators" out of the state. It had now been proven beyond doubt, he observed, that the union was supplying Winchester rifles, revolvers, and ammunition in large quantities to the "sluggers" it had brought into the field from other states and to the "bloodthirsty" Greeks, who had just returned from the "Turkish" war.[26] Bowers did not tell Rockefeller that CF&I and other coal companies were also purchasing large quantities of weapons and ammunition to arm their augmented force of mine guards. During the strike, CF&I alone spent $25,000 to $30,000 for guns and ammunition to arm its mine guards and sheriff's deputies, compared to the UMWA's total expenditure of $7,500 for arms and ammunition.[27] The Victor-American and Rocky Mountain Fuel companies also contributed to the purchase of arms, including eight machine guns. That purchase was necessary, Osgood told the Foster Congressional Committee, to protect mine property and personnel. "[W]hen we were unable to get protection from the sheriff and when the governor refused to order out the troops," he said, "then we ordered the machine guns, and I want to take all the responsibility coming to me for my part." He emphatically stated that the guns were purchased for defensive purposes. "They were not meant to kill anybody," he asserted, but were intended solely "to protect our property, and we believed that it was the most effective way to give us defense. . . . Those guns were not used anywhere except as the sheriff used them, and if the strikers had not come to our boundaries they would never have gotten in contact with them."[28]

Osgood's testimony did not square with the historical record. Even before the guns were turned over to the state militia, mine guards and Baldwin-Felts agents employed by the companies frequently used the machine guns

The "Death Special." Courtesy, Denver Public Library, Western History Collection, call no. X-60380.

purchased by CF&I and Victor-American in attacks on the tent colonies. A machine gun was mounted in the rear of the "Death Special," an early version of an armored car constructed at the CF&I steelworks in Pueblo. The tent colonists were filled with awe and apprehension, as was intended, at the sight of the Death Special with its mounted machine gun as it approached their camps.

With or without the Death Special, armed sheriff's deputies and mine guards engaged in pitched battles with strikers at or around the Ludlow and Forbes tent colonies on several occasions. During the afternoon and early evening of October 7, 1913, to cite one incident, seventeen mounted mine guards exchanged gunfire with strikers at Ludlow. Although each side accused the other of starting the firefight, the battle appeared to be a well-planned act of provocation on the part of mine guards employed by the coal operators.

The attacks convinced union leaders that it was the coal companies' policy to incite the strikers to fight. While trying to keep the strikers under control, John Lawson initiated measures to protect the Ludlow colony. He organized the colony along military lines and appointed a leader for each of the twenty-one ethnic groups. He posted guards on a twenty-four-hour basis. Breastworks were constructed around the colony, and pits were dug under most of the tents to provide shelter for women and children in case of an attack. The union leaders also wrote letters to the coal operators and Governor Ammons protesting the companies' purchase and deployment of machine guns in the strike zone. They received no replies. The operators wrote a letter to the governor, however, in which they blamed the strikers for the violence and cited recent incidents as justification for their refusal to acknowledge the union leaders. They advocated moving the Ludlow tent colony farther from the mines and deporting Mother Jones from Colorado as ways to restore peace.[29]

On October 17, ten days after the skirmish at Ludlow, a dozen deputies arrived at the Forbes tent colony to disarm anyone illegally possessing weapons. A series of nighttime sniping attacks had forced the removal of women and children from the main part of the colony. There is no impartial account of what happened, but both sides began shooting. The arrival of the Death Special with its machine gun firing into the camp forced the defenders to take refuge in an arroyo nearby. Around 600 rounds from the machine gun riddled the canvas tents, broke crockery, and shattered furniture. A Slav striker was killed and a mine guard was wounded. An eighteen-year-old boy with nine wounds in his legs lay sprawled on the ground unattended all afternoon in drenching rain until he could be rescued. The Foster Congressional Committee judged the attack on the Forbes camp by armed guards using machine guns as "unjustifiable from any standpoint."[30]

The arrival of the Death Special in the strike zone marked the high point in the arms race between mine guards and Baldwin-Felts detectives sponsored by the coal operators on the one side and the strikers armed by the UMWA on the other. A feeling of terror as well as an unconditional hatred for the mine guards and the Baldwin-Felts agents began to pervade the tent colonies following the attack at Forbes. "What if machine guns were turned on Ludlow with its 150 women and 300 children?" asked Don MacGregor, reporter and soon-to-be comrade of the strikers. "The strikers swore by their various gods that neither armored automobile nor force of deputies would ever be permitted near enough Ludlow to allow this to happen." It seemed to Ethelbert Stewart that "the only language common to all, and which all understand in Southern Colorado, is the voice of the gun."[31]

The coal operators used the Ludlow and Forbes incidents—described by Bowers as unprovoked attacks by outside "agitators, armed sluggers, and bloodthirsty, murderous Greeks" on innocent mine guards and sheriff's deputies—to intensify their pressure on Governor Ammons to send the National Guard into the strike field.[32] From the beginning of the strike, the operators were convinced that they could co-opt Ammons, even though he was a Democrat and had been elected with union support, as they had Governor James Peabody in 1903 through the same combination of financial support, political dealing, and gentlemanly cooperation. Ammons was a man of average intelligence and limited resourcefulness whom veteran observers of Colorado politics described as weak-kneed and irresolute during times of crisis. Eager to be seen as fair to everybody, he was unwilling at the start of the strike to take any action that would force the union and coal operators to resolve their dispute. Instead, he sought only to make both sides comply with state statutes covering everything from the importation of strikebreakers to the operations and conditions of the workplace.[33] His failure to take more resolute action at the beginning helped turn the conflict into a prolonged and violent struggle between operators and miners in the southern Colorado coalfields.

In a formal statement issued two days after the strike began, Ammons warned both sides that he would not tolerate disorder. He still insisted that local authorities could handle the situation; but if they were unable to do so, he added, "the state will intervene and take any steps that may appear to be necessary to protect life and property, prevent intimidation and abuse of all kinds, and restore and enforce order and law." Although Ammons hoped to assuage the miners' apprehension over the possible dispatch of state troops to the strike zone, his statement had the opposite effect. The governor's comments that he would not hesitate to use National Guard troops both to prevent rioting if the operators attempted to import strikebreakers and "to put an end to the inflammatory statements of Mother Jones" convinced the strikers that sooner or later he would cave in to the operators' demand to send the militia into the strike zone in support of their campaign to break the strike and crush the union. The operators reached the same conclusion. They believed the "cowboy" governor would soon be in their pocket.[34]

LaMont Bowers certainly thought so. "We have here a pin-head governor who could put the troops into the territory and end the strike in twenty-four hours," Bowers wrote on October 10, 1913.[35] Shortly after the beginning of the strike, the operators through one of their attorneys, Judge Jesse G. Northcutt, owner of the *Trinidad Chronicle-News,* circulated a petition among Trinidad merchants calling for mobilization of the militia. The sheriffs of Las Animas and Huerfano counties as well as other local officials, many of them beholden to the coal companies, joined the chorus for militia intervention. The mayor of Trinidad, M. T. Dunlavy, was not one of them.

Governor Elias Ammons. Courtesy, Denver Public Library, Western History Collection, call no. Z-8805.

"We can handle the situation as far as Trinidad is concerned," he told the governor in late September. "At Ludlow, however, where the strikers are gathering in a great camp, I fear there may be trouble," he added. He was certain that trouble would come when "the operators start up their mines again with the strike-breakers they are constantly importing." Then, he lamented, the governor would have to send in the militia.[36]

The operators were relentless in their campaign to force the governor's hand. "There probably has never been such pressure brought to bear upon the governor of this state by the strongest men in it, as has been brought to bear upon Governor Ammons," Bowers boasted to John Rockefeller Jr.. Bowers noted that the operators had secured the cooperation of the Chamber of Commerce, the real-estate exchange, other business people, and fourteen newspaper editors who have visited "our hesitating governor" to urge him "to drive the vicious agitators from the state." Bowers then underscored the most important point: "We have been able to secure the cooperation of all the banks in the city, who have had three or four conferences with our little cowboy governor, agreeing to back the state and lend it all the funds necessary to maintain the militia and afford ample protection."[37]

That financial arrangement removed one of the major obstacles the governor had cited as contributing to his hesitation to send the National Guard into the strike zone—that no state funds were available for military intervention. Osgood played a key and perhaps the most important role in arranging the agreement. The details of the way the military campaign was ultimately financed can be ascertained in Osgood's testimony before the Foster Congressional Committee.

Governor Ammons, Osgood testified, had decided that the only way to pay for the troops in the field was to issue certificates of indebtedness. Osgood told the governor that the operators were willing to assist in financing the campaign by carrying the certificates. The governor demurred. Under the circumstances, he responded, it was not proper to permit the operators to do anything to help finance the militia. Instead, he had decided to ask the Clearing House Association if it would cash the warrants to a specified amount. Although the governor refused to accept any financial assistance from the operators, Osgood made it clear that he was ready to do his part to carry the certificates of indebtedness until the Colorado General Assembly appropriated the money for the campaign.[38]

With Osgood's assistance, the matter was resolved as the governor proposed. The Clearing House Association's agreement to finance the certificates of indebtedness in the amount of $250,000, with banks in Denver, Colorado Springs, and Pueblo furnishing most of the money, obviated the operators' need to finance the military campaign directly. Although Osgood played down his involvement in the negotiations with the association before the Foster Congressional Committee, he was at the center of the matter and helped consummate the arrangement the governor wanted. The association needed little urging, Osgood noted, for it, as well as the banks that financed the certificates of indebtedness, considered it "purely and simply a public spirited matter on their [the association's] part to furnish this money and carry these certificates." Therefore, Osgood added, the operators did not have to make any arrangement with the banks "to take care of them in this matter." Everyone involved in the transactions assumed that the state would eventually appropriate the money to compensate the banks, plus 4 percent interest.[39]

Even with the funds guaranteed, Ammons, still hoping the strike could be settled, was not yet ready to send the militia troops into the strike zone. His hesitancy stirred the operators' anger to a fever pitch by late October. *Metropolitan Magazine* reported that newspaper reporters at the state capitol overheard a group of operators reviling Ammons: "You God damned coward," they said. "We are not going to stand for this much longer. You have got to do something, and do it quick, or we'll get you!" Ammons responded, "I'm doing it as fast as I can."[40]

After receiving conflicting reports about the need for troops, Ammons decided to travel to Trinidad to inspect conditions in the strike zone for himself. On the morning of October 21, the day of the governor's arrival, 4,000 strikers and their families assembled in Trinidad to demonstrate against bringing the militia to the southern coalfields. Don MacGregor of the *Denver Express* reported that the miners believed the militia would help the mine guards break the strike, as they had done in 1904: "[T]hey would do as the deputies had done and raze their [strikers'] tent colonies, tear them from their families, load them on trains and dump them on the prairies of Kansas, Texas and New Mexico, threatening them with death if they ever returned to Colorado."[41]

That afternoon, strikers, women, and children led by Mother Jones marched from union headquarters in Trinidad to the governor's hotel, the Cardenas, singing union songs and carrying large banners that read WE REPRESENT CFI SLAVES; WE WILL NOT BE WHIPPED INTO CITIZENSHIP BY THE SHERIFF AND GATLING GUNS; SOME OF MOTHER JONES'S CHILDREN; and, more pointedly for the governor, THE DEMOCRATIC PARTY IS ON TRIAL. A band followed by hundreds of women carrying small babies, women with baby buggies, and toddling youngsters barely able to keep up followed Mother Jones at the front of the parade. More than a thousand coalminers, many of them carrying children, marched behind the women. When the marchers reached the Cardenas, Mother Jones shouted to the governor, who was still in his room, that the women wanted to see him. Refusing to meet Mother Jones and the delegation outside, Ammons descended only as far as the hotel lobby. There he was met by John Lawson and John McLennan representing the union and by E. H. Weitzel, CF&I's fuel manager, and other coal company officials, who quickly ushered him out of the hotel to begin his tour of the region.[42] To his relief, he had avoided a direct confrontation with Mother Jones and the crowd.

All was peaceful during the governor's two-day automobile tour of the region from Trinidad to Walsenburg. The only real incident was an embarrassing one. Near the end of his tour, the governor and his party were stopped by an armed mine guard on a public highway at the gates of the Victor-American Ravenwood mine. The guard refused to allow the party to enter the property until the mine superintendent could verify the governor's identity. Ammons, pressed for time, declined to wait. He departed for Denver soon after the incident, still undecided about calling out the militia. He stated to the press that he had "found a strong sentiment that the situation is serious and that something should be done, but a variance of opinion as to the best methods of procedure."[43] Edward Doyle had offered a suggestion to the governor: "Why don't you throw Welborn, Osgood, Brown, McLennan, Lawson, and myself in jail and keep us there until we can agree to come out and sit down in a conference like gentlemen?"[44] Ammons's vacillation also displeased the operators. It seemed that only another wave of violence would persuade the governor to do their bidding.

Violence was bound to occur when two armed bodies of men, between whom an inplacable hatred existed, faced one another. The strikers had erected their main tent colonies near the mines or at the entrances of canyons leading to the mines to prevent strikebreakers from entering them. It was inevitable that the strikers would clash with the mine guards who had the duty of protecting workers still on the job and bringing in strikebreakers to fill the ranks depleted by the strike. Regarding the guards as professional fighters hired by the companies to defeat and subjugate them, the strikers developed a desperate hatred of them. For their part, the hired guns and desperados from out of state who served the operators had developed a hatred for miners through their participation in a series of labor conflicts throughout the country. "There was war between the two," John Fitch stated in an article in *The Survey*, "and neither side waited passively to be attacked." Nor could either side claim innocence as the violence escalated.[45]

The large contingency of Greeks, harboring deep resentments of their own, made Ludlow the most volatile of the strikers' tent colonies. The Greeks lived in their own section of the camp. As the last major ethnic group to arrive in the coalfields of southern Colorado, they suffered from rampant discrimination. As a result of their bitter experiences, they strove for self-respect. They had their own code of behavior, their *philotimo*—love of honor—and they were quick to turn their sense of grievance into action to seek revenge for any perceived or real slight.[46] On August 28, 1913, less than a month before the beginning of the strike, Louis Tikas, the Greek leader, described the spirit of his 350 countrymen in the southern district: "They are ready at any time unless conditions improve to engage in an industrial war and to fight, just as their fathers and brothers in the fatherland have fought the Turks until their freedom has been obtained, so these men are ready even at the sacrifice of their lives to fight until their industrial freedom has been obtained."[47]

In the battles ahead against the mine guards and the militia, a legend grew up around the Greeks—that they formed a little Balkan army among the strikers that was armed, efficient, and ruthless. Much of the trouble and violence that occurred, especially around Ludlow, was blamed on the

Greeks who refused to give up their guns. They believed they were fighting a just war against the hated mine guards, who overtly expressed their determination to put down the "inferior foreigners."

Karl "Monte" Linderfelt, the most notorious company man on the field of battle, best expressed the attitude of those who believed they were entrusted with the duty of suppressing the strikers' insurrection. Among the mine guards, he was the most hated by residents of the Ludlow tent colony. Asked about him years later, Mike Livoda responded: "Well, he was a son of a bitch. A man that if you don't believe and do like he does, he thinks you ought to be dead."[48] This cruel, mean, swaggering, blustering man, as Barron Beshoar noted, was a rare combination of bully and bulldog. Later, as a lieutenant in the Colorado National Guard, he set out to defend the state against "agitators, wops, and rednecks."[49] Under his leadership, the mine guards intensified their efforts to intimidate and harass the strikers.

Governor Ammons's departure from the strike district served as a signal for the mine guards and sheriff's deputies to adopt a more aggressive policy against the strikers. The purpose of the campaign was clear: to plunge the strike district into a state of chaos and violence. The sheriffs of the two southern counties deputized scores of mine guards and increased their presence at key locations near the tent colonies. "In the earlier period of violence," John Fitch stated, "guards and deputy sheriffs went hunting for strikers and . . . fired on them in cold blood."[50] This seemed to be the case in Walsenburg on October 24 when mine guards, commissioned as deputies, fired into a crowd of angry protestors—including women and children—killing three strikers. Evidence presented in the report prepared by the Commission on Industrial Relations indicated that there was no provocation for the shooting and that the guards were likely under the influence of alcohol.[51] The violent act in Walsenburg precipitated a three-day war in the Ludlow vicinity as the strikers sought revenge and acted to defend themselves against anticipated attacks on their tent colony.

News of the Walsenburg incident, according to Don MacGregor, "set the tent colony to seething." The strikers believed the mine guards planned to wipe them out completely. Rumors fed their fears, throwing "the entire colony into the wildest excitement. . . . Hysterical women demanded that their men take steps to protect them." The men took the women and children to the arroyo north of the colony in anticipation of the coming of the deputies and mine guards: "There was despairing talk of cleaning out the two canyons, of killing every mine guard in them."[52] The mine guards and deputies did not come that night. The next morning the tent people, tired, cold, and still frightened, returned to their makeshift homes.

Fighting between armed strikers and a detachment of twenty guards and deputies under the command of Karl Linderfelt broke out the following afternoon and continued the next day, Sunday, October 26. Driven in part by the desire to avenge the Walsenburg killings and in part by determination to prevent what they feared most—an attack on their tent colony—heavily armed Ludlow strikers set out to lay siege to the important mines at Hastings, Delagua, Berwind, and Tabasco. They first seized and burned down the section house south of Ludlow that Linderfelt and his troops had vacated the night before. The strikers then advanced along Berwind Canyon toward CF&I's Berwind and Tabasco mines. Once in their positions overlooking the camps, the strikers kept up a barrage of rifle fire into the buildings below.[53]

Informed of the attack on his company's mine property, Welborn, in the midst of heated discussions with the governor, urged Albert Felts of the Baldwin-Felts Agency to rush to Trinidad to organize a relief force for the besieged properties. In the superintendent's office at Tabasco, where he had set up headquarters after leaving Ludlow, Linderfelt sent telegrams to Adjutant General John Chase, commander of the National Guard, in which he described a desperate situation. He urged the general to send state troops to the troubled area as quickly as possible. One telegram read: "There has been a continuous battle for 40 hours. We have no expectation of ever receiving any help from Sheriff [James] Gresham [sic]. Too damned much politics to do anything from Trinidad. We must have ammunition and high-power rifles to hold this place and protect women and children. The only solution is troops, and at once."[54] The situation was hardly desperate, but Linderfelt knew the strikers had played into the coal operators' hands at last, and he seized the opportunity to take advantage of it.

Unable to send state troops without the governor's approval, General Chase could only assure Linderfelt that the force mustered by Albert Felts and Sheriff Grisham of about fifty deputies and company guards, including thirty-six newly deputized coal company guards sent from Walsenburg to Trinidad, would soon arrive in Berwind. However, the union locomotive crew's refusal to transport the relief detail delayed the departure of the special train. Finally, on the morning of October 27, with mine guards and deputies entrained with two machine guns, the locomotive driven by a Baldwin-Felts detective left Trinidad pulling three steel coal cars, a boxcar, and a caboose. An official at union headquarters in Trinidad telephoned the leaders at the Ludlow colony to announce that the train was on its way northward.[55]

The miners, meanwhile, had returned from their shooting spree at Berwind and Tabasco in a celebratory mood, only to find the Ludlow colonists terrified by the news of the northbound train carrying machine guns. Convinced that the Ludlow tent colony was the train's destination, Lawson hastily assembled 500 men with red bandannas tied around their necks and guns in their hands to stop it. What motivated the men as they took positions along the crest of a hill overlooking the tracks south of Ludlow, Don MacGregor observed, was a mixture of terror and semi-hysterical determination that the deputies and mine guards would never get near the tent colony with machine guns. The strikers began to fire on the railway cars as the train approached and slowly made its way toward the Tabasco railroad switch. Unknown to the strikers, Albert Felts had no intention of moving the train northward to Ludlow. After backing it four miles to Forbes junction to escape the strikers' rifle fire, the guards and deputies detrained with their machine guns and made their way on foot over the hills to Tabasco.[56]

The strikers, believing they had prevented the train from reaching Ludlow, were more jubilant than ever as they returned to camp after their "steel train victory." While some of the colonists celebrated, about 300 strikers slipped out of camp before dawn on October 28 to attack Berwind and Hastings. Their pent-up hatred was manifested in the ferocity of their attack. Their deadly fire felled ten mine guards and deputies before noon. They cut telephone and telegraph wires and blew up the railroad tracks. Another detachment of miners attacked Tabasco, driving the guards and their families into the mine. The mine guards' machine gun fire finally forced the strikers to retreat, leaving two of their fellow Greeks dead. Some of the gunmen regrouped in the hills above Hastings, where they began sniping at the camp once again.[57]

Previous to the attacks, Linderfelt's scouts and company spies had reported that the strikers were intent upon "cleaning up Berwind and Hastings." Linderfelt immediately wired General Chase once again to send state troops to quell the "rebellion": "Large body of men leaving Aguilar to reinforce. . . . Situation looks hopeless. No hope can be expected only from troops, as there is nothing left to hope for."[58] One can imagine the exultation Linderfelt must have felt in talking about the beginning of armed insurrection. He knew the strikers had finally taken the bait and that the trap was sprung. Back in the Ludlow camp, Lawson knew it too.

General Chase shared Linderfelt's urgent pleas for state troops with Governor Ammons. The governor also received "the almost frantic appeal" from the sheriffs of the two southern counties, boards of county commissioners, mayors, judges, and other civil authorities, as well as hundreds of private citizens, pleading with him to call out the National Guard.[59] The news of the ongoing battle in the hills around Ludlow moved him closer to military intervention. Still, sick and exhausted, he made a last-ditch effort to resolve the conflict. He invited John White and Frank Hayes to meet with him and Thomas Patterson, the pro-labor former U.S. senator and publisher of the *Rocky Mountain News*. The two national union executives, who were in Denver conferring with local District 15 officials, quickly accepted the invitation.

Patterson worked indefatigably for three days and nights to bring about a conference between the principal mine operators and leading union officials. With the strikers in Ludlow out of control, he gained the acquiescence of White, Lawson, and Hayes for the governor to dispatch the state militia to the strike zone to keep the strikers within the bounds of law. In return, the union leaders insisted on a conference with the operators to attempt a settlement of the strike, a request Patterson and Ammons urged the operators to accept. In their response, the operators again emphatically stated that they would never "confer with murderers and interlopers." Nothing, Patterson lamented, "could change the determination of Messrs. Osgood, Brown, Welborn, and S. M. Perry [president of the Moffat and Leyden coal companies], speaking for themselves and the rest of the operators, not to confer with the miners' representatives, whatever might be the outcome." The operators even declared, Patterson added, that "if White, Hayes, Lawson, and the others should come into the room they would leave it. At that very time White, Lawson, Hayes, and the others were in an adjoining room hoping to be admitted for a conference."[60]

The operators knew they were on the verge of success in getting the governor to call out the militia, and they did not want to give the union any excuse to call off the strike. They had no intention of settling the strike on any terms other than their own. The key, as it had been in 1903–1904, was to get the militia in the field to protect their mining operations and to allow them to replace the strikers with strikebreakers. Public opinion, they believed, was on their side. Representatives of the five largest banks in Denver had again assured the governor that he could have the money he needed for the militia in thirty days. With all this in their favor, the operators stepped up pressure on the governor to send the militia to the strike zone. Welborn observed that they "had been pressuring the governor very hard for over twenty-four hours to save our mines."[61]

The intense pressuring Welborn spoke of began during a meeting between the governor and a group of operators at the Brown Palace Hotel in Denver on October 25. Fortunately for the historical record, Gene Fowler, a young newspaper reporter for the *Denver Republican*, surreptitiously recorded the conversation that occurred during the "secret" conference. Before the governor arrived, Fowler, who was hiding in a bedroom adjacent to the conference room where the meeting was taking place, observed that Osgood interrupted the casual conversation about golf and trout fishing among the coal executives and their legal representatives in attendance to announce that they must compel Ammons to declare martial law and that he and Welborn would do the talking. Welborn began the session as soon as the governor arrived by demanding that he call out the militia to subdue the strikers. Ammons said that he could not agree to such a demand. Labor, he explained, had been very instrumental in his election, and he did not want to defy the miners. Osgood reacted angrily, cursing and shouting insults at Ammons and threatening his political future. The other coal executives joined in, and the verbal abuse of the governor lasted for over an hour as they continued to pressure him to call out the militia. Finally, Ammons, described by Fowler as "a portrait of defeat painted in ochre and sallow green," succumbed to his "browbeaters" and promised to send the National Guard to the strike zone on October 28.[62]

Fowler was discovered when the meeting broke up. According to his account, as he pocketed his notes and tried to depart, he was stopped by Osgood, who shouted, "Why, you Goddamned, sneaking bastard! I'll . . ." "You'll what?" Fowler interrupted. Before he could reply, Fowler, right in Osgood's face, said: "I've heard you call the Governor names. . . . You'd never call Theodore Roosevelt names! And what's more, if you call me names, you pompous old bastard, I'll smack you on the chin. I didn't sneak in here, and I've got a story that will make the whole country sit up." Running to the newspaper office with what he considered "the biggest story in the world," Fowler found when he arrived that Osgood, or some other opera-tor, had already convinced the managing editor to suppress it. "You can't go around calling important people like Mr. Osgood names," the editor "petulantly" told the young reporter. "My God!" Fowler exclaimed in total disbelief. "You mean to throw away this scoop just because old Osgood or some other coal operator telephoned you?" The editor's response was an emphatic "yes."[63]

Recounted many years after the fact, some aspects of Fowler's anecdote might be questioned, particularly his boast that he got the best of Osgood. Yet the story rings true in terms of reflecting the personality of the men involved and Osgood and the coal executives' relentless determination to force Ammons to send National Guard troops to the strike district.

Notwithstanding his concession to the operators, Ammons did not abandon his efforts to settle the strike. He telephoned Welborn at the Denver Club on the evening of October 26 to request another meeting with him, Osgood, and Brown. He told Welborn he had been conferring with union leaders and Senator Patterson, who had assured him that the strike could be settled if the operators met with them. He added that he believed the union would waive the issues of recognition and a pay raise. Emphasizing the union leaders' expressed eagerness to end the strike, he pleaded with Welborn to get the operators to make a small concession to help him, which was to meet with union leaders in the governor's office. Welborn replied that the companies would never make a concession "to that murderous element" but indicated that the operators would gladly sign a letter from him requesting that they obey the law relative to the strikers' demands. Left with this slight glimmer of hope, Ammons called a meeting for the following morning with the purpose of drafting the letter.[64]

Senator Patterson took the initiative in writing a letter addressed to the operators over the governor's signature that he hoped would be acceptable to both sides. His draft dismissed the recognition issue, required the operators to abide by the statutes of law in the operation of their businesses, and established the right of strikers to return to their jobs without discrimination. When presented with the draft in the governor's office that afternoon, Osgood, Welborn, and Brown reacted with such anger that it was reported their voices were heard in distant corners of the statehouse. They protested Patterson's description of the laws, particularly the one establishing the miners' right to organize. More important, they rejected categorically the provision that allowed strikers to return to work after the strike ended.[65]

The operators immediately drafted their own letter for the governor to sign and send them. It simply cited the numbers and titles of state mining laws without describing their provisions and stated that the operators would continue to obey those laws. The operators agreed to take back only those employees whose positions had not been filled and who could prove that they had not participated in any unlawful actions. Thus, they reiterated their contention that they were scrupulously law-abiding citizens and that the union had no legitimate demands. They also made it clear that they intended to replace all strikers with strikebreakers, as they had done in 1904.[66]

As everyone expected, John White and Frank Hayes rejected the operators' draft letter. To accept it would mean a complete capitulation to their demands. In rejecting the letter, the union leaders knew the governor would call out the National Guard. They preferred to take the chance that the militia would be able to separate the militant strikers from the hated mine guards and sheriff's deputies. If the militia remained neutral and did not facilitate the importation of strikebreakers, they believed there was an excellent chance of ultimately forcing the operators to the negotiating table. The operators, for their part, were determined to use the militia as an instrument to break the strike and deal a crushing blow to the union.

With all his attempts to settle the strike ending in failure, Ammons believed he had no choice but to send the National Guard into the strike zone. He had come to the conclusion that the tent colonies, located in positions that commanded the approaches to the important mines, were actually silent pickets in violation of Colorado law. He also believed the operators had the legal right to employ armed mine guards on their properties to protect them and their workers from aggression. Additionally, he had concluded that the strikers' fear of attack by mine guards, which was their justification for arming themselves, was unfounded, "though it may have been honestly entertained." With "a tumult threatened," it was time, the governor stated, for the state "to assert its authority through its military arm."[67] Therefore, at 1:30 A.M. on October 28, Ammons signed the executive order to send the National Guard into the southern Colorado strike field.

The governor's order calling out the militia reached Ludlow around midnight. Lawson immediately sent word to the men in the hills to stop fighting and return to their tents. They reluctantly put down their guns and descended the hills to the tent colony. Many were hysterical and filled with despair. Some recalled with a mix of bitterness and apprehension their experiences during previous strikes, particularly in 1903–1904. The coming of the militia, they feared, meant more men and guns to back up the mine guards and the company men. The machine guns would still be there to clean them out. Lawson's assurance that the governor had promised that the militia would be impartial and would not help bring scabs into the strike area eased the tension in the camp, for some but not for all. There were many who would never surrender their guns.[68]

NOTES

1. McGovern and Guttridge, *Coalfield War*, 104.

2. Ibid.; Andrews, "Road to Ludlow," 2–3, 496.

3. *Denver Express*, September 24, 1913.

4. Ibid. McGregor's sympathy for the strikers eventually led him to quit the left-leaning *Denver Express* and volunteer his services to the striking miners.

5. West, *Report on the Colorado Strike*, 32.

6. Long, *Where the Sun Never Shines*, 273–275; McGovern and Guttridge, *Coalfield War*, 105–106.

7. Priscilla Long, "The Voice of the Gun: Colorado's Great Coalfield War of 1913–1914," *Labor's Heritage* 1, no. 4 (October 1989): 12–13.

8. Bazanelle quoted in Margolis, "Western Coal Mining," 77.

9. Helen Ring Robinson's testimony, CIR/FR 8: 7212; Bazanelle quoted in Andrews, "Road to Ludlow," 505, citing John and Caroline Tomsic oral history.

10. Long, "Voice of the Gun," 13, citing interview with Livoda, January 1977; Margolis, "Western Coal Mining," 77, citing his interview with Livoda, August 1975; last quote in Beshoar, *Out of the Depths*, 74.

11. *Denver Express*, September 23, 1913.

12. Long, *Where the Sun Never Shines*, 276.

13. *Denver Express*, September 22, 1913.

14. *Trinidad Chronicle-News*, September 15, 25, 1913. It was reported in the *Denver Daily News* on September 23, 1913, that the entire workforce of 135 men at Victor-American's Radiant camp joined the union en masse on September 22 and obeyed the strike call the next day. The term "taken out their tools" was the miners' vernacular for leaving work or going out on strike.

15. Ibid., September 23, 1913; *Denver Express*, September 24, 1913. Ed Doyle, UMWA District 15 secretary-treasurer, reported "that large numbers of Italians, Polish, and Slavs are leaving for the old country" (Doyle to William Green, UMWA secretary-treasurer, September 30, 1913, Edward S. Doyle Papers, Envelope 4, Box 1, WH126, Western History Collection, Denver Public Library, Denver, Colo.).

16. Andrews, "Road to Ludlow," 499.

17. McGovern and Guttridge, *Coalfield War*, 108. "Sent down the canyon," meant being fired.

18. McGovern, "Colorado Strike," 167–168.

19. See, for example, "The Cause of the Colorado Strike," *Coal Age*, 5, no. 26 (June 27, 1914): 1058.

20. Frank E. Gove letter to editors, September 27, 1913, in Ammons Papers, Box 26751, FF-5, "Corres. with Mine Operators, A-O, 1913–1915."

21. *Brief of the Coal Mining Operators*, 5.

22. These were the views of the author of an unsigned letter (copy) to Ammons, November 18, 1913, Ammons Papers, Box 26751, FF-6, "Corres. with Mine Operators, P-Z, 1913–1915." Although the author of this letter is unknown, the views therein reflect those expressed by Osgood and Jesse Welborn over the course of the strike. Either one could have written the letter. Osgood expressed similar views and used some of the same terms as those in the letter at the editors' conference on November 13, 1913, five days before the letter was written.

23. Osgood's testimony, SMM, 419.

24. Stewart to Louis Post, November 21, 1913, in *The Papers of Woodrow Wilson*, ed. Arthur S. Link, vol. 28 (Princeton, N.J.: Princeton University Press, 1978), 581; hereafter cited as PWW; last quote in Martelle, *Blood Passion*, 84, quoting Stewart to Wilson, September 26, 1913, Record of the Bureau of Labor Statistics, Office of Ethelbert Stewart, 1904–1931, RG 257.3, National Archives, Washington, D.C.

25. Bowers to Rockefeller, September 29, October 3, 11, 21, 1913, and Rockefeller to Bowers, October 6, 1913, in CIR/FR 9: 8417–8421.

26. Bowers to Rockefeller, October 11, 1913, in ibid., 8421.

27. Long, *Where the Sun Never Shines,* 278.

28. Osgood's testimony, SMM, 408–409.

29. *Rocky Mountain News,* October 12, 15, 1913; McGovern, "Colorado Strike," 189–190; Beshoar, *Out of the Depths,* 68–74.

30. *Report on the Colorado Strike Investigation,* in Stein and Taft, *Massacre at Ludlow,* 17 (source of the quote); McGovern and Guttridge, *Coalfield War,* 122–123; Long, *Where the Sun Never Shines,* 278; Papanikolas, *Buried Unsung,* 90–91; and Beshoar, *Out of the Depths,* 71–73, all have varying accounts of the attack on the Forbes tent colony. The wounded boy survived but was crippled for life. Walter Belk and George Belcher, both Baldwin-Felts agents, were in the Death Special during the Forbes incident.

31. MacGregor quoted in Long, *Where the Sun Never Shines,* 278; McGovern and Guttridge, *Coalfield War,* 119; Stewart to Post, November 21, 1913, in PWW 28: 583.

32. Bowers to M. B. Streeter, October 10, 1913, in Andrews, "Road to Ludlow," 508.

33. *Rocky Mountain News,* September 18, 1913.

34. Ammons's statement and quotations in the *Denver Express,* September 25, 1913.

35. Bowers to M. B. Streeter, October 10, 1913, in Andrews, "Road to Ludlow," 508.

36. Dunlavy quoted in *Denver Express,* September 30, 1913.

37. Bowers to Rockefeller, November 18, 1913, in CIR/FR 9: 8421–8422.

38. Osgood's testimony, SMM, 616, 619–620.

39. Ibid., 618–620.

40. *Metropolitan Magazine* (July 1914): 13.

41. MacGregor quoted in Long, *Where the Sun Never Shines,* 279.

42. Ibid., 279–280; *Rocky Mountain News,* October 22, 1913.

43. Ammons quoted in *Rocky Mountain News,* October 22, 1913.

44. Doyle quoted in Beshoar, *Out of the Depths,* 77.

45. Fitch, "Law and Order," 252, 254.

46. Papanikolas, *Buried Unsung,* 80–81, 116.

47. Louis Tikas to Ed Doyle, August 28, 1913, in ibid., 72.

48. Livoda quoted in Margolis, "Western Coal Mining," 83.

49. Beshoar, *Out of the Depths,* 75; quote in McGovern and Guttridge, *Coalfield War,* 124. Linderfelt's background no doubt had a lot to do with his character. He had served as a member of the Fourth U.S. Cavalry during the Philippine Insurrection of 1899–1900. McGovern and Guttridge suggest that the brutal nature of that campaign probably left a deep impression on him. Subsequently, he joined a force of foreign mercenaries and Mexican insurgents in the revolt against President Porfirio Díaz in

Mexico. As a soldier of fortune, he served under Sherman Bell during the 1903–1904 strike at Cripple Creek, and he eagerly volunteered for strikebreaking duty in the southern coalfields in 1913 (McGovern and Guttridge, *Coalfield War,* 166–168).

50. Fitch, "Law and Order," 254.

51. Eugene O. Porter, "The Colorado Coal Strike of 1913—an Interpretation," *The Historian* 12 (Autumn 1949): 7–8.

52. MacGregor quoted in Long, *Where the Sun Never Shines,* 280.

53. McGovern and Guttrridge, *Coalfield War,* 127–128.

54. Linderfelt telegram to General Chase, October 27, 1913, in Linderfelt's testimony, CIR/FR 7: 6873.

55. Beshoar, *Out of the Depths,* 85–86; McGovern and Guttridge, *Coalfield War,* 130–131. Besides the engineer, another Baldwin-Felts agent was the fireman and Albert Felts himself was the conductor.

56. Papanikolas, *Buried Unsung,* 102–103; Beshoar, *Out of the Depths,* 86; Mac-Gregor quoted in McGovern and Guttridge, *Coalfield War,* 131–132. Five guards were wounded by shrapnel while still in the rail cars. Lawson instructed every striker to wear a red bandanna around his neck. "It is our uniform," he stated (quoted in Beshoar, *Out of the Depths,* 74). The term "redneck," used by the mine guards and militia, was derived from the red bandannas.

57. Beshoar, *Out of the Depths,* 86–37; McGovern and Guttridge, *Coalfield War,* 132.

58. Linderfelt to Chase, October 28, 1913, in Linderfelt's testimony, CIR/FR 7: 6873.

59. Elias M. Ammons, "The Colorado Strike," *North American Review* 200 (July 1914): 37.

60. Thomas M. Patterson, "The Strike in Colorado," *Rocky Mountain Sentinel,* June 6, 1914, in U.S. Congress, *Congressional Record* (Washington, D.C.: Government Printing Office, June 12, 1914), 3–4.

61. Welborn statement cited in CIR/FR 7: 6601.

62. Gene Fowler, *A Solo in Tom-Toms* (New York: Viking, 1946), 330–332.

63. Ibid., 332–333.

64. McGovern and Guttridge, *Coalfield War,* 129.

65. Ibid., 130.

66. Ibid., 133–134.

67. Ibid., 134; quotes in Ammons, "Colorado Strike," 37.

68. Papanikolas, *Buried Unsung,* 104–105.

The Editors' and Governor's Conferences

Believing they were finally protected from the hated mine guards, most of the strikers and their families welcomed the state troops under the command of General John Chase with cautious enthusiasm. The Ludlow colonists received the pompous general and his detachment of troops in full regalia, with festivities that included an improvised band playing "The Battle Cry of Freedom" and little children singing and waving American flags. Many in the crowd appeared in native Greek, Montenegrin, Serbian, and Bulgarian costumes. The festive atmosphere soon changed, however, when the militia officer in charge ordered the strikers to surrender their weapons. The strikers responded with thirty-seven rusty rifles and a child's popgun.[1]

John Lawson deserved credit for making the occasion as peaceful as it was. With difficulty, he had gained control over the more militant strikers by assuring them that the governor had instructed the militia to act with strict impartiality and had banned it from helping the coal companies bring in strikebreakers. In addition, the governor had ordered the militia to disarm the mine guards and prohibit them from leaving company property. The dreaded machine guns were also to be turned over to the militia. Under these circumstances, the union leaders believed they could keep the mines closed, something they hoped would inflict a heavy financial cost on the operators and raise public fears of a coal shortage. If this happened, the union leaders thought they could force the coal companies to accept their demands.[2]

The operators were not happy with Governor Elias Ammons's terms for sending the 1,000 National Guard troops to the strike zone. Thomas Patterson had admonished the governor not to allow the importation of strikebreakers as long as the operators refused to confer with union leaders. Still hopeful of arranging a conference between John Osgood, Jesse Welborn, and David Brown on the one side and United Mine Workers of America (UMWA) leaders on the other, Ammons agreed with Patterson; consequently, the governor's orders to General Chase reflected the former senator's pro-labor views more than those of the operators.[3]

Although General Chase had agreed to the terms the governor set— that the militia would be strictly neutral and that company guards and gunmen would not be enlisted in the militia under any circumstance—neither he nor the operators intended to adhere strictly to the provisions, particularly the one that restricted the operators' objective of hiring new workers to fill the ranks depleted by the strike.[4] Within days of the militia's arrival in the strike zone, the operators began to pressure the governor to lift the ban on the importation of strikebreakers, and Chase found ways to subvert some of the stipulations of the order. From the beginning of the occupation, the adjutant general made it clear that he was completely in the coal companies' pocket. There was no attempt to conceal the multitude of connections and interrelationships between the general, who signed his directives "Commanding General, Military District of Colorado," and the companies, particularly Colorado Fuel and Iron (CF&I) and Victor-American. State troops were quartered in company buildings and furnished with company supplies. The two companies made loans to impoverished militiamen and cashed the certificates of indebtedness issued to the militia when Roady Kenehan, the state auditor, held up their pay. CF&I alone paid out up to $80,000, reimbursable with interest from the state, for salaries and supplies

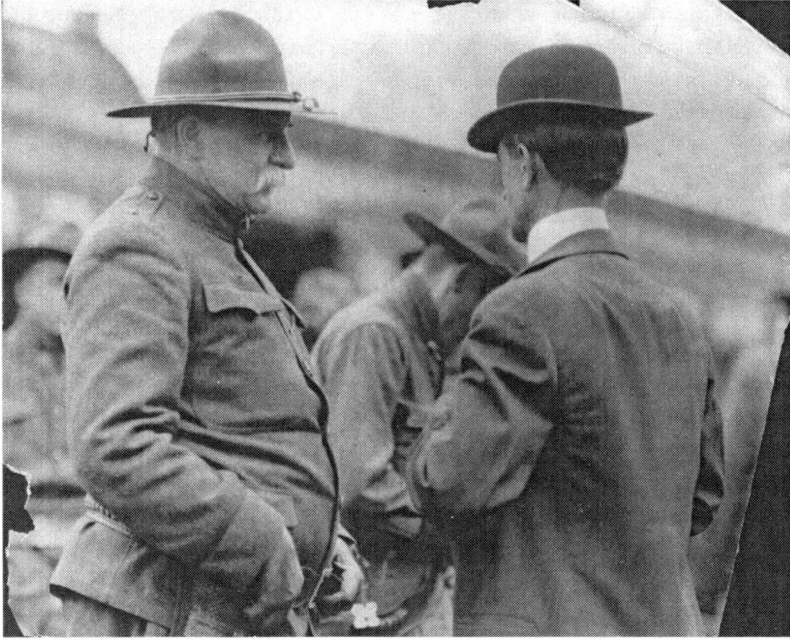

General John Chase (left) and Frank E. Gove, lawyer for the coal companies. Courtesy, Denver Public Library, Western History Collection, call no. X-60525.

for the troops.[5] Contrary to Governor Ammons's order, the National Guard began to enroll mine guards within two weeks of its arrival in the strike zone. "The bitterness of the miners was intense," Don MacGregor reported, as they saw mine guards whom they regarded as murderous thugs returning to the field in National Guard uniforms.[6] Seeing their old enemies, including Karl Linderfelt, in militia uniforms made the strikers more determined than ever to keep their weapons.

Although Governor Ammons was aware of the close relationship between the militia and coal company officials, particularly the National Guard's recruitment of mine guards and Baldwin-Felts detectives, he took no action to restore impartiality within the militia. In fact, the cooperation between the militia and the operators was permitted to continue openly. With good reason, the strikers and their union leaders believed the relationship constituted a conspiracy against them. Yet they held their fire, and relative calm persisted in the southern Colorado coalfield through the remainder of the year. John Lawson was once again the peacemaker who kept the "hotheads," especially the Greeks, among the strikers in the Ludlow camp under control. He persuaded the colonists to refrain from provoking the militiamen. Perhaps his greatest tool for persuasion was the possibility that the conflict would be resolved through federal intervention, for at the very moment the state militia gathered in the field, President Woodrow Wilson became involved in the stalemated crisis.

In late October, President Wilson read Ethelbert Stewart's report recommending a congressional investigation of the Colorado coal strike. Stewart blamed the conflict on the operators' absolute intransigence. Because he knew he would receive a request for an investigation from Congress, the president, "deeply disappointed" by the mine executives' refusal to confer with the miners, addressed a letter to Jesse Welborn asking for "a full and frank statement of the reasons" CF&I officials had rejected the "counsels of peace and accommodation in a matter now grown so critical." Although the letter was addressed to Welborn, LaMont Bowers was the first to answer it. He denied that the operators had treated Stewart churlishly. In fact, he told the president, Stewart was biased and opinionated and only interested in obtaining the right of recognition for the union. To this demand "we shall never consent, [not even] if every mine is closed, the equipment destroyed, and the investment made worthless." Welborn's later response contained the standard litany of company claims about the good conditions under which miners worked and the infamy of the unionists.[7]

Both Stewart and Louis Post, the assistant secretary of labor, commented on Bowers's and Welborn's letters. In their estimation, the struggle was a strike by modern labor against antiquated labor policies and absentee ownership. The operators' unwillingness to negotiate, Stewart wrote, put them in a position that was contrary to contemporary practices of industrial democracy and collective bargaining. Stewart scathingly rejected Welborn's contention that the workers were satisfied: "Theoretically, perhaps, the case of having nothing to do in this world but work, ought to have made these men of many tongues, as happy and contented as the managers claim to think they were." But in reality, the companies had deprived their employees of basic freedoms and rights and had "created a condition which they considered satisfactory to themselves, and ought to be to the workman, and jammed the workman into it, and thought they were philanthropists. That men have rebelled grows out of the fact that they are men, and can only be satisfied with conditions which they create, or in the creation of which they have a voice and [a] share." The operators must be made to realize, Stewart concluded, that "feudalism is no longer acceptable" and that southern Colorado must be "placed industrially where it is geographically, as a part of the United States, and not of the Hanseatic League."[8]

Clearly, President Wilson was rapidly losing patience with the Colorado coalmine executives. He was tired of receiving long letters from CF&I officials explaining why they refused to enter into discussions with "assassins and violators of law" or to accept arbitration. "I can only say this," he told Bowers curtly, "that a word from you would bring the strike to an end, and all that is asked is that you agree to arbitration by an unbiased board." It was a reasonable request, the president said, "conceived in the spirit of the times." Defending the members of the Department of Labor, especially Stewart and Secretary of Labor William Wilson, he stressed that he would back their request for arbitration "with the greatest earnestness and solemnity" so the dispute between the mine owners and the strikers could be settled on its merits.[9]

President Wilson's rebuke only riled Bowers further. In reply, he informed the president that Stewart and Wilson were engaged in a conspiracy with the UMWA leaders and other labor officials to destroy the open shop in America. They had made the strike in Colorado a national issue. The American people, he warned the president, would not tolerate the use of the Department of Labor in support of labor unions in a movement to close open shops throughout the country. Bowers also told John D. Rockefeller Jr. that the Colorado coalmine executives, supported by "men in high positions" throughout the country, would fight "to a finish" in defense of the open shop. In a letter to Starr Murphy, Bowers stated that the operators were ready to take their chances with a congressional investigation of the strike rather than agree to arbitration that would force them to recognize the union.[10]

The notion of a congressional investigation was already on President Wilson's mind. He had been conferring with Representative Edward Keating and his colleagues in the Colorado congressional delegation about the appointment of such an investigative body. Keating, known for his pro-labor sympathies, was busy trying to win approval in the House of Representatives for a resolution calling for a strike investigation. His activities made the operators and Governor Ammons nervous. Uncertainty about how the Denver business community would react to a possible congressional investigation held in Colorado particularly worried the governor. Several banks had already canceled their pledges to underwrite certificates of indebtedness he had counted on to keep the militia deployed in the strike zone. Equally concerned, the operators sent a committee of four men to Washington to lobby against the appointment of an investigative committee.[11]

To make matters worse for Ammons and the operators, the price of coal was increasing. On November 19 Ammons sent simultaneous telegrams to

President Wilson and Secretary William Wilson urging them to intervene in a situation that was "growing worse hourly." Responding to the request, the president advised his secretary of labor to travel to Colorado to take part in discussions with Ammons and anyone else willing to participate.[12]

A few days earlier, a group of prominent Colorado newspaper editors had met at the Brown Palace Hotel in Denver at the invitation of John C. Shaffer, the editor and publisher of the *Rocky Mountain News*. Shaffer stated that the purpose of the meeting, which included representatives from several civic bodies throughout the state, was to learn more about the strike and, it was hoped, devise some means for ending it. Realizing the importance of the press in shaping public opinion, members of the operators' policy committee had agreed to meet with the editors on the condition that they would not be brought into any contact with leaders of the UMWA. Shaffer accepted the operators' terms and agreed to notify the union leaders that they were not to be present when the operators addressed the conference. However, when he arrived at the meeting, Osgood discovered that John McLennan, UMWA president of District 15, was in the room, whereupon he chastised Shaffer for not carrying out his intention of keeping the union leaders away. At Osgood's insistence, Shaffer ordered the labor leader to leave.[13]

With McLennan out of the room, the conference heard first from Governor Ammons. He urged the editors, through their newspapers, to help bring about a settlement or at least a temporary agreement until legislation was enacted during the legislature's next session to provide "some means for compulsory arbitration in such cases as this." After the governor spoke, Shaffer introduced three veteran miners to present the strikers' case. Ford Cornwell was presently employed at the Valdez mine and had worked for Rocky Mountain Fuel, CF&I, and Victor-American Fuel. Dennison (first name unknown) worked for the Valdez mine, and A. Lamont worked for the Oakdale mine. Although each had been in the United States and had worked in various coalmines belonging to all three of the major companies for more than twenty years, they were not proficient in English. Each in turn complained of being forced to do timbering and other forms of dead work without pay, being compelled to trade at the company store where prices were very high, being cheated at the scales by short weights, being docked for rock in the coal, and being forced to work in unsafe conditions.[14]

All three miners described how they had been fired for registering complaints, or, as they put it, "making a kick." The only recourse a miner had, they said, was to pack his tools and get out. They stressed that the miners had asked the national union to come in to protect them, and each of the three men strongly demanded recognition of the union. Without the union, they stated, they would have nothing. Contrary to the owners' assertion that the union officials had called the strike, the miners noted that it was the men themselves who demanded the walkout. "We elected our delegates from the different places and they voted for a strike," observed the first miner who spoke, "and the strike is on, and the way it looks to me, it will never be settled until there is recognition of the union." The last of the miners to speak was more blunt: "If we have no union, I don't care what Mr. Operator promised to us it would not mean nothing."

Following the miners' brief appearance before the conference, the operators presented their view of the strike. Osgood, Welborn, and Brown, the three members of the operators' executive committee, represented the coalmine owners. As the group's leader, Osgood presented the operators' case in a speech that lasted more than three hours. After reciting a history of the coal industry in Colorado and the causes of previous strikes, Osgood disputed the claim made earlier by the three miners that they and their fellow workers had asked the UMWA for protection and demanded the strike. The miners' convention in Trinidad, Osgood charged, was "simply a convention of the United Mine Workers of America officials under the leadership of Mr. Hayes, and never a representative convention of the men called on [to] strike." Most of the mine employees were never consulted, Osgood claimed, and once the strike was called, they were forced through intimidation to leave the mines. The workers who remained at work were abused verbally and threatened with violence.[15]

Osgood went through each of the union's demands in the strike call. He began with the demand for recognition of the union, which if granted, he argued, would put the union in possession of the mines. He and the other operators would never consent to this. He called the demand for a 10 percent increase in wages totally unjustified. There was no economic reason, he contended, why the Colorado operators should make their pay scale competitive with Wyoming, a unionized state where the UMWA had made the wage scale particularly high. The eight-hour law applied to miners working underground but not to men working on the surface and at the coke ovens. The law had little relevance to the miner who, as a contractor, "never did work eight hours . . . going in [the mine] when he pleases and out when he pleases." In addition, Osgood explained, miners were not entitled to extra pay for dead work, which they agreed to do when they signed a contract to work.[16]

Osgood repudiated the charges that his company denied the right of employees to trade and board where they pleased. These complaints were heard only before or during a strike, he asserted, "and [were] seldom or never a source of grievance when the men are working." He was not aware of any mine where these conditions existed: "I know it would be a short sighted policy on the part of any operator to coerce their men in any such way. It is not a matter of argument even. Every man should be allowed to board and trade where he pleases and to what extent he pleases in the company store or elsewhere." Osgood said nothing about the use of scrip in his company's Western Stores.[17]

Osgood brushed aside the complaint made by the miner who spoke immediately before him about being charged a dollar a month for medical coverage, whether ill or not, without being able to see a doctor of his choice. "We have had a system in vogue at our mines for [the] thirty years that I have been connected with them," Osgood noted, "and I have never heard one solitary word of complaint until this complaint was made by this man." For the dollar a month, the men "receive the services of a doctor for themselves and [their] family, all the medicines required, and in case of injury or sickness sufficiently serious they are sent to the hospital at the expense of the company, and they are kept there any length of time necessary." There had never been any epidemics in the mining camps, and conditions in them were splendid—an amazing fact, Osgood thought, in that "[t]here are a great many foreigners not careful in their habits."[18]

The reports in the press and talk in the halls of Congress of "horrible conditions" in the mine camps rankled Osgood. The Colorado mines and camps, he asserted, were as good as or better than any of the mines he had visited in the United States or overseas in England and Germany. "Our mines—you know the character of country we have in Colorado, where there is no water on the soil, and we have very little water in southern Colorado—naturally the mining districts are not attractive looking places . . . but they are clean." Certainly, faults could be found: "If you went down there with your camera you could take one of the most squalid looking pictures you ever saw; of course, they have the shanty towns connected with the mines, tin cans for stove pipes and so on and so on, with the pig and the goat and the chickens, but if you took our payroll you would probably find the man that occupies that kind of house drawing the largest wages." He emphasized that no matter what the companies did, "[t]he men simply insist on living as they please." Although the camps were not beautiful, the charge that there were harmful conditions was "simply the imagination or the lying slander of men who have a purpose to gain and do not care for the facts."[19]

Osgood addressed the other main issues at length. He declared that the new mining law was being enforced by the state, and "if the operators are not enforcing it they can be made to enforce it and it does not take a strike to bring it about." He denied that the mine managers refused to allow the miners to have a check-weighman of their own choosing at each mine, stressing that the operators preferred such an arrangement: "If we could get the correct weight it would take a great deal of trouble off of our hands." The main problem was that the men could never find anyone they could trust to serve in that capacity or anyone who would keep the job for long: "I stated with assurance [a few moments ago] that the company is not robbing its men. We are not petty thieves. We are trying to give them full weight, full credit, but there are chances of error in the weight. I would like to see a check weighman there, and we are willing to do all we can to get a check weighman to keep the place."[20]

Continuing in his defensive tone, Osgood turned to the volatile topic of mine guards. The miners wanted the guard system abolished, and "[s]o do I," he exclaimed. That would be possible only when the strikers no longer threatened the mines and the workers who wanted to work in them. In his view, the main source of the current trouble was the Ludlow tent colony, situated on the main road from Trinidad to his mines of Hastings and Delagua and the CF&I mines to the south. After the start of the strike "there was an absolute reign of terror," he said, as the strikers fired on every vehicle traveling down the road past the tent colony. With this state of affairs, the operators had no choice but to hire guards and have them deputized by the sheriffs. With the outbreak of violence, he added, the operators had advised the governor that National Guard troops should have been sent into the field immediately: "Four hundred men could then have handled the situation, whereas it takes the entire militia now."[21]

Osgood also expressed his opinion regarding strikebreakers. He and the other operators argued that Governor Ammons's determination to prohibit the National Guard from bringing in workers from outside the strike zone to replace miners who had either left the state or vacated their positions by going on strike only prolonged the conflict. Osgood refused to call these potential employees strikebreakers. They were seeking permanent employment and therefore were not professional strikebreakers who sought temporary work in order to break the strike.[22] It was the labor shortage rather than the operators seeking to gain an advantage from the strike that was causing the spike in the price of coal. In fact, the operators were operating their mines at a loss: "It would have been infinitely more profitable for us to close down the mines and we might have saved lives, but we believe it would have worked an unendurable hardship to the public, and we have endeavored to operate our mines as best we could, and as soon as we can [we will] bring them back to normal prices and the people would thereby be benefited." For this to happen, he believed the governor had to lift his ban on the importation of workers to the area: "The strongest point we make is that there is only one condition necessary to the return of normal prices of coal and the end of this strike and that is the maintenance of law and order and the right of every man, whether now employed or heretofore employed, to work if he wants to work, under the statutes of right which our constitution gives us."[23]

Osgood next reiterated all the reasons the operators had refused to meet with union leaders—the bogus nature of their demands, the ineffectiveness of a conference to restore law and order, the operators' unwillingness to enter into a contract with the union that would end thirty years of open-shop business operations, and the unlawful and irresponsible nature of the union—and he added the most severe charge of all: the operators would never enter into talks with the UMWA officials who had instigated a reign of terror in the coalfields of southern Colorado. "They have purchased and distributed arms to the men on strike and by anarchistic and incendiary speeches and advice have caused the killing of . . . ten of our employes [sic] . . . and we hold Mr. Hayes, Mr. Lawson, and Mr. McLennan and all their subordinate organizers as thoroughly guilty of these murders." Therefore, the coal magnate proclaimed, "[w]e do not want to meet with men who have brought about the conditions that caused this condition of anarchy in our state."[24]

Osgood ended his lengthy discourse by expressing his ideas on how to end the strike. First, he requested that the parties involved drop the word "settlement." The conflict should be concluded purely on its own merits and existing conditions, not on the basis of some arbitrary arrangement. The merits of the operators' case were obvious to him, as was the bogus nature of the miners' complaints and demands. The miners' claims, in his opinion, were neither specific nor substantial and could be found in any other type of employment. In essence, he argued, "[t]here was no grievance that was real presented to you gentlemen this morning that was of a character to justify a strike, or justify the suffering and loss to the public, and the bloodshed and reign of terror that exist." To terminate the strike, he concluded, Governor Ammons should go even further in carrying out his policy by giving the operators "all the protection that the law can give us for the operation of our mines and the protection of any man who wants [to] work in these mines. . . . We also ask him, as we have asked him in a letter which we have published with his consent, to rigidly enforce all the state laws referred to by the miners, and have given him our assurance that we would cordially cooperate with him and would obey those laws." If the strike could not be ended any other way, he advised, the governor should be supported in invoking martial law and "arresting every one of those men who are guilty of instituting these acts of violence that are a disgrace to the state." With a strong hand and martial law, he concluded, "your strike is over."[25]

Although Osgood's antiunion diatribe and acutely partisan defense of the coal operators against the strikers pleased the majority of those in attendance at the editors' conference, some of the editors wanted to hear from a union leader. They pointed out that the conference had listened to Osgood and Ammons for several hours but to the three miners for only a few minutes. When the conference voted unanimously to invite John McLennan to address the audience, Osgood, Welborn, and Brown stalked out of the room. Readmitted to the conference room, McLennan emphasized in a short speech the need for a union to prevent the operators from taking away what they had promised their employees at the last minute in an attempt to prevent the strike. The miners, he stressed, had always been willing to go into conference with representatives of the operators or the operators themselves to discuss each and every issue. Had the operators met with the miners, he admonished, they would not have found them unreasonable, as they were presumed to be.[26]

Following McLennan's speech, the editors selected a committee from among the group to formulate recommendations for resolution of the strike. After deliberating, the committee recommended granting the strike demands for an eight-hour day for all classes of labor in and around coal-mines and at coke ovens, the employment of check-weighmen, the right to trade freely, and the right of miners to belong to a union. The miners' demands for recognition of the UMWA, a 10 percent wage increase, established rates of pay for dead work, and the abolition of the mine guard system were rejected. In essence, the committee recommended granting only those demands already covered by state law. They stressed that it was the duty of the governor to enforce the mining laws "to obtain for the miners every right to which they are entitled under the law." The editors approved the recommendations and called for an immediate end to the strike, with miners who had not committed any law violations reinstated in their old jobs. The editors also backed the militia and supported whatever police action Governor Ammons thought necessary to maintain peace in the strike district.[27]

Not surprisingly, the union officials rejected the recommendations, while the operators, for the most part, expressed great delight with them. In a letter to the editors' committee accepting the recommendations, the operators made another pitch for ending the ban on the importation of workers from outside the strike zone, one of the issues the editors had failed to endorse. The letter read: "When the operators receive the protection from the civil authorities for the men who desire to work and for their properties to which they are entitled, are not interfered with in employing men to replace those now on strike or who left before the strike was called, and are enabled to operate their mines under normal conditions to normal capacity, on the open shop principle, which has prevailed in Colorado for more than thirty years, we will put into effect the scale of prices for coal heretofore prevailing."[28] The operators' letter was cleverly crafted to use the public's anguish over the rising price of coal to put additional heat on the governor to lift the ban on the importation of strikebreakers.

John Lawson observed that the editors' conference had been nothing more than another propaganda tool for the operators. He noted that eleven of the fourteen editors who participated in the meeting were either "subsidized or bulldozed" by the coal companies. They were antiunion and had framed the conference to aid the coal operators for business or other reasons. John D. Rockefeller, Lawson had reason to believe, had subjected John Shaffer of the *Rocky Mountain News*, the conference organizer, to intimidation.[29] Undoubtedly, the operators, supported by Denver commercial organizations, had used the editors' conference as yet another means of gaining public support for their position.

A few days after the editors' conference, Secretary Wilson arrived in Denver with President Wilson's mandate to intervene in the labor dispute in an attempt to restore industrial peace to Colorado. The secretary was determined to get the operators and union leaders together to discuss his plan for establishing an arbitration committee to deal periodically with miners' grievances. Wilson faced a difficult task, however, for Rockefeller had already rejected the secretary's invitation to support the effort. Taking his cue from Bowers, Rockefeller told Secretary Wilson that the Colorado affair was entirely in the hands of company officials there and that Governor Ammons had only to "protect the lives of the bona fide miners to bring the strike to a speedy termination."[30]

Secretary Wilson had more success with Governor Ammons, who, stung by criticism from all sides, decided to try once more to negotiate a settlement of the strike. The governor urgently requested that Osgood, Welborn, and Brown accept Wilson's invitation to meet privately with three striking miners on the understanding that union recognition would not be mentioned. Wilson had settled on the three miners after the operators refused yet again to meet with union leaders. Although he had suggested to the latter that the demand for union recognition should be withdrawn if there was to be any chance for an agreement on arbitration, the union officials instructed the miners to settle for nothing short of full recognition. Accepting the governor's terms, the three operators agreed to meet at the statehouse on November 26, the day before Thanksgiving.[31]

Now that recognition of the union had been dropped, or so Ammons thought, he was confident that a settlement could be reached. "Governor Ammons hopes that the strike will be settled within twenty-four hours from the time the two sides go into conference," the *Rocky Mountain News* reported, "and that the order for the recall of the militia will have been issued by that time." The governor and other state officials thought a "man-to-man talk . . . will do more toward wiping out misunderstandings and re-establishing peace and prosperity than any thing that has yet been done," the reporter wrote. "The entire state is hopefully [a]waiting the outcome because of the evident intention of the parties to the conference to give the situation a judicial, earnest consideration."[32]

In the governor's mind, the path to success was for each side to concentrate on the present by ignoring the contentious history of labor-management conflict in the coalfields. As an editorial in the *Rocky Mountain News* stated: "Forget the passions, the bitterness and the promptings of retaliation that have disfigured this splendid state since the first raucous note of class warfare went hurtling through the chain of coal-seamed hills of the south. . . . Send the dogs of industrial war back to their kennels, and 800,000 people will bless and thank you with their most expressive gratitude."[33] The striking miners, however, could not forget about the past, for it was the history of their struggles that made them fight in the present for the future. The operators were also unwilling to "send the dogs of industrial war" back to the kennels.[34]

Miners T. X. Evans, Archie Allison, and David Hamman were chosen to represent the striking miners at the conference. The first two were former employees of CF&I, and the latter was a former employee of Osgood's Victor-American Fuel Company. These three practical miners with a combined fifty-two years' experience faced Osgood, Welborn, and Brown—the three most powerful coal executives in the state—in a meeting that lasted fifteen hours. From the very beginning, Osgood and the other two operators made it clear that they had agreed to come to the meeting to discuss the grievances of the three miners as individuals and former employees, not as representatives of the union. Although Ammons at first intended to leave the room and let the six men have a "man-to-man" talk, both sides asked him to stay and serve as chair, a position the governor gladly accepted. Secretary Wilson also attended the meeting. It is easy to discern from the transcript of the proceedings why it was virtually impossible for the operators and miners to resolve their differences. The transcript also reveals Osgood's commanding position as leader of the "big three" coal operators.[35]

Despite Ammons's wish to keep the issue of union recognition off the table, Osgood immediately brought it to the fore. By getting it out of the way, he said, "we will save a lot of time." Osgood argued that the UMWA's desire to organize the state "was the real inception of the strike, and we had better discuss that feature if it is agreeable." Although Ammons attempted to move the conversation past the issue, Osgood would not relent. "[W]e have come up against a rock as far as recognition of the Union is concerned," he contended. "We have very strong opinions in regard to this organization; we insist on the right of men to join a Union if they so desire; we recognize that they have the same right that we have to join capital in corporations in order to put business in shape, but there are unions and unions just as there are men and men, and corporations and corporations, and from our standpoint and the knowledge that we have we do not think that the underlying principles of this Union are correct." Osgood added that he would have no business dealings with any organization—union or corporation—that did not live up to its contracts and imposed unfair practices. In his opinion, the UMWA was such an organization; therefore, as far as he was concerned, it had "no business with us nor we with [it]."[36]

Addressing the miners directly, Osgood told them "the day will come when there will be Unions that we would be mighty glad to see you join, but their purposes would be to build men up and not break them down, as is the case today." The UMWA's ideals were those of mutualism—"the cause of one is the cause of all"—ideals that deprived honest workers of their sacrosanct right to upward mobility and robbed businessmen of their ability to control their enterprises and enjoy their rightful rewards. It would be impossible, he proclaimed, "to build up the civilization that we want until those ideals [of mutualism] are abolished." He believed the miners should give their sons the opportunity to succeed rather than hold them back at the lowest level. To make his point, Osgood told his own Horatio Alger story: "I started as poor as you; I had to leave school and earn my own living at fourteen years of age and there is no country that gives the opportunity that this does, and the Union to my mind is the thing that is checking it. The biggest men in the United States are men that worked their way up from the ranks, and they did not work their way up by joining organizations where they could not, by their merit or skill, advance."[37] Such was the worldview of Osgood and his fellow operators. It was the rationale behind their irrepressible hatred of the UMWA.[38]

The three miners did not bear Osgood's rebukes in silence. They were experienced miners who took immense pride in their work. Evans stated that he did not have to bow his head "to any man in Colorado" as far as mining was concerned.[39] The miners based their arguments on their vast knowledge of the state's coalmines as well as on their expertise as skilled colliers. Several times during the meeting they told the operators how they should be operating, or should have operated, some of their mines. They related numerous instances when they had told pit bosses or mine superintendents what to do. On occasion, they lost their jobs when they complained or criticized what was happening. Evans stated that he had once complained to a superintendent about miners paying bribes to their superiors in exchange for good locations in the mines. The superintendent fired and blacklisted him; he "put me on the bum," Evans said. "I was not wanted and for ten years I travelled the state."[40]

The issue of widespread graft was only part of the reason for the miners' unhappiness with the power arrangement in the mines. This complaint more broadly included indictments of pit bosses and superintendents as incompetent, tyrannical, and corrupt. Besides the charge of bosses demanding bribes for good places in the mines, all three miners related accounts of corrupt foremen and managers who shorted their weights or credited other men with the coal they had mined. Corrupt politics also corroded the work atmosphere. "The result was," Allison explained, "that there were a good many people getting connected with the mines that were unscrupulous." He was willing to produce a notebook he had kept over the years to document that the entire system discriminated against good miners. The skilled miners, he stated, "always come in the way of the boss or the supers get jealous of a good man or intelligent men and what we think is that you people [operators] . . . don't really know what is going on."[41] Osgood replied by stating that he and the other operators always chose the pit bosses and superintendents from the ranks of the men. Hamman countered: "[T]hese men who were raised up from the mine, they have changed a whole lot since they were working; since they got in this position it seems that they do not take interest in it, not in the work, [they] just take an interest in the job."[42]

The miners had two other major concerns regarding mine management in southern Colorado. The first was their conviction that the coal companies had not done enough to prevent mine accidents. All three miners recounted firsthand accounts of mine disasters and argued vehemently that the companies had done far too little to prevent them. Again and again, Osgood defended mine management, but the miners rebutted with examples of their own. "[I]t would be to the best interests [of everyone] to have an organization," Evans suggested, and "a better class of people" working in the mines.[43] David Brown interjected by stating that the companies were doing everything in their power to improve conditions: "When we have an explosion we pay dearly for it," he exclaimed. "Yes," Evans retorted, "and we pay dear too—with our lives."[44]

The second concern centered on dead or deficiency work. "There is a good deal of advantage taken on deficiency work all over the state," Evans complained. "If a boss takes exception to a man, don't want him, he will put him up against deficient places, and it will cripple him probably a dollar or two dollars a day and he had no way in the world to get out of it only to quit and get out, and if he quits the same thing will happen somewhere else."[45] The three miners, along with almost all other miners throughout the coalfields, rejected the operators' argument that flat tonnage rates on coal constituted fair compensation regardless of the difference in mining conditions.

At every chance, the miners pressed the point that the operators' system of management had failed. "[Y]ou people don't know what is going on," Hamman reiterated a point made frequently, "and if you people were in closer touch with what is going on at these mines I believe you would change your minds yourself."[46] The miners argued that the fault with the companies' managerial system was that all power flowed downward—from the executive offices in Denver, through the various departments and mid-level officials, to the superintendents and pit bosses at the mines—with no information flowing upward. As a consequence, officials in Denver were ignorant of what went on in their mines. Their authority, therefore, had become arbitrary and unjust. Corporate hierarchy at the mines, the miners believed, must be replaced with a form of workers' democracy. The advantages of such a system over the one currently in place were obvious to the three miners, as was the realization that recognition of the UMWA was essential in achieving their goal.[47]

The three miners argued that the UMWA was essential for ensuring workplace safety, educating inexperienced miners, and settling grievances. Like other miners, they blamed the companies for the mine disasters and viewed the union as an organization that could prevent further tragedy.[48] Allison emphasized the importance of educating inexperienced miners: "The English speaking people there [in the mines] were predominant because this foreign element are illiterate and do not understand the customs very well and down in the mines the intelligent miner has a great deal to contend with from them and . . . they have to be educated, not only to read and write, but to do their work; they have to be taught . . . [to] do right."[49] In these miners' view, inexperienced miners needed to be educated in the unwritten laws of the mines, which were superior to company rules and state statutes: "It is the law of the mines that I am speaking about, not the State laws; the laws that the mines ought to be ruled by." The union could help turn unskilled workers into practical miners by teaching them the miners' laws and customs, Allison explained. Puzzled, Osgood asked what these laws were and how they differed from state laws, to which Hamman replied: "To have the mines [be] safe."[50] The implication was that each mine was unique and that only experienced miners could discern the dangers that lurked underground in each individual mine.

The three miners argued that the UMWA was also essential in protecting the pit committees the workers wanted to establish. Such committees had existed among Anglo-American miners in the past and had functioned as conduits, carrying grievances from the miners to the pit bosses or superintendents. Pit committees could also serve as arbiters between disputing parties. Through this system, the power of the union could counterbalance that of the company to produce a democratic workplace. Operators and miners alike, they stressed, would benefit from such a system.[51]

The operators responded angrily to the miners' view of the art of mining and to their reform recommendations, particularly the establishment of pit committees. "It is human nature that you would want to settle your own grievances," Osgood retorted, "but is that just to the operators? It does not seem to me that it is. . . . . I think we might as well fight this proposition out, with the consent of the Governor, right now. That the proper man to settle grievances is the superintendent of the mines and not a committee of the men. . . . I have to have a certain amount of control over my property and that control must be exercised through the superintendent I choose."[52]

Ammons tried to prevent the talks from ending on that note by turning the conversation to the enforcement of state laws dealing with the coalmine industry. However, neither the miners nor the operators were willing to drop the insoluble question of union recognition. The operators reiterated their refusal to recognize the UMWA. The three miners were equally adamant in insisting that the union was the only way to resolve grievances and ensure workplace safety. In reply to the governor's question about what he would recommend to his fellow workers, Allison stated: "In going back to the mine, we, as the men, want the Union to begin with, the pit committees, and the recognition of the Union." "And that," David Brown shouted, "you will never get."[53]

Evans once again appealed to the operators: "You gentlemen seem to be so fair and, if you are sincere, what objection would you have to drawing a contract so we could go on in peace?" Welborn answered by stating that the miners had enjoyed "ten years of peace at very good wages." Angrily, Evans responded: "We are in no position without an organization to defend ourselves. We are at the mercy of them [local mine officials]."[54]

With this exchange, Ammons adjourned the meeting. Despite the intensity of the proceedings, he still believed the differences between the two sides were reconcilable. With union recognition apparently the only "insurmountable obstacle" to an agreement, he was convinced that a settlement could be reached. He could not understand why the union was so important to the striking miners and their families. He concurred with the operators that the issue of union recognition was not a legitimate basis for striking, and he regarded Allison's and Evans's statements as a petty refusal to consider any settlement proffered that did not include such recognition.[55]

With these views in mind, he proposed a settlement based on the operators' November 5 letter, in which they stipulated that they would continue to operate their mines on the open-shop principle and agreed to observe state statutes pertaining to the coal mining industry. Ammons's settlement plan, which he presented at the close of the conference, completely mirrored the operators' views. It called on both sides to end the strike on the basis that the companies would agree to abide by the state mining laws and re-employ strikers whose places had not been filled and who had not committed violent or unlawful acts. The miners were asked to give up the recognition issue and the demand for higher wages in return for the operators' promise to obey the law.[56]

Without hesitation, Welborn, Brown, and Osgood accepted the governor's proposal. The three miners indicated that they were not authorized to agree to any plan that did not include recognition of the union. They told Secretary Wilson that since the plan was identical to the operators' original offer, it would be useless to submit it to the strikers, who, they said, would most assuredly reject it. Wilson, however, agreed with the governor and the operators that the proposal should be submitted to the miners for consideration.[57]

In an effort to achieve something out of the conference and to placate the miners, Wilson drew up an arbitration plan that would address both the current and future labor disputes. He proposed an arbitration panel consisting of seven members—three selected by the operators, three chosen by the miners, and one chosen by the six members previously selected. Wilson sent his proposal—signed by the governor—to the operators, who refused to consider it until the result of a miners' referendum on Ammons's proposal was known. Although the operators were prepared to reject Wilson's plan, which to them was a step toward bringing union recognition closer, they did not want to go on public record as rejecting it. Their strategy was to force Wilson to withdraw his plan until after the rank-and-file miners had voted on Ammons's proposal. Welborn later informed John McClement in New York that the operators had no intention of submitting the dispute to arbitration, but by forcing a miners' referendum, they had found a way to respond to Wilson's request in "a more effective way than by absolutely declining to consider arbitration."[58] The operators adopted this strategy again the next year with regard to President Wilson's truce plan, which did not contain recognition, only to be shocked when they learned that the union and strikers had accepted it.

In the present case, however, the strategy worked. Seeing no alternative, Wilson withdrew his arbitration proposal and urged the union to accept the operators' demand to put Ammons's proposal to a vote of the striking miners. In deference to Wilson, the union leaders agreed. Subsequently, mass meetings were held in the tent colonies, where the strikers unanimously rejected the governor's proposal because it omitted union recognition and wage issues. The outcome of the vote was clearly anticipated by the operators, who charged that the miners would have accepted the plan had they not been subjected to intimidation by the union's agents.[59]

The outcome of the vote, which he had also expected, convinced Wilson that it would be futile to offer any further ideas about settling the strike, although he brought up the subject of appointing an arbitration board once again during a meeting with Osgood, Welborn, and Brown on December 4, the last day of his stay in Colorado. In his testimony before the Foster Congressional Committee in 1914, Osgood disputed Wilson's claim that he had raised the matter of arbitration during the meeting and denied that the operators had refused to discuss it. The meeting was, Osgood insisted, "simply a pleasant chat in which he [Wilson] asked us if we had any suggestion to make as to how the strike should be brought to an end. He made no suggestion himself, and at no time, other than what information he gave during this conference with the miners, did he make any inquiry from us as to strike conditions or our view—our point of view—with regard to the strike conditions."[60] Osgood and his two colleagues continued to assert that they had never refused to consider Wilson's arbitration plan. No such plan had been offered to them, they insisted, a point that was technically true.

Wilson left for Washington still convinced that the union would have given up its bid for recognition in exchange for the creation of an arbitration board to resolve grievances. He realized, however, that the operators never had any intention of accepting arbitration and would accept nothing but total surrender by the union. Correspondence between Denver and New York City confirmed that view. Welborn informed McClement that the operators did not want an agreement with the union, for "had an understanding between the miners and ourselves been reached it would have received the stamp of approval of the officers of the [union] organization and in that way been twisted into an arrangement between us and the organization." Bowers told Rockefeller much the same thing, assuring him that he and the other Colorado operators would never give the union a victory by accepting arbitration.[61]

Secretary Wilson's trip to Colorado and his effort to resolve the conflict through arbitration convinced Osgood, Welborn, and Brown that the Wilson administration was committed to helping organized labor defeat the open-shop principle. Although they realized that their rejection of arbitration greatly enhanced the chances of a congressional investigation of the strike, which Secretary Wilson told them he would advocate as the only way to get the facts before the public, they were determined to defend the open shop, even in the face of adverse publicity. The operators justified their position by stressing that they had accepted and the union had rejected Governor Ammons's November 27 proposal. They made an effort—a very successful one—to convince the public that in accepting the proposal they had conceded everything that was reasonable and that by rejecting the proposal the strikers were responsible for an unjustifiable continuation of the strike and for all the violence and disorder that occurred after that date.[62]

Governor Ammons also considered the strikers' rejection of his plan to be the final straw. With the failure of his conference, the governor gave up all hope of brokering a settlement of the strike. The operators' incessant demands combined with mounting public pressure to end the strike finally convinced him to throw the weight of the state entirely behind the mine owners. Without waiting for the outcome of the referendum to confirm the strikers' rejection of his November 27 proposal of settlement, Ammons rescinded his policy against bringing in strikebreakers. From all appearances, the governor had washed his hands of the entire affair, leaving the operators to resolve the matter. "There is no excuse now for high [coal] prices," he stated, "because the mines can be operated."[63] Regardless of whether the governor fully appreciated it, his decision sealed the strikers' fate, for with his latest action it was just a matter of time before the operators prevailed. But it was a time filled with horrible violence and bloodshed.

NOTES

1. Philip Van Cise's testimony, CIR/FR 7: 6806; McGovern and Guttridge, *Coalfield War*, 139; Papanikolas, *Buried Unsung*, 113; "The Southern Colorado Coal Strike," *Outlook* 106 (January 3, 1914): 24–26.

2. McGovern and Guttridge, *Coalfield War*, 138–139.

3. Patterson, "Strike in Colorado," 4–5.

4. Beshoar, *Out of the Depths*, 89–90. The stipulation against enrolling mine guards in the militia was based on the precedent of the 1903–1904 strike, when CF&I and Victor Fuel had shifted gunmen from their own payrolls to that of the state.

5. McGovern and Guttridge, *Coalfield War*, 140–142. The Colorado Supreme Court later ordered Kenehan to issue the certificates of indebtedness.

6. MacGregor quoted in Long, *Where the Sun Never Shines*, 281.

7. President Wilson to Welborn, October 30, 1913, in PWW 28: 475; Bowers to President Wilson, November 8, 1913, in ibid., 507–514, and November 25, 1913, in ibid., 589–590, quote on 589; Welborn to President Wilson, November 10, 1913, in ibid., 518–524.

8. Stewart to Post, November 21, 1913, in ibid., 580–584; Post to Joseph P. Tumulty, November 15, 1913, in ibid., 546–556.

9. President Wilson to Bowers, November 18, 1913, in ibid., 28: 563.

10. Bowers to President Wilson, November 25, 1913, in ibid., 28: 589–590; Bowers to Rockefeller, November 28, 1913, in CIR/FR 9: 8425; Bowers to Starr Murphy, December 6, 1913, in CIR/FR 9: 8426.

11. McGovern and Guttridge, *Coalfield War*, 146, 155; *Rocky Mountain News*, October 22, 1913; Edward Keating, *The Gentleman from Colorado: A Memoir* (Denver: Sage Books, 1964), 379–381.

12. McGovern and Guttridge, *Coalfield War*, 146; Keating, *Gentleman from Colorado*, 380–381.

13. Osgood's testimony, SMM, 457–458; "Colorado Editors Confer on Coal Strike," *The Survey* 31, no. 10 (December 6, 1913): 232. Shaffer had recently purchased the *Rocky Mountain News* from Patterson. The paper turned from being pro-labor to pro-business, especially pro–coal operator, after Shaffer bought it.

14. The entire proceedings of the conference were published in the *Rocky Mountain News*, November 13, 1913, and the *Pueblo Star-Journal*, November 16, 1913. These newspaper accounts are the sources for the material in the next several paragraphs pertaining to the conference.

15. On the eve of the strike, Osgood issued a public statement in which he claimed the state's "real" coalminers were satisfied with their conditions and did

not want to strike but had been coerced into the movement by "outside agitators" (*Trinidad Chronicle-News*, September 22, 1913).

16. *Pueblo Star-Journal*, November 16, 1913.

17. Ibid.

18. Ibid.

19. Ibid.

20. Ibid.

21. Ibid.

22. Osgood stated that the true definition of a strikebreaker was a professional who made breaking strikes his business and who worked in place of men on strike until the strike was broken. In the present situation, he argued, the men seeking employment in the mines were not professional strikebreakers.

23. *Pueblo Star-Journal*, November 16, 1913.

24. Ibid.

25. Ibid. The views Osgood expressed in this talk were almost identical to those contained in the unsigned letter to Governor Ammons dated November 18, 1913, leading me to believe Osgood wrote the letter.

26. Ibid.

27. Recommendations of the Editors' Association, November 13, 1913, in *Brief of the Coal Mining Operators*, 23–26.

28. Operators to editors John C. Shaffer, Frank S. Hoag, H. E. Bowden, L. C. Paddock, and Fred Marvin, November 14, 1913, in ibid., 26; "Statement of Union," in CBLS, *Fourteenth Biennial Report*, 154–155.

29. Beshoar, *Out of the Depths*, 99. There was merit to the union's claim that the conference was stacked against them. The three editors who dissented from the conference report were from the *Colorado Springs Gazette*, the *Denver Express*, and the *Fort Morgan Herald*—the only pro-labor papers in attendance.

30. Manfred F. Boemeke, "The Wilson Administration, Organized Labor, and the Colorado Coal Strike, 1913–1914" (unpublished Ph.D. diss., Princeton University, 1983), 145; Rockefeller to Bowers, containing Rockefeller to William Wilson, November 21, 1913, in CIR/FR 9: 8422.

31. *Rocky Mountain News*, November 26, 1913; William Wilson to President Wilson, May 11, 1914, in PWW 30: 17; Boemeke, "Wilson Administration," 145.

32. *Rocky Mountain News*, November 26, 1913.

33. Ibid., November 25, 1913.

34. Andrews, "Road to Ludlow," 513.

35. Ibid., 514. A copy of the transcript is in "Proceedings of Joint Conference Held in the State Capitol, Denver, Colorado, November 26, 1913," Folder 212A, Box 23, Business Interests series, Record Group 2, Office of the Messrs. Rockefeller (OMR), Rockefeller Family Archives, Rockefeller Archive Center; hereafter cited as "Proceedings of Joint Conference."

36. "Proceedings of Joint Conference," 13.

37. Ibid., 16–17.

38. Andrews, "Road to Ludlow," 516.

39. "Proceedings of Joint Conference," 12.

40. Ibid., 27.

41. Ibid., 113.

42. Ibid., 77.

43. Ibid., 21.

44. Ibid., 29.

45. Ibid., 71–72.

46. Ibid., 76.

47. Andrews, "Road to Ludlow," 521–522.

48. Ibid., 519.

49. "Proceedings of Joint Conference," 113.

50. Ibid., 56–57.

51. Andrews, "Road to Ludlow," 523.

52. "Proceedings of Joint Conference," 89.

53. Ibid., 247.

54. Ibid., 254–255.

55. Andrews, "Road to Ludlow," 525.

56. Ammons to Welborn, Osgood, Brown, Evans, Allison, Hamnan, November 27, 1913, in CIR/FR 7: 7037; operators' letter to Ammons, November 5, 1913, in *Brief of the Coal Mining Operators,* 22; Boemeke, "Wilson Administration," 146.

57. McGovern and Guttridge, *Coalfield War,* 153; William Wilson Memorandum to President Wilson, December 10, 1913, in PWW 29: 31; Welborn, Brown, Osgood (copy) to Ammons, November 27, 1913, Ammons Papers, FF-5.

58. Welborn, Brown, Osgood (copy) to Ammons, November 30, 1913, Ammons Papers, FF–5; Welborn to McClement, December 4, 1913, in CIR/FR 8: 7118.

59. Welborn to McClement, December 4, 1913, in CIR/FR 8: 7118; *Rocky Mountain News,* December 4, 1913; Witt Bowden, "New Developments in the Colorado Strike Situation," *The Survey* 31, no. 20 (February 14, 1914): 613; W. B. Wilson (copy) to Welborn, Brown, Osgood, December 1, 1913, Ammons Papers, FF-5.

60. Osgood's testimony, SMM, 419.

61. Welborn to McClement, December 4, 1913, in CIR/FR 8: 7118; Bowers to Rockefeller, November 22, 28, 1913, in ibid., 9: 8423, 8424–8425.

62. Bowers to Starr Murphy, December 6, 1913, in CIR/FR 9: 8426; West, *Report on the Colorado Strike,* 90; Secretary Wilson Memorandum of December 10, 1913, in PWW 29: 32; Boemeke, "Wilson Administration," 150.

63. Ammons quoted in McGovern and Guttridge, *Coalfield War,* 156.

Congressional Investigation

In the years following his term as governor, Elias Ammons was unsure whether he had actually declared martial law or assumed that it automatically applied when he ordered the militia into the southern Colorado strike zone. The governor had directed General John Chase to use his own "judgment and discretion . . . in conjunction with, or independently of, the civil authorities" to maintain peace and order in the southern Colorado coal district and to bring about the speedy reopening and full operation of the coalmines. Chase believed the governor's instructions gave him authority to take any action he pleased. Therefore, the general, rather than the governor, actually declared martial law in the strike zone. The declaration of martial law allowed Chase to establish a military commission to prosecute civilians arrested under his authority. According to George McGovern, there was likely never "a more complete abdication of civil authority in peace time to a military commander so temperamentally ill-suited for his responsibility."[1]

General Chase acted with utmost speed in rounding up and incarcerating leading unionists. Hundreds of people, some not even union members or miners, were arrested by the end of the year, and many were held incommunicado for long periods as "military prisoners." Most of the arrests were a form of intimidation. Judge Advocate Major Edward Boughton, the chief legal officer who led the proceedings, admitted that General Chase was indifferent to whether the men his military commission held in jail were guilty or innocent. What was important to the general was to fulfill his duty, as he saw it, to use the militia to break the strike.[2] Incarceration under the most horrible conditions broke neither the spirit nor the will of the most stalwart unionists, however. Instead, the general's dictatorial tactics raised the ire of members of the State Federation of Labor, who, at the urging of John Lawson and Frank Hayes, called a special convention for December 16 in Denver for the purpose of protecting both "the rights of every worker in this state" and "the public from the unbridled greed and outrages of the coal operators."[3]

Approximately 500 delegates representing nearly 250 unions answered the call, including most local and national United Mine Workers of America (UMWA) officers and Mother Jones. On the first day of the convention, the delegates began to debate resolutions for the recall of Governor Ammons and the retirement of General Chase. During the debate, Mother Jones, demanding that Governor Ammons be hanged forthwith, challenged the delegation to march with her to the statehouse to confront the governor. The delegates, joined by hundreds of other persons, filed behind her and Louis Tikas, the Greek leader of the Ludlow tent colony, carrying a Ludlow banner, to make their way through Denver's snow-banked streets to the capitol.[4]

Governor Ammons agreed to meet the convention delegates in the House of Representatives chamber, where he answered several questions from a written list handed to him. However, the governor became agitated when the delegates expressed disapproval of his answers to questions dealing with General Chase and the holding of prisoners incommunicado. He demanded proof of the charge that Chase and Boughton were tyrants who were "mere tools and lickspittles for the mine owners." Angered by the shouts of disapproval, the governor abruptly ended the meeting.[5]

On the last day of the convention the delegates passed a lengthy resolution that demanded the release of all military prisoners and the removal of

Chase and Boughton. The delegates gave Ammons five days to carry out the resolution's intent or face a recall petition. They also empowered the federation's executive board to call a statewide strike at any time it saw fit. "We call upon the great body of Americans to not drive workingmen into the ranks of the anarchists," the resolution stated. "The law was not made simply for the rich. There is not a man who will read this declaration but knows that [if] Osgood, Brown, and Rockefeller, who are fighting the strikers with a malignity hitherto unknown in American history, were arrested, they would not be held *incommunicado* or denied counsel. Can any fair-minded man blame us for bitterness when the laborer is thus, by the officers of the law, denied the rights granted to the rich?" The convention attendees demanded that the laborer be granted "every privilege before the law which the rich man" enjoyed and vowed to acquire those privileges "lawfully" if they could. "Again, we say, if this be treason, let the coal operators make the most of it."[6]

Among other resolutions passed by the convention was one condemning the editors' position in support of the operators during their November conference. Another resolution specifically condemned John Osgood's "[b]latant hypocrisy" in accusing the union of lawlessness at that conference as a way to "besmirch the characters" of the members of the UMWA. "J. C. Osgood," the resolution stipulated, "has for many years openly and flagrantly defied and broken many of the laws of the land, both in his commercial and private life."[7]

Governor Ammons ignored both the threats and the demands in the resolution, and at the end of the five-day grace period the federation's executive board did not initiate a recall of the governor or call a statewide labor strike. Instead, the board accepted the governor's challenge to conduct a probe of the militia by naming an investigating committee with John Lawson as chair. With the governor's assurance that the National Guard would cooperate, the members of the committee left at once for the southern Colorado coalfield.[8]

Contrary to the governor's instruction, however, General Chase refused to cooperate with the investigating committee. He would not allow the committee to interview any members of the National Guard and instructed that all information about the militia come directly from him. Undeterred, the committee members went to the various tent colonies, nearby ranches, residences, and towns—including Aguilar and Trinidad—and interviewed more than 160 persons. While they were at Ludlow, a score of witnesses—including one of the committee members—saw and heard Karl Linderfelt, recently commissioned as a lieutenant in the militia, verbally and physically assault Louis Tikas and verbally assault a young boy who had no connection to the strike or the colony. Linderfelt shouted to Tikas: "I am Jesus Christ, and my men on horses are Jesus Christs, and we must be obeyed." According to several witnesses in the Ludlow depot where the confrontation between the two men occurred, Linderfelt swore at Tikas and told him he had a bunch of soldiers who had just returned from Mexico and they were going "to clean out every goddamn striker and Dago in the country."[9]

After the committee had returned to Trinidad, Lawson wired Governor Ammons to report the incidents. Linderfelt "rages violently upon little or no provocation," the wire said, "and is wholly an unfit man to bear arms and command men as he has no control over himself. We have reason to believe that it is his deliberate purpose to provoke the strikers to bloodshed. He has threatened to kill Louis Tikas. . . . In the interest of peace and justice, we ask immediate action in his case." At about the same time, militiaman Captain W. C. Danks suggested to Major Boughton that it might be a good idea to dismiss Linderfelt from the National Guard. Neither the governor nor the major took any action on Lawson's and Dank's advice. One can only wonder what the course of history in the southern Colorado coalfields in 1914 would have been if they had done so.[10]

Lawson's investigating committee finished its report in January 1914 and sent it to the governor, along with a complete transcript of testimony. The report contained testimonials describing the militia's various activities, including illegal searches of strikers' quarters and the theft of their money and property. The militia was also charged with violating the law by escorting strikebreakers to the mines and keeping them there by force of arms and of using cruel and inquisitorial methods against prisoners. Based on these findings, the report recommended the resignation of General Chase, the discharge of all mine guards and Baldwin-Felts detectives serving in the militia, enforcement of the law prohibiting the importation of strikebreakers, and an end to the practice of militia companies selecting their own officers. Governor Ammons dismissed the report with the comment that the testimony the committee had gathered had not been sworn.[11]

Congressman Edward Keating of Colorado was much more interested in the report than the governor was. Before it was completed, the investigating committee had notified Keating and the other members of the Colorado congressional delegation that the report would document the militia's "gross violations" of the strikers' constitutional rights. "[W]e earnestly urge," they wired Keating, "that every effort be made to secure a full congressional investigation, not only of the real causes of the strike in Colorado, but also of the conduct of the state militia in violating federal constitutional rights under General Chase's orders." In his response, Keating told the committee members he believed he could secure a federal investigation as soon as Congress reconvened.[12] With disillusionment setting in at the union offices in Colorado and Indianapolis, leaders in both places increasingly pinned their hopes on a congressional investigation to save them from defeat.

Meanwhile, the union leaders faced a legal challenge of their own. The federal grand jury appointed to investigate the strike at the demand of the coal operators issued its report on December 2, 1913. It indicted twenty-five members of the UMWA—including John White, the national president, and John Lawson, Adolph Germer, and Robert Uhlich among the Colorado strike leaders—for violation of the Sherman Anti-Trust Law. "This marks the first attempt of capital to destroy all organized labor by means of the anti-trust law," the *Denver Express* declared. "The indictments charge the miners with violating a federal law by doing something the Colorado law recognizes as legal." The *Express* headlined the story by observing that the coal barons who had commanded the indictment of union officials were themselves described in the report as having violated state laws in the past. Although the grand jury did not bring indictments against them, the jury findings included significant legal confirmation of industry malpractice. The report stipulated that the coal companies had not observed state laws; that they had nominated, elected, and controlled county officials; and that company camp marshals had resorted to arbitrary police powers and had brutally assaulted miners. Furthermore, the report found that the scrip system was still in effect at some properties, that miners were obliged to trade at company stores, and that the hiring of check-weighmen had been denied.[13]

The union officials took the indictments in stride. Frank Hayes stated that the principles upon which the union leaders stood could never be indicted and would "prevail until human slavery ceases to exist." He continued: "We are accused of violating the Sherman Anti-trust law and of organizing a conspiracy in restraint of trade. If they mean by the term 'restraint of trade' that we have restrained John D. Rockefeller and a few other eastern millionaires from plundering the miners of Colorado, then we plead guilty to the indictment and we are proud of the achievement." It was now evident, Hayes concluded, "that these coal companies are greater than the state government, and that they can do as they please, so far as the law is concerned."[14]

The union men under indictment need not have worried. Upon the advice of District Attorney Harry E. Kelly, the Department of Justice quashed the indictments before any warrants were served.[15] To the coal operators' dismay, the only result of the grand jury report was to provide damaging information against them to the congressional committee soon appointed to investigate conditions in the coalmines and camps in southern Colorado.

John Lawson and the other union strike leaders in Colorado were too busy with other matters to pay much attention to the grand jury indictments. Lawson in particular was involved in collecting the affidavits of scores of alleged victims of militia abuse to correct the error cited by Governor Ammons in the investigative committee's report. He was also helping the colonists dig out from the early December snowfall, one of the heaviest in the state's history, which had buried the tent colonies under four to six feet of snow. Many of the tents had collapsed under the weight of the snow or from winds that formed drifts twelve to fifteen feet high. "This ought to cause a good many of the strikers who are living in the tents provided by the [union] organization to seek comfortable houses and employment at the mines," Jesse Welborn wrote with obvious glee to Rockefeller's office in New York.[16] As always, he was wrong about the will of the strikers. Although the suffering in the camps was great, not a single person left. The hardships brought by the storm only strengthened the strikers' determination to continue their struggle against the coal companies.

Isolated in their snowbound tents, the strikers and their families were consumed by a fierce hatred of the militia. The strikers observed the liaison between the militia and the mine owners that the authorities, including the governor, allowed to develop openly. They saw the ranks of the militia increasingly filled with Baldwin-Felts agents and former camp marshals or mine guards, who continued to be paid by the coal companies in spite of the governor's prohibition against such enlistment. They saw General Chase on the roads in an automobile owned by Colorado Fuel and Iron (CF&I), and they stood by helplessly as militiamen and mine guards raided their camps, abusing young girls and stealing money and jewelry from their tents while pretending to search for arms and ammunition. They witnessed a reign of terror unleashed against them, with scores of their leaders and comrades arrested and held as military prisoners. Worst of all, they saw the militia escorting strikebreakers to the mines, an act that destroyed the last vestige of goodwill between the strikers and militia troops.[17]

The coal operators made sure the militia had an abundant supply of labor to escort to the mines. When they learned from General Chase that Governor Ammons had given him oral permission to permit the importation of strikebreakers, the operators immediately swung into action long before the governor officially lifted the ban prohibiting such activity in late

November 1913. Earlier in the month, the coal companies had opened a recruiting office in Joplin, Missouri, where hundreds of men were promised the opportunity to purchase fertile land for ridiculously low prices in the West provided they went to Colorado and worked at a steady job for at least thirty days. They were promised $3.08 or more in pay per day and free railroad passage. They were not told that they would be employed in strike-bound coalmines. Besides, many who signed up could not read the purported contracts between them and the companies. If the testimony of some of these men before the congressional investigating committee was truthful, they did not know they were being hired as scabs. The recruitment campaign was later extended to Chicago, Cincinnati, Toledo, and Pittsburgh. From Joplin alone, more than 100 men, mostly recent immigrants, were transported to Colorado. Hundreds more left from the other cities where recruitment had taken place, primarily in bars. Mine guards boarded trains at the Kansas-Colorado line to complete the trip, then escorted the new recruits to the mines from where there was little chance of escape.[18]

The sworn affidavit of four immigrant Italian workers illustrates the procedure for importing strikebreakers followed by Osgood's Victor-American Fuel Company. According to the document, the four were stopped on a Pittsburgh street and asked whether they wanted work. They said yes and were taken to an employment agency where they were told their railroad fare would be paid to a job in Colorado that paid five or six dollars a day. They were assured that everything was "Ok, no strike and no trouble." With that assurance, they boarded a train bound for Trinidad, along with forty-eight other Italians and over a hundred other foreigners. They arrived the evening of December 17, 1913. A body of soldiers met them, gave them a card or paper with a wage scale for work, and told them there was a strike on. After being held in Trinidad for about twenty minutes, they were marched to the train for Delagua and "asinged [sic] a place to board." On December 19, the statement continued, "they put us to work in the mines, we worked every day untill [sic] the 25th of January, 1914, at which time we called for our time and was told there was nothing coming." They tried to get out of the camp but were told they could not leave without a pass. After several attempts to secure a pass, they were finally granted permission to leave and were escorted out of town. "When we left," the workers stated, "the company claimed we were indebt to them. Allthough [sic] their statement shows there was money due us."[19] With no money or food, they walked thirty-five miles to Walsenburg.

The contract presented to the imported workers outlined the lowest wages to be paid for each category of worker as well as expenses and terms of employment. The scale for pick mining ranged from 55 to 60 cents per ton; blacksmiths were paid $3.25 per day; drivers, rope riders, and motormen $3.08 per day; and trackmen, timbermen, and rock men $3.10 per day. The terms of employment included an eight-hour workday underground and a biweekly payday. Expenses included $2.00 per room per month, 35 to 40 cents per month for electricity, 50 cents per month for blacksmith costs, and $1.00 per month for doctor and hospital care. It was explicitly stated that any worker who chose to leave the mine to which he had been shipped within thirty days would forfeit the cost of his transportation and would be required to pay back the transportation cost of any family member who had accompanied him at the rate of $5.00 per month until fully paid. The bold print on the form declaring that a coal strike was on in Colorado meant nothing to the imported workers, for as recent immigrants from southern and southeastern Europe, few of them could read or write. Two of the four men who signed the affidavit previously discussed did so with the mark "X." Like the majority of their cohorts, it is doubtful that they understood the terms of the contract they were forced to sign.[20]

Strikebreakers began to arrive in large numbers in mid-November 1913, at least two weeks before the governor lifted the ban on their importation. With their arrival the strikers' picketers became more aggressive, particularly the women at Ludlow, who were determined to "clean up" the scabs. But despite their aggressive actions, they were able to block only a few strikebreakers from reaching the mines. On the morning of November 30, 1913, it appeared that the entire Ludlow tent colony—men, women, and children—assembled to turn back a train reputed to have strikebreakers aboard. The women brandished ball bats, clubs with spikes driven through them, or sharpened branches. A detail of National Guard troops with fixed bayonets managed to clear the depot and grounds. "We drove them out rather easily," Captain Philip Van Cise, officer in charge of the detail, reported. "Then they lined up in the road east of the depot and the women all formed in the front rank, with the men behind. The women were brandishing their war clubs and were very violent, but the men were generally quiet; the women were cursing in violent fashion." Van Cise rounded up three of the strikers' leaders and threatened to shoot them if any violence broke out. The train arrived with five or six strikebreakers aboard, but, unlike other occasions, Van Cise ordered that the strikebreakers be sent back to Trinidad on the same train.[21]

With the ban against importing strikebreakers lifted and the militia authorized to escort them to the mines, the strikers could do little but jeer the scabs at the depots. By the end of the year, the coal companies had imported 1,400 strikebreakers to work their mines. With such success, the operators faced the new year with increased optimism. "Since we commenced to ship men from the east," Jesse Welborn reported to the CF&I executive board, "our forces have increased rapidly, and unless some unforeseen interference develops, we should be able to take care of practically all demands on us for coal late in January." Publicly, the operators downplayed the number of strikebreakers they had brought in. Of the 9,600 men the operators reported at work, they claimed the vast majority were old employees who had deserted the union cause and returned to work. At the same time, the union reported 19,300 men, women, and children on strike relief. If the union's figures were correct, it would seem that few had deserted the tent colonies.[22]

Unlike the glow of optimism in the coal industrialists' offices, the mood among union leaders and strikers was gloomy as 1913 ended. They had failed to shut down the mines, and the strike was having little effect on coal production or the state's economy. They had failed to garner public support. General Chase was still holding many unionists as military prisoners without charging them with any crime. National union officials were increasingly losing hope for victory. "We have a serious situation out here," Frank Hayes wrote to Mother Jones from Trinidad. "The operators are doing everything imaginable to break the spirit of the men."[23] In typical fashion, Mother Jones refused to bow to defeatism. With uncanny timing, she took center stage in the confrontation between the union on the one side and General Chase and Governor Ammons on the other. Her intervention raised the strikers' spirits and put them in a fighting mood once again.

The incident, or series of incidents, occurred in early 1914. On January 4, in defiance of General Chase's announcement that she would be jailed if she returned to the southern Colorado coalfields, Mother Jones left Denver and traveled to Trinidad. She was arrested upon her arrival and, with a military escort, immediately put on a train back to Denver. General Chase ordered her to leave the state and threatened to hold her incommunicado if she returned to the strike zone. "I am not going to give her a chance to make any more speeches here," the general said. "She is dangerous because she inflames the minds of the strikers."[24]

On January 11, Mother Jones slipped past the guards posted at Union Station in Denver and boarded a southbound train. She got off the train at an unscheduled stop on the outskirts of Trinidad and made her way to the Toltec Hotel, where General Chase eventually arrested her in person. Although the governor wanted her deported, Chase, who knew she wanted to go to jail, instead had her confined under "military surveillance" at Mount

San Rafael Hospital on the eastern outskirts of Trinidad. There she would remain under guard and be denied visitors, Chase told her, until she agreed to leave the strike zone permanently.[25]

General Chase had shown more sensitivity to public opinion concerning Mother Jones than the governor had, but to no avail. The union, to Mother Jones's delight, made the most of her incarceration, which drew national attention. Political cartoons depicted the coal operators and the militia in a bad light. As the notoriety grew, several hundred coalminers from Fremont County threatened to march on Trinidad to liberate Mother Jones if Governor Ammons refused to do so himself. Women from Las Animas County took up the strikers' cause by organizing a demonstration and parade in Trinidad on January 23 to protest Mother Jones's confinement. That morning people from all parts of the state arrived at the depot, and shortly after 2 P.M. more than a thousand women and children marched up Commercial Street and then east on Main toward Mount San Rafael Hospital—more than likely, General Chase suspected, in an attempt to free the celebrated prisoner.[26]

The marchers were stopped opposite the post office by a cordon of National Guard cavalrymen. General Chase, mounted on his cavalry horse in front of his men, ordered the women and children to turn back. After hesitating momentarily, the women at the front of the marching column moved forward toward the mounted troopers. As the women advanced, General Chase's horse brushed a young girl who was watching the event. According to witnesses, the general kicked at the girl, hitting her in the breast with his spurred boot. The general's horse became frightened and either stumbled or bolted into a horse and buggy, causing General Chase to fall to the ground. The women screeched with derisive laughter at the sight of the embarrassed general sprawled on the street.[27]

What followed was later called "the Mother Jones riot." Witnesses swore that an angry Chase yelled at his men to "ride down the women." The general rode into the crowd yelling like a madman and swinging his pistol back and forth as his cavalrymen charged the women with drawn sabers. With screams of terror, the women and children scurried to the safety of porches and yards. Three women were severely cut in the melee. Several other protestors suffered blows from troopers' fists or rifle butts.[28]

The cavalry charge was a propaganda bonanza for the strikers. "GREAT CZAR FELL! AND IN FURY TOLD TROOPS TO TRAMPLE WOMEN" was the headline in the *Denver Express* that day. The lead story sensationalized the incident: "A craven general tumbled from his nag in a street of Trinidad. . . . In fifteen minutes there was turmoil, soldiers with swords were striking at fleeing women and children; all in the name of the Sovereign State of Colorado. For Gen. Chase, having lost his poise on his horse, also lost his temper and cried, 'Ride down the women!' A throng of mothers and wives intent only on a mass meeting of sympathy for Mother Jones, had laughed at Chase's fall."[29]

The riot aroused the passions of coalminers throughout the state and revived support for the strike, at least momentarily. Hundreds of angry strikers decided to annihilate the militiamen and mine guards. The Greeks, led by Louis Tikas, stealthily moved in the darkness of night to positions in the hills above militia headquarters near Trinidad. The plan called for an attack, in which the Greek fighters and other miners would close in on the militia from all sides and destroy them with one mighty blow. Other groups of miners from Segundo, Tercio, and Sopris had quietly slipped into Trinidad and unobtrusively manned the rooftops of business buildings. A hundred sharpshooters took up sniping positions around General Chase's headquarters. Hidden in buildings below were detachments of twenty-five to thirty men ready to spring into action when the signal was given. A telegram from Congressman Edward Keating arrived just in time to change the course of history.[30]

Through his tireless efforts and the support of President Wilson, on January 27 Keating won approval of his resolution calling for a congressional investigation of the Colorado strike. Perhaps the wave of popular sympathy for coalminers unleashed by the Mother Jones riot was a factor in the passage of the resolution. Whatever the case, it was a major victory for a first-term congressman over seasoned pro-business conservatives in Congress.[31] Keating immediately wired the news to Trinidad. Lawson received the telegram at about the same time he learned of the contemplated attack on the militia and General Chase's headquarters. With little time to spare, Lawson found Tikas and demanded that the attack be called off. Reluctantly, Tikas complied, and the miners returned to their camps. The arrival of his telegram, Keating correctly observed, had narrowly prevented "an appalling tragedy."[32]

The U.S. House Subcommittee on Mines and Mining began its hearings in Denver on February 9, 1914. Dr. Martin D. Foster, a retired physician from Illinois, was chair of the five-member committee, which also included James F. Byrnes of South Carolina, John M. Evans of Montana, Richard W. Austin of Tennessee, and Howard Sutherland of West Virginia. During the hearings, the committee allowed the attorneys representing the "big three" coal companies, the UMWA, and the National Guard to cross-examine witnesses.[33] The exhaustive, painstaking investigation would produce one of the most complete historical records of the strike. Unfortunately for the miners, it did not bring public opinion over to their side and force the mine owners to end the strike.

John Osgood was called to testify before the committee on February 12, 1914. Under the friendly examination of his company's own lawyer, Frank Gove, he related his version of the history of labor unrest in Colorado during the past twenty years and the causes of the present strike. In his lengthy opening argument, he dismissed each of the union demands as groundless, as mere tools to put public pressure on the mine owners to force them to recognize the union. He reiterated his determination never to have any business relations with the union.[34]

Although he "was characteristically harsh and uncompromising," Barron Beshoar described Osgood's frank dissertation as "[p]erhaps the clearest and most explicit statement of coal company policy and attitude toward working men" presented during the investigation.[35] Since most of his opinions and policies have already been discussed in this study, they need not be repeated here. For the most part, he merely reiterated what he had said during the newspaper editors' conference the previous November. However, he introduced a new interpretation as to why many more men had gone on strike than were UMWA members. "A large number of our men are Slavs and Italians," he said, "and they belong to benevolent organizations of their own workingmen and the rules of these organizations prohibit a member from working in a territory where there is a strike going on. The men are not members of the United Mine Workers of America, but of this society and would not work under strike conditions." Osgood implied that these men had no attachment to the union but had joined the strike for practical reasons: they did not want to jeopardize their own lives or the fraternal organization to which they belonged.[36]

Edward Costigan, representing the UMWA, took over the questioning during the second day of Osgood's testimony. He quickly turned the committee's attention to the Pueblo federal grand jury report of December 2, 1913, about which Osgood had not previously testified. Characterizing the report as "reflecting severely upon the coal operators," Costigan asked Osgood to respond to specific charges in the report. In answering whether the charge was true that the coal companies "discouraged and opposed the organization of labor unions and fraternal societies in the camps in fear of the effect of such organizations in taking from them the control and

John C. Osgood, David W. Brown (center), president of Rocky Mountain Fuel Company, and Jesse F. Welborn, president of CF&I, testifying before the Foster Congressional Committee in Denver, February 1914. Courtesy, Denver Public Library, Western History Collection, call no. Osgood Biography, F 23636.

discipline of their men," Osgood simply said, "I think so." To statements in the report that the eight-hour law was frequently violated by both operators and miners, that many miners believed mine officials frequently discharged employees for requesting check-weighman, and that coal companies had used their political influence to control many county officials, Osgood answered either that to his knowledge Victor-American Fuel Company had always obeyed the law or that he was not personally aware of any complaints of the nature contained in the report. As to how many check-weighmen were employed in his mines, Osgood stated that the law provided the opportunity for the men themselves to select the check-weighmen, but "in none of the mines that I know of have they done it." Therefore, he added, no mines with which he was familiar had appointed check-weighmen.[37]

Costigan had other questions about the grand jury report. He started with camp saloons. "Many of the coal companies," he quoted from the report, "maintain camp saloons and collect from the keepers of such saloons a per capita sum of 25 to 40 cents per month for each person whose name appears upon the company pay roll as a charge against the saloon keeper for the privilege of enjoying the exclusive saloon business of the camp." The report, Costigan continued, noted that the saloons produced "a deplorable situation among the miners, addicting them to the use of strong drink and thereby impairing their efficiency by lessening the production and increasing the hazard in operating the mine." The union lawyer asked Osgood to explain the connection between coal companies and the saloons. "We regulate their hours of closing and regulate the manner of their selling liquor to men who are already intoxicated and to minors," Osgood responded, "and from my personal observation and from reports that have been made to me, we are as orderly there in our saloons as can be found anywhere, and they [saloons] seem to us to be a necessity of camp life." Osgood tried to deflect criticism of the saloons' negative influence by stating that those mentioned in the grand jury report were beyond the control of his Victor-American camps.[38]

Costigan turned to the subject of how Osgood and the Victor-American Fuel Company dealt with employee grievances. Asked if he had ever instituted an investigation into complaints registered against his company, Osgood observed that the only complaints he had heard were general in character and were leveled only during strikes. Therefore, he stated, "I made no investigations, because I had no specific complaint, and from information received, I believe that we have fair-minded and competent men in charge." Elaborating, he said: "I think there is an intention on the part of our superintendent[s] to find out the merits of any grievances complained of and if possible to cure them." Although he was not sure whether the company's general manager had instructed the superintendents regarding the investigation and redress of grievances, he knew it was "in the spirit and practice of the company to have all such cases investigated."[39]

Osgood's testimony contributed to the committee's conclusion that company officials in Denver and New York City did not know what was happening at their mines and camps and did not care enough to find out. They simply trusted and accepted the reports of their camp managers and superintendents. "Absentee owners or directors by their absence from the scene of such disturbances," the majority members of the committee stated, "can not escape their moral responsibility for conditions in and about the properties in which they are interested."[40] Although directed at John D. Rockefeller Jr., the statement could have applied to Osgood just as well, for his concept of corporate business and his labor-management policies were little different from those of either Rockefeller or his father at the time of the 1913–1914 Colorado strike. The main difference between Osgood and the younger Rockefeller was that the latter had never been exposed to the everyday concerns and conditions of the workingman. Apparently, though, what Osgood had learned about workingmen during his forty-three years in the coal business was irrelevant at this juncture of his career when everything was secondary to defeating and destroying the UMWA.

Near the end of Osgood's second day of testimony, James Byrnes, acting as chair of the committee, asked if he would agree to a board of conciliation that would include representatives of the employees to resolve grievances not settled on the local level. Osgood responded with a resounding "no." He insisted that he must be the final person to decide all issues regarding the operation of his company: "When I operate the property, after giving a fair hearing to these men with reference to their grievances, in an earnest desire to correct anything that is not fair, I want to decide how that matter shall be treated, in connection with my mine and business enterprise, the dead work to be paid for, and such questions as are largely brought up, I want to be the one to decide." For the good of everybody, Osgood reiterated, he and his appointed company officials must determine the reasonableness of all employee grievances.[41]

This exchange ended with Osgood emphatically stating once again that he would never consent to submitting labor disputes, especially ones over wage scales, to arbitration. There could have been no doubt in the minds of the committee members that Osgood was one of the most, if not the most, reactionary of the Colorado coal operators. But he was not the main target of the investigation. Although they acknowledged Osgood's leadership role on the operators' policy committee, members of the congressional committee placed most of the blame for the troubles in Colorado's coalfields on the junior Rockefeller and CF&I officials. In a curious rebuttal of the charge, counsel for the operators argued that Rockefeller should not be charged with being the sole offending party responsible for "all the imaginary ills" of miners in Colorado. Osgood, they stressed, had been one of the most active parties in formulating the operators' policy during the present strike, policy Rockefeller accepted as his own. As the oldest and most experienced coal operator in the state, no one was in a better position to know the business of coal mining than Osgood, they stated, adding: "[T]hose who know that gentleman's character, and who heard him testify from the witness stand, or who read his testimony, can not be led to believe that Mr. Rockefeller or any other individual shapes his line of thought or dictates what he shall do in his association with the United Mine Workers of America. Moreover, no one could accuse him of not being thoroughly familiar with all the conditions which obtain in the mines of Colorado and as they have changed from the inception of the mining industry in the State."[42]

With this statement, the counsel for the operators asserted that the coal operators' strike policy had been formulated in Colorado and not in New York and that Osgood had played a leading role in devising it. Most members of both the Foster Congressional Committee and the Commission on Industrial Relations, which would report on the strike situation in 1915, refused to accept this assertion. Instead, they continued to place most of the responsibility on Rockefeller for the events that happened in Colorado.

Regardless of who bore most of the blame for the Colorado troubles, Osgood, Rockefeller, and the other coal operators shared a passionate belief in the open-shop philosophy. In practice, the principle meant every man had a guaranteed right to work for whom and for what pay he pleased under the conditions that seemed best to him. The majority on the investigating committee, however, had a different view of the open-shop principle and the operators' "right-to-work" concept. They concluded that the operators advocated the open-shop principle "only for the purpose of holding in control their workmen and compelling them to work for them under such conditions as they chose to give them, and such wages as they might feel like paying." The operators' assertion that they were fighting for the liberty of the workingman would not "bear investigation," the majority report stated. Although the report singled out Rockefeller, references to "operators" throughout the text clearly indicate that nearly everything attributed to the New York financier applied equally to the Colorado coal barons. The strike could have been settled without the operators recognizing the union, the committee believed, had they been willing to meet with union leaders, as they should have done, or had they agreed to arbitration. Instead, they chose force as the method for settling the industrial dispute, something that, the majority members declared, "should be a thing of the past."[43]

After hearing from the governor and the coal officials in Denver, the investigating committee transferred the hearings to Trinidad to question miners, union officials, and local company officials. On their way south, the five committee members visited the Ludlow tent colony, where the strikers gave them a warm welcome.[44] During the hearings in Trinidad's West Theater, Chairman Foster permitted the committee considerable latitude in taking evidence in investigating probable causes of the strike. Taking advantage of that latitude, union leaders used the affidavits they had collected from strikers and former strikebreakers to prove their case against the coal operators. Over the objection of Representative Byrnes, the majority on the committee agreed to include this testimony in a report to Congress. In arguing his case, Byrnes expressed his opinion that an investigation of the causes of the industrial unrest in Colorado and of the relations between capital and labor was beyond the mandate of the congressional resolution authorizing the hearings, which, he reminded his colleagues, was limited to whether any federal laws had been violated. Although he agreed with many of the findings, he believed much of the testimony was unauthorized; therefore, since the committee in his estimation had found no violation of federal law, he was opposed to submitting a report to Congress. He did not want to contribute to the impression being created throughout the nation that Colorado was "inhabited exclusively by oppressive coal barons and lawless bloodthirsty strikers."[45] Fortunately for the historical record, the other committee members did not share Byrnes's opinion.

For the most part, the majority report was an indictment of the coal operators, state authorities, and the Colorado National Guard. The report stated that the militia was on the side of the operators and had not acted impartially in its duty to restore peace, protect property, and prevent violence. Had the militia been impartial and performed its duty as it should have, the committee members concluded, much of the loss of life and destruction of property that had occurred could have been prevented. The members criticized the coal companies for hiring private guards, including Baldwin-Felts agents, and stated that only proper peace officials should have been relied upon to maintain law and order. Furthermore, the report concluded that the manner of selecting juries in the two southern Colorado counties of Las Animas and Huerfano appeared to be against the law. The committee also stressed that although martial law might be a military necessity, the wholesale arrest of men without some stated charge against them and their imprisonment for long periods without benefit of a court trial "seems contrary to our idea of justice and a usurpation of civil law." If it was necessary to put men in prison to prevent violence, why, the majority members asked, was it not just as necessary for state authorities to prevent the sale of arms and ammunition to the contending parties? The testimony heard by the committee, the report stated in one of its most striking passages, "leaves little doubt as to the deplorable conditions existing there [southern Colorado] as to the denial of social, industrial, and political justice. No thinking person can read the testimony . . . without being convinced that fundamentally and underlying all these disturbances there must be some evil which right thinking and acting people would be able to correct."[46]

The situation that existed in the closed camps, the majority report stated, "was like a system of feudalism, with such regulations by law as the operators were willing should be put into operation." As long as those conditions existed, the congressmen stated, no permanent order could be established. The constant oppression, neglect, and arbitrary conduct of coal company officials "were prolific causes of the dissatisfaction which resulted in this disturbance and the consequent destruction of life and property."[47] It was unfortunate for the people of Colorado, the report continued, that these periodic strikes had occurred with no apparent way of settling them except by force. The committee again stressed that arbitration was the only solution to labor disputes of this nature. All "parties to such a dispute must not be permitted to embroil a State or States in a prolonged and bloody warfare that disturbs so disastrously the peace and welfare of the Nation."[48]

Realizing that they had done all they could under the terms of their charge, the committee members ended their investigation with the recognition that a more thorough inquiry into the underlying causes of the Colorado strike and specific recommendations to Congress for the remedy of labor disputes would have to be undertaken by the U.S. Commission on Industrial Relations. That investigation began in December 1914 and continued into the spring of 1915, resulting in further condemnation of the Colorado coal operators.[49]

The strike zone had remained relatively peaceful while the Foster Congressional Committee remained in Colorado. Taking advantage of the calm and unable to bear the expense of keeping the militia in the field any longer, Governor Ammons withdrew all but 200 troops from the strike zone on February 27, 1914. The calm did not last, however, as strife broke out again within days following the congressional delegation's departure. The first instance occurred at the Forbes tent colony. General Chase accused strikers there of killing a non-union miner named Neil Smith, although a Colorado and Southern Railroad crew reported that the victim had staggered drunk into the path of their locomotive. Following Sheriff James Grisham's arrest of sixteen strikers on the charge of killing Smith, a militia detachment tore down the tents at the Forbes camp on March 10, leaving about two dozen families exposed to the cold weather. The colonists were given forty-eight hours to leave the camp and take their household effects with them or face deportation. The *Trinidad Chronicle-News* reported that Chase had long advocated breaking up the tent colonies—"hotbeds of dissension"—as a means of restoring peace and that the dismantling of the Forbes tent colony was the first step in removing all the strikers' camps. The paper asserted that General Chase had conferred with Ammons and had the governor's approval to tear down the tents. To justify his act, Chase assured President Wilson that he had given the order for removal of the tents "to forestall further outlawry."[50]

"How long, Oh God, how long?" was the headline in the Trinidad *Free Press,* the union's local newspaper, in reporting the Forbes incident. "How long must we endure the tyranny of these military poltroons and cravens?" Where would the general's "mailed fist" fall next? "Will Ludlow be the next to suffer?" These were questions the "kow-towing" governor needed to answer. "He does not know what the next order of the coal barons will be, but he knows that he will probably obey that command as he has sniffingly and cringingly obeyed every order that has come to him from the offices of the Colorado Fuel & Iron Company and the Victor American Fuel Company— his masters. He does not know what his militia will do, for he is fully aware, in his puny heart, that the militia has got[ten] beyond his control."[51]

Governor Ammons tried to calm the union leaders by disclaiming any responsibility for what had happened at Forbes and assuring them that no other tents would be torn down. Meanwhile, the Mother Jones saga resurfaced. Released on March 15 after being held incommunicado at Mount San Rafael Hospital for ten weeks, Mother Jones, once again exiled to Denver, boarded a southbound train intent on going back to Trinidad. She got as far as Walsenburg, where General Chase had her arrested and put in jail again. Faced with the prospect of an unfavorable hearing on the habeas corpus proceedings on her behalf before the Colorado Supreme Court, Ammons ordered her release in mid-April. The governor and the militia commander were relieved to see her leave the state on an eastbound train.[52]

Other incidents threatened to disrupt the peace and calm that generally prevailed in the strike zone. One incident occurred with the release of the sixteen men held in connection with the death of Neil Smith. They promptly returned to their camp at Forbes and began to rebuild the tent colony. Just as promptly, Lieutenant Linderfelt and his mounted troops tore down the tents once again, then camped on the ground to make sure the tents stayed down. The state attorney general's opinion that the strikers had a legal right to pitch their tents on ground they had leased did not stop the militia from removing a tent erected by union leaders Lawson and McLennan on March 25. Although the strikers remained calm, an atmosphere of dread prevailed. Many feared the demolition of the tents at Forbes was the prelude to a planned attack on Ludlow and the other colonies. Union officials were convinced that General Chase and some National Guard officers shared the coal operators' desire to see the remaining tent colonies dismantled as a way to drive the striking miners back to work.[53] The recall of most of the militia did not assuage the Ludlow strikers' fears, for Monte Linderfelt's hated Company B remained camped nearby.

NOTES

1. McGovern, "Colorado Strike," 261.

2. Papanikolas, *Buried Unsung*, 134; Bowden, "New Developments in the Colorado Strike Situation," 614.

3. Quote in Beshoar, *Out of the Depths*, 115.

4. Ibid.; McGovern and Guttridge, *Coalfield War*, 162–163.

5. McGovern and Guttridge, *Coalfield War*, 163–164 (quote on 164).

6. *Proceedings of the Special Convention of the Colorado State Federation of Labor*, Denver, December 16, 1913, 33–34.

7. Ibid., 37.

8. "State Federation of Labor Calls a Special Convention," in CBLS, *Fourteenth Biennial Report*, 177. The executive board decided that the $8,000 cost for circulating the recall petitions would be better put to use in supporting the strikers and their families (Beshoar, *Out of the Depths*, 118).

9. Linderfelt quoted in Papanikolas, *Buried Unsung*, 147–148. The incidents occurred on December 20, 1913. Linderfelt called Tikas and the Greeks a "bunch of bootblacks" down from Denver who were not miners but fighting men living off union dole in the colony. The term "bootblacks" is in reference to the story that Tikas had possibly formed a syndicate of bootblacks in Denver shortly after he arrived in the city. Like many of his countrymen, Tikas entered the northern Colorado coalfield as a scab before joining the strike in the south. Tikas and the Greeks "ragged" Linderfelt on the Trinidad streets whenever they had the chance. The men's animosity toward one another developed over a period of several months.

10. Lawson quoted in Beshoar, *Out of the Depths*, 126; Danks quoted in McGovern and Guttridge, *Coalfield War*, 168–169.

11. John Lawson et al. to Ammons, January 20, 1914, in CBLS, *Fourteenth Biennial Report*, 177–187; Bowden, "New Developments in the Colorado Strike Situation," 614; Papanikolas, *Buried Unsung*, 153. The report covered 760 pages of typewritten statements of 163 witnesses examined by Lawson's committee.

12. Quoted in Beshoar, *Out of the Depths*, 129.

13. *Denver Express*, December 2, 1913; Bowden, "New Developments in the Colorado Strike Situation," 614.

14. Hayes quoted in *Denver Express*, December 2, 1913.

15. McGovern and Guttridge, *Coalfield War*, 161.

16. Welborn to McClement, December 4, 1913, in CIR/FR 8: 7119.

17. Beshoar, *Out of the Depths*, 122; McGovern and Guttridge, *Coalfield War*, 146, 168–170; Helen Ring Robinson's testimony, CIR/FR 8: 7211.

18. Beshoar, *Out of the Depths*, 117, 127; McGovern and Guttridge, *Coalfield War*, 158.

19. Affidavit in Doyle Papers, Box 1, FF 38, January 1914.

20. Victor-American Fuel Company form, in ibid., FF 40.

21. Van Cise's testimony, CIR/FR 7: 6809. Papanikolas, *Buried Unsung*, 136–137, gives the date of November 13, 1913.

22. McGovern and Guttridge, *Coalfield War*, 158–159 (Welborn quote on 158); Osgood's testimony, CIR/FR 7: 6450.

23. Hayes quoted in McGovern and Guttridge, *Coalfield War*, 160.

24. Chase quoted in Beshoar, *Out of the Depths*, 128.

25. Ibid., 130; Bowden, "New Developments in the Colorado Strike Situation," 614.

26. Margolis, "Western Coal Mining," 86, his interview with Bill Lloyd, May 18, 1978.

27. Beshoar, *Out of the Depths*, 132–133. According to other testimony, General Chase kicked the girl after he remounted his horse.

28. Ibid., 133–134; *Denver Express*, January 23, 1914.

29. *Denver Express*, January 23, 1914.

30. Beshoar, *Out of the Depths*, 138–139.

31. Although he had the support of President Wilson, who told him that only a congressional investigation would "shake . . . [t]hose damned operators [who] won't yield an inch," Keating succeeded by gaining the Democratic caucus's support for his petition ordering the House Rules Committee to report out his resolution establishing the investigative committee (Keating, *Gentleman from Colorado*, 381–382).

32. Ibid., 384.

33. The lawyers for the coal companies were Fred Herrington, CF&I; Frank Gove, Victor-American Fuel Company; and J. V. Sickman, Rocky Mountain Fuel Company. Jesse G. Northcutt acted as general attorney for all three coal companies. Professor James H. Brewster, Horace N. Hawkins, and Edward P. Costigan represented the UMWA. Major Edward Boughton and Captain W. C. Danks represented the National Guard.

34. Osgood's testimony, SMM, 395–405.

35. First quote in McGovern and Guttridge, *Coalfield War*, 179; second quote in Beshoar, *Out of the Depths*, 149.

36. Osgood's testimony, SMM, 413.

37. Ibid., 422–426.

38. Ibid., 424.

39. Ibid., 426.

40. Committee members quoted in Stein and Taft, *Massacre at Ludlow*, 31.

41. Osgood's testimony, SMM, 476–477.

42. Quoted in *Brief of the Coal Mining Operators*, 31.

43. Stein and Taft, *Massacre at Ludlow*, 40–42. "Judged by their past performance the operators of Colorado are not fighting for the 'open shop.' They have stoutly

maintained a closed shop—closed to organized labor—in violation of a law of the state" (John Fitch, "When Peace Comes to Colorado," *The Survey* 32, no. 8 [May 16, 1914]: 206).

44. *Rocky Mountain News*, February 19, 1914.

45. "Views of Representative Byrnes," in Stein and Taft, *Massacre at Ludlow*, 48–49.

46. Ibid., 16–17, 31.

47. Ibid., 40.

48. Ibid., 43.

49. Ibid.

59. *Trinidad Chronicle-News*, March 10, 11, 1914; McGovern and Guttridge, *Coalfield War*, 189.

51. *Free Press* quoted in Beshoar, *Out of the Depths*, 155.

52. McGovern and Guttridge, *Coalfield War*, 189–192; Long, *Where the Sun Never Shines*, 289.

53. Doyle to Green, March 11, 1914, Doyle Papers, Box 1, FF 8.

The Ludlow Massacre

Information contained in a penciled letter from a secret agent to Edward Doyle at union headquarters in Denver indicated that in early March 1914 the "big three" coal operators wanted Lieutenant Karl Linderfelt to take charge of all secret surveillance operations in the strike district. "I can get a pass and letter of introduction to any of the Supts' or foremen any place from Linderfelt," the informant wrote. "He wants me to join his outfit and help him get rid of the B & Fs [Baldwin-Felts] men. . . . The Big 3 [John Osgood, Jesse Welborn, and David Brown] told Linderfelt that B & F. had not lived up to their contracts, and that their notoriety was influencing public opoinon [sic] against them—the operators." The informant mentioned the matter again in a letter a few days later. "Reno [William "Billy," supervisor of Colorado Fuel and Iron (CF&I) spies] says he is disgusted with the B & Fs [sic] work." Linderfelt, however, the agent noted, was still undecided about accepting the "big three's" contract, "as he is in hopes of trouble breaking in Mexico, and don't want to be tied up here, if it does."[1]

Doyle's informant was evidently well-placed, which added credibility to the information he sent to union headquarters. He talked about being in the (CF&I?) company's inner offices and socializing with the "big three's" men at the (Denver?) club who "always have plenty of chang[e] and are free with it." He had only been with them on two occasions on their account, but if the union allowed him $5 or $10 a week for incidentals and drinks, he suggested to Doyle, he would be better able to take advantage of these opportunities.[2]

Governor Elias Ammons also received information concerning the operators' offer to Linderfelt. A report from an agent in Trinidad sent to the governor on the letterhead of the Globe Inspection Service noted that the operators had offered Linderfelt a contract for "$400 a month for four years and expenses after the National Guard troops were withdrawn," a sum that exactly equaled General John Chase's salary.[3] No evidence proves that Linderfelt accepted the operators' offer, but his actions in April leading up to and including the fateful events at Ludlow on April 20 indicate that he operated as a paid agent of the coal companies. Otherwise, his presence in the Ludlow area that day would be difficult to explain.

Allegedly, Linderfelt's militia service in the strike zone had been terminated when he was relieved of his command of Company B on April 8, a few days before Governor Ammons, faced with a crippling financial burden that threatened to bankrupt the state, ordered the withdrawal of most militia troops. The governor retained thirty-five men of Company B, which was placed under the command of Major Patrick C. Hamrock. Captain Philip Van Cise later testified that Linderfelt was relieved of his command of Company B because his life was in peril as a result of the "deadly hatred" of the Ludlow tent colony's "large foreign population."[4]

Linderfelt was scheduled to leave the strike zone with General Chase and the recalled troops on April 17, either to be mustered out of the militia or assigned to recruiting service. However, he never left the area, and he continued to act as a National Guard officer. Even before the militia troops departed, he was instrumental in enrolling mine guards, pit bosses, clerks, engineers, and foremen employed by the CF&I and Victor-American fuel companies into a hastily organized cavalry troop, the notorious Troop A, that would replace the troops of Company B at Ludlow when that company was recalled. The idea of enrolling mine employees in a state militia unit originated with coal company officials, General Chase, or both in concert. The urgency of organizing the auxiliary troop was likely caused in part by Governor Ammons's order to recall Company B by April 22 or 23 and was justified in the eyes of the operators, Linderfelt, and Chase because of the alarming reports they received of a planned attack by gunmen from the Ludlow tent colony on the coalmines and nearby camps on or about April 20.[5] With the sanction of coal company officials and General Chase, Doctor Edwin M. Curry, surgeon from the Victor-American mine at Hastings, and E. J. Welch, editor of one of Judge Jesse G. Northcutt's anti-labor newspapers, organized Troop A. Linderfelt, presumably on the CF&I and Victor-American payroll, helped in this endeavor.[6]

At the Trinidad armory the night of April 14, Lieutenant Linderfelt administered the oath to over 130 men enrolled in the new unit. With this enrollment, George West later asserted, "the Colorado National Guard no longer offered even a pretense of fairness or impartially, and . . . had degenerated into a force of professional gunmen and adventurers who were economically dependent on and subservient to the will of the coal operators."[7] Only six days after they were sworn in, General Chase urgently summoned these "independent militiamen," as LaMont Bowers called them, from the CF&I and Victor-American coal camps, courthouses, sheriffs' offices, and saloons in Aguilar and Trinidad to relieve the troops of Company B during the battle at Ludlow. About fifty from Trinidad—some of the most notorious labor baiters among them—answered the call without any training, uniforms, officers, or regular arms. Their main purpose, as reported in testimony by witnesses who overheard conversations among them, was to clear out the colonists and burn their tents.[8]

Strikers at the Ludlow tent colony reacted to the formation of Troop A with dread. "All that is left now," a striker observed of the remaining militia, "are the gunmen, the scum of the earth, barrel house bums, professional killers from every part of the country who think nothing of human life."[9] State senator Helen Ring Robinson, on a visit to the colony on April 18, noted an atmosphere of desperation in the camp. The anxiety arose from the hastily assembled Troop A, which the colonists believed was organized for the sole purpose of destroying the camp. She gained the impression that the stage was being set for action. James Fyler and Louis Tikas, two of the most important camp leaders, said little to her, but the women shared their apprehension that something was definitely going to happen. They took her inside the tents and showed her the pits under the floorboards where they were going to hide if the militia attacked. The feeling in the camp, the senator sensed, was that an attack was imminent.[10]

National Guard troops in front of a Ludlow saloon, 1914. Courtesy, Denver Public Library, Western History Collection, call no. X-60540.

During her investigation in Trinidad and Ludlow, Senator Robinson "found a vortex of mad, swirling hate" she had not known existed in the world until she "went down there." The situation between the strikers and the militia was bitter, "with the open saloon always between them," she told the Commission on Industrial Relations. Bitterness among the strikers was fed by the memory of ten years earlier, when miners were deported from the Colorado coalmines and dumped on the prairies of Kansas, Oklahoma, and New Mexico. "That sort of thing," the senator cautioned, "arouses hatred in a community, and I believe that that hatred does not die with the objects that caused it, but that it gathers compound interest; I found that it had gathered that interest at Trinidad." Even Ludlow children were seized by this hatred toward the militia. When a militiaman approached the camp, Robinson noted, "the little child who a moment before had looked like one of Raphael's cherubs immediately became a little fiend in his appearance and would call out 'Tin Willie,' or 'Scab herder,' or something similar, to the militiaman." Similarly, the militiamen with whom she spoke were strongly opposed to organized labor and expressed bitterness toward the strikers. They felt a combination of racial and class hatred, a hatred that, Senator Robinson pointed out, was "fearfully strong in Colorado at that time and particularly in the southern coal fields." The militiamen continually referred to the strikers as men of "inferior character" and "low intelligence."[11]

Both sides had a feeling of inevitability that one side or the other had to be destroyed before peace could be restored in southern Colorado. Both the strikers and the militia fanned the flame of increasing enmity. "There was a condition of tenseness which was likely to break out in some demonstration at any moment," John Fitch wrote in *The Survey* in late 1914. An officer in the National Guard, "the fairest member of the guard" with whom he had spoken, told him "that Linderfelt had sworn 'to get' Louis Tikas. Word was brought back to Linderfelt that Tikas would 'get' Linderfelt. Rumors of that sort were flying in the air all of the time." With this "condition of tenseness" created by the fear of being attacked, a "demonstration" or confrontation was bound to happen. Therefore, Fitch reasoned, it was immaterial who fired the first shot when the fighting actually broke out.[12]

On Sunday, April 19, the day after Senator Robinson left the strikers' camp, Greeks in the Ludlow tent colony celebrated the Greek Orthodox Easter. The entire tent community participated in the events. Men, women, and children of several southeastern European nationalities dressed in national costumes or their Sunday best to help the Greeks celebrate. After a church service, women dressed in "gym bloomers" played a game of baseball. The game was followed by a community dinner of roasted lamb and another game of baseball, this time between men and women. Suddenly, four militiamen with rifles appeared. After a few tense moments, the women began to shout insults at them. "If we women would start after you with BB guns you'd drop your rifles and run," one of the women shouted at the men, to the delight of the crowd. Corporal Patton, the only one of the four militiamen who was mounted, calmly replied: "That is all right, girlie, you have your big Sunday to-day, but we will have the roast to-morrow. It would only take me and three or four men out there to clean out all the bunch."[13]

Although an exchange of insults and threats between the two sides was commonplace, the appearance of soldiers with their rifles was not. The return of the same militiamen that night while the strikers were enjoying a dance in the big tent further heightened tensions. A rumor spread that they were trying to blow up the camp. Chased off by camp guards, they retreated to the depot where they found the fight they had been looking for all day. The story, retold sixty years later, that Louis Tikas was one of the strikers beaten by the soldiers at the depot that night was likely the result of a faulty memory.[14]

That evening, Linderfelt was with his old company on Cedar Hill about two miles from the Ludlow tent colony. He was no longer in command of the company, and his presence at Cedar Hill was variously explained as a weekend visit with his two brothers, both fellow officers; a visit to the CF&I superintendent at nearby Tabasco; or, his own explanation, a military mission in search of storage facilities for state property at Hastings. Claiming he was under orders from General Chase, he implied that the mission was connected with the armament of the newly formed Troop A. He also noted that he was later to go to Tercio, Segundo, and other places on the same mission. Rather than return to the Columbian Hotel in Trinidad that Sunday evening, as he said he had originally planned, he stayed at Cedar Hill. There he received word from Hamrock that a large consignment of arms had been shipped to Aguilar and that the major wanted him and the Cedar Hill troops to go there early Monday morning to confiscate it. Hamrock cancelled the Aguilar plans that evening, but Linderfelt claimed it was too late for him to catch the night train to Trinidad. Consequently, Linderfelt was still at Cedar Hill on Monday morning, the day of the Ludlow Massacre, with eight men of Company B.[15] Whether by design or coincidence, he found himself at center stage during the momentous events of that fateful day.

Louis Tikas's fears that something major was about to happen were fueled by reports that were reaching him. He had heard that Linderfelt had boasted about his intention to wipe out the Ludlow colony. Certainly, he had read the articles in Judge Northcutt's *Trinidad Chronicle-News*, the mine owners' mouthpiece, calling almost daily for the expulsion of the "alien agitators" whose presence was "an offense to the community."[16] A union spy had told him that mine guards were reporting to the coal company officials that the strikers were planning an attack on the militia volunteers now that the latter were vastly outnumbered, followed by a seizure of the mines, expulsion of the strikebreakers, and infliction of vengeance on the mine guards. The attack, so the reports indicated, was initially planned for April 20 but had been deferred until the next day because of the Greek Easter celebration. The militiamen were also on edge because of reports that the strikers had recently dug up weapons they had long hidden. Tikas did not know if the militia officers and operators took these reports seriously or if they were using them as a pretext for an attack on the Ludlow colony. He suspected, however, that the militia's demand for the release of a man from the colony who was no longer there was a pretext for the militia to search the tent colony. The strikers were determined never to allow them to conduct that search.[17]

On Sunday evening, April 19, Lieutenant Linderfelt claimed he had received a message at the Cedar Hill camp from a woman at the Berwind coal camp stating that her husband was being held at the Ludlow tent colony against his will. The fact that Linderfelt rather than Hamrock received a letter allegedly written by a woman who spoke no English strongly suggests that the letter was a plant and that Linderfelt himself might have been behind the entire scheme.[18] He had previously acted as an agent for the coal companies and General Chase, and his actions now seemed too calculated to be anything less than the execution of a plan designed to draw the Ludlow fighters into battle with the militia. He had played this game successfully the previous October, and it was no secret that he had long wanted to destroy the tent colony. With rumors of an imminent attack by strikers on the militia, the conditions and timing for destroying the colony could not have been better for Linderfelt than they were that April day.

Linderfelt waited until early the next morning to send the letter to Major Hamrock at Ludlow militia headquarters. Hamrock then sent Corporal Patton and the three men who had been with him at the ballgame the previous day to confront Tikas about the man alleged to be held in the colony against his will. Tikas told them the man was no longer there and asked Patton on what authority they were acting. It was his understanding, he told Patton, that they had no authority to search the tents, since the military commission in Las Animas County had been suspended. Failing to get a satisfactory response, Tikas indicated that he would like to talk to Hamrock about the matter. Patton simply stated that he would be back.[19]

Shortly thereafter, Hamrock summoned Tikas to meet him at the militia camp. Tikas refused, wanting the meeting to take place on neutral ground. Finally, both men agreed to meet at the railroad depot. Hamrock then called Linderfelt to tell him he had sent for the Greek and that he might need help when they searched the colony for the man they wanted released. Expecting trouble, the major instructed Linderfelt to bring the Cedar Hill troops to Water Tank Hill, approximately 1,000 yards south of the tent colony, and deploy them conspicuously along its crest overlooking the camp. With this order, Linderfelt once again assumed command of Company B.[20]

Before departing for the depot, Tikas brought the men of the camp together and, with difficulty, obtained a promise from them that they would remain calm and not act rashly while he conferred with Hamrock. Despite assurances from Tikas that nothing was going to happen, the strikers were

National Guard Officers involved in the battle of Ludlow, April 20, 1914. Left to right: *Captain R. J. Linderfelt, Lieutenant T. C. Linderfelt, Lieutenant Karl (Monte) Linderfelt, Lieutenant G. S. Lawrence, and Major Patrick Hamrock. Courtesy, Denver Public Library, Western History Collection, call no. X-60539.*

almost certain the militia planned to conduct another search of the tent colony. They had vowed never again to see their tents searched and torn up, their weapons confiscated, their jewelry and small keepsakes stolen, and their women insulted. The Greeks especially were angry and determined to resist with guns to prevent the search. Tikas set out for the depot uncertain whether he could control them. He was also aware that he might be walking into a trap.[21]

While waiting for Tikas, Hamrock observed the Greek leader talking to the assembled men. He construed the gathering as a mobilization of the Ludlow fighters, which prompted him to telephone Cedar Hill again. "Put the baby in the buggy and bring it along," he ordered. Lieutenant Gerry S. Lawrence, who was on the other end of the line, quickly informed Linderfelt that Hamrock wanted the machine gun. Linderfelt issued the order to hitch a couple of mules to a wagon and load the gun and ammunition on it. Within minutes of Hamrock's call, Lieutenant Lawrence set off for Water Tank Hill with the gun.[22]

Tikas arrived at the depot a few minutes before nine A.M. to find Hamrock and the woman who was looking for her husband waiting. The Greek leader recognized the woman and told her that her husband had been in the colony Saturday night but was no longer there. He had searched the camp and made certain of that. Tikas also said the man, an Italian named Carindo Tuttoilmando, was a cripple and of no use to the strikers or the companies. He was not welcome in the tent colony, Tikas added, vowing to kick him out the next time he came through.[23]

At that point, Lieutenant Lawrence, who had delivered "the baby" to Water Tank Hill, appeared at the depot on horseback to warn Major Hamrock of what he considered a mass exodus of armed men from the colony. "My God, Major, look at those men," he exclaimed; "we are in for it."[24] Hamrock and Tikas saw several armed strikers taking up positions in a sandbank cut along the Colorado and Southeastern tracks southeast of the tent colony. From that position, the strikers could fire on the militiamen on Water Tank Hill. What Tikas and Hamrock could not see from their vantage point was that a much larger force of armed strikers was moving north of the tent colony into Delagua Arroyo. Tikas immediately started back to the tents, waving a white handkerchief and shouting at the strikers to return to the camp, but to no avail. They had seen the militia troops assemble on Water Tank Hill with the machine gun and observed the men constructing breastworks around it. They had been told of other militiamen armed with Springfield rifles stationed along the railroad tracks south of the depot.[25] They needed no further evidence to prove to them that the militia was about to attack their tent colony. They trusted their instincts rather than the Greek leader of their camp.

As Tikas dashed toward the strikers' tents, Major Hamrock hurried to his headquarters to call General Chase. He urged the general to summon Troop A to Ludlow. The major calculated that approximately 450 men resided in the tent colony, and of that number over 100 were believed to be hard-core Greek fighters. If the Greeks attacked, Hamrock feared his small band of 35 would be no match for them, even though the machine gun gave them superior firepower. He urgently pleaded with Chase to mobilize as many of the 130 new recruits as he could and dispatch them to Ludlow as quickly as possible. Agreeing, Chase instructed Captain Edwin Carson, officer in charge of the new "independent militia," to take his company to Ludlow and to bring his company's machine gun, a gift from CF&I.[26]

Thoughts of being overwhelmed by a superior force were not on the minds of the militiamen on Water Tank Hill. They pleaded with Linderfelt for permission to fire on the strikers as they ran for the sandbank railroad cut. They became more anxious as they received fire from the strikers' position. Linderfelt finally ordered his men to return fire. As the exchange quickened, three bombs exploded at sixty-second intervals from behind the militia tents. The colonists were certain that the signal had been given to the militia to launch an all-out attack. Linderfelt, who had prepared the dynamite bombs, later testified that Major Hamrock ordered the detonation to announce that the militia was under attack and to summon the new recruits of Troop A at Berwind, Hastings, and Delagua.[27]

The bomb explosions, which the strikers thought were cannon shots, and the beginning of machine gun fire forced the men, women, and children who were still in the tents to flee for shelter. Around seventy women and children rushed to the pump station and boiler house next to the Colorado and Southern Railroad's track northwest of the colony. The overcrowded structures soon became targets for the militiamen. The railroad's pump man directed the refugees to a deep well measuring about twenty feet wide and ninety feet deep. The well had three interior platforms connected by a rotten, crumbling stairway. The prospect of crashing through the wood platforms and drowning in the putrid water below did not deter the women and children from descending the stairway to the platforms to escape the militia bullets. There they would remain, caught in a cross fire between militia forces and Ludlow fighters, until almost dark, when they escaped to the arroyo a few yards to the north.[28]

Not all the tent residents fled the colony. A number of them, mainly women and children, took refuge in the pits under the floorboards of their own tents or in those of neighbors. The record of the names of those known to have descended into the underground pits has helped humanize the tragic story of Ludlow. Clorinda Padilla and her four children shared their pit with Juanita Hernandez and her family. In her final weeks of pregnancy, Mrs. Ed Tonner entered the pit beneath her tent with her five children. Cedi Costa and her two children and Patria Valdez and her four children joined Alcarita Pedregone and her two children in the latter's pit. The three women and eight children remained in the pit, which measured approximately eight feet long, six feet deep, and four and a half feet wide, for most of the day. Toward evening, with her tent on fire, Mary Petrucci and her three children raced to the Pedregone tent and squeezed into the pit with the eleven others. Nearby, William Snyder and his wife and six children occupied a pit under a tent that measured sixteen by twenty-four feet. The Snyders had made the pit their home since the first day of the walkout. At the first sign of trouble, John Bartolotti had pushed his wife, Virginia, and their three children into the cellar beneath their tent. When a bullet shattered the oatmeal pot simmering on the stove, Virginia gathered up the children and joined the James Fyler family in a dash toward the pump house.[29]

The question of who fired the first shot at Ludlow—whether strikers or militia—was never officially answered and remains a mystery to this day. However, the firing became general and sustained after the three bomb explosions. The strikers in the sandbank cut fired their rifles at the guard troops on Water Tank Hill; other strikers fired from positions along the arroyo north of their tents or from rifle pits at guardsmen deployed in and under steel railroad cars on the Colorado and Southeastern track southwest of the tent colony. The militia returned fire on the sandbank cut with the machine gun as well as rifles. At about ten A.M., Lieutenant Linderfelt sent two details forward in an attempt to dislodge the strikers from the cut and to prevent any more strikers from reaching that position. Both details were stopped by heavy rifle fire before they could reach the cut and were forced to retreat with two wounded, one mortally. The badly mutilated body of Private Alfred Martin was not recovered until nine that evening.[30]

A little later that morning, Linderfelt led a group of eight or ten men from Water Tank Hill northward along the Colorado and Southern tracks toward the Ludlow depot. Linderfelt's ultimate objective was to dislodge the strikers from their position at the steel bridge across the arroyo a few yards north of the pump station and northwest of the tent colony. When the militiamen reached the depot, they were able to fire on the strikers in the sandbank cut about 300 yards to the east. A combination of rifle and machine gun volleys from Water Tank Hill forced the strikers to abandon their position in the cut and retreat eastward into the Black Hills. With the railroad cut cleared of gunmen, Linderfelt's detachment was able to move forward up the tracks toward the bridge across the arroyo, all the while firing at the pump station and the tents until a shortage of ammunition forced the troops to stop just north of the depot.[31]

With the strikers' retreat from the sandbank cut, the machine gun detail, under the charge of Lieutenant Lawrence, turned its fire on the strikers' tents, shredding canvas and shattering furniture and utensils. Those who had taken shelter in the pits or cellars beneath their tents remained pinned down, unable to retrieve food or water for themselves or their children. During a lull in the firing, Frank Snyder, the eleven-year-old eldest son of William Snyder, was fatally shot in the head when he emerged from his family's pit to get food and drink for himself and his baby sister. In the midst of the chaos, Louis Tikas and Pearl Jolly, a twenty-one-year-old nurse who wore improvised red crosses on her chest and each of her arms, raced from tent to tent to see if people were safe underground or had evacuated. They were fired on constantly. The militiamen "took it [the red cross] for to be a good target," Jolly later remarked, "and shot at me as hard as they could. I started to run for protection, and one of the bullets took the heel off my shoe."[32] The militiamen also fired on Mary Thomas as she carried food and drink from the pump house to the arroyo a short distance to the north. Near the same arroyo, Charles Costa, the Italian leader within the strikers' colony, was felled by a fatal gunshot wound to the head.

During the early afternoon, both sides waited anxiously for reinforcements and a new supply of ammunition. Captain Carson and his Troop A detachment of about fifty men from Trinidad arrived south of Ludlow at around four in the afternoon on a special train arranged by Sheriff James Grisham. They made the trek to Water Tank Hill with their machine gun and ammunition in a commandeered automobile. Linderfelt immediately instructed Carson and his troops to join the regular militia for an assault on the strikers at the bridge over the arroyo northwest of the colony.[33]

Earlier in the day, Tikas had placed an urgent call to Lawson in Trinidad requesting reinforcements. In response, Lawson ordered his aides to enlist all the volunteers who could be gathered for a relief army as quickly as possible. He then set off for Ludlow, where, after a harrowing trip over open prairie to dodge militia gunfire, he met Tikas at the steel bridge. Although the situation was grim, Tikas still believed the strikers outnumbered the militiamen and could hold on to the tent colony. Lawson assured Tikas that help was on the way and told him to hold out until the relief force arrived.

He then returned to Trinidad to take command of the hastily summoned relief force, which arrived too late to save the colony.[34]

Late in the afternoon, Major Hamrock ordered the operators of the machine guns on Water Tank Hill to direct their fire at the pump house and steel bridge across the arroyo, from where the armed strikers were firing at the advancing militia force. Just before sunset, a tent in the southwest corner of the colony closest to the militiamen caught fire. At dusk the machine guns ceased firing, and the militia troops assaulted the tent colony. With battle cries and war whoops, the men, led by Lieutenant Linderfelt, rushed through the tents and took "whatever appealed to their fancy . . . clothes, bedding, articles of jewelry, bicycles, tools, and utensils."[35] One woman still in the camp saw her husband's accordion stolen, and another cried as men in civilian clothes carried off her sewing machine. To no avail, Captain Carson tried to stop his members of Troop A from looting. The National Guard had "ceased to be an army and [had] become a mob," later testimony established. Then, with at least one tent on fire, a militia officer reported, "men and soldiers swarmed into the colony and deliberately assisted the conflagration by spreading the fire from tent to tent. . . . Beyond a doubt, it was seen to, intentionally, that the fire should destroy the whole of the colony." Despite Lieutenant Linderfelt's testimony that wind had carried the flames and sparks of exploding ammunition from one tent to another, other witnesses saw men with lit oil-soaked brooms setting fire to the tents until the entire camp was ablaze.[36]

As the flames progressed, some of the colony's trapped occupants began to emerge from their underground shelters. William Snyder and his family appeared just as five or six militiamen were setting fire to their tent. With his dead son draped over his shoulder and his daughter on the other arm, William and his family headed for the railroad depot. It was reported that George Titsworth Sr., a deputy sheriff and former mine guard for CF&I, threatened Snyder with a gun, saying, "God damn you, you have fired as many shots as anybody, you red neck son of a bitch. I have a notion to kill you right now." Snyder was then confronted by Lieutenant Linderfelt, who asked: "What God damn red neck have we got now?"[37] Mrs. Tonner ran from tent to tent with her five children as militiamen set fire to the tents. Dressed only in a thin shift and an apron and wearing worn-out shoes, she and her exhausted and screaming children finally made it to safety in the arroyo north of the camp. Mrs. James Fyler, the paymaster's wife, also fled to safety. Shortly thereafter, her husband was captured and shot by the militia.[38]

Along with Tikas, Fyler was one of the few men who had remained in or returned to the camp. Tikas and Pearl Jolly had succeeded in helping women and children escape to the arroyo, but, along with a handful of strikers, they were prevented by militia gunfire from returning to the camp after the tents on the southern edge of the colony were set ablaze. Those still trapped in pits beneath the burning tents were entirely at the mercy of the troops. A few soldiers helped colonists out of the camp, but not the number claimed by Linderfelt, who in the official militia report described his men as gallant rescuers of thirty-six "wretched" humans. It was the heroic rescue efforts of Tikas and Jolly rather than the humanitarianism of the militia that had prevented the tragedy at Ludlow from being worse than it was.[39]

The arrival at Ludlow of a southbound local freight train at about 7:20 P.M. also undoubtedly saved many lives. Moving slowly, the thirty-six freight cars provided a temporary shield between the camp refugees and the militia on the west side of the tracks. When the train stopped and began switching cars in the rail yard, scores of women and children ran from the tents, pump station, and well and scrambled to safety in the arroyo. The train's brakeman witnessed the entire scene and later swore that he saw a uniformed man in the colony torching tents. The train crew perhaps could have seen more had militiamen not pointed their rifles at the engineer and ordered him to move on.

Once safely in the deep arroyo, the refugees separated into two groups. The smaller group followed the arroyo eastward toward the low, piñon-covered Black Hills three miles away to join strikers who had earlier fled the railroad cut. The larger group, following Louis Tikas's advice, walked westward to Frank Bayes's ranch less than a mile away. Tikas then ordered the fighters who had been firing at the militia from the arroyo to retreat to the Black Hills. Without ammunition or reinforcements, there was no reason for them to stay.[40]

Although the men pleaded with him to join them in the retreat, Tikas turned back to the camp, unarmed, to continue his rescue efforts. Strikers would later say that Tikas had decided to surrender himself to stop the shooting and save what was left of the colony. He was captured somewhere near the pump station. Nearby, Lieutenant Linderfelt heard a triumphal cry, "We've got Louie the Greek!" James Fyler and John Bartolotti were also captured. The three prisoners were brought before Linderfelt sometime after nine that evening.[41] What happened next is clouded in the confusion of conflicting testimony, almost all of it from the militia's point of view.

Linderfelt's version was the one officially accepted. He admitted that he had cursed Tikas for not stopping the conflict and that he struck Tikas over the head with his Springfield rifle after the Greek called him "a name that no man will take." Even though Tikas's arm slightly cushioned the blow, it

245

landed with such force that the stock of the gun snapped. Tikas staggered but did not fall. The fifty or more men, mainly irregulars from Troop A, who had rushed to the scene implored Linderfelt to hang Tikas. Some in the crowd even threw a rope over a telegraph pole. Linderfelt, however, refused to hand the prisoner over to the mob. Instead, he turned Tikas and the other prisoners over to a militia detail for protection. He then left to organize the final assault on the strikers' remaining positions. Within minutes of his departure, there was a fierce resumption of gunfire from the east. When the militia guards scrambled for cover, the three prisoners made a dash for the tents. They were caught in the cross fire and killed. When the bodies were taken away on the "dead wagon," Linderfelt was astonished to see Tikas's body among them. So read Linderfelt's testimony.[42]

Other accounts contradicted Linderfelt's version. Ed Doyle recounted what he had heard of the incident to John White: "Louis Tikas the Greek organizer was captured by these guards, and they discussed whether they should hang him or not and finally decided to shoot him; but before doing so, Lieutenant Linderfelt struck him with a rifle and made the remark when going up the track, that he spoiled a d— good rifle on him."[43]

The most damaging account against Linderfelt and the militia came from Captain Philip Van Cise, who was deeply troubled by what he had learned through his own investigation when he was recalled to Ludlow a few days after the battle. Van Cise, a Denver attorney, had been in command of Company K, which was stationed across the tracks a few hundred yards southwest of the Ludlow tent colony when the militia was first deployed to the strike zone. He and his company of "college boys" had been on good terms with the strikers, frequently sharing meals and playing baseball with them. Van Cise later described Tikas as "the greatest single agent for peace during the strike."[44] During his private investigation, Van Cise had concluded that Tikas and the other two prisoners had been murdered. He obtained a sworn affidavit from a sergeant in Linderfelt's company stating that the lieutenant had ordered that Tikas and the other prisoners be shot. The sergeant stated that Linderfelt, after breaking the stock of his rifle over Tikas's head, had at first wanted the mob to hang the Greek but was dissuaded from doing so. Instead, Linderfelt called out to his men, "Shoot the prisoners." The prisoners were pushed over the railroad track against their will and shot in the back. This version of Tikas's death was never made public, for the National Guard, with the support of Governor Ammons, suppressed all the evidence Van Cise had collected.[45]

Shortly after his return from Ludlow, Van Cise recorded his thoughts in an unpublished account in which he praised the uniformed soldiers and condemned the strikers for attacking the troops and thus engaging in an "assault upon the Government." But his assessment of the National Guard's role in the Tikas affair was far different. "The assault upon Tikas and the murder of the three prisoners can not be too severely condemned," he wrote. "As the men were outlaws they could have been shot in their tracks and never captured, but once taken they were entitled to be kept inviolate. These murders by this mine-guard group should be as severely punished as should the murders by the strikers, and both should receive the extreme penalty of the law."[46] Although Van Cise advocated prosecuting perpetrators of violence from both sides, Osgood and his cohorts, as discussed in Chapter 13, were only interested in bringing the strikers to justice.

Sporadic gunfire continued throughout the night of the battle. Stragglers continued to leave the burning camp and the nearby arroyos. A small group of strikers east of Ludlow found John Lawson and the reinforcements who had finally arrived from Trinidad. They told him the colony had been destroyed, that most of the strikers had gone to the Black Hills, and that a group of refugees had gathered at Frank Bayes's ranch northwest of the colony. Lawson instructed the men to stay where they were while he and a companion checked on the women and children, but he quickly returned after seeing that Bayes and his wife were caring for them. Lawson contemplated ordering his men to charge the militia but realized that his poorly armed and untrained men would be no match for the superior militia force. Reluctantly, he turned away from the burning tents and led the men to the Black Hills. Along the way, they found many hungry and terror-stricken refugees scattered along the slopes. As they reached the Black Hills, they saw the early morning sunshine fall on the smoking ruins of the Ludlow colony.[47]

Major Hamrock withdrew the soldiers and their irregular allies from the destroyed tent camp at around midnight. Some headed for the railroad depot, where they boasted about the day's events. They believed they had done a fair day's work. One said he had killed a redneck at the bridge and was eager to try to get another as soon as it was daylight. Another soldier began to play the accordion he had taken from one of the tents, and yet another soldier joined in on a violin. Juanita Hernandez and Clorinda Padilla were also at the depot. The soldiers had dragged them out of a pit where they had been hiding all day. In the depot's baggage room, William Snyder tried to comfort his weeping wife while their five children slept on the floor. Wrapped in a gunnysack next to them was the body of their brother Frank.[48]

In the smoldering ruins of the tent colony, Mary Petrucci regained consciousness sometime after dawn and staggered out of the pit under what remained of the Pedregone tent. She had huddled in the cramped hole throughout the night with her three children, Patria Valdez and her four children, Cedi Costa and her two children, and Alcarita Pedregone and her two children. In a daze, she wandered through the ruins of the camp, not knowing where she was or where her children were. Her only thought was to go to Trinidad to see her mother. Susan Hallearine, the Ludlow postmistress, found both Petrucci and Alcarita Pedregone, who had also emerged from the hole in an incoherent state, while inspecting the charred remains of the colony. After promising she would search for their children, Susan put both women on the train to Trinidad. It would be nine days before Mary Petrucci realized that her children were dead.[49]

Hallearine anxiously searched through the ruins for the missing children, but the pit openings were blocked by debris. Later that afternoon, someone uncovered the Pedregone pit and discovered the bodies of the two women and eleven children who had perished in the inferno. The shocking discovery was kept as quiet as possible. Only Dr. Edwin Curry, the Victor-American Company physician, was permitted to visit the death pit and inspect the bodies. Under orders from General Chase, Major Hamrock prohibited the Red Cross or any other doctors, inspectors, or reporters from entering the destroyed camp until Wednesday, two days after the attack, when the bodies were finally removed from what soon came to be called "the Black Hole of Ludlow."[50]

The bodies of Tikas, Fyler, and Bartolotti lay for three days near the railroad tracks where they had fallen. They were plainly visible to passengers on passing trains. So were the charred remains of the tent colony: the twisted bedsteads and coils of springs, broken furniture, scorched floorboards, burned clothing, and heavy cast-iron stoves still stood in place. The militia kept the colony closed. Major Hamrock, acting on General Chase's orders, refused to let a party of correspondents enter the camp. Chase was quoted as charging one of the correspondents with having written articles denouncing the militia. Late Tuesday afternoon, union officials in Trinidad, perhaps still unaware of the thirteen bodies recovered from the Black Hole, arranged for deputy coroners to collect the bodies of the Ludlow victims. A shower of machine gun bullets stopped the three "dead wagons" shortly after they had passed Cedar Hill, and the drivers immediately turned around and raced back to Trinidad. Investigators using field glasses claimed to have

Hole Where Bodies
Of 11 Children And
2 Women Were
Recovered From
After Fire At Ludlow
Tent Coloney
D
Dold

Black Hole where two women and eleven children died during the battle of Ludlow, April 20, 1914. Courtesy, Denver Public Library, Western History Collection, call no. X-60481.

collected evidence that the soldiers were hiding bodies. These reports and incidents convinced John Lawson that the militia was destroying or carrying off the bodies and "trying to obliterate traces of the slaughter."[51]

With scores of women and children unaccounted for during the hours immediately following the attack on the colony, it was not difficult for the strikers and union officials to believe there were many more victims than first reported. "Thirty-three will not be one-half the dead at Ludlow," Lawson told union headquarters in Trinidad. A telegraphic wire from representatives of the Colorado and Southern Trainmen and Engineers in Rugby on Wednesday afternoon might have been the first news Lawson heard about the bodies from the Black Hole. The wire read: "Bodies of women and children exposed in tent colony at Ludlow[.] Death from suffocation the cause[.] Please do something with the bodies for God's sake for they are human souls and deserving of decent burial."[52]

Pearl Jolly later recounted a story to the Commission on Industrial Relations that clearly revealed the strikers' confusion as well as their suspicions of the militia's activities in the immediate aftermath of the Ludlow battle. Jolly reached a neighboring farmhouse early Tuesday morning. There was a telephone in the house, and she decided to eavesdrop to see if she could find out what had happened the day before and how many people had died. Such eavesdropping was "not a very nice thing to do," she said,

> but they tell me that at a time of war everything goes. So we eaves-
> dropped . . . and we heard Dr. Curry's wife and the superintendent's wife
> having a talk. Dr. Curry is a doctor for the Victor Fuel Co., and at that
> time he was wearing a militia uniform; and his wife was talking over the
> telephone to the superintendent's wife. And she says to her, "Why, what
> do you think of yesterday's work? Wasn't that fine?" Then she mentioned
> about them killing this old man Feiler [Fyler]. . . . So she says, "They got
> that old Jim Feiler [Fyler] and they got Louis, the Greek." She says,
> speaking now of the time of the burning of the tent colony, "We burned
> down that dirty tent town, and you know there are 28 of the dirty brutes
> roasted alive in it." That was as much as I could stand. I think when she
> said that there were 28 of them roasted in there alive she knew what
> she was talking about. We got only 13 out; but I think if the coke ovens
> around there could tell their story, there would be a much clearer story.[53]

Jolly's account underscored a belief held by Lawson and many of the strikers that the militia would cremate the bodies and destroy as much evidence as possible. Coke ovens had frequently been used as crematoriums in the past. Suspicion also surrounded the deaths of the women and children found in the Black Hole. Some of the miners never accepted the official report that they died from suffocation. Instead, as they recounted many years later, they believed they were victims of blood-crazed militiamen. "And then the floor started burning," Dan DeSantis recalled in 1978, "the smoke got down there, so was forced to come out. When they come out of there, there was women with their children, there was one woman with [a] three or four months [old] baby. . . . [W]hen the women come out, he was to hear them and with a bayonet, he kill them all . . . and he hold them [babies] up in the air with it." Victor Bazanelle broke down in tears several times as he recounted his version of the affair in 1976. "Miss Costa," he said, "she was pregnant six months. She had bayonet wound in her belly too. Because I remember, I said, 'We want to see Miss Costa for the last time.' He said, 'You can't. It's impossible, she's all wounded, full of blood and stuff.' "[54]

It is impossible to discern whether General Chase and Major Hamrock contemplated trying to cover up the discovery of the bodies of the women and children. More than likely, it was confusion and uncertainty that explained the militia's refusal to allow a prompt inspection of the camp and removal of the dead. Undoubtedly, Chase needed time to gather information and confer with others before he allowed union officials or independent investigators into the camp. He wasted no time in meeting with acting governor Stephen R. Fitzgarrald, Jesse Welborn, David Brown, Frank Gove (counsel for Victor-American Fuel Company), and Fred Herrington (counsel for CF&I) at the statehouse. After the meeting, Fitzgarrald promised a sweeping investigation of the Ludlow casualties. Instructions were also sent to Major Hamrock to allow Red Cross nurses, doctors, reporters, and undertakers into the charred ruins.[55]

Once recovered, the bodies were taken to a mortuary in Trinidad. Suspicions about the cause of death of the victims were raised once again when the bodies had to be hauled into the street after a fire mysteriously broke out in the mortuary. How the fire started was never ascertained, but it was whispered that someone wanted the evidence those bodies held destroyed before the truth about the massacre reached people in the highest places.[56] Despite convincing evidence to the contrary, many still continued to believe the real story of the massacre had been concealed from the public.

The pit beneath the Pedregone tent had become a death trap for two women and eleven children.[57] Other pits, however, had protected many other women and children from the militia's machine gun and rifle fire that raked the tents during the daylong battle. Determined to destroy the tent colony completely, the militia troops were merciless in their attack.[58] Yet, were the militiamen solely responsible for the Ludlow tragedy? John Fitch of *The Survey* thought not. Of the deaths of the two women and eleven children he wrote:

> Nothing so completely illustrates the unspeakable horrors of industrial warfare carried to the utmost extreme [as the Ludlow Massacre]. As to responsibility for this tragedy, the evidence is again hopelessly conflicting. I can only record my belief—and I confess that an apparently good case can be made against this belief—that despite the despicable and criminal acts of some of the militiamen that day, they were not responsible for these deaths. . . . In my opinion the militia did not murder them. They were innocent victims of one of the most cruel and barbarous and unnecessary of industrial wars.[59]

Although Fitch was too willing to accept the militia's side of the story, it is hard to disagree with his overall statement, The coal operators, not the militia who served them in their determination to destroy the tent colonies and eliminate the "foreign agitators," were responsible for the "cruel and barbarous and unnecessary" industrial conflict that resulted in the Ludlow Massacre.

Train cars and wagons carried scores of refugees from farms, ranches, and rail junctions near Ludlow to Trinidad during the days after the attack on the tent colony. The refugees were mostly women and children, scantily clad and some shoeless. The men stayed behind in the hills beyond the burned-out camp with their Winchester 30-30s. Revenge was on their minds.

NOTES

1. Doyle Papers, Box 1, FF 1, March 2, 1914, and undated letter, ca. mid-March 1914. The letters are signed "Respectfully, Dick."

2. Ibid., undated letter, ca. mid-March 1914.

3. McGovern and Guttridge, *Coalfield War*, 184. The letter is dated March 21, 1914.

4. Van Cise's testimony, CIR/FR 8: 7315.

5. Ammons indicated in his testimony before the Commission on Industrial Relations that he had issued the order to recall Company B by April 22 or 23 (CIR/FR 7: 6416).

6. Bowers to Rockefeller, April 18, 1914, in CIR/FR 9: 8429–8430; McGovern and Guttridge, *Coalfield War*, 205. Curry frequently referred to the strikers as "outlaws, bums and gunmen."

7. West, *Report on the Colorado Strike*, 126.

8. McGovern and Guttridge, *Coalfield War*, 219–220.

9. Quoted in Long, *Where the Sun Never Shines*, 290.

10. Robinson's testimony, CIR/FR 8: 7213.

11. Ibid., 7211–7213.

12. Fitch, "Law and Order," 257. Van Cise testified that strikers had told him many times that they intended to get Linderfelt (Van Cise's testimony, CIR/FR 7: 6813). Van Cise was probably the officer to whom Fitch referred.

13. Jolly's testimony, CIR/FR 7: 6349. By virtue of being based on oral history, the accounts of the day's events vary somewhat. Another version of what was said on the ball diamond is quoted in Papanikolas, *Buried Unsung*, 213: "Never mind, girlie. You have your big Sunday today and tomorrow we'll get the roast." As Patton turned to ride off, he said: "It would only take me and my four men to clean out this bunch." According to Baron Beshoar, *Out of the Depths*, 168, Patton's words were: "Oh, that's all right. Have your fun today, we'll have our roast tomorrow."

14. Papanikolas, *Buried Unsung*, 213–214. Mary Thomas claimed the soldiers attacked Tikas because of his relationship with Pearl Jolly.

15. Linderfelt's testimony, CIR/FR 7: 6888. Linderfelt's wife accompanied him on the trip; the lieutenant later claimed it was her slowness in dressing that caused him to miss the Sunday train to Trinidad (McGovern and Guttridge, *Coalfield War*, 211).

16. Quoted in Beshoar, *Out of the Depths*, 167.

17. Ibid.; McGovern and Guttridge, *Coalfield War*, 212. The report of the military commission appointed to investigate the Ludlow affair accepted the assertion that the Greek strikers planned to attack the militia on Tuesday, April 21. The report also stated that the Greeks, who had resented the searching of the colony and seizure of their arms in the past, "swore that their arms should never be taken from them again" ("Report of Military Commission," in CIR/FR 8: 7316; hereafter cited as "Report of Military Commission").

18. Papanikolas described her as "an old woman who did not speak any English and who didn't know anything except that she wanted her husband back" (*Buried Unsung*, 215).

19. Ibid., 214–215; Jolly's testimony, CIR/FR 7: 6349–6350.

20. Linderfelt's testimony, CIR/FR 7: 6888. The machine gun had been purchased by CF&I and placed under Linderfelt's supervision when he was a mine guard for the company. Linderfelt brought the gun with him when he was commissioned as an officer in the National Guard, and it was still under his supervision on the day of the Ludlow battle (McGovern and Guttridge, *Coalfield War*, 214).

21. Linderfelt's testimony, CIR/FR 7: 6888; McGovern and Guttridge, *Coalfield War*, 213–214; Papanikolas, *Buried Unsung*, 215.

22. Papanikolas, *Buried Unsung*, 217; McGovern and Guttridge, *Coalfield War*, 214.

23. Papanikolas, *Buried Unsung*, 217.

24. "Report of Military Commission," 7318.

25. Ibid.; McGovern and Guttridge, *Coalfield War*, 215; Papanikolas, *Buried Unsung*, 218.

26. McGovern and Guttridge, *Coalfield War*, 200.

27. Linderfelt's testimony, CIR/FR 7: 6890–6891.

28. McGovern and Guttridge, *Coalfield War*, 216–217.

29. Ibid., 216–217, 227; Papanikolas, *Buried Unsung*, 220.

30. "Report of Military Commission," 7318–7320; Linderfelt's testimony, CIR/FR 7: 6892–6893. Martin was one of the four militiamen who had appeared at the baseball game the previous day and was involved in beating strikers at the depot that night.

31. "Report of Military Commission," 7320; Linderfelt's testimony, CIR/FR 7: 6892–6893.

32. Jolly's testimony, CIR/FR 7: 6350.

33. McGovern and Guttridge, *Coalfield War*, 219–220; "Report of Military Commission," 7319.

34. McGovern and Guttridge, *Coalfield War*, 220–221; Beshoar, *Out of the Depths*, 170–173.

35. "Report of Military Commission," 7321–7322.

36. Ibid.

37. Quotes from Report of the Military Board in Bowers's testimony, in CIR/FR 9: 8776–8777; also quoted in Papanikolas, *Buried Unsung*, 225. Snyder did not own a gun and never took part in any of the fighting.

38. McGovern and Guttridge, *Coalfield War*, 225.

39. McGovern, "Colorado Strike," 228; "Report of Military Commission," 7321; Jolly's testimony, CIR/FR 7: 6351.

40. McGovern and Guttridge, *Coalfield War*, 115; Beshoar, *Out of the Depths*, 176.

41. Papanikolas, *Buried Unsung*, 226; McGovern and Guttridge, *Coalfield War*, 228–229.

42. "Report of Military Commission," 7322. Evidence collected by the Las Animas County physician during the inquest indicated that Tikas had been shot three times in the back. The fact that two of the bullets had passed all the way through his body indicated that they were probably the steel-jacket type fired from the Springfield rifles used by the militia. The scalp wound from the rifle-butt blow was deep enough to show bone. James Fyler died from a gunshot wound to the head. His widow accused the militiamen of taking a ring, gold watch, union documents, and $300 in cash from her husband's body.

43. Doyle to John White, April 27, 1914, Doyle Papers, Box 1, FF 20.

44. Van Cise quoted in McGovern and Guttridge, *Coalfield War*, 214.

45. Papanikolas, *Buried Unsung*, 235; Van Cise's testimony, CIR/FR 7: 6816–6819.

46. Van Cise, "The Colorado Strike Situation," in CIR/FR 8: 7328.

47. Beshoar, *Out of the Depths*, 178–179.

48. Papanikolas, *Buried Unsung*, 226–227.

49. Long, *Where the Sun Never Shines*, 292–293; Martelle, *Blood Passion*, 178.

50. *Denver Times*, April 22, 1914; McGovern and Guttridge, *Coalfield War*, 235.

51. *Denver Times*, April 22, 1914.

52. Telegram quoted in ibid.

53. Jolly's testimony, CIR/FR 7: 6352.

54. DeSantis and Bazanelle quoted in Margolis, "Western Coal Mining," 93–94.

55. *Denver Times*, April 22, 1914; *Rocky Mountain News,* April 22, 1914.

56. Sampson, *Remember Ludlow*, 25.

57. Besides the two women and eleven children, the Ludlow Massacre claimed the lives of five strikers and the Snyder boy. Two militiamen were also killed during the ten-hour gun battle.

58. McGovern, "Colorado Strike," 277, 284.

59. Fitch, "Law and Order," 253–254.

The Ten Days' War

Ed Doyle was stunned by the reports from Ludlow that reached him at his office in Denver. "For God's sake," he wired United Mine Workers of America (UMWA) president John White, "urge the chief executive of this nation to use his power to protect the helpless men, women and children from being slaughtered in southern Colorado." White forwarded the telegram to President Woodrow Wilson, adding: "On behalf of five hundred thousand organized miners we earnestly request you to take prompt action in order that lives of innocent men, women and children will not continue to be ruthlessly sacrificed on the altar of greed." Doyle also telegraphed national and international labor union headquarters throughout the country, urging them "to call upon" their membership "to demand of the President of the United States and both houses of Congress to leave Mexico alone and come into Colorado to relieve these miners, their wives and children, who are being slaughtered by the dozen by murderous mine guards." Appealing directly to the president, Doyle asked, "Will you for God's sake stop this slaughter?" Unless something was done quickly, he warned, union officials were ready to take matters into their own hands.[1]

To underscore the point that the union was ready to take action, Doyle enclosed a copy of the circular entitled "Call to Arms" in his letter to the president. Drafted by Doyle, John Lawson, and John McLennan of the local UMWA policy committee and other union leaders, including William T. Hickey, secretary of the State Federation of Labor, the circular was sent to all Colorado labor organizations as a clarion call for action in defense of the striking miners. It asked for donations of guns and ammunition and requested that the labor leaders organize volunteers in their communities into companies "to protect the workers of Colorado against the murder and cremation of men, women and children by armed assassins in the employ of coal corporations, serving under the guise of state militiamen." The statement continued: "We seek no quarrel with the state and we expect to break no law; we intend to exercise our lawful right as citizens, to defend our homes and our constitutional rights."[2]

The "Call to Arms" appeared on the front page of almost every newspaper in Colorado as well as in many publications throughout the nation. It had an immediate effect. Offers of armed assistance reached UMWA union headquarters in Denver from all over the United States, and more than $20,000 in cash donations arrived by telegraph, mail, and messenger within the next few days. Coalminers throughout the country were enraged when they heard about the Ludlow Massacre. Thousands of miners in Illinois, Pennsylvania, Wyoming, Missouri, and Texas threatened to march on Colorado to protect the rights of their fellow miners unless President Wilson stopped the bloodshed. Miners in Arnot, Pennsylvania, wired the president to demand that he "stop this wanton carnage which is not only a blot on the state of Colorado but on the government of the United States."[3] Horace Hawkins, attorney for the UMWA in Colorado, received telephone calls from trade union officials offering to raise an army of 10,000 volunteers to fight in Colorado. Hundreds of UMWA locals across the country petitioned the national office in Indianapolis to call a nationwide strike to protest the killings at Ludlow, a request the national executive board rejected.[4] Thousands of miners across the nation waited for either a notice to stop work or a call for an armed march on Colorado. Neither came.

Strikers in the hills around Ludlow and Aguilar did not wait for out-side help before seeking revenge for the destruction of the Ludlow tent colony and the killing of innocents. After the Ludlow Massacre, John Fitch exclaimed, "the strikers went mad. For a week they were bereft of reason. The belief that the Ludlow tent colony had been deliberately attacked by the soldiers of the state, and the fact that women and children were dead as a result, led them to believe that a war of extermination was on." They believed they must become the aggressors.[5] Badly shaken by the events at Ludlow, John Lawson became an inspirational force for aggressive action. "It is unthinkable and unbelievable," he said in a statement printed in the *Rocky Mountain News*, "that there are fiends in human form that could be induced to commit these hellish acts." He blamed John D. Rockefeller Jr., who, Lawson proclaimed, "may ease his conscience by attending Sunday School regularly in New York but . . . will never be acquitted of commit-ting the horrible atrocities." He continued: "We now have the sinews of war backed by guns and ammunition and the faith and financial backing of every union-labor man in the country. . . . The murder of men and women at Ludlow . . . has cinched the determination to fight to a finish."[6] With this statement, both the UMWA's pacifistic hierarchy and the coal operators damned Lawson, who became public enemy number one in the latter's eyes. Lawson's fiery words and support for aggressive action, however, inspired the strikers in their campaign to burn, wreck, and kill.[7]

What became known as the Ten Days' War or Coalfield War, which has been termed the only incidence of class warfare in American history,[8] began at daybreak on Wednesday, April 22, when 160 strikers attacked the Victor-American mines at Delagua and Hastings. Although they failed to capture the Delagua mine after repeated attempts, the attackers killed three mine guards, dynamited the reservoir that supplied water to all the major mines and camps in the area—Delagua, Hastings, Tabasco, and Berwind—and left the Delagua and Hastings coal camps in flames. Other strikers attacked the Southwestern Fuel Company's Empire mine west of Aguilar. The compa-ny's president, J. W. Siple, along with 35 mine officials, employees, wives, and children, took shelter in the mine. The strikers dynamited the shaft house and tipple and set fire to all the mine buildings on the property, including the houses. The women and children were allowed to leave the mine and were escorted to safety. With the augmentation of militia forces under General John Chase's command, a detachment of 75 cavalrymen finally rescued Siple and 20 of his employees nearly fifty hours later.[9]

The strikers and their allies attacked several other mines and installa-tions over the next three days. Besides the Delagua, Hastings, and Empire mines, they set fire to buildings and tipples at the Southwestern, Green Canyon, Royal, and Broadhead mines. Approximately $200,000 worth of property was destroyed by fire and dynamite in the attacks. By April 25, between 1,000 and 1,500 strikers with red bandannas tied around their necks and bandoleers filled with ammunition slung over their shoulders roamed freely in an area about five miles wide and eighteen miles long bounded on the south by Ludlow, where the militia still retained control of the station, and on the north by Rouse, a strongly fortified Colorado Fuel and Iron (CF&I) mine. As they destroyed or wrecked every mine property within this area, the strikers shouted "Remember Ludlow" and sang "Union Forever," but they changed the words from "Down with the militia, up with the law" to "Down with the militia, to hell with the law."[10] While the rampage went on, Major Patrick Hamrock and his National Guard troops remained in a purely defensive position at Ludlow, unable to prevent the attacks on mine properties.

At the outset of the strikers' rebellion, General Chase appealed to Lieutenant Governor Stephen R. Fitzgarrald, acting in place of the absent Governor Elias Ammons, to rush 600 National Guard troops to the war zone. Fitzgarrald told the general the state did not have the money to send troops and that he would not call a special session of the legislature unless Ammons instructed him to do so. On the morning of April 22—the day the strikers attacked the Delagua and Hastings mines—Jesse Welborn, David Brown, Frank Gove (representing John Osgood), and a number of small coal operators conferred with members of the Denver Chamber of Commerce in Osgood's office. The businessmen agreed to support a call for a special legislative session to obtain the funds to send National Guard troops back to the strike zone. At noon, Chase joined the coal operators and their legal representatives for a closed meeting with Fitzgarrald. The meeting lasted until ten that evening, at which time 30 members of the Denver Chamber of Commerce, led by President Thomas B. Stearns, descended on the acting governor to demand that he order the troops out at once.[11]

Although the press had been barred from the meeting, Fitzgarrald later told the *Rocky Mountain News* that the coal operators had offered to advance the money necessary to support the militia in the strike field. "They told me the money could be deposited in a bank and that nothing need be known of it," the acting governor said, "but I told them the militia would not be farmed out to them."[12] With regard to calling a special legislative session, Fitzgarrald had resisted making any decision on his own. He insisted that Governor Ammons was the only person who could summon the legislature and order the National Guard into the field. The operators applied "heavy pressure," as Welborn described it, on Fitzgarrald, who finally urged Ammons to accede to their wish. Ammons agreed only to arrange for the troops' temporary pay when he returned to Denver. That was good enough for Fitzgarrald, who ordered General Chase back into the strike zone "with such forces as in your judgment may be necessary to create laws, suppress insurrection and repel invasion." Ammons telegraphed his approval of Fitzgarrald's action the next morning.[13]

Although he had pledged to raise a force of 600, General Chase could muster only 362 men. The mutineers, "dirty, black-hearted cowards" the general called them, vowed not to answer the summons until they received their back pay. Obviously displeased with the governor's unwillingness to call a special session to fund the militia, Chase declared that "[u]nless pay can be arranged, I would advocate the closing down of every coal mine in the state until the difficulty is settled."[14] Disgruntled, the general headed south with his depleted force shortly after noon on April 23. The strikers, motivated more by the desire to destroy than to fight, allowed the train carrying the troops to proceed through the eighteen-mile war zone without opposition. After freeing the entrapped men at the Empire mine, Chase and his troops reached Ludlow at dusk on Thursday, April 24. There they would remain under strict orders from Fitzgarrald to proceed no farther south. The troops were also under orders not to fire unless fired upon while a forty-eight-hour truce arranged by Horace Hawkins, Fitzgarrald, and George W. Musser, chief justice of the Colorado Supreme Court, was in effect.[15]

In seeking the truce, Hawkins was motivated by the realization that prolonged fighting would plunge southern Colorado further into anarchy. George West noted that the situation had "approached a condition of absolute prostration of government and of actual revolution." The state of Colorado had been rendered helpless to maintain law and order because its military arm, the National Guard, had acted as an agent of the coal operators against the strikers.[16]

Hawkins believed that with this breakdown of the state's authority, there could be no peace as long as the National Guard troops and their mine guard allies remained in the field and until the basic issues of the strike were resolved through negotiations. In a conference with Ammons shortly after the governor's return from Washington, Hawkins recommended appointing Chief Justice Musser as a commissioner with full power to effect the cessation of fighting between the strikers and the militia and to force representatives of both factions to "get together" with him to settle the strike without further delay on terms that would serve justice for all concerned. Hawkins stated publicly that the strikers were willing to place the entire matter of a definitive settlement in Musser's hands as long as his "dictum did not surmount their demands for the deportation of mine guards and for the retention of arms by the strikers for their own protection." The strike leaders also demanded that Ammons appoint a committee to thoroughly investigate the Ludlow site. Such an investigation was needed, they believed, to place the blame for the battle where it belonged and "to prove or disprove the stories that victims of Monday's battle were burned and buried where they fell to conceal the evidence. We want to know if all of the bodies of the dead have been recovered."[17]

Many of the strikers were unhappy with the truce. The same was true of the operators—"nothing short of a conspiracy," Welborn called it—and the mine guards, who were still eager to "clean out" the strikers.[18] Governor Ammons, however, was more than happy to support the truce and to do everything in his power to continue it. Besieged from all sides, the governor welcomed any move that would stop the shooting, burning, and killing. On the morning of April 25, the day the truce was officially declared, Ammons was confronted at the statehouse by nearly 1,000 women who demanded that he send a telegram to President Wilson asking for federal intervention in Colorado's strike war. The Women's Peace Organization, which had organized the demonstration, also urged that Major Hamrock and Lieutenant Karl Linderfelt be arrested and brought to Denver to answer charges of being responsible for the deaths of women and children at Ludlow.[19]

Senator Helen Ring Robinson, chosen as chair of a committee of five to ask the governor to meet with the women, confronted the governor, who answered her "in a most hysterical way," she later told the Commission on Industrial Relations. "'I can not come now,'" the senator quoted the governor, "'because I have men with me in the inner office,'" and he pointed to the inner office where many representatives of the mine operators were assembled, 'Men who were desirous of helping me establish peace. They are men who have great stakes down there.'" The senator retorted that she and the committee represented a convention of women who also had "great stakes down there."[20] Cowed, the governor finally agreed to meet the large delegation assembled in the legislative chamber.

The chair of the convention, Mrs. Robert W. Steele, presented the resolutions to the governor. With respect to the demand that he telegraph President Wilson to request federal troops, Ammons at first demurred, pleading that he needed more time. "I assure you that I haven't been on any picnic and that I am trying to perform the duties of my office," he explained, "but I can do nothing unless public sentiment is back of me." The women remained defiant and vowed to stay at the statehouse until the governor wired the president and acceded to their other demands. Exhausted and at the end of his patience, Ammons finally wired President Wilson requesting federal troops at nine that evening.[21]

It was evident that public sentiment was not behind Ammons and that he was clearly on the defensive after the battle at Ludlow. So were the coal operators. Some of the most influential newspapers in the state, which had previously treated the governor and the operators kindly and the strikers harshly, changed their editorial point of view after Ludlow. The *Rocky Mountain News* made the most radical shift of all. Ammons was now depicted as the lackey of the coal barons. In its leading editorial on April 22, 1914, entitled "The Massacre of the Innocents," William Chenery called the "foul deed" done at Ludlow worse than Villa's barbarities in Mexico. "Villa is a barbarian," Chenery wrote, "but in his maddest excess Villa has not turned machine guns on imprisoned women and children. Where is the outlaw so far beyond the pale of human kind as to burn the tent over the heads of nursing mothers and helpless little babies?" Chenery described the mine guards, most of whom were members of the militia, as "the gunmen of the great cities, the offscourings of humanity whom a bitter heritage has made the wastrels of the world. Warped by the wrongs of their own upbringings, they know no justice and they care not for mercy. They are hardly human in intelligence, and not as high in the scale of human kindness as domestic animals." But they were not the guilty ones, Chenery declared, even though they had fired into the tents before setting them on fire. "The blood of the innocent women and children rests on the hands of those who for the greed of dollars employed such men and bought such machines of murder. The world has not been hard on these; theirs has been a gentle upbringing. Yet they reck not of human life when pecuniary interests are involved."[22]

Chenery believed Ludlow was a battleground in a private war financed by Rockefeller, "the richest man in the world." "Once and for all time," he asserted, "the right to employ armed guards must be taken away from private individuals and corporations. To the state, and the state alone, belongs the right to maintain peace. Anything else is anarchy." Private warfare must be stopped either by stronger state laws or the intervention of the federal government, Chenery believed. "The blood of the women and children, burned and shot like rats, cries aloud from the ground. The great state of Colorado has failed them. It has betrayed them. Her militia, which should have been impartial protectors of the peace, have acted as murderous gunmen. . . . Does the bloodiest page of the French Revolution approach this in hideousness?"[23]

Chenery closed with a passionate appeal to President Wilson: "Think, Mr. President, of the captain of the strikers, Louis Tikas, whose truce with the gunmen was ended with his murder. . . . Think of his body, which has lain exposed since his infamous killing. Then, with that vast power which has been committed to you as the executive of a great nation, attend to the misery wrought by an anarchistic lust for dollars. Without your speedy aid the poor and the needy, betrayed by the state, may be slaughtered to the last smiling babe."[24]

Members of the Denver Chamber of Commerce responded to this inflammatory editorial by storming the *Rocky Mountain News* offices and threatening to withdraw their advertising unless Chenery was silenced and Harvey Deuell, the *News* correspondent covering the strike, was transferred to another assignment.[25] Chenery stood his ground, even after CF&I filed a $500,000 libel suit against the paper and the *Denver Times*. "The Colorado Fuel and Iron Company and its allied coal operators," he wrote in a front-page editorial, "have bulldozed and brow-beaten Governor Ammons all through this shameful crisis. They cannot bulldoze The News and The Times."[26]

Chenery vowed to continue to publish the truth about the activities and policies of the governor and his allies among the coal operators and the Chamber of Commerce. To begin with, he suggested, the governor should do his duty and tell the full story of the coal situation, such as "[h]ow he was asked by the operators to keep facts from the public; how, after he yielded to their demand to send out the militia, they recruited mine guards, placed them in the state's uniform, and used them for the 'restoration of peace and order' with machine guns bought by the operators; how they blocked effort after effort to settle the strike at conferences." He promised that if Governor Ammons would write the story, the *News* and the *Times* would publish it, but "[i]f he doesn't write it and send it out, that the people of Colorado may know the truth, we shall bring it out anyway when the $500,000 damage case comes to trial." Most of all, Chenery wanted the public to know that the coal operators had brought the suit and threatened a boycott against the papers for not going "down the line for them."[27] Fortunately for him, the threat of a boycott receded when the *Denver Post* allied itself with the *News* and the *Times*. In addition, CF&I dropped its suit against the two papers. Chenery had survived, but only for the short term. Although he had briefly trebled his paper's circulation with his "Massacre" editorial, he ultimately lost his job.[28]

The coal operators fought back against their critics. In their official statement, released four days after the destruction of the Ludlow tent colony,

Osgood and the coal executives placed all the blame on the strikers, who, they argued, planned the attack on the militia as a preliminary step in their campaign to capture and destroy the mines in the area. They asserted that the National Guard troops had fought courageously against a band of vicious attackers who outnumbered them and used the machine gun in their possession only to stop the strikers' advance. Additionally, the operators rejected the charge that the militiamen were employed by the mine owners to protect their property or were in any way under their control. Finally, they declared that the soldiers had not purposely set fire to the tents.[29]

The argument that most infuriated the strikers and union leaders was the one that blamed the strikers for the deaths of the women and children:

> After the firing ceased they noticed that one of the tents was blazing, and soon other tents began to blaze. The soldiers ran into the colony of burning tents. It was not known to them that there were any women and children in any of the tents, and they did not believe the strikers had exposed their women and children to danger which they had invited upon themselves.
>
> While the soldiers were attempting to save what property they could they heard the screams of a woman and children and saved them. It was not known until the following day that women and children were in the caves beneath the tents. The strikers made no effort to save their imprisoned families, and that they did not do so is a question for them to answer.[30]

There was no mention of Louis Tikas in the statement, which ended with the declaration that the owners had accepted every one of the miners' demands months ago except "the demand that they practically turn the control of the mines over to the unions."[31] The declaration was timed to take advantage of the current turmoil in the strike zone. With the miners on a rampage, attacking mines and coal camps in southern Colorado, the owners hoped their version of the Ludlow battle—that it was the opening battle in the strikers' campaign to capture and destroy the coalmines in the region—would carry some plausibility.

While the charges and countercharges over Ludlow were being exchanged, the attention of the strikers and their families turned to burying their dead. On Saturday, April 24, 1,500 people attended the funeral held in Trinidad for all those killed at Ludlow except Louis Tikas, who was buried the following

Showing Coffins Of Victims In Front Of Catholic Church Trinidad Colo

Funeral of the two women (black coffins) and eleven children (white coffins) who died in the Black Hole, April 20, 1914. Courtesy, Denver Public Library, Western History Collection, call no. X-60444.

Monday. The little white coffins of the eleven children and the black ones of the two women who had perished in the Black Hole were put on a large dray pulled by horses and taken to Holy Trinity Catholic Church for the requiem. The church bell tolled, as it frequently did when dead miners were recovered from the mines. "The manifestations of grief on the women's part was [sic] pathetic," reported the *Rocky Mountain News*, "but for the most part, the men watched the services grim-jawed and silent." Charles Costa's aging father vowed vengeance as the caskets of his son and his son's family were taken from the morgue to the church.[32]

The funeral for Tikas was even more solemn. "Grim-faced riflemen of the armies of Aguilar and Ludlow stacked their arms this morning and buried Louis Tikas, known as Louis the Greek, who, the report of the coroner's autopsy tomorrow will show, died in the strike war at Ludlow with three bullets in his back and a gaping wound in his head," Harvey Deuell began his account of the funeral in the *Rocky Mountain News*. Four Greeks with rifles on their shoulders forced their way through the crowd into the undertaker's chapel before the Mass for the Dead began. They halted in a line in front of Tikas's body and stared at the lifeless Greek leader for a moment or

265

two. Then they lifted their hats, swore an oath to "avenge Louie's death," and ritually pounded their rifle butts on the floor four times before filing out of the chapel. Outside the chapel, 578 riflemen representing almost a dozen nationalities waited to join hundreds of miners in the mile-long procession behind the casket to the Knights of Pythias cemetery. The miners marched silently without the customary band, which the union leaders had canceled at the last moment fearing that martial music would create unnecessary excitement.[33]

Even with the victims buried, controversy persisted over the cause of death of the two women and eleven children. Dr. Edwin Curry, the Victor-American Company physician who had first examined the bodies, was a star witness at the coroner's inquest. In his opinion, the space in the pit where the victims died was too small to sustain the lives of thirteen people for more than two hours; therefore, he concluded, since they had been in the pit all day, they had suffocated long before the tent was set on fire. Neither he nor the National Guard report mentioned any survivors. The personal accounts of Mary Petrucci and Alcarita Pedregone were ignored. According to her statement, Pedregone had seen a militiaman set fire to the tent above her, Petrucci, and the victims, and she and Petrucci had watched the other occupants suffocate until they themselves fell unconscious.[34] Disregarding this evidence, guard officials doggedly insisted that the strikers had caused the deaths of the women and children by sending them into the pit at the beginning of the battle. The coroner, however, disputed that claim. His verdict stated that the victims "came to their deaths by asphyxiation or fire, or both, caused by the burning of the tents of the Ludlow colony and that the fire that burnt the tents was started by militiamen under Major Hamrock and Lieutenant Linderfelt, or mine guards, or both."[35] Tenaciously clinging to their own conclusions, which exonerated them from any blame for the Ludlow tragedy, the militia and spokespersons for the coal companies ignored the coroner's verdict.

On Sunday afternoon, the day between the Saturday and Monday funerals in Trinidad, more than 5,000 men and women stood in the pouring rain before the state capitol to protest the Ludlow Massacre. "It was a scene," the *Rocky Mountain News* observed, "that never in the history of Colorado, possibly in the United States, has had a parallel." The crowd cheered loudly when UMWA officials arrived, marching behind the American flag and the scorched and tattered Ludlow flag that had waved over the camp only a week before. As a band played, the crowd sang the battle song of the union. After the crowd had fallen silent, Jesse Vetter of the machinists' union read the demands Colorado labor was proposing for ratification: the impeachment or recall of Governor Ammons and Lieutenant Governor Fitzgarrald as traitors and accessories to the murder of babies, the arrest for murder of Major Hamrock and Lieutenant Linderfelt, immediate seizure of all coal properties by the state, the revocation of 13,276 acres of state school lands held by the coal companies, the repudiation of the $1 million in debt incurred by the state in sending the militia to the strike fields, and the immediate arming of every laboring man in Colorado.[36]

The featured speaker was George Creel, a social reformer and newspaper writer who would later head the Office of War Information during World War I. Creel unleashed a scathing attack against the Rockefellers, Colorado coal operators, and National Guard officers. "Those like the Rockefellers," he shouted, "who profess Christ in public and crucify Him privately, have been unmasked, and never again will the patter of prayers be permitted to excuse Judas' greed. . . . Private ownership of natural resources and public utilities is seen as a thing that corrupts officials, poisons the law and makes murderers, and we will have no more of it." He continued:

> These, then, are Ludlow's challenges to those who sit in the seats of the mighty, wrapping the flag about their profits, putting their assassins in the country's uniforms, buying law and legislators, and crying out against class prejudice, even while they draw class lines with a bayonet's point. But is there not a message from those graves to you yourselves, oh brothers, in all callings? The blood of children is on the hands of Rockefeller, Welborn, Osgood and Ammons, but can we count ourselves entirely free from blame? . . . Let this solemn occasion mark regret for past failures and stern resolve for future unity. March as an army, toilers, and fear no defeat.
>
> Drag down such traitors as Ammons and Fitzgarrald, banish your Welborns and your Osgoods, jail Chase, Hamrock and Linderfelt on the charge of murder, and pursue the Stearnses and Johnsons into obscurity with your loathing.

Creel implored the people to unite to "take back the privileges" that had been "stolen" from them and to destroy the evil and transform Colorado into "a haven for the oppressed of the world" based on "love and equal justice. It is the command of Ludlow's living dead."[37]

Other speakers followed Creel, but none could match his brilliant performance. Even Mother Jones, who rushed in from Union Station, was something of an anticlimax. "Here I am again, boys, just back from Washington," she exclaimed. "Washington is aroused and there is help coming. . . . Go home, boys. Mind me now and keep cool. Stay out of the saloons, save your money, and when I want you I'll call you." A tremendous cheer arose when she finished, and "then the 'boys' and their wives obediently turned and, through the pouring rain, went home."[38]

Fighting had already broken out again in some areas of southern Colorado, where the truce announced on April 25 had never taken hold. At daybreak that morning, several hundred armed strikers from the coal camps in Fremont County attacked the Victor-American mine at Chandler seven miles south of Cañon City. The company had been preparing for an attack for several days, and the guards were well entrenched, with two machine guns covering the main approaches to the camp. The strikers took up positions in the hills overlooking the camp and fired rounds into it for most of the day. Hawkins and the strike leaders attempted to stop the attack, but to no avail. "We are trying to bring peace and end the strike," John Lawson said after hearing about fighting at the Chandler mine as well as around Delagua and Walsenburg. "We are constantly receiving offers of volunteers, arms, ammunition and money from various parts of Colorado and from outside the state. But I think we should be humble in victory and I will gladly meet General Chase or anyone else and talk over plans for preventing any further bloodshed. I want peace, but I want peace with justice."[39]

Under orders from Governor Ammons to work out the details with the strike leaders for implementing the truce, General Chase received Lawson and three other union leaders at his Ludlow headquarters later that afternoon. Despite the outbreak of fighting at Chandler, the general reluctantly agreed to continue the truce until the conferences going on in Denver concerning the strike had been terminated. However, he demanded that the attack on Chandler and further disorders be stopped at once. He censured the *Rocky Mountain News* and the *Denver Times* for their coverage of the strike war zone. "A sentiment has been created against law and order," he said of the papers' reporting, "and I am tempted to move all the troops out of here and to let the people down here cut each other's throats until peace has been restored." Standing their ground, the strike leaders again stated that their concurrence with the truce was predicated on the acceptance of their demands that no force be used to make the strikers disarm and that mine guards and gunmen be disarmed and deported.[40]

Meanwhile, the strikers had taken control of Trinidad and established a new tent colony on the site of the old militia camp near Mount San Rafael Hospital. The new Camp San Rafael was the largest and most completely equipped of the miners' tent colonies in the southern coalfield. Its 300 tents housed 600 strikers and their families who had been displaced from Ludlow and other tent colonies. The strikers in the camp were determined to fight to hold Trinidad if General Chase and the militia attacked the city. Although the general pledged not to send troops unless disorder was sufficiently serious to warrant intervention, uneasiness and fear of an approaching battle gripped not only the strikers but all the residents of Trinidad.[41]

The resumption of the attack on the Chandler mine on April 26 shattered what was left of the truce, forcing Ammons to order Chase to take 200 troops to the besieged mining camp. That afternoon, hundreds of strikers— an estimated 800 to 1,000—captured the mine property and looted offices, stores, and houses; sabotaged equipment; and destroyed mine records. The camp was completely torn up, with furniture and fixtures demolished, glass windows broken, and doors torn from their hinges.[42] General Chase found the camp deserted when he and his cavalry troop arrived the next morning.

Violence quickly spread to other mining camps. Hundreds of strikers attacked CF&I's McNally mine near Walsenburg. By nightfall on April 27 the attackers had driven the mine guards from the mine and set fire to the bunkhouse, tipple, and shaft house. The strikers turned next to the nearby Walsen mine, the largest in the area. Scores of strikers from the Trinidad district rushed northward to join their companions on the Walsenburg firing line. The strikers were still on the Hogback, a long ridge near the mine, forty-eight hours later after a detachment of 60 soldiers from Ludlow under the command of Colonel Edward Verdeckburg had failed to dislodge them.[43]

Further complicating matters for the militia, General Chase found it necessary to divide his troops by sending a detachment to Louisville in the northern coalfield to help protect the Rocky Mountain Fuel Company's Hecla and Vulcan properties. With the situation in the field becoming desperate, on April 26 Governor Ammons sent a telegram to Colorado congressman Edward T. Taylor begging the Colorado delegation to give President Wilson additional facts beyond those he had conveyed to the president the previous day. The telegram read: "A truce made some days ago between state authorities and strikers absolutely violated by strikers. . . . Militia altogether inadequate to protect persons and property. . . . Trinidad is overrun with armed strikers, police and sheriff helpless. Citizens in imminent danger. Principal mine operators wired request [for troops] to president."[44]

Taylor presented the telegram to President Wilson. After he read it, the president immediately consulted with the Colorado congressional delegation and other key individuals about the situation.[45] Ultimately, he decided to send federal troops to Colorado. The decision was not an easy one for him, and it had taken considerable deliberation over several days for him to reach this resolution.

The deliberation had begun on April 23, when Secretary of Labor William Wilson, after meeting with the Colorado delegation and Congressman Martin Foster, agreed to raise the matter of federal intervention at a White House cabinet meeting the next morning. Although the subject of federal intervention was put on the agenda merely as an informational item, President Wilson expressed his view that there was no precedent to warrant federal intervention in a strike that did not involve a federal issue. The president's statement implied his conviction that the state of Colorado should not be allowed to shift its responsibility to the federal government. Another issue besides upholding state's rights put the president in a cautionary mood. He feared his administration would be criticized for intervening on the side of capital in a labor dispute.[46]

The Mexican venture also weighed heavily on the president's mind. It had been less than a week since he sent troops to occupy Vera Cruz, and he did not believe he had troops to spare to send to Colorado. Yet the pressure mounted, and the telegrams demanding federal intervention multiplied. He still hoped to defuse the situation by sending the Foster Congressional Committee back to Colorado, a proposition events in the state had already made unrealistic. He also decided to contact the elder Rockefeller in an attempt to get him directly involved in solving the trouble, but that course of action had no chance of succeeding. Rockefeller, declaring that he had turned his interests in Colorado over to his son and that he knew nothing about CF&I's business, refused to become involved. In another telegram, however, the financier agreed to ask his son to meet with Congressman Foster.[47]

President Wilson pondered Rockefeller's telegrams as well as the one he received from Governor Ammons requesting federal troops during a meeting on Sunday afternoon, April 26, with the Colorado senators and house delegation, Representative Foster, and Secretary Wilson. The men brought scores of telegrams they had received to show the president, including ones from Horace Hawkins and Frank Gove, principal attorneys for the two opposing sides in the Colorado labor dispute. Senator Charles Thomas, overwrought and weeping, told the president what he had heard about the militia shooting women and children and "the clubbing of mothers with nursing babes in their arms by the paid agents of the mine owners." He also read the latest telegram he had received from Denver, which relayed the alarming news that the strikers were on the move everywhere and purchasing all the guns and ammunition they could find.[48]

Persuaded by the testimonial accounts, after the meeting the president sent for Lindley M. Garrison, the secretary of war. Garrison told the president that 200 or 300 regular troops could be rushed to the strike district within a few hours from bases in neighboring states without disturbing the troops on the border with Mexico. Governor Ammons's description of the struggle in Colorado as "an industrial controversy between interstate organizations with headquarters outside Colorado" apparently removed President Wilson's concern about federal intervention in a purely state matter. By the evening of April 26, he was ready to sign the order sending troops to the strike zone. Before doing so, however, he wanted to pursue one last effort, hopeless as it seemed, to resolve the Colorado strike. He sent Congressman Foster to New York City for a conference with the junior Rockefeller and John Osgood.[49]

A little before one o'clock on Monday afternoon, April 27, Martin Foster walked out of Rockefeller's New York office to find newspaper reporters waiting. "Nothing has been accomplished," he told them, "and I am not sure that I will come again. There is nothing of immediate promise in the air."[50] During his meeting with Rockefeller, Foster had unsuccessfully urged him to submit the strike issue to a board of arbitration. Counseled by LaMont Bowers, Rockefeller wrote to President Wilson later that afternoon to say that the question of arbitration was nonnegotiable as far as the Colorado operators were concerned and that any withholding of federal troops would be "exceedingly detrimental and unwise." Greatly disappointed by Rockefeller's refusal to intervene in the "distressing situation in Colorado," President Wilson tersely suggested that Rockefeller should be guided by a higher purpose. "It seemed to me," the president wrote, "a great opportunity for some large action which would show the way not only in this case but in many others."[51] The president's call to a higher duty, however, was lost on Rockefeller.

With the last alternative to military intervention rejected by Rockefeller, President Wilson, after conferring with Garrison, ordered federal troops into the strike district on April 28, 1914. White House officials stated that the president had acted because all parties, including Colorado's congressional delegation, the governor, mine owners, and union officials, had requested the federal soldiers.[52]

President Wilson wired Governor Ammons to stipulate clearly that the federal troops would confine themselves to maintaining order only until the state could "reassert its authority and resume the enforcement thereof." The president emphasized that the soldiers would not interfere in the strike controversy. The settlement of that controversy, he stressed, fell "strictly within the field of state power." Wilson asked that the state militia be temporarily withdrawn until the state legislature considered the entire strike situation and arranged for the militia to resume its police duties. In the proclamation that publicly announced the intervention, Wilson ordered all persons engaged in domestic violence to disperse and go home peaceably on or before April 30, 1914.[53]

The people of Colorado generally welcomed the president's decision to send federal troops into the strike zone. General Chase and Major Edward Boughton of the National Guard, however, were furious. They knew the presence of federal troops in Colorado reflected badly on their own ability to preserve order in the state and would give the strikers new hope for a settlement of the strike favorable to them. Nor was the news welcomed by Frank Gove, lead attorney for Osgood and the major coal companies. Although he and the leaders of CF&I had campaigned for federal troop intervention, they sided with Chase and Boughton against withdrawing the militia from the field. Gove's attitude, shared by the coal operators, remained one of crushing the UMWA, not of finding a settlement to the labor conflict. "You will never get a statement from the operators agreeing to any sort of truce," Gove declared angrily to a group of reporters outside General Chase's office in Denver. "The coal operators will fight the miners until every last one of them is in jail."[54] The operators also made it clear that they would fight any move to nationalize their properties just as tenaciously as they had resisted unionization.

Believing federal intervention would stabilize the situation in the coalfields and provide an opportunity to end the strike, national union officials welcomed federal intervention with enthusiasm. On the local level, union leaders in Colorado rejoiced over President Wilson's assurance that the troops would not be used for strikebreaking. However, word that federal troops were on the way and that the president had ordered the removal of the militia did not deter strikers from making last-minute raids in their campaign of vengeance to destroy mine property. On April 29, more than 100 strikers left Trinidad and were joined by 200 other fighters in the hills to take up positions at dawn overlooking the Forbes mine and camp. Mike Livoda, one of the group's leaders, recalled the attack years later: "I told the fellows not to bother women and children. . . . If there's any men that's up, use your own judgment about what to do about it. Leave women and children alone. And they did."[55] The attackers quickly overwhelmed the few mine guards and swarmed through the camp, setting fire to the tipple and other company buildings. Twelve camp buildings were set ablaze, one of which was a shack in which four Japanese miners died. The strikers left the gutted camp

Miners who marched from the Black Hills after the Ludlow Massacre awaiting the arrival of federal troops at Trinidad, Colorado. Courtesy, Denver Public Library, Western History Collection, call no. X-60417.

at ten A.M., just two hours before 125 men from the Twelfth U.S. Cavalry from Fort Robinson, Nebraska, reached Cañon City.[56]

Despite Horace Hawkins's efforts to arrange a cease-fire in the ongoing battle of the Hogback near Walsenburg, strikers under the command of Don MacGregor, former journalist for the *Denver Express* turned guerrilla fighter, continued to fire at the militia and the Walsen mine guards. Hawkins urgently wanted the shooting stopped before the U.S. troops arrived. MacGregor and his troops would have none of it, and the gunfire intensified during the afternoon of April 29, finally ending after seven that evening. By eleven the next morning a detachment of soldiers from the Fifth U.S. Cavalry was in Walsenburg, where the troops arrested six members of the Colorado National Guard for looting a saloon. The strikers came down off the Hogback and surrendered their guns. MacGregor disappeared, never to be heard from again.[57]

The Ten Days' War was over. For ten days, terror had reigned in the southern Colorado coalfield. The strikers had unleashed a fierce guerrilla campaign that spread "indescribable" terror among militiamen and mine guards, strikebreakers, and company people residing in the mining camps. "Remember Ludlow" was the strikers' battle cry, although they declared to a

273

newspaper reporter that they were not fighting for revenge alone. They also fought for liberty and freedom from oppression. By the war's conclusion, the strikers had killed thirty-three people—fifteen more than the militia had killed at Ludlow—and suffered at least two dozen casualties of their own.[58] Revenge they might have gained, but John Osgood and the other major coal operators were determined to use the Ten Days' War against the miners to reclaim the moral high ground they had lost so decisively with the Ludlow Massacre.

NOTES

1. Doyle to White, April 21, 1914, Doyle Papers, Box 1, FF 20; White to President Wilson, April 21, 1914, in WPP 29: 479; Doyle to national and international labor union headquarters, April 21, 1914, in CBLS, *Fourteenth Biennial Report,* 188; Doyle to President Wilson, April 21, 22, 1914, cited in McGovern, "Colorado Strike," 298. The reference to Mexico was in regard to President Wilson's dispatch of a U.S. military force to seize the port of Vera Cruz after refusing to recognize the Huerta regime.

2. "Call to Arms," (copy), Doyle Papers, Box 1, FF 3.

3. Quoted in Long, *Where the Sun Never Shines,* 296.

4. *Denver Times,* April 25, 1914. Priscilla Long has argued that in all the union's history there was never a better time for a nationwide strike than in the immediate aftermath of the Ludlow Massacre. She stated that coalminers everywhere would have laid down their tools and that money to finance the strike would have poured in. In opposing the strike, the national UMWA officers "lacked the visionary boldness that . . . such a dramatic step required" (*Where the Sun Never Shines,* 298).

5. Fitch, "Law and Order," 254.

6. Lawson quoted in *Rocky Mountain News,* April 22, 1914.

7. McGovern and Guttridge, *Coalfield War,* 240.

8. Margolis, "Western Coal Mining," 95.

9. *Denver Times,* April 22, 1914; *Rocky Mountain News,* April 25, 1914.

10. Margolis, "Western Coal Mining," 98; Beshoar, *Out of the Depths,* 190.

11. *Denver Times,* April 22, 1914.

12. *Rocky Mountain News,* April 24, 1914.

13. Quoted in McGovern and Guttridge, *Coalfield War,* 242; Welborn to McClement, May 27, 1914, in CIR/FR 8: 7121; Welborn, Brown, and Gove to Ammons, April 22, 1914, Ammons Papers, FF 5; Beshoar, *Out of the Depths,* 191–192 (Ammons telegraph).

14. Chase quoted in *Denver Times,* April 25, 1914.

15. Ibid.; *Rocky Mountain News,* April 25, 1914.

16. West, *Report on the Colorado Strike,* 136–137.

17. Quotes in *Denver Times,* April 25, 1914.

18. Welborn to McClement, May 27, 1914, in CIR/FR 8: 7121; McGovern, "Colorado Strike," 303.

19. *Rocky Mountain News,* April 25, 1915.

20. Senator Robinson's testimony, CIR/FR 8: 7214.

21. Ammons quoted in *Denver Times,* April 25, 1914; *Rocky Mountain News,* April 26, 1914; Ammons telegram to President Wilson, April 25, 1914, in PWW 29: 501–502.

22. William Chenery, "The Massacre of the Innocents," *Rocky Mountain News,* April 22, 1914.

23. Ibid.

24. Ibid.

25. McGovern and Guttridge, *Coalfield War,* 246. The authors observed, "Deuell employed the same journalistic mix of emotion and objectivity that Damon Runyon had once effectively blended for the paper" (ibid., 245).

26. *Rocky Mountain News,* April 28, 1914.

27. Ibid.

28. McGovern and Guttridge, *Coalfield War,* 246. Chenery later became editor of *Colliers* (Beshoar, *Out of the Depths,* 187).

29. "Operators' Statement on Ludlow," in CBLS, *Fourteenth Bienniel Report,* 189.

30. Ibid.

31. Ibid.

32. *Rocky Mountain News,* April 25, 1914.

33. Ibid., April 28, 1914; Beshoar, *Out of the Depths,* 213.

34. West, *Report on the Colorado Strike,* 130–131; Petrucci's testimony, CIR/FR 8: 8195–8196. Alcarita Pedregone told her story about the Black Hole as early as April 23 ("And Then We Had to See All the Children Die, One by One, in Death Hole," *Denver Express,* April 23, 1914, cited in Martelle, *Blood Passion,* 244).

35. Quoted in McGovern and Guttridge, *Coalfield War,* 239.

36. *Rocky Mountain News,* April 27, 1914.

37. Creel quoted in ibid. Fred P. Johnson was head of the Denver Stockyard.

38. Mother Jones quoted in ibid.

39. Lawson quoted in *Denver Times,* April 25, 1914.

40. Chase quoted in ibid.; *Rocky Mountain News,* April 26, 1914.

41. *Rocky Mountain News,* April 27, 1914.

42. Ibid., April 27, 28, 1914.

43. Ibid., April 28, 1914.

44. Ammons to Taylor, April 26, 1914, in ibid.

45. Ibid.

46. Ibid.; *Denver Times,* April 25, 1914; President Wilson to Ammons, April 25, 1914, in WPP 29: 503.

47. *Denver Times,* April 27, 1914; McGovern and Guttridge, *Coalfield War,* 252, 256; President Wilson to Rockefeller Sr., April 25, 1914, and Rockefeller telegrams to President Wilson, April 25, 26, 1914, in PWW 29: 503–504, 512.

48. *Rocky Mountain News*, April 27, 1914.

49. Ibid., April 26, 27, 1914; Ammons telegram to President Wilson, April 25, 1914, in PWW 29: 502; Bowers to Rockefeller, April 27, 1914, in CIR/FR 9: 8433. Although Bowers mentioned that Foster was to meet with Osgood, who was in New York at the time, there is no record of the meeting.

50. Foster quoted in *Denver Times*, April 27, 1914.

51. Rockefeller Jr. to President Wilson, April 27, 1914, and President Wilson telegram to Rockefeller Jr., April 29, 1914, in PWW 29: 513, 533; McGovern and Guttridge, *Coalfield War*, 257.

52. *Rocky Mountain News*, April 29, 1914.

53. President Wilson telegram to Ammons, April 28, 1914, in PWW 29: 528–529.

54. Gove quoted in Beshoar, *Out of the Depths*, 224.

55. Livoda interview with Margolis, September 20, 1980, in Margolis, "Western Coal Mining," 99.

56. McGovern and Guttridge, *Coalfield War*, 263–264; Beshoar, *Out of the Depths*, 217–219. Nine of Forbes's men and four strikers died in the battle.

57. McGovern and Guttridge, *Coalfield War*, 265–267.

58. *Denver Times*, April 22, 24, 1914. Martelle stated that "no fewer than fifty-four men, women, and children had been killed" during the Ten Days' War (*Blood Passion*, 210).

Federal Intervention

John Lawson and Horace Hawkins were on hand to greet Major W. A. Holbrook, commander of the Trinidad district, and the U.S. cavalrymen when they pulled into the Trinidad station at eight A.M. on April 30, 1914. William Murray, general manager of the Victor-American Fuel Company, was also present. Murray, the only coal company official who had remained in Las Animas County during the Ten Days' War, was the first person to reach Holbrook as he stepped off the train. Along with Max Kahn, acting city mayor, Murray ushered Holbrook into a waiting Colorado Fuel and Iron (CF&I) automobile to give him a tour of possible sites for the establishment of a camp and headquarters for the federal troops. Ed Doyle recounted the incident in a telegram to John White: "Murray Victor-American operator reported to have made attempt to force his services upon federal troops in the strike zone and was given to understand by officer his service was not needed." Returning to the station nearly two hours later, Major Holbrook announced that he would not use any of the proffered buildings in the city but would quarter his troops at the fairgrounds northeast of the business district. He also told the union leaders that the federal troops would be absolutely neutral and that the strikers could rebuild their tent colonies at Forbes and Ludlow.[1]

The union leaders were delighted that Major Holbrook had overridden Governor Elias Ammons's refusal to allow the reconstruction of the tent colonies. Shortly after receiving approval to reconstruct the camps, Doyle appealed to the union's national officials for money to cover the unavoidable expenditures incurred by the Ludlow affair. In a telegram to President John White, he noted that the expense of housing hundreds of strikers and their families in hotels in Trinidad was a tremendous burden on District 15.[2] William Green, United Mine Workers of America (UMWA) secretary-treasurer, eventually wired Doyle $15,000 to care for the wounded, bury the dead, and rebuild the Ludlow tent colony. However, with the union almost bankrupt, officials in Indianapolis pressed for an end to the strike as soon as possible. In an attempt to facilitate mediation, Green stated publicly in late April that since unionization was not the issue in contention, the UMWA would waive any recognition of the union as a condition for settling the strike. With the removal of recognition from the list of union demands, Green indicated that the remaining issues for mediation involved the manner in which the company stores were conducted, the demand for check-weighmen at mine tipples, and the general conditions of peonage.[3]

President Wilson and Congressman Martin Foster, chair of the congressional investigating committee, were as eager to see the strike end as the union leaders were. Immediately after hearing Green's statement, Foster wired John D. Rockefeller Jr. to notify him of the union's compromise offer. "Are you willing," Foster asked, "to enter into negotiations for settlement of strike on that basis and stop [the] killing of men, women, and children? I strongly urge you to do so, and believe that the strike can be ended without recognition of the union and all the other differences can be amicably settled. In my judgment, it is your duty to do so."[4] Rockefeller, still refusing to become involved in the strike, forwarded the telegraph message to Jesse Welborn and LaMont Bowers, who immediately consulted with John Osgood, David Brown, and several other operators. Their response, wired directly to Foster rather than to Rockefeller, was emphatic: "We cannot enter into negotiations of any character with the officers and agents of the United

Mine Workers of America, who alone are responsible for the terrible reign of disorder and bloodshed, which has disgraced this State." It was not their duty to call off the strike; rather, it was that of the union that had called it in the first place, they added. "In no event," the operators concluded, "will the American people, when fully advised, permit 1200 or 1500 armed strikers to continue their unlawful efforts to prevent 10,000 law-abiding and industrious men from working for whom, when, and upon such terms as they see fit."[5]

In a second telegram to Foster sent the next day, Osgood, Welborn, and Brown told the congressman that the basis for settlement had been established in Governor Ammons's letter of November 27, 1913, the terms of which, they stressed, had been accepted by the operators but rejected by the miners. They enclosed a copy of that letter and concluded by saying that "all the disorder and bloodshed in this State since November 27" had resulted from the UMWA officials' refusal to accept the governor's settlement offer. Foster responded forcefully, stating that he was no longer interested in explanations as to who was responsible for the disturbances in Colorado but was only interested in getting the parties to submit the dispute to an arbitration board. "Why can not all other questions [save recognition of the union] be now submitted to arbitration regardless of failure to adjust differences in the past?" he asked the operators.[6]

Rockefeller was delighted with the way the three leading coal operators had responded to Foster. In a letter addressed to Welborn and Bowers, he "strongly" urged them "to take a vigorously active position" in trying to get all parties concerned to agree to Governor Ammons's proposal: "Such action will demonstrate what has always been the fact, namely, that the operators are earnestly desirous of doing all in their power to restore harmony." He thought it would be wise for them to seek "the good offices of the President and the governor in bringing about the above result." In response, Bowers advised that it was Secretary William Wilson rather than the president they needed to enlist to help them force the union to accept Ammons's proposal. Foster, "doubtless a cat's-paw for Washington officials and the union leaders," was of no use to them, Bowers added. Osgood, Welborn, and Brown thus concluded their negotiations with Foster by telling him that Secretary Wilson had agreed with the Ammons proposal and that they believed Wilson needed to use his influence with the union leaders to end the strike. To make sure Foster understood that they would not settle with the union on any other terms, they noted that they had all the miners they needed to operate their mines and, further, that they would not discharge any of these "loyal workmen" and replace them with "those responsible for the destruction of our property and the killing of our men."[7]

It was ironic that the operators were now turning to Secretary Wilson, whom they had previously scorned for supporting arbitration, to help bring about a settlement of the strike on the basis of Ammons's proposal. They deliberately misrepresented Wilson's position and were unrealistic in arguing that he would pressure the strikers and union leaders to accept the proposal at the expense of arbitration. But realizing that they were open to criticism, the three leading Colorado coal operators, with the cooperation of Rockefeller and Bowers, devised a strategy to combat the widespread condemnation they had received following the Ludlow Massacre as well as any anticipated adversity caused by their rejection of Foster's request for arbitration. It was a simple stratagem: place all the blame on the strikers for the continuation of the conflict and the violence that had occurred after November 27, 1913, when they rejected Governor Ammons's terms for settlement of the strike. In short, they argued, the men on strike, coerced by intimidation or influenced by the "incendiary and anarchistic" speeches of union officials, had become criminals by causing "a state of insurrection and anarchy to prevail in this commonwealth."[8] It was a cynical ploy, but the operators knew that with the union desperately short of funds, they had time on their side. With the aid of a publicity blitz they hoped would counter the damage to their reputations caused by the Ludlow Massacre, Osgood and his two colleagues resolved to oppose any proposal for arbitration. If they had their way, the strike would end only with the complete capitulation of the union.

Defiantly defending their position against arbitration, Osgood and Brown, joined by seventeen other operators—excluding Welborn and any CF&I official—presented their views in a telegram to President Wilson on May 5. The unionists, they wrote, "have burned our mines, driven law abiding citizens and their families from their homes, and murdered our employes [sic]. They have denied to us and to our employes [sic] all rights and privileges accorded by the laws and constitutions of the state of Colorado and of the United States. . . . We submit with all deference that we ought not to be asked to deal with an organization whose officers, leaders and members have been guilty of these acts." The operators insisted that from its inception the strike had only been about union recognition. It had "ceased to be, if it ever was, one between capital and labor." No issue "of the rights of organized labor" was involved in the conflict; further, by committing criminal acts, the UMWA had "forfeited any claim" it might have had "to be considered a labor union." The only issue in Colorado, they maintained, "is one of law and order and the maintenance of the Constitutional privilege of every man to work when, where, for whom and upon such terms as he sees fit. Shall government prevail or shall anarchy and lawlessness rule?"[9]

The telegram, published in full in the *Rocky Mountain News* and signed by coal operators representing nineteen of the largest companies in Colorado exclusive of CF&I, was not only a defense of Rockefeller and CF&I officials but also a declaration of independence from that corporation. Osgood and Brown, along with their allies who signed the telegram, noted that their position with respect to the UMWA was absolutely independent from that taken by the Rockefellers or officials at CF&I. Furthermore, the operators noted that they deplored "the unjust attacks" on the younger Rockefeller: "It is neither fair nor just to him nor to us to place the burden upon, nor give him sole credit for[,] the position we are maintaining. Independent of any stand he has taken or may take, we have endeavored to strive and must continue to fight for the maintenance of fundamental principles of government and law."[10]

These words must have been comforting to Rockefeller Jr., who bristled at references to the strife in Colorado as "Rockefeller's War." He knew he was not alone in his antiunion position, for he noted that Osgood had stated publicly his refusal to ever recognize or even negotiate with the UMWA regardless of CF&I's policy. Rockefeller, however, had already begun efforts to dissociate himself from the unsavory events in Colorado and from Osgood and the more extreme operators.[11] The statement by the executives of nineteen coal companies gave him an opportunity to chart a new course for CF&I independent from Osgood and those operators who chose to stay with him. Rockefeller eventually seized the opportunity, which became even greater as a result of the divergence of opinion between Osgood and Brown on the one hand and the Rockefeller team on the other over how to respond to President Wilson's truce plan. This dispute between these former comrades in arms is discussed in Chapter 14.

The Rockefellers' negative responses to his implorations to arbitrate the Colorado strike led President Wilson to conclude that it was hopeless to continue the dialogue with them. Instead, he sent Hywel Davies and William R. Fairley to Colorado to meet directly with officials of CF&I and the other Colorado coal operators. Davies, a retired coal operator, was president of the Kentucky Mine Operators Association. Fairley was a former member of the UMWA executive board. The two conciliators would spend the summer in Colorado, with Fairley negotiating mainly with the operators and Davies with the miners.[12]

Other mediators and investigators made their way to Colorado as well. Francis Patrick (Frank) Walsh, head of the U.S. Commission on Industrial Relations, sent five members of the commission's staff, including George P. West, to confer with Davies and Fairley and conduct their own investigation. Two members of the commission, John Lennon and S. Thurston Ballard, accompanied the staff members. They found the situation still extremely critical. "The ranks of the operators, as well as those of the miners," they reported, "are as solid as the day the contest opened." The entire population was divided into two warring camps. "There were several days," the commissioners asserted, "when there was positive danger of a national revolution growing out of this Colorado strike." Had the federal troops not arrived, a commission researcher noted, "one side or the other would have been annihilated."[13] Walsh heard much the same thing from West, who wrote: "They [the mediators] say the situation is as full of dynamite as ever and that not the Lord Himself could come here and exert a spirit or influence that would soften the attitude of either side." The operators became "wild men" when they discussed the strike, West continued. "They fly into a rage, curse the federal government, and froth at the mouth." The situation in Colorado "appalled" and "disgusted" both federal mediators, and one of them told West "the state ought to be disenfranchised."[14]

The reports from Colorado convinced Walsh that the strike situation there warranted the Commission on Industrial Relations's immediate attention. Despite the objections of Governor Ammons and Governor-elect George A. Carlson that the probe would only "serve to inflame passion and endanger the peace," Walsh scheduled the opening of the commission's hearings in Denver for December 2, 1914. "This will be the most important and significant hearing that we will have," he told Commissioner Ballard. "If we have a good hearing there, it will stamp our commission all over with success."[15]

President Wilson had also expressed reservations about Walsh's plans to hold hearings in Colorado, lest they upset the fragile labor peace that had been achieved following the arrival of federal troops. Such peace as now existed in the strike zone was a result of the judicious policies outlined by Washington. Instructed by the president, the army had ordered the Colorado National Guard out of the strike zone and demanded that both sides relinquish their arms. The army troops were under instructions to treat the strikers with courtesy. They were not to be searched, a policy that allowed many to keep their weapons despite pleas from union officials to disarm. The president and his secretary of war had also decreed that only the mines operating at the time of the Ludlow battle would be allowed to continue or reopen and that the importation of strikebreakers was strictly forbidden. Although Osgood and Welborn strenuously protested the last of these decrees, Secretary of War Lindley M. Garrison refused to lift it. The ban, however, seemed to make little difference, as strikebreakers continued to find their way to the coal camps.[16]

Federal occupation of the Colorado coalfields was overwhelmingly supported by almost everyone, including mine owners, unionists, and politicians; and petitions flooded the White House demanding that they be kept there until the strike was resolved and peace completely restored. President Wilson, however, was determined to withdraw the troops as soon as he was convinced the state could maintain law and order. When he learned that Governor Ammons had summoned the Colorado legislature to a special session, he advised the governor to impress upon that body the "imperative necessity" of taking action to resolve the strike and the urgency of restoring Colorado's sovereign power in the strike district so he could withdraw federal troops as soon as possible.[17] The president's implorations, however, fell on deaf ears in the statehouse.

At the outset, the members of the legislature had been more interested in debating a resolution demanding Governor Ammons's resignation than in taking up the other measures introduced in the governor's call for a special session. Also, the measure authorizing the governor to compel the arbitration of strikes was not introduced because, according to Ammons, Attorney General Fred Farrar had ruled that it did not fall within the scope of the special session. In addition, a bill authorizing the establishment of a state constabulary, a measure the governor supported, was defeated. Instead, the legislature passed an appropriation bill for a $1 million bond issue to clear the militia's indebtedness, which paved the way for the governor to send the National Guard back to the strike zone if the opportunity arose.[18]

The *Rocky Mountain News* charged that the coal operators had dominated the special session and prevented the passage of any legislation designed to end the strike through arbitration or any other means. Senator Helen Ring Robinson added credence to this charge when she later testified before the Commission on Industrial Relations. She challenged Ammons's contention that Farrar's ruling had prevented him from doing anything about the strike situation. The governor was mistaken, she asserted, for a resolution was passed in the Senate asking him to extend the call of the special session to allow the introduction of an arbitration measure that might prevent another strike from occurring. The resolution passed by a conclusive margin, but shortly thereafter she observed representatives of the coal executives as well as the governor's secretary talking with legislators who were easily influenced. "I suppose they are going to reconsider that resolution?" she asked one of the men. He replied, "Oh, yes, we will have to." It was reconsidered, and the second vote rescinded the previous action.[19]

Having failed to persuade Ammons and the majority of the legislature to take a more active role in seeking a solution to the strike, Senator Robinson and a few of her Senate colleagues petitioned President Wilson to intervene more actively in the Colorado situation and to retain federal troops in the field until the strike was settled.[20] Among the numerous telegrams from labor and union leaders pleading with the president to keep federal troops in the strike zone was one from John White of the UMWA. "Colorado legislature adjourned," he wrote, "having done nothing except appropriate money to pay debts of militia who murdered our men, women and children at Ludlow, and other places. Acting upon request of our Colorado officials we recommend that federal troops be not withdrawn at this time for if militia returns they fear repetition of Ludlow outrages. We further recommend that steps be taken to close down those mines [all those still operating in the southern field]."[21]

The debate during the special session had been impassioned. Legislators yelled at one another while the public peeked in windows from the corridor to view the spectacle. Senator John I. Tierney, one of the most outspoken legislators who believed the legislature had failed to do its duty, cried out in the Senate chamber, "Colorado is cruelly wronged and undeservedly shamed" and was "paying the price of a national stupidity that has permitted the private exploitation of natural resources, and has bred a powerful and unscrupulous group of financiers who seek their wealth in special privilege instead of honest industry." Referring to President Wilson's rebuke to Governor Ammons, Tierney shouted at the governor, "How much stronger a spur do you need? What more stinging lash must crack over your shoulder?"[22]

The rebuke Tierney referred to came in a telegram President Wilson sent to Ammons the day the president learned that the Colorado legislature was about to adjourn without taking any action directed at settling the strike. "Am disturbed to hear of the probability of the adjournment of your legislature and feel bound to remind you that my constitutional obligations with regard to the maintenance of order in Colorado are not to be indefinitely continued by the inaction of the state legislature," the president wrote. The federal troops were there only until Colorado could "resume complete sovereignty and control in the matter." He closed emphatically: "I can not conceive that the state is willing to forego her sovereignty or to throw herself entirely upon the Government of the United States and I am quite clear that she has no constitutional right to do so when it is within the power of her legislature to take effective action."[23]

Having failed to keep President Wilson's stinging reprimand a secret, Ammons turned to the top coal executives and their political allies to draft a response. In the reply, the governor assured the president that he had been misinformed about the legislature's accomplishments. Besides laws empowering the governor to close saloons in times of disorder and to prohibit the sale of firearms in strike districts, Ammons noted that the General Assembly had appropriated the funds necessary to pay off the militia's indebtedness and to meet expenses that might be necessary to suppress insurrection and defend the state in the future. Furthermore, the governor mentioned the approval of a resolution calling for the General Assembly to appoint a joint committee to work with state officials to find a way to end the strike. In a supplemental telegram sent two days later, Ammons told President Wilson that the state would be able to take care of the strike situation as soon as the bonds were issued and that the joint committee would make an "earnest effort" to end the strike. Ammons admitted apologetically that the state could not settle the strike without assistance from Washington, which, he emphasized, would require keeping federal troops in Colorado for some time.[24]

President Wilson was not pleased with the governor's response. He told Ammons that he was "not entirely reassured" by the measures the Colorado General Assembly had adopted, and he was concerned that the bond issue provided $300,000 beyond what was required to pay the militia's debt. He assumed, correctly, that the additional amount appropriated indicated that Ammons and the state authorities were contemplating sending the National Guard back to the strike zone. Such a move, he warned, was "apt to kindle the flame again into its old violence." Greatly concerned, he asked Ammons several questions. What steps did the governor plan to take in an effort to settle the strike? What was the program immediately ahead of him? What prospect of success was there for settling the strike? And most important, he asked: "Will the operators consent to enter into negotiations which will cover the whole matter in controversy? If they will not, what course do you think it will be feasible for you to pursue?"[25]

In all probability, President Wilson knew the answers to these questions before he asked them. Besieged by appeals from every quarter to maintain the federal military presence in Colorado, the president was forced to abandon his original plan for early withdrawal of the troops. Doubtful that Governor Ammons and the state authorities were able or even willing to take the necessary action to end the strike and despite the opposition of the

Colorado coal operators, he accepted the task for himself and his administration of ending the conflict through federal mediation.

The smoke had barely cleared from Ludlow before a propaganda blitz was launched to exonerate the operators and militia and place responsibility for the battle and the violence and bloodshed in its aftermath on the strikers and union leaders. One of the first organized efforts was initiated by the Law and Order League of Women, a group composed of members of Denver's "Sacred Thirty-Six" and wives of coal managers and National Guard officers, including the wife of John Chase. While debate continued in the legislature during the special session, the women met to express sympathy for the governor and the militia in "their great ordeal." They passed a resolution decrying anarchy and denouncing the "vicious people and a prejudiced and inaccurate press corrupted either by money or by the influence of the labor vote." The organization later delivered a statement signed by 1,200 citizens to President Wilson, which placed the blame for the Ludlow tragedy entirely on the strikers.[26] Such support undoubtedly strengthened the resolve of the governor and operators to refuse to use arbitration to end the strike.

John Osgood and Jesse Welborn did not wait long to join the propaganda blitz. Articles signed by Welborn blaming the union for the continuation of the strike and for all the violence and deaths that had occurred appeared in the Chicago *Herald-Record*. Osgood's statement published in the *Christian Herald* [Denver] was one of the harshest condemnations of the UMWA and the strikers. It recapitulated the operators' position on the strike and presented his response to the Ludlow Massacre, which he blamed entirely on the strikers, who had precipitated the battle "in a final and desperate effort to win the strike." Again mirroring the operators' statement made earlier, he argued that the deaths of the innocents at Ludlow had been caused by "the heartlessness of the strikers who exposed their families to danger in attacking the militia." "Unprincipled politicians and newspapers" had used the strike leaders' "lying reports" about the militia shooting and killing "defenseless women and children" to add "fuel to the flames . . . [that] produced a condition of anarchy which necessitated the calling in of the federal troops." In reference to Washington's attempt to force the operators to submit to arbitration, Osgood observed: "The impossibility of arbitrating the matter . . . must be apparent to every right thinking man." Noting that much of the pressure for arbitration was being applied to Rockefeller Jr.,

Osgood stated defiantly that nothing the New York financier did could force him and the other operators to follow his lead.[27]

Osgood borrowed selectively from the report of the special military board appointed to investigate the Ludlow affair in writing this letter. However, the board's report, recently released, was not quite the exoneration of the militia that Osgood and other apologists of the coal operators implied. In fact, its publication brought additional disquietude to the militia. The report, *Coal Age* admitted, made it difficult to exonerate the militia, "even if we grant that the citizen force had every reason to attack and remove the tent colony as being an encampment of armed forces occupying a strategic position and constantly used as a vantage point in lawless attacks on the militia and strike breakers."[28] Since the report was not the anticipated thorough whitewash of the National Guard, General Chase and Governor Ammons had tried to suppress it. Although it strongly defended the National Guard and put the blame for the battle squarely on the Greek fighters in the Ludlow camp, it contradicted several of Major Patrick Hamrock's earlier assertions and confirmed some of the strikers' charges. It also recommended the appointment of a general court-martial to try all officers and enlisted men who had participated in looting, burning tents, or killing prisoners during the battle of Ludlow.[29]

General Chase had reluctantly appointed the investigating board when it was learned that Captain Philip Van Cise was determined to inform the editors of large daily papers about what he had discovered concerning alleged "unbelievable atrocities" committed at Ludlow unless the reports were officially investigated. "There had been a tremendous amount of talk in the papers about the alleged murder of the women and children," Van Cise later told the Commission on Industrial Relations. "I was absolutely convinced that [it] was an accident . . . but I thought that the stories about the murder of the prisoners [Louis Tikas and the other two prisoners] were very serious and should be investigated." Van Cise and his friend Captain W. C. Danks took the matter to Governor Ammons. "I was quite insistent [with the governor] that some action should be taken, because it was my opinion that if murder had been committed it should not be concealed," Van Cise testified.[30]

Danks informed Major Edward Boughton about Van Cise's threat to go public with the information concerning the alleged atrocities. They deplored their colleague's "hot-headedness," which they believed would likely inflame public sentiment. Between them, they persuaded Van Cise to abandon his "foolish notion." However, agreeing that an investigation could not be avoided, the two suggested to the governor that an investigative committee be appointed. The outcome of their meeting was expressed in a telegram Boughton sent to General Chase informing him that they had successfully suppressed Van Cise's story and that the governor had approved the committee, which would allow the general to do his own investigation "and publish the real facts before any others." General Chase dutifully appointed the board of inquiry, which consisted of Boughton, Danks, and Van Cise.[31]

Van Cise did not want to serve on the board, especially since Boughton was to be a member, but the governor ordered him to do so. Van Cise's suspicions of the major were well-founded. Although Van Cise was bound by oath not to discuss the proceedings of the inquiry, it was later ascertained that Boughton had ruled that no member of the board should seek testimony unilaterally and that men from Lieutenant Linderfelt's company were not to be questioned individually. As a result of these stipulations, Van Cise was not able to introduce the testimony of the sergeant in Linderfelt's company who swore that the lieutenant had ordered the shooting of Tikas and the other prisoners. Van Cise had to settle for a statement purporting that the prisoners were shot while they were running toward the tents. "The evidence is conflicting," the report read, as to "whether they were made to run or tried to escape." Tikas, the report conceded, was shot in the back by fire from the soldiers' side.[32]

In the first instance, the board of inquiry found that the remote cause of the Ludlow battle was the coal operators' employment of a "class of ignorant, lawless, and savage south-European peasants." Of the strikers, the Greek fighters were the most vicious, and their plan to attack the soldiers, seize the mines, expel non-union workmen, and inflict vengeance on the mine guards made the conflict at Ludlow inevitable. "As is usual with such inevitable conflicts," the report concluded, "the battle was unexpectedly precipitated and by a trifling incident [the strikers' misinterpretation of the troop movement on Monday morning]. Two facts in this connection stand out very clearly. One is that the conflict was contemplated, prepared against, deliberately planned and intended by some of the strikers, and was feared and expected by the soldiers and inhabitants of the mining villages. The other fact, equally clear, is that neither side expected it to fall at the time nor in the manner that it did."[33]

The officers concluded by stating that they did not "presume even to hint where the ultimate responsibility lies in the present strike. It may be that the coal operators or the union are wholly to blame for the conditions that have made such results possible; it may be that both sides are partly at fault." However, they added, "The conditions having been brought about and being actually existent, whatever the cause, we feel that for their treason and rebellion against organized society, with the horrible consequences of anarchy that followed, certain union leaders must take the responsibility before man and God."[34]

The charges in the report that Major Hamrock had allowed machine guns to be fired into the colony, that militiamen had deliberately spread the fire to the tents, that Lieutenant Karl Linderfelt was chiefly responsible for the enmity that led to the fighting, that soldiers had participated in widespread looting, and that it had been hinted that murder might have been committed all required a hearing before a court-martial. Although the major coal operators, local political officials, and the state attorney general were not in favor of the court-martial, they were more than ready to pursue the last of the board's recommendations—to make certain that union leaders took responsibility for their acts.[35]

The recommendation that a general court-martial be appointed to try cases involving the militia could not be denied. However, by manipulating the proceedings, General Chase made sure the military court resulted in a complete whitewash of the National Guard. Captains Van Cise and Danks and a few other officers refused to take part in the proceedings after they were told the National Guard had to "take care of these men of ours" by vaccinating them "so no court in the land can touch them at some future date."[36] Sixty-two charges of murder, looting, arson, and larceny were introduced; in the space of two weeks, ten officers and a dozen men were tried. Not one of the mine guards who had served in the militia at the time of the Ludlow battle was accused of any of the charges, even though the extent to which they and coal company employees dominated the ranks of the militia was revealed when General Chase released the rosters of Troop A and Company B during the trials. According to the rosters, 122 of the 130 men in the two units were coal company employees: 71 were employed by CF&I, 50 by the Victor-American Fuel Company, and 1 by the Rocky Mountain Fuel Company. During the proceedings all the evidence presented was ex parte except for the testimony of John Lawson, who was subpoenaed after union officials decided not to participate in what they considered a show trial in which exoneration had been predetermined.[37]

As expected, everyone was acquitted. The accused militiamen claimed they fired at the strikers only after they had been fired upon or that they were doing only what they were told. No one questioned Dr. Edwin Curry's testimony that the women and children in the pit had died hours before the tents caught fire. The charges of arson, looting, and larceny were swept aside or completely lost in the conflicting testimony, based mainly on hearsay. No cross-examination of witnesses was allowed, and irrelevancies, such as Pearl Jolly and Mary Thomas's alleged immoral character, were introduced solely to malign the strikers.[38]

The trial of Lieutenant Karl Linderfelt was the most absurd of all. Besides being charged with the murder of Louis Tikas, the lieutenant faced an additional charge of assault with a deadly weapon. Linderfelt admitted striking Tikas with a rifle and conceded that such conduct was unbecoming of a soldier. The verdict against him was entirely in character with the entire proceeding: the court found Linderfelt guilty of striking Tikas with a Springfield rifle "but attaches no criminality thereto," thus acquitting him of the charge of assault as well as all other charges, including murder.[39]

Absolved from guilt for the Ludlow Massacre by this preposterous display of military justice, the National Guard leaders, coal operators, and their allies intensified their efforts to blame union leaders and strikers for the violence in the southern Colorado coalfield. During the summer of 1914, the alliance launched a ruthless campaign of prosecution of strikers and union officers under the "law-and-order" banner. The sheriffs of Huerfano and Las Animas counties arrested scores of miners and union officials. State attorney general Fred Farrar worked with grand juries in various coal counties to bring indictments against strikers charged with participating in the violent events following the battle of Ludlow. The most important grand jury was the one established in Trinidad at the instigation of Judge Jesse Northcutt, an attorney in the coal operators' pay. The jury of twelve men, personally selected by Sheriff James Grisham, consisted of three former CF&I employees, three deputy sheriffs who had fought against the strikers, and six local merchants who depended on coal company patronage. On June 23, 1914, Farrar began the secret inquiry in person.[40]

With much of the evidence collected through bribery, intimidation, and exploitation of divisions among union officials, the grand jury made its report on August 29, 1914. The report read like a coal company bulletin. It showed that "the crimes under consideration were committed by armed mobs, acting in pursuance of well-defined, carefully matured plans, having for their object the destruction of property and human life." The "mobs" were either members of or sympathizers with the UMWA, which, "through its chief officers in this state, bought and paid for and furnished to its members the arms and ammunition used, organized and led the mobs[,] and directed the execution of various crimes." Local union officials were also charged with collecting money from outside the state under the false pretenses of aiding persons made destitute by the strike and using the money to purchase firearms and ammunition used by strikers in their campaign of violence to achieve "their demands through terror induced by the destruction of life and property."[41]

The grand jury indicted 124 labor leaders and union members in Las Animas County alone. John Lawson, with nineteen indictments filed against him—fourteen for murder, two for assault with intent to kill, one for arson, and two for conspiracy in restraint of trade—was the most important person in this group. The coal operators, with the help of trusted allies, had unleashed another weapon from their strikebreaking, union-busting arsenal—criminal prosecution of strikers. The legal proceedings had a chilling effect on the strikers. Frank West, Fred Farrar's assistant, observed that there was panic within the Greek ranks and a general stampede to confess.[42]

Supporters of the strikers and the union were not idle as the grand jury prosecutions progressed. One of their most sensational endeavors in their effort to win the publicity war was Judge Benjamin Barr Lindsey's sojourn to the East Coast with an entourage of strikers' wives and supporters. The tour had been suggested by Upton Sinclair, author of *The Jungle* and the dandy of the muckrakers, who later used many events of the Colorado conflict in writing his novel *King Coal*. Sinclair deemed the trip a unique opportunity to further the miners' cause. By giving those most directly involved in the strike a chance to tell their own stories, he hoped to gain the support of the American public and persuade President Wilson to intervene in the dispute on behalf of the strikers. He persuaded Lindsey, judge of Denver's juvenile court, to lead the expedition, which included Pearl Jolly, Mary Thomas and her two children, Margaret Dominiske, and Mary Petrucci, whose three children had died in the infamous Black Hole of Ludlow. The group traveled from Denver to the East Coast, making publicity stops at major cities before reaching Washington.[43]

Lindsey's party arrived at the White House on May 21, where President Wilson received them cordially. The president listened to stories about Ludlow and the coal operators' oppressive actions. In response to Lindsey's assertion that the federal government should compel the coal operators to arbitrate, the president said he and his government would do all they could within their legal rights to bring peace and order to Colorado.[44]

The group then traveled to New York, where Lindsey was told that John D. Rockefeller Jr. would not leave his home in Tarrytown to come to the city to meet with them. In response, Mary Thomas and Pearl Jolly picketed Rockefeller's New York office until an official told them Rockefeller would not see anybody about the Colorado matter and resented being made its "goat."[45] Despite the rebuke, the party believed their efforts had generally brought public attention to the atrocities in Colorado. Lindsey's group had enjoyed enough success in gaining sympathy for the strikers and their families that the operators and their supporters were prompted to send their own delegation on a publicity tour of the East.[46]

On the same day Judge Lindsey's group left New York to return to Denver, Major Boughton of the Colorado National Guard arrived in the city with an invitation to visit Rockefeller. A letter of introduction from Bowers explained that the major's mission was conducted at the request of Governor Ammons and state attorney general Fred Farrar and was financed by CF&I and "one or two other operators," presumably John Osgood and David Brown. Now that the agitators and muckrakers had "blown off their hot air," it was time for the coal operators and their allies to "begin a conservative and carefully planned campaign of publicity" to explain "the real facts of the mine war" to the people of the United States, Rockefeller's trusted official in Colorado wrote.[47]

Rockefeller had anticipated the need for such a campaign, not only to refurbish CF&I's image but also to correct what he believed was a misunderstanding regarding him and his father by the press and the public. He felt unjustly pilloried by some of the country's most important newspapers. Ludlow had placed him and CF&I at the center of the national debate over industrial conflict, and popular criticism and resentment of the Rockefellers had turned extremely hateful. In May 1914, nearly every major paper and magazine in the country carried stories about the events in Colorado, most of them unfavorable to the multimillionaires—particularly to Rockefeller Jr. and CF&I. Even the pro-business *New York Times* editorialized that "somebody blundered" at Ludlow, and the *Wall Street Journal* observed that a "reign of terror" existed in southern Colorado.[48]

Jerome Greene, secretary of the Rockefeller Foundation and a director of CF&I, advised Rockefeller to view the situation as a serious social and economic problem that must be solved to save the country from a great danger. He advised that they "must beat the unions in the wicked game" they were playing and that the best way of doing so was to "work through public opinion until the pressure becomes so strong that the United Mine Workers Union will have to slink off and acknowledge itself beaten."[49] Rockefeller took Greene's advice seriously. He hired Ivy Ledbetter Lee, a master of propaganda and a pioneer in corporate public relations, to undertake the task of wiping out the stain of Ludlow, restoring CF&I's image, and providing justification for the Colorado coal operators in their struggle against the UMWA. He hoped his own reputation would be restored as well.

Before serving as publicity agent for various corporations and organizations, including the Pennsylvania Railroad and the anthracite coal operators, Lee had been a reporter for several large newspapers. In 1915, after his assignment as publicity agent for CF&I and the Colorado coal operators, the Rockefellers gave him a full-time position.[50]

When Rockefeller hired Lee in 1914, he informed Welborn that Lee would work on behalf of the executive committee of Colorado operators—Osgood, Welborn, and Brown—and not exclusively for CF&I, even though the firm would bear most of the cost of the publicity campaign and John D. Rockefeller Sr. would pay Lee's salary of $1,000 a month. The publicity work would be conducted by the operators' committee and would originate in Denver.[51] It was evident from this arrangement that Rockefeller wanted to conceal from the public both his and Lee's association with the work. At first, it was planned that the information Lee collected would be sent to every newspaper in the country over Governor Ammons's signature. Lee would also ghostwrite an additional statement "setting forth the situation as Governor Ammons saw it," with information provided mainly by the members of the operators' policy committee. The statement was to be addressed "To the American People" and distributed all over the United States. For some reason, the statement was never sent out. But Lee did draft letters for Ammons and Welborn addressed to President Wilson.[52]

As an alternative to the original plan, Lee and the operators' policy committee decided to publish a series of bulletins entitled *Facts Concerning the Struggle in Colorado for Industrial Freedom* over the signatures of Welborn, Osgood, and Brown. Between June 22 and September 4, 1914, fifteen bulletins were published from information put together by representatives of the three operators and edited and printed by Lee in his Philadelphia office. The bulletins were sent to members of Congress, governors, editors, journalists, college presidents, professional leaders, and church ministers. The fifteen bulletins were reprinted in a single volume in late September with a cover letter signed by the three operators and a twelve-page history of the strike from the operators' point of view. "It is to be hoped that a knowledge by the American people of the *facts* may promote permanent and healthy industrial peace throughout the United States," the operators wrote.[53]

The bulletins mainly contained information already circulated in advertisements the coal operators' policy committee had been running in regional newspapers. They maligned the UMWA while defending the coal operators and the Colorado National Guard. The first bulletin, entitled "The Principle at Stake," was a reprint of the coal operators' letter to President Wilson on May 4 [5], 1914. Bulletin no. 5, "The Real Meaning of the Colorado Strike," provided extracts from the operators' summary of conditions in the Colorado coalmines sent to Congressman Martin Foster's subcommittee on mines and mining. General Chase's report to Governor Ammons on the military occupation of the strike zone was the source for two of the bulletins. In the first, Chase referred to the strikers' "bad faith" in refusing to disarm. In the second, "The Activities in Colorado of 'Mother Jones,'" the general justified his incarceration of her by stating that he confidently believed "that most of the murders and other acts of violent crime committed in the strike region . . . [had] been inspired by this woman's incendiary utterances (63)." Other bulletins included the statement by Senator Charles Thomas relating information he had received from W. F. Oakes of the Sunnyside Mining Company and the statement by Congressman George Kindel of Colorado before the U.S. House of Representatives supporting the coal operators. Reprints of partisan articles, reports, and sermons were included in other bulletins.

Although he claimed his publicity endeavor was a quest for truth, Lee never questioned the operators' information or opinions before he reproduced the material. One of the most blatantly incorrect statements he published was one from the Law and Order League of Women. "No machine gun was at any time directed against the colony," the women asserted in the tract entitled "No 'Massacre' of Women and Children in Colorado Strike." For Lee, the truth of the bulletins was, as one federal investigator described it, "the truth as the man you were serving saw it."[54] But he was caught in a lie when he published the operators' claim that the union officials had been paid huge salaries while strike relief was meager. The union opened its books to disprove the assertion, and the radical press soon labeled Lee a paid liar and dubbed him "Poison Ivy."[55]

The operators' policy committee, however, continued to send material to Lee, which he published in bulletins in November 1914 as Series II of the *Facts.* Some bulletins in the new series were even more vicious against the strikers and union leaders than those in the first series. A prime example was an account of the Colorado strike by the Reverend A. A. Berle, which the operators reprinted and circulated extensively in two bulletins under the title *The Colorado Mine War.* Berle described the strike as an "invasion of the State by a group of men who seek, with irresponsible and unlimited funds, to supply arms and ammunition to ignorant men and urge them to commence a bloody assault upon the laws and orderly administration of public affairs."[56] A public appeal to Secretary Wilson to end the strike, signed by six prominent Colorado religious and education leaders, formed the basis of another bulletin. "Let the agitators, brought from other states, be withdrawn," the dignitaries pleaded.[57]

Instead of silencing the criticism from the popular press, Lee's public relations campaign fanned the flames of muckraking journalism. Such national magazines as *McClure's, Everybody's, Success, Hampton's, Arena,* and *Colliers* published articles extremely critical of Rockefeller and the Colorado operators. Bowers, among others, believed more drastic measures than those pursued by Lee were needed to counter the influence of these publications. The withdrawing of advertising, as he advocated, and the purchase of "unfriendly" magazines by "friendly" corporations were two methods eventually used to silence the muckrakers.[58]

Despite the controversy stirred by Lee's propaganda campaign, the Rockefeller camp was highly encouraged by the responses to his bulletins from such groups as chambers of commerce, manufacture associations, churches, and educators. By early September 1914, 37,000 copies of the bulletins had been printed and circulated; by March 1915 CF&I had spent $19,000 on publicity—excluding Lee's salary, which the senior Rockefeller still paid. That amount was almost as much as the company had spent on guns the previous year.[59]

Pleased with the bulletins' success, Lee emphasized the importance of continuing the propaganda campaign. But Rockefeller Jr. had something else in mind. Painfully aware of his isolation from the American public, he had begun to change his thinking about the situation in Colorado during the summer of 1914. He sent Lee to Colorado to tour the mines and camps in an attempt to gain deeper insight into the situation. Lee's reports, in important particulars, undercut some of the opinions proffered by Bowers and Welborn concerning the strike situation, especially their conviction that union agitation was behind all the state's labor troubles. As a result, Rockefeller's confidence in the local CF&I management weakened. What became uppermost in importance to the financier was to find out what had caused the miners to go out on strike and to find a way to avoid a repetition of such a conflict. He saw that the company's attitude and policy needed to be scrutinized thoroughly and that new methods and improved labor policies had to be implemented. For these reasons, he needed the help of a trained, objective expert in industrial relations who was not personally involved in the conflict to find the basic cause of the trouble and to offer solutions to solve it. The man he turned to for this mission was William Lyon Mackezie King.[60]

NOTES

1. Beshoar, *Out of the Depths,* 222–224; Doyle to White, April 30, 1914, Doyle Papers, Box 1, FF 20.

2. Doyle to White, May 6, 1914, Doyle Papers, Box 1, FF 20.

3. *Rocky Mountain News*, May 2, 1914.

4. Foster to Rockefeller, April 29, 1914, in "Statement of Colorado Operators," *Coal Age* 5, no. 19 (May 9, 1914): 775; Fosdick, *John D. Rockefeller*, 151.

5. Coal operators to Foster, April 30, 1914, in CIR/FR 7: 6713–6714. In addition to representatives of the "big three" coal companies, the telegram was signed by sixteen other operators.

6. Foster to Welborn, May 2, 1914, in ibid., 7: 6716–6717; coal operators to Foster, May 1, 1914, in ibid., 6715–6716; Bowers to Rockefeller, May 2, 1914, in ibid., 9: 8435.

7. Osgood, Welborn, and Brown to Foster, May 4, 1914, in ibid. 7: 6717–6718; Bowers to Rockefeller, May 4, 1914, in ibid., 9: 8436; Rockefeller to Welborn and Bowers, May 3, 1914, in ibid.

8. Colorado operators' telegram to President Wilson, May 5, 1914, in PWW 29: 547.

9. Ibid., 546–549. Secretary Wilson rebutted the operators' statement in a lengthy telegram to President Wilson. The secretary, a former UMWA member and officer, stated that the union was a lawful and responsible organization that had approximately 430,000 members in the United States. Since 1897, he noted, the organization had made wage contracts with all mine employers in Ohio, Indiana, Illinois, Iowa, Missouri, Kansas, Arkansas, and Texas and with some of the operators in Pennsylvania, Kentucky, Tennessee, and Alabama. The Colorado operators' justification for refusing to have business dealings with the UMWA because it was a lawless organization whose "officers, leaders, and members have encouraged intimidation, assaults, arson, murder, armed resistance to organized government, and anarchy in general" was baseless. The charge, he said, "would have greater force if it came from men who themselves have been conservators of the peace, but these companies have not been" (Secretary Wilson to President Wilson, May 11, 1914, in ibid., 30: 16–20).

10. Ibid., 29: 546; *Rocky Mountain News,* May 5, 1914.

11. McGovern and Guttridge, *Coalfield War*, 274–275.

12. Ibid., 299; *Rocky Mountain News*, May 2, 1914. Davies, in addition to being a mine owner, was a mine engineer who had taken a prominent role in negotiations between employers and employees. Fairley was well-known in the South for his sociological work with miners. He had been instrumental in the enactment of legislation that compelled mine owners to take steps to improve mine safety. He was also interested in mine rescue work and had given valuable aid to the Bureau of Mines in connection with that work.

13. Lennon, Ballard, and another commission researcher quoted in Graham Adams Jr., *Age of Industrial Violence, 1910–15* (New York: Columbia University Press, 1966), 147, 161.

14. West to Walsh, June 26, 27, 1914, quoted in ibid., 147.

15. Ammons and Carlson to Walsh, May 24, 1914, and Walsh to Ballard, Garretson, and Weinstock [commissioners], November 16, 1914, quoted in ibid., 147–148; last quotation in McGovern and Guttridge, *Coalfield War*, 314.

16. McGovern, "Colorado Strike," 323–324; Welborn testimony, CIR/FR 7: 6722; Doyle testimony, CIR/FR 8: 6987.

17. President Wilson to Ammons, April 28, 1914, in PWW 29: 529.

18. Beshoar, *Out of the Depths,* 228–229.

19. Senator Robinson's testimony, CIR/FR 8: 7217; *Rocky Mountain News,* cited in McGovern and Guttridge, *Coalfield War,* 280.

20. McGovern, "Colorado Strike," 338.

21. White to President Wilson, May 18, 1914, in PWW 30: 46.

22. Tierney quoted in McGovern and Guttridge, *Coalfield War,* 279–280.

23. President Wilson to Ammons, May 16, 1914, in PWW 30: 37.

24. Ammons to President Wilson, May 16, 18, 1914, in ibid. 37–38, 45–46.

25. President Wilson to Ammons, May 20, 1914, in ibid., 48–49.

26. Quote in Beshoar, *Out of the Depths,* 229; McGovern, "Colorado Strike," 408. McGovern noted that Ivy Lee later used the statement as the basis for Bulletin 4 in the July 25, 1914, issue of *The Struggle in Colorado for Industrial Freedom* (ibid.).

27. Beshoar, *Out of the Depths,* 229 (Welborn quote); J. C. Osgood, "History of the Coal Strike in Colorado, 1913–1914," letter to the editor of the *Christian Herald,* May 5, 1914, Western History Collection, Denver Public Library.

28. "Colorado Strike," *Coal Age,* May 9, 1914, 771.

29. *Denver Express,* May 1, 1914; "Report of Military Commission," in CIR/FR 8: 7313.

30. Van Cise's testimony, CIR/FR 7: 6816–6817.

31. McGovern and Guttridge, *Coalfield War,* 250.

32. Van Cise's testimony, CIR/FR 7: 6817; "Report of Military Commission," in ibid., 8: 7312, 7322. McGovern and Guttridge observed that Van Cise solicited testimony in secret in defiance of Major Boughton's order and that the major conferred privately with Linderfelt and Major Hamrock (*Coalfield War,* 251). Van Cise's charges relating to Tikas's killing were made formally at a secret court of inquiry into alleged malpractices by members of the Colorado National Guard. The hearings, held in August 1915, were never made public.

33. "Report of Military Commission," in CIR/FR 8: 7316.

34. Ibid., 7311–7323.

35. McGovern and Guttridge, *Coalfield War,* 287.

36. Quoted in Beshoar, *Out of the Depths,* 230.

37. Ibid., 231; McGovern and Guttridge, *Coalfield War,* 285.

38. McGovern and Guttridge, *Coalfield War,* 285–286.

39. Ibid., 286–287.

40. Ibid., 287.

41. Quotations in Beshoar, *Out of the Depths,* 239–240.

42. Ibid., 240; McGovern and Guttridge, *Coalfield War,* 288.

43. McGovern and Guttridge, *Coalfield War,* 276; Lindsey to Joseph Tumulty, May 16, 1914, in PWW 30: 38–39.

44. Beshoar, *Out of the Depths*, 233; McGovern and Guttridge, *Coalfield War,* 276–278.

45. McGovern and Guttridge, *Coalfield War*, 278; *New York Times,* May 18, 22, 1914. Through the efforts of Jane Addams of Hull House, the Lindsey delegation while in New York secured a hearing before the Commission on Industrial Relations months before the commission opened its hearings in Denver to investigate the Colorado strike (McGovern, "Colorado Strike," 422).

46. McGovern, "Colorado Strike," 422–423.

47. Quotes in McGovern and Guttridge, *Coalfield War,* 281.

48. *New York Times* and *Wall Street Journal* quoted in Long, *Where the Sun Never Shines*, 308–309; R. MacGregor Dawson, *William Lyon Mackenzie King: A Political Biography, 1874–1923* (Toronto: University of Toronto Press, 1958), 233.

49. Jerome Greene to Rockefeller, May 21, 1914, quoted in Long, *Where the Sun Never Shines,* 308.

50. Ibid., 310–311.

51. John D. Rockefeller Jr. to Welborn, June 8, 1914, Jesse Floyd Welborn Papers, FF 2, File 2, Colorado Historical Society, Denver.

52. Beshoar, *Out of the Depths*, 231–232.

53. Coal Mine Managers, *Facts Concerning the Struggle in Colorado for Industrial Freedom*, Series I (Denver, September 21, 1914), 1 (original emphasis). Information in the next paragraph is also from this source.

54. Official quoted in Long, *Where the Sun Never Shines*, 310.

55. McGovern and Guttridge, *Coalfield War,* 291.

56. A. A. Berle, *The Colorado Mine War,* 571, cited in McGovern, "Colorado Strike," 412.

57. Quoted in McGovern, "Colorado Strike," 413.

58. Quoted in Long, *Where the Sun Never Shines*, 311. The UMWA put out its own series of pamphlets titled *The Struggle in Colorado for Industrial Freedom*. The first issue focused on the dangerous conditions in Colorado coalmines based on statistics from the U.S. Bureau of Mines (McGovern and Guttridge, *Coalfield War,* 292).

59. Howard M. Gitelman, *The Legacy of the Ludlow Massacre: A Chapter in American Industrial Relations* (Philadelphia: University of Pennsylvania Press, 1988), 35; Long, *Where the Sun Never Shines,* 310.

60. Fosdick, *John D. Rockefeller,* 153.

F O U R T E E N

The Strike Ends

John D. Rockefeller Jr.'s choice of Mackenzie King to conduct an investigation of industrial relations for the Rockefeller Foundation was an excellent one. King was a Canadian citizen thoroughly trained in that field. He had been a resident fellow at Hull House and had studied political economy under Thorsten Veblen at the University of Chicago and Frank Taussig at Harvard, two professors extensively involved in social and industrial matters. In England he had attended lectures by Sidney and Beatrice Webb of the Fabian Society, who influenced him, as did the teachings of Arnold Toynbee. After returning to Canada in 1900, he was assigned to organize a department of labor for the Canadian government. In 1909 he was elected a Member of Parliament and appointed minister of labor. During his tenure as labor minister, he drafted the Industrial Disputes Investigations Act. He lost his ministerial post and parliamentary seat in 1911. Forced into private life once again, the Rockefeller Foundation appointment rescued him from financial difficulties and professional insecurity.

King was a liberal in the Christian Socialist tradition. He did not agree with the conservative laissez-faire philosophy of allowing social forces to function without intervention. He regarded unions as an important component of industrial society and believed state intervention in economic and social affairs was justified as long as it was limited in scope. He also believed there were good reasons for the state to limit the power of private citizens, especially when that power was bound up in great concentrations of wealth. Such intervention was needed to assure the upward mobility of the talented and ambitious among the common people who provided the driving force of capitalistic society and human progress. King was contemptuous of the wealthy class's conspicuous consumption, an attitude doubtlessly formed from his association with Veblen. The ostentatious display of wealth and lavish lifestyles of the rich, he felt, were made possible at the expense of the struggling working class. Through their desire for self-gratification, the wealthy lost their strength of character and thus their moral integrity and their mandate to shape and reform society.[1] King's judgment of John Osgood, as discussed in Chapter 15, was strongly influenced by his view of the relationship between character and social and political conduct.

Believing what he did about wealth and society, it is paradoxical that Mackenzie King and John D. Rockefeller Jr. developed a relationship that became a lifelong friendship. To King, their relationship seemed preordained to accomplish a noble endeavor. "I shall always feel that there was nothing of 'chance' at our having been brought together at the time we were," King would write.[2] Rockefeller, for his part, felt he had never met a man more qualified than King to draft a new industrial relations policy. At their first meeting in early June 1914, Rockefeller asked King if he could devise a representation plan that would provide a means for employees to air their grievances. Although interested, King remained conflicted over the job offer. He was not certain that the heart and soul of Colorado Fuel and Iron (CF&I) could be transformed enough to prevent him, if he took money from that interest, from being branded an enemy of the working class. In early August, Rockefeller once again appealed to King to help him develop a system of representation that would provide employees with opportunities for collective bargaining, discussion of grievances, "and any other advantages which may be derived from membership in the union."[3] King replied with a brief proposal in which he recommended the establishment of a

William Lyon Mackenzie King. Courtesy, William James Topley / Library and Archives, Canada / PA-028136, Ottawa, Ontario.

company board of conciliation, made up of representatives of both managers and workers, that would meet at stated intervals to discuss grievances and working conditions. The plan, King advised, would give the workers everything they asked for except what King regarded as the hollow victory of union recognition. The outline of the plan pleased Rockefeller, and in mid-August the Rockefeller Foundation officially put King on its payroll.[4]

Rockefeller promptly sent King's proposal to LaMont Bowers and Jesse Welborn in Denver. Both men reacted unfavorably. Welborn believed acceptance of the plan would constitute an admission that workers' grievances existed in the first place. Moreover, he insisted that it was unwise to introduce such a plan at a time when the strike was turning in their favor and there was every chance to force the United Mine Workers of America (UMWA) into unconditional surrender. "To take [the plan] up at the moment," Bowers told Rockefeller, "would be most unwise in my opinion from every viewpoint; I feel certain the other operators would balk, the socialistic papers would charge us with dodging and hiding behind this eleventh hour scheme to save our faces. The union leaders would use it as a club to drive us into some other corner. Our rugged stand has won us every foot we have gained . . . so to move an inch from our stand at the time that defeat seems certain for the enemy, would be decidedly unwise in my opinion." If the operators adopted King's plan, Bowers added, the union would claim victory and miners would join the UMWA in droves.[5]

Ivy Lee concurred with Bowers and Welborn that the time was not right to introduce King's plan, although he agreed with King that some kind of grievance machinery was needed. Lee reported to Rockefeller that he had found CF&I's management "most enlightened as to all important subjects. But the mine superintendents and petty bosses have all the faults of their kind and the Company has no assurance that its policies are being carried out. There is no appeal (in practice) from the decision of the pit boss," and the men were "afraid to complain or appeal."[6]

Lee also told Rockefeller that it was not a good time for King to visit Colorado, as originally planned, for there was growing dissension within the ranks of the leading operators. Osgood, the dominant voice directing the operators' strike strategy, was a major problem. For one thing, Lee noted that Welborn, who began his career as a bookkeeper for Osgood, allowed himself to be dominated by the senior coal operator in the state. Osgood was rabidly antiunion and inflexible in his opinions, Lee added. He was totally oblivious to the arguments of others and to the consequences his actions might have. This was particularly troublesome for the Rockefellers, Lee warned, for they alone had to answer for anything done on behalf of the operators. Whereas Osgood was still greatly respected in Colorado, local sentiment was strongly biased against the Rockefellers, who many believed had exploited Colorado for their own pecuniary gain. Therefore the Rockefellers, rather than the Colorado operators, were blamed for all that was wrong with regard to the strike situation. They needed to find a way to correct this false impression, Lee suggested.[7]

For the time being, Rockefeller succumbed to the views of those who wanted to postpone any reforms until the union had capitulated. He was aware that, as Lee hinted, introducing a representation plan before the strike ended would shatter the unity among the major operators at a time when unity was needed to defeat the union. Lee's report that Hywel Davies and William Fairley, whom President Wilson had earlier sent to Colorado as conciliators, had reached an agreement with local and national union leaders on a plan for settlement of the strike brought Rockefeller's attention back to the immediate problem at hand.[8]

Davies and Fairley's plan called for a three-year truce, subject to the strict enforcement of Colorado mining and labor laws; reemployment of all strikers not guilty of a crime; prohibition of intimidation of union and non-union workers; posting of current wage scales, rules, and regulations in each mine; establishment of a grievance committee in each mine; and creation of an arbitration commission consisting of three members appointed by the president of the United States to resolve all issues on which agreement could not be reached in the grievance committees. The plan further stipulated that the union waive its recognition demand; that there be no picketing, parading, colonizing, or mass campaigning (organizing) by representatives of the union when such activities interfered with working operations in the mines; that no mine guards be employed, except those necessary as watchmen; and that all decisions of the commission in cases submitted to it would be final and binding on both employers and employees.[9]

On September 5, 1914, President Wilson submitted the Fairley-Davies plan to Osgood, Welborn, and Brown—the members of the operators' policy committee—and to UMWA's international officers. "I feel justified in addressing you with regard to the present strike situation in Colorado because it has lasted so long, has gone through so many serious stages, and is fraught with so many possibilities that it has become of national importance," the president wrote in a letter accompanying the proposed plan. He had earlier hoped, he told the operators and union leaders, that they would have shown some willingness "to consider proposals of accommodation and settlement," but it had become apparent to him that no one was willing to act, compromise, or even consider any terms of settlement. Therefore, since he could not use the U.S. Army indefinitely as a police force in the strike zone, he was compelled to submit the Fairley-Davies "truce" plan to the leaders of the two warring parties. He implored them to consider the plan "as if you were acting for the whole country" and begged them to regard its acceptance "with very deep earnestness."[10]

The union officials quickly agreed to the plan, subject to its approval by the strikers' representatives. On September 15, ninety-six miners representing the locals of District 15 met in Trinidad to consider what was now called President Wilson's truce plan. They heard arguments from the principal Colorado strike leaders. Frank Hayes told the miners that the strike was lost and that the international executive board wanted it to end as soon as possible. Accepting the president's proposal, he stressed, was the best way out of their desperate situation. Ed Doyle and John Lawson, however, spoke in favor of continuing the strike. Mother Jones countered with a warning that rejecting the plan would constitute a repudiation of the president. Despite Doyle and Lawson's plea to continue the strike, the vote was almost unanimous for approval. The local union leaders told President Wilson that the miners would immediately terminate the strike and return to work when they received notice that the coal operators had accepted the plan.[11]

According to one of Doyle's informants, the news of the miners' approval of the president's plan was "quite a jolt" to the "big three" operators, who had counted on the miners rejecting the plan to save them the trouble of having to address it. They had wanted to stall until after the upcoming state election, in which they felt certain of electing a governor they could control or one who was favorable to them. They could then force the UMWA to agree to their terms "or be deported as fast as the trains could take them out." The "big three" operators, the informant continued, were using the whip to keep the small operators in line. They declared that President Wilson "could not force arbitration no matter how much he would like to," and they were "not going to stand for the independent operators agreeing to the truce."[12]

The information from the informant was essentially correct. William Fairley told Secretary William Wilson that the Colorado operators held several "stormy" sessions over the next two weeks to decide how best to reject the truce plan. Unwilling either to accept or openly reject it, the operators, clearly under Osgood's influence, decided to delay, during which time they would block a negotiated settlement with the miners but avoid the appearance of rejecting President Wilson's urgent appeal for a settlement of the strike. They realized that their problem was magnified by Rockefeller and his New York advisers' decision to chart their own course separate from the rest of the operators.[13]

The first indication that officials in the New York office were considering an independent course of action for CF&I came in a letter Starr J. Murphy, Rockefeller Jr.'s legal adviser, addressed to Welborn on September 8. Murphy told Welborn that President Wilson had put the coal operators in "a delicate situation" by making the Fairley-Davies plan public and that the union's acceptance of the proposal deprived the operators of any delaying tactics. Although he counseled that they reject the plan, he thought it imperative for CF&I to offer counterproposals for President Wilson to consider. "It seems to me clear that public opinion will demand either the acceptance of the President's proposition or some constructive suggestion from the operators," he wrote. "A mere refusal to do anything would be disastrous." Earlier, Murphy had agreed with Welborn and Bowers that Mackenzie King's proposal for employee representation should be deferred while the strike was still pending; but, he told Welborn on September 16, "in view . . . of the President's action, and particularly in view of the fact that the plan which he suggests is stated in his letter to be tentative, I think the time has come for the operators to bring forward their constructive suggestions." Therefore, he suggested that a passage be included in the letter to President Wilson indicating that CF&I intended in the near future to develop a grievance system that would involve workers in the settlement of company problems.[14]

Murphy also suggested to Welborn that President Wilson's proposal gave CF&I the perfect opportunity to cut ties with the other Colorado operators and chart its own course. Ivy Lee's comments about Osgood's dominance of the operators' committee no doubt helped shape Murphy's argument, as did the realization that Osgood, with his reactionary views, would never accept new ideas that might help settle the strike. Welborn made the last point absolutely clear in a letter to Rockefeller. He stressed that Osgood and the other operators would never accept the truce plan because they believed settling grievances through a commission appointed by the president would take too much power away from them. This information strengthened Murphy's conviction that CF&I had to take an independent course to end the strike and restore Rockefeller's public image. A letter to the president in response to his truce plan signed by CF&I independent of the other operators, Murphy assured Welborn, would not mean an end to the united resistance to the union or preclude other Colorado operators from independently exercising their own judgments.[15]

Murphy's recommendations arrived in Denver after Welborn and Lee had already drafted CF&I's response to President Wilson's truce plan. Reluctantly, after receiving Murphy's detailed suggestions for what to include in the letter, Welborn agreed to incorporate a reference to the company's current intention of developing plans for dealing with grievances. He told Murphy that the reference would be vague, for he preferred to discuss such plans in a private meeting with President Wilson when he went to Washington to present the "true facts" of the Colorado situation to him.[16]

In the letter to President Wilson, largely written by Lee, Welborn stated emphatically that CF&I would never enter into a truce with lawless agitators: "[I]f men are determined to attain their ends by violence, it is axiomatic that government cannot make concessions of principle merely to induce such men to refrain from riot. . . . [N]o surrender, merely for temporary peace, should be made to those who incited and directed the lawlessness which has taken place in Colorado." The principle CF&I would not sacrifice was the company's assurance to its employees that its mines were open shops. Arbitration boards were not applicable to conditions in the mines of southern Colorado and were a threat to the company's power and authority. CF&I was unwilling to take back strikers, even those not guilty of legal violations. Finally, in the statement suggested by Murphy, Welborn wrote: "We [CF&I] are now developing an even more comprehensive plan, embodying the results of our practical experience, which will, we feel confident, result in a closer understanding between ourselves and our men. This plan contemplates not only provision for the redress of grievances but for a continuous effort to promote the welfare and the good will of our employees."[17] The last sentence satisfied Murphy's suggestion that Welborn include something positive and constructive in a letter that otherwise rejected the truce plan.

Although Welborn had not intended it, publication of the letter in major newspapers with the reference to the development of an "even more comprehensive plan" than the one presented in the Fairley-Davies proposal put the company on the course outlined by Mackenzie King. The company's commitment to a new course of action was now a matter of public record.[18]

Rockefeller expressed approval of the CF&I statement in a telegram to President Wilson on the eve of Welborn's visit to the White House to confer directly with the president. Rockefeller's comments portended a major change in the role he would play in the settlement of the Colorado strike. Since Welborn's reply was made on behalf of CF&I alone, Rockefeller wrote, "I feel at liberty both as one of its directors and as representative [of] a substantial minority interest to take a more active part in the matter than I did when it was in the hands of a committee representing all of the operators." Furthermore, he stated, "I sincerely hope that as a result of the interview you have granted Mr. Welborn some practical plan may be envolved [evolved] which will be adapted to the peculiar situation of our company and be acceptable to our employees."[19] Clearly, Rockefeller was heeding the advice of some of his principal New York advisers—namely, Ivy Lee, Starr Murphy, and Mackenzie King—to break with Osgood and the other Colorado coal operators and chart an independent course for CF&I.

Rockefeller's hope that the two men could reach an understanding beneficial to CF&I was dashed, however, for President Wilson used the meeting with Welborn to press his point that it was the operators' duty to accept the Fairley-Davies proposal as drafted and approved by the miners. Public interest demanded the end of the strike, he proclaimed, and "it was the patriotic duty of the mine operators to accept the proposal." In addition, the president instructed Welborn to tell the other operators that he could not accept a refusal of the plan. Although not verified officially, it was reported that President Wilson vowed to withdraw federal troops unless a satisfactory settlement was reached.[20]

Despite President Wilson's refusal to make any concessions, Welborn left the White House still convinced that the operators should seek modification of the truce plan. However, at lunch with Rockefeller, Murphy, Lee, and King the next day, he described his interview with the president as fruitless.[21] He wired that view to Osgood and Brown. Ed Doyle's informant was present in Osgood's office when Welborn's telegram arrived. "A number of operators blowed [sic] up yesterday [September 23] when a wire from Welborn arrived giving the results of the interview with Pres. Wilson," the informant wrote in describing the scene. Welborn, the informant continued, expected to meet with the president again and "still hoped to make Wilson see the unfairness of certain parts of his plan." Welborn advised Osgood and Brown to make preparations to protect their properties with civilian guards, "as the situation might take on a serious aspect at any hour." As far as the informant could make out, this meant Welborn saw the danger inherent in withdrawing federal troops from the strike zone.[22]

When Welborn's wire arrived, several operators representing other coal companies were meeting with Osgood, Brown, and the Victor-American attorneys to finalize the draft of their letter to President Wilson in reply to his settlement proposal. With CF&I officials apparently charting their own course with respect to the strike situation, Osgood and Brown had assumed leadership of forty-six coal operators in the state, who, along with them, subsequently signed the letter to President Wilson. In the letter, the operators expressed regret that the president had been misinformed about the strike by Secretary Wilson's representatives, who were partisans of the union leaders and strikers who had made it necessary to send federal troops to the strike district. They singled out William Fairley in particular, accusing him of having been a UMWA organizer and agitator in Colorado in 1904. For many reasons, they believed it would be "imprudent" to enter into an agreement with the union, whose leaders, they warned, could not be trusted: "We feel . . . that a mere 'truce', even if it could be enforced against this voluntary, unincorporated association and its irresponsible leaders, is but a palliative measure and can lead to nothing other than what the term itself implies—a renewal of trouble at its termination." Therefore, they would never enter into an agreement that did not secure the principles for which they stood. The majority of the people in Colorado, they argued, agreed with them that the sole issue in the state was "the preservation of law and order . . . and the maintenance of the constitutional right of every man to work when, where, for whom, and upon such terms as he sees fit. . . . Whether the responsibility for what has taken place in Colorado is chargeable to the operators or to the striking miners and their leaders, the plan proposed involves a bargain between government and law on the one side and violators of the law on the other." They would never agree to such a bargain.[23]

Osgood's influence in drafting this letter was paramount. The contrast between law and order on the one side and anarchy on the other and the reference to the right to work in an open shop were standard features in his statements. The dogmatism was also an Osgood trademark. Although the tone of the letter was uncompromising overall, the operators did agree to the first four stipulations of the draft plan—enforcement of all mining laws, no intimidation of union or non-union men, posting of all wage scales and mine regulations, and reemployment of all strikers not convicted of a crime. The operators accepted the last point with reservations. They agreed to employ as many of the strikers as possible after the strike ended, but they would never employ men who had participated in violence even if they had not been prosecuted or found guilty of any violation of the law. This group included men presently residing in the tent colonies, who, the operators asserted, had been imported by the union to keep up the semblance of a strike and had never been employed in Colorado mines.[24]

Other parts of the proposal were absolutely unacceptable to the operators. Osgood told the *Denver Post* that they were adamantly opposed to the election of a grievance committee for each mine and the appointment by President Wilson of a commission to hear all grievances not resolved by those committees. The creation of grievance committees was one of the union's favorite methods "to foment trouble and provoke strife." It was the practice of such committees "to magnify trifling and unjust complaints into great grievances, and interfere with the discipline necessary for the safety of the employes [sic] and company property, and to destroy the authority of the officers responsible for the operation of the mines."[25]

Most assuredly influenced by Welborn's declaration of a new plan proposed by CF&I for the redress of grievances, Osgood and the other operators who drafted the letter to the president informed him that they, too, were preparing an alternative to the proposed creation of grievance committees. Although they had always been ready to correct their employees' grievances, they were now working with the governor to devise a plan that would protect their workers "against any possible injustice on the part of mine bosses, and to investigate and correct real or dissipate imaginary grievances, if any such exist." They believed this plan would satisfy their employees "without destroying the necessary authority or influence of our superintendents and without depriving us of the reasonable control of our business."[26]

The details of their plan were never revealed, but Osgood and his cohorts vehemently objected to the appointment of a presidential commission to serve as the final authority in disputes affecting wages and working and social conditions. They argued that the unlimited authority of such a commission would deprive them of control over the most important aspects of their business. Without the power to regulate their employees' wages, they would be unable to make any estimate of the cost of production. The unwise use of this power, they believed, could bring financial ruin to any operator. Furthermore, they stressed, the commission's authority to adjust issues affecting working and social conditions would destroy individuals' personal liberty. It was unfair to place their "business in a position where it can, under any circumstance, be subjected to the unappealable mandates of any men or body of men however well meaning and experienced."[27]

The operators urged the president not to withdraw federal troops until the strikers were completely disarmed and the UMWA had ceased supporting them in idleness and inciting them to lawlessness. Concluding, Osgood and the operators pledged to cooperate with the president "in any practical measures having for their object the termination of the unfortunate labor conditions which, to some extent, still exist in this State." The termination of these conditions could only be achieved by the strict and impartial enforcement of state laws. To accomplish this, they argued, federal authorities needed to cooperate with the governor to enforce the laws recently passed by the state legislature and "to repeat our frequent requests that the orders to the officers in command of the Federal troops in this State restricting the mine operators in the employment of labor, be so modified as to permit the employment of workmen as in normal times."[28] The last point meant lifting the ban against the importation and hiring of strikebreakers.

After reading the letter, there could have been little doubt in the president's mind that Osgood and his band of operators were demanding nothing short of complete victory and would never accept arbitration. Nonetheless, at a press conference he stated that the matter was not closed, and over the next three weeks he persisted in trying to reach a settlement of the strike on the basis of the truce plan. "Just now," he wrote to Columbia University professor Edwin R.A. Seligman, "we are in the throes of discovering whether the operators are willing to do anything at all or not."[29]

Osgood was confident that President Wilson would eventually give in to the operators. According to Doyle's informant, whom Doyle considered a "reliable source," Osgood believed the president was only making a play for the support and sympathy of labor and that he "would take in his horns on the truce plans shortly." The informant continued to flood Doyle's office with letters. In a letter dated September 28, he noted that Welborn told the operators he had inside information that President Wilson would accept any reasonable change in his truce plan that would facilitate a settlement.[30] On this occasion the informant's information was accurate, for Hywel Davies had assured Welborn that he could get substantial modification of the president's proposal if it was handled quietly.[31] On October 16 the informant notified Doyle that the operators were delighted to hear that the president had agreed to consider their settlement plan. A few of them met that afternoon, sending word to operators throughout the state that President Wilson had acceded to some of their points and was sure to agree to their plan. There was also considerable comment at the meeting about the rumor that the president had finally agreed to rescind the rule forbidding the hiring of men who had not previously worked for the companies.[32]

The operators were badly misinformed, for by mid-October President Wilson had given up hope of reaching a settlement with them. The operators' tactics and obstinacy had tried his patience. He was convinced beyond doubt that they were responsible for the failure to reach a settlement of the strike. By refusing to compromise, they had humiliated the UMWA officials, who had sacrificed the principle of unionization to accept the truce plan, and had rekindled the explosive situation in southern Colorado. A letter he had received from Davies reinforced his conclusions. Davies found the operators' actions inexcusable, and he questioned their judgment. Could they not understand that they had dashed the best hope for "the assurance of peace, prosperity, possibilities of forgetfulness and a period of goodwill [that meant] larger dividends to the employer, more work to the employee, good will among all concerned and the saving of the state of Colorado from bankruptcy?"[33]

The operators saw the situation differently. They were more confident than ever of achieving peace by destroying the UMWA and driving the unionists out of the state. They were still absolutely committed to that goal. Adding to President Wilson's consternation, Governor Ammons announced that the Colorado National Guard would soon be ready to resume its duty in the strike field. With the operators' rejection of the truce plan, the president reluctantly accepted the reality that he could not pull the federal troops out of Colorado until the operators changed their views or the strike came to an end.[34]

The operators were once again misinformed about the president's intentions, believing instead a rumor that he would pull federal troops out of Colorado by November 15. According to Doyle's informant, by mid-October the talk among the operators and their allies had turned from forcing President Wilson to accept their views for a settlement of the strike to that of guns, ammunition, mine guards, gunmen, and militiamen. The informants' reports arrived in Doyle's office almost daily between mid-October and mid-November. He mentioned his conversations with gunmen and deputy sheriffs about their intention to attack strikers if the opportunity arose, with Major Patrick Hamrock about the possibility of the militia returning to the field with the anticipated withdrawal of federal troops, and with other National Guard personnel about the shipment of guns, ammunition, and other equipment to Colorado. On October 27 he mentioned that he had been told that Springfield rifles, Colt automatics, and an ample supply of ammunition were being shipped to the National Guard for use by coal operators to arm private mine guards. The companies were also making arrangements to employ militiamen as civilian mine guards. On November 12 he informed Doyle that CF&I had shipped eight machine guns into the district during the last three weeks. Although consigned to the state, they were delivered directly to CF&I. Militiamen were also leaving for the Trinidad district at the rate of about twenty a day and were being assigned to various coal companies as mine guards.[35]

Doyle compiled the informant's reports for UMWA president John White to use during the union leaders' meeting with President Wilson on November 19. It is not known whether White shared the contents of the reports with the president or, if he did, whether the information contributed to strengthening the president's resolve to keep federal troops in the Colorado coalfields.

The picture the reports painted of imminent danger of renewed fighting between strikers and mine guards or militiamen in the event of the premature withdrawal of federal forces was replicated in the reports presented to the other side, for the coal companies also had informants. General John Chase, for instance, announced in the *Trinidad Advertiser* that he had received a report that 3,000 armed strikers in Colorado and adjoining states "were prepared to attack the militiamen should they return to police the strike zone."[36] William Murray of the Victor-American Fuel Company received information that increased his fear that the Ludlow colony was being rebuilt as a major staging area for union fighters. He reported to Governor Ammons that 85 of the 131 men in the Ludlow tent colony were fighters armed with Krag Joergeson, Mauser, and Winchester "351" automatics or Winchester 30-30 rifles. All 60 of the Greeks in the camp were fighters, Murray was told, with 45 of them arriving since mid-October after rumors spread regarding the withdrawal of federal soldiers. Most of the rest of the armed men were Slavs and Montenegros, the report indicated, while only 3 of the 46 Italians were armed fighters.[37]

Governor Ammons took these reports seriously. He had informed President Wilson that the strikers in the southern district were "in a very rebellious mood" and threatened to harm non-union men and destroy the mines in which they worked. This sentiment, he believed, was largely brought about by the strike leaders and existed especially among foreigners, "who have been led to believe that they are martyrs to a principle and would go to any length to keep the fire burning." The angry mood would eventually pass, the governor thought, but he urged the president to keep federal troops in the southern Colorado coalfield until the state was capable of relieving them.[38] Ammons's assessment was essentially correct. The talk of renewed armed conflict died down once it became apparent that President Wilson was not going to withdraw federal troops from the strike zone.

In early November, the operators had turned their attention to the state elections. Believing that a successful resolution of the strike rested on the outcome of those elections, the coal operators and their allies had invested a large sum of money and expended considerable effort to secure the election of their candidates in key races. Foremost was that of governor. Their candidate was the Republican George A. Carlson, who was pitted against the liberal reformer and former senator Thomas Patterson on the Democratic ticket and Edward P. Costigan, the Progressive Party candidate. Carlson, a temperance crusader, and his supporters turned the campaign away from labor troubles and industrial strife and focused instead on prohibition. Carlson, in fact, said nothing about the strike or industrial problems during the campaign. Nor did the evangelist Billy Sunday, brought in at great expense by the coal operators to fight Demon Rum and bring religion to the state. Booze, the evangelist preached relentlessly, was the source of poverty and distress, not industrial greed.[39]

On election day, the major coal operators sent their office workers to distribute literature and campaign for a prohibition amendment to the state constitution. Bowers later conceded during the Commission on Industrial Relations hearings that the operators had used prohibition sentiment to gain support for a law-and-order platform designed to help them in their prosecution of strikers and union officers.[40] The strategy was successful. Carlson decisively defeated Patterson, while Costigan ran a distant third.

The operators also celebrated the reelection of Attorney General Fred Farrar. Although a Democrat, Farrar had gained their support by his active involvement with the grand juries that had brought indictments against strikers accused of participating in rioting. Under his direction, in August 1914 the Trinidad grand jury had returned indictments against 124 strikers and their leaders. As a reliable force for law and order, Farrar was more than worthy of the operators' support, Welborn explained to Rockefeller: "His re-election serves to emphasize the sentiment in favor of law and order, expressed in the election of the main part of the Republican ticket."[41] The operators especially rewarded him for his valuable service in aiding their campaign to expunge the union effort in Colorado.

Governor Carlson and Attorney General Farrar repaid the operators and their corporate allies by pursuing a "law-and-order" policy, which, as George West described, "was the ruthless suppression of the strike and imprisonment or execution of the men who dared to lead it, this to serve as an object lesson to others who might attempt to lead a similar revolt in the future."[42] Their biggest prize was John Lawson, convicted on the charge of murder in the first degree and sentenced to life imprisonment at hard labor. This conviction, West judged,

> marked the lowest depths of the prostitution of Colorado's government to the will of the Colorado Fuel & Iron Company and its associates [Victor-American and Rocky Mountain Fuel companies]. It is the crowning infamy of all the infamous record in Colorado of American institutions perverted and debauched by selfish private interests. It is anarchism stripped of every pretense of even that chimerical idealism that fires the

> unbalanced mind of the bomb thrower. It is anarchism for profits and revenge, and it menaces the security and integrity of American institutions as they seldom have been menaced before.[43]

With the "law-and-order" officials working on their behalf, Osgood and most of the coal operators and their allies were more determined than ever to finish the job of driving the UMWA out of Colorado.

Doyle's informant had learned on the eve of the election that the operators had decided to agree to President Wilson's truce plan before the end of the year if either Patterson or Costigan was elected governor. Carlson's victory made any thought of compromising with the president moot. Talk among the operators, the informant wrote shortly after the election, turned to speculation that the reports issued by government officials from the Justice and War departments who had been sent to Colorado would support their position. "Some investigation committee appointed at Washington and just now finishing their investigations in the Southern field reported to the 'Big Three' that their reports to Wilson would be favorable to them, and against the U. M. W. A. and the operators believe this will [have] the effect of deciding Wilsons [sic] attitude toward them," the informant wrote on November 11. The next day he added that Governor-elect George Carlson planned to deport all active strikers when he assumed office.[44]

President Wilson, however, listened to other voices than those mentioned by the informant. On November 19 he met with the UMWA leaders, who urged him once again to seize the Colorado coalmines and put them under government operation. The president reminded them that he lacked the constitutional authority to take such action. Frank Hayes then admitted that the union no longer had the financial resources to continue the strike. President Wilson again expressed his regret that the operators had refused to consider his settlement plan. Encouraged by his remarks, the union leaders urged him to make his position known in a public statement and to appoint the mediation commission proposed in the settlement plan. The president agreed.[45]

On December 1 President Wilson released a public statement in which he placed the blame for rejection of the settlement plan squarely on the mine owners. "I think the country regretted their decision, and was disappointed that they should have taken so uncompromising a position," he wrote. He continued,

I have waited and hoped for a change in their attitude but now fear that there will be none. . . . I have, therefore, determined to appoint the commission contemplated in the plan of temporary settlement, notwithstanding the rejection of the plan by the mine operators, and thus at least to create the instrumentality by which like troubles and disputes may be amicably and honorably settled in the future, in the hope, the very earnest and sincere hope, that both parties may see it to be not merely to their own best interest but also a duty which they owe to the communities they serve and to the Nation itself to make use of this instrumentality of peace and render strife of the kind which has threatened the order and prosperity of the great State of Colorado a thing of the past, impossible of repetition so long as everything that is done is done in good temper and with the genuine purpose to do justice and observe every public as well as every private obligation.[46]

President Wilson appointed Seth Low, president of the National Civic Federation; Charles W. Mills, a manufacturer; and Patrick Gilday, UMWA president of Pennsylvania District 2, to the new presidential commission, referred to as the Seth Low Commission.

Although President Wilson had future conflicts in mind when appointing the commission, its appointment provided the cover the UMWA needed to end the present strike. The UMWA headquarters sent a copy of the president's statement to each local office in Colorado, along with a plea to bring the strike to an end. "In view of this urgent request, coming as it does from the Chief executive of the Nation, we deem it the part of wisdom to accept his suggestion and to terminate the strike," the union's statement read. "In our opinion, to wage the strike further would not mean additional gain to our members. In taking this position . . . we believe we are doing the best thing possible for the men on strike, who have suffered so long that justice might be done. . . . [O]ut of the martyrdom of our people will come the dawn of a better day for the suffering miners and their families. . . . We recognize no surrender and shall continue to propagate the principles of our humanitarian movement throughout the coal fields of Colorado." The union officials urged the strikers to return to work and promised to provide legal protection to strikers and union members who were "being prosecuted by the hirelings of organized greed."[47]

On December 7, 1914, union delegates from the Colorado coalfields voted unanimously to end the strike. The strike officially ended three days later. Frank Hayes lamented: "Thus passed into history one of the greatest conflicts ever waged by any body of workers on this continent."[48] Few strikes, if any, had been waged with such ferocity and bitterness. To the miners at the time, it seemed they had gained nothing from a conflict in which they had paid dearly in terms of sacrifice and suffering. But Ed Doyle saw it otherwise. "The operators," he said, "have learned that the miners can and will strike, and know that there is a limit to what they will endure of abuse and oppression put upon them. And though the strike has been called off, the spirit of the men will never permit again such impositions to be heaped upon them as heretofore."[49] Doyle was right. To avoid the mistakes of 1913, the operators eventually realized that they had to confer with officials of the UMWA.

The federal soldiers were withdrawn from Colorado in early 1915, thus ending the most successful police action by federal troops in U.S. labor history. The United States Army and the federal government had been forced to fill a vacuum left by the virtual collapse of a discredited state government.[50] From a historical perspective, John Osgood, LaMont Bowers, Jesse Welborn, and David Brown were the men most instrumental in causing the collapse of government authority in Colorado.

The end of the strike left hundreds of strikers stranded without strike benefits. Some stayed with their families in tents for a short time. Others left the state, as many miners had done after the 1903–1904 strike. Only a few returned to the mines they had left over a year ago, in September 1913. Scores more waited under indictments for trials to decide their fate. Frank Hayes observed:

> It seemed to be the purpose of the operators, when the strike was concluded, to railroad as many of our men into the penitentiary as possible, and after the termination of the strike scores of our people were indicted by grand juries in sympathy with the coal operators, several notorious gunmen and guards sitting in judgment upon our people. This action of the civil authorities in the strike counties was a travesty upon justice and a disgrace to the State of Colorado. In confirmation of this view let me say that not one single mine guard has ever been brought to justice for the murder of our people. I regret to chronicle that thirty-eight of our men, women and children lost their lives at the hands of the mine guards and subsidized militiamen during the Colorado strike, and yet no one has ever been indicted or tried for these murders, and it is a well-known fact that no mine owner, mine guard or militiaman will ever have to answer for this awful slaughter.[51]

Those who had fought the desperate fight against the operators knew they could not expect pity or mercy from the victors. Once again, the operators of CF&I and Victor-American Fuel were the complete and undisputed masters of the southern coalfields of Colorado. Only the arrival in Denver of the Commission on Industrial Relations tempered the operators' joy.

NOTES

1. The background information on Mackenzie King is from Gitelman, *Legacy of the Ludlow Massacre*, 40–44.

2. King quoted in Fosdick, *John D. Rockefeller*, 154.

3. Rockefeller to King, August 1, 1914, in CIR/FR 9: 8441; McGovern and Guttridge, *Coalfield War*, 295–296.

4. Gitelman, *Legacy of the Ludlow Massacre*, 52; "Extract from Letter of Mr. King to Mr. Rockefeller," August 6, 1914, *The Survey* 33, no. 16 (January 16, 1915): 426–427.

5. Bowers to Rockefeller, August 16, 1914, in CIR/FR 9: 8442; Welborn to Rockefeller, August 20, 1914, in *The Survey* 33, no. 16 (January 16, 1915): 428–429; Rockefeller to Welborn, August 11, 1914, in *The Survey* 33, no. 16 (January 16, 1915): 426.

6. Lee quoted in Gitelman, *Legacy of the Ludlow Massacre*, 52–53.

7. Ibid., 53.

8. Ibid.

9. "Draft of a Tentative Basis for the Adjustment of the Colorado Strike," Colorado Fuel and Iron Company Papers, MSS 1057, Box 7, FF 142, Colorado Historical Society; Enclosure in President Wilson to John White and Others, September 5, 1914, in PWW 30: 486–488.

10. Printed copy of letter from President Wilson to Welborn, Osgood, and Brown, September 5, 1914, Colorado Fuel and Iron Company Papers, MSS 1057, Box 7, FF 142, Colorado Historical Society; President Wilson to John White and Others, September 5, 1914, in PWW 30: 485–486.

11. John White and Others to President Wilson, September 14, 1914, in PWW 31: 31–32; Frank Hayes and Others to President Wilson, September 16, 1914, in ibid., 37; McGovern and Guttridge, *Coalfield War*, 301–302; Boemeke, "Wilson Administration," 199.

12. Doyle to John White, November 13, 1914, relaying information from an informant contained in reports dated September 12, 16, 24, 1914, Doyle Papers, Box 1, FF 20. The Republican candidate whom the operators supported was George A. Carlson, who, with their help, was elected governor.

13. Fairley to William Wilson, September 30, 1914, in Boemeke, "Wilson Administration," 202; McGovern, "Colorado Strike," 344–345.

14. Starr Murphy to Welborn, September 8, 15, 16, 1914, in CIR/FR 7: 6688–6691.

15. Murphy to Welborn, September 15, 1914, in ibid., 6689–6690; Welborn to Rockefeller, September 10, 1914, in ibid., 6688–6689.

16. Welborn to Murphy, September 18, 1914, in ibid., 6691.

17. Welborn to President Wilson, September 18, 1914, in PWW 31: 48–54; *Rocky Mountain News*, September 23, 1914. McGovern called the letter "a masterpiece of half truths, deceit, and hypocrisy" ("Colorado Strike," 348).

18. Gitelman, *Legacy of the Ludlow Massacre*, 56.

19. Rockefeller Jr. to President Wilson, September 22, 1914, in PWW 31: 77.

20. *Denver Post*, September 23, 1914; McGovern, "Colorado Strike," 350.

21. *Denver Post*, September 23, 1914; Gitelman, *Legacy of the Ludlow Massacre*, 56.

22. Doyle to John White, November 13, 1914, relaying information from informant contained in report dated September 24, 1914, Doyle Papers, Box 1, FF 20. There is no indication of who the informant was; however, there is a strong possibility that it is the same person who had earlier corresponded with Doyle and signed his letters "Dick."

23. Osgood and Others to President Wilson, September 23, 1914, Colorado Fuel and Iron Company Papers, MSS 1057, Box 7, FF 142, Colorado Historical Society; hereafter cited as Osgood and Others to President Wilson; letter printed in *New York Times*, September 28, 1914.

24. Osgood and Others to President Wilson.

25. *Denver Post*, September 23, 1914.

26. Osgood and Others to President Wilson.

27. Ibid.

28. Ibid.

29. President Wilson's remarks at a press conference, September 28, 1914, in PWW 31: 87; Wilson quoted in Boemeke, "Wilson Administration," 213.

30. Doyle to John White, November 13, 1914, relaying information contained in the informant's letters to Doyle dated September 28, October 6 (quote), 1914, Doyle Papers, Box 1, FF 20.

31. Gitelman, *Legacy of the Ludlow Massacre*, 56.

32. Doyle to White, November 13, 1914, relaying information contained in the informant's letter to Doyle dated October 16, 1914, Doyle Papers, Box 1, FF 20. White had learned from press reports and "otherwise" that the coal operators were insisting on modifications in the truce plan. On September 29 he told President Wilson that the union supported the truce plan without change, "providing only that the same will be agreed to by the coal operators of Colorado in like manner" (White to President Wilson, September 29, 1914, in PWW 31: 99).

33. Davies to President Wilson, October 3, 1914, in McGovern, "Colorado Strike," 353.

34. McGovern and Guttridge, *Coalfield War*, 305.

35. Doyle to White, November 13, 1914, relaying information contained in the informant's letters to Doyle dated October 17, 20, 21, 25, 27 and November 4, 12, 1914, Doyle Papers, Box 1, FF 20.

36. Chase quoted in Andrews, "Road to Ludlow," 381, note 69.

37. Murray to Ammons, November 25, 1914, Ammons Papers, FF 5.

38. Ammons to President Wilson, November 6, 1914, in PWW 31: 272–273.

39. Beshoar, *Out of the Depths*, 241–242.

40. West, *Report on the Colorado Strike*, 19–20; Bowers's testimony, CIR/FR 9: 8773.

41. Welborn to Rockefeller, November 6, 1914, in West, *Report on the Colorado Strike,* 20.

42. West, *Report on the Colorado Strike,* 23.

43. Ibid., 27.

44. Doyle to White, November 13, 1914, relaying information contained in the informant's letter to Doyle dated November 11, 1914, and Doyle telegram to White, November 12, 1914, Doyle Papers, Box 1, FF 20.

45. McGovern, "Colorado Strike," 354–355.

46. "A Statement on the Colorado Coal Strike," November 29, 1914, in PWW 31: 367–369.

47. Quotes in Beshoar, *Out of the Depths,* 246.

48. Hayes quoted in McGovern and Guttridge, *Coalfield War,* 310.

49. Doyle testimony, CIR/FR 8: 6997.

50. McGovern and Guttridge, *Coalfield War,* 310.

51. Hayes quoted in Proceedings of the U.M.W. Convention, 1916, I, 102, in McGovern, "Colorado Strike," 361.

King's Verdict

Chairman Frank Walsh convened the Commission on Industrial Relations in Denver on December 2, 1914, to begin its investigation of the Colorado strike. Of the nine commission members, there were three each representing capital, labor, and the public. To some degree, they were all committed to social reform, with everyone but Walsh a member of the National Civic Federation (NCF). The makeup of the commission satisfied conservative labor, corporate businesses associated with the NCF, and progressive reformers. Interests aligned with the National Association of Manufacturers (NAM) and radical labor—socialists and the International Workers of the World (IWW)—were excluded from representation. The NCF condemned the fanatical open-shop "business anarchism" of the NAM and the anticapitalism of the socialists and the IWW. These groups, in the eyes of moderate business interests and social reformers, represented the "radical irresponsibles" the commission was determined to investigate.[1]

Walsh was profoundly concerned about social justice. He was a close friend of George Creel and other progressive journalists and social reformers whom Ralph Easley of the NCF called a "crazy bunch of Socialists." Walsh agreed with the social engineering concept of reducing social tensions and improving social conditions through such measures as minimum wages, workmen's compensation, industrial insurance, and social security. He shared the vision of social reformers and NCF officials of a society in which cooperation and accommodation would exist between social classes. He also agreed with the NCF that responsible unionism was an important ingredient in a more rational capitalistic society. But it was his obsession with establishing "the absolute and inalienable right of workers" to have "a compelling voice" in determining their working conditions that drove him during the commission's proceedings. Only "industrial democracy," he argued, could solve the nation's labor problems. Thus, the call for industrial democracy became the central theme of Walsh's campaign to change labor relations in the nation's workplaces.[2]

With good reason, John Osgood and the other coal operators and their allies, including General John Chase, both disliked and distrusted Walsh. They had supported Governor Elias Ammons and his successor, George Carlson, in an unsuccessful appeal to President Woodrow Wilson to keep the commission out of Colorado. They realized that the hearings would provide additional national exposure of their policies and actions. They also anticipated that Walsh and the commission's NCF members would use the hearings as a sounding board for the support of unionism. Their worst fears were realized. The commission's *Final Report* presented a case for responsible unionism and exposed what Walsh called the "industrial feudalism" of those communities "in which the employees are unorganized."[3] Osgood's and David Brown's only consolation was that Walsh and the commission focused on Colorado Fuel and Iron (CF&I) and laid most of the blame for the events in Colorado on John D. Rockefeller Jr.

During its two-week stint in Colorado, the commission took public testimony from Ammons, Carlson (governor-elect), state mining officials, union leaders, strikers, and coal company executives. The commissioners and their staff had access to the extensive reports and transcripts of the Foster Congressional Committee, and much of the testimony presented to the commission in Denver was an extension or clarification of the earlier evidence. This was particularly true of Ammons's and Osgood's testimony.

Spending only a total of one day with these two men, Ammons in the morning and Osgood in the afternoon, Walsh seemed eager to get to Jesse Welborn and CF&I as quickly as he could. Walsh kept Welborn on the stand for three days, questioning him closely on every aspect of CF&I activity concerning the strike. Walsh's intention to go after the New York multimillionaire was made absolutely clear when he served Welborn notice to produce all the correspondence relating to the strike between CF&I officials in Denver and Rockefeller and his officials in New York.[4]

Much of the information contained in Osgood's testimony is scattered throughout this study and will not be recounted here in depth. The information he related and the appearance he presented were much the same as they were before the Foster and Walsh investigating bodies. His "domineering attitude toward men on his payroll," John Fitch of *The Survey* observed of Osgood's performance on the witness stand, exceeded the "choleric resentment against public interference in company affairs" expressed by such men as LaMont Bowers. One aspect of his testimony, Fitch singled out, showed "how completely unmoved and uninfluenced" Osgood was with regard to liability for industrial accidents, which, Fitch noted, had become a movement within the past few years that "has completely changed the attitude of most of the leading employers of the country."[5] Besides the issue of liability, Osgood remained defiant in his view that his workers had no complaints against either his company or local mine management. The men employed by the Victor-American Fuel Company were perfectly satisfied with the wages they were paid and the conditions under which they worked, he contended. To prove this point, he noted that with the union attempting to organize the company's miners, "we were very anxious to know, as were our superintendents and our general managers and others, what the attitude of the men was so that by all means that were possible we were trying to keep in touch with the disposition of the men working in the mines and of the conditions in the mines."[6] He stressed several times during his testimony that the superintendents and pit bosses never reported any grievances or dissatisfaction among the men to him.

Osgood admitted that he had not visited his company's mines for several years and that he depended on William Murray, the company's vice president and general manager, for information. Murray in turn, he explained, depended on the pit bosses and mine superintendents for information about the everyday operations of the mines and conditions in the camps. The superintendents and pit bosses were all former miners and had "a good deal of sympathy" for the men they supervised. He opined, "I think the superintendents themselves are interested to prevent injustice and dissatisfaction on the part of the men. . . . There are men of course who are constant fault finders and grumblers and make themselves very disagreeable and I think they have some justification perhaps for feeling that the superintendent is getting tired of them and says, 'You had better go.' "[7]

Although Osgood denied the charge that miners were reluctant to voice complaints for fear of being marked as agitators, he confessed that his company hired "spotters," or detectives, whenever there was a hint of trouble. Albert C. Felts of the Baldwin-Felts firm was one of the detectives hired to determine if there were "any men who were attempting to agitate and create trouble in the mine." Osgood emphasized, however, that detectives were not employed as mine guards or used to ferret out union members. Pressed on this point by Walsh, Osgood admitted that he had received many reports from Felts, but he insisted that no individual miners had been discharged as a result of those reports.[8]

In other matters, Osgood insisted that the 100 men Victor-American hired to guard its mines and property after the strike began were reputable; the majority were ranchers from the vicinity of the mines. Although they were armed with weapons purchased by the company, they did not participate in any attacks on strikers or their tent colonies. The indictment of over 300 strikers and union men, Osgood argued, proved that they, rather than mine guards, had committed the acts of violence during the period leading up to the arrival of the National Guard in the strike zone. Furthermore, he countered the union's charge that the coal companies had been violating state mining laws by noting that no cases against his or any other company had been brought before the courts, and he denied emphatically that the absence of prosecutions against the coal companies was a result of the power and influence they exerted over local county officials, particularly in Huerfano and Las Animas counties.[9]

Osgood's testimony did little to absolve him from blame for the tragic events in Colorado. In fact, his comments strengthened Commissioner Austin B. Garretson's conviction that Osgood was the man most responsible for the state's labor troubles. Garretson expressed this view in a conversation with the junior Rockefeller and Mackenzie King in late January 1915, which the latter recorded in his diary. What had caused most of the trouble, Garretson told them, "was simply closing the door to any kind of communication." It was Osgood, he said, who was really responsible. He had dominated Welborn, Garretson believed. Had Welborn and Brown handled the situation without Osgood, the strife could have been avoided. Now Osgood and his crowd were making Rockefeller "the scapegoat for the whole situation." In connection with the Colorado conflict, Garretson asserted, "most people were guided by their feelings more than by their reason." They "laid emphasis wholly on human nature . . . [and] said that all men were prejudiced and were open-minded only to the degree to which their own natures, despite the limitations which circumstances had placed around them, made possible."[10] King kept these thoughts about Osgood and human nature in mind when he traveled to Colorado to investigate the situation there for himself.

As the commissioners headed east to New York to resume their hearings, Mackenzie King prepared to go west to begin his investigation of the southern Colorado coalfield. King had expressed his wish to go to Colorado soon after his appointment by the Rockefeller Foundation in August 1914. He was confident that he could work with the Denver CF&I officials to adopt changes in labor relations that would resolve the strike and prevent future ones from occurring. However, Welborn and Bowers made it clear that they did not want him to visit Colorado and were unwilling to consider changes in company policy while the strike was in progress. King deferred to their wishes. After the strike was over, King's trip was postponed again when John D. Rockefeller Jr. was summoned to appear before the Commission on Industrial Relations in January 1915. Although eager to get to Colorado, King believed his first duty was to prepare his new employer for the coming ordeal. Even at this time, he preached the need for CF&I to improve labor relations and persuaded Rockefeller to announce his own plans to go to Colorado as soon as he could. "I look forward to seeing Mr. R. ultimately get a great reception from the workingmen in Colorado," King confided to his diary.[11]

King spent the last part of January and almost the entire month of February briefing himself on the Colorado situation. In late January he had several conferences in New York with Welborn, during which he softened the CF&I president's objections to a new industrial plan for employee representation. He also succeeded in convincing Rockefeller to demand Bowers's resignation. On January 28 he arranged a meeting in New York between Rockefeller on the one side and Frank Hayes and Ed Doyle of the United Mine Workers of America (UMWA) on the other. During the meeting, which King and Starr Murphy also attended, the two labor leaders reviewed the miners' complaints. Doyle told Rockefeller that dishonest superintendents and pit bosses were mainly responsible for the injustices in the coalfield.[12]

King was impressed by what the union leaders had to say during the meeting. "The impression I got, in listening to their representation of their views," he recorded in his diary, "was that the whole strike might have been avoided had Welborn been willing to discuss with a few of them at the outset possible grievances. It was the closing of the door to them absolutely that had precipitated the trouble, and had helped to keep it up." The main problem in Colorado, he concluded from listening to the union leaders and Mother Jones, whom he had talked with earlier, was the closed camp system, which he believed was "genuinely feudalistic." From what he had heard from Hayes and Doyle, King concluded that the crisis in Colorado had resulted from the lack of machinery for the proper representation of employees in shaping the conditions under which they worked.[13] Thus, before he even set foot in Colorado, he thought he had ascertained the cause of the labor troubles in the state's coalfields. He also believed he had a solution—a representation plan—for preventing the troubles from recurring. King would use the Colorado situation to mold and test his plan for labor-management reconciliation and confirm his theory of social conflict.

The meeting between Rockefeller and the union leaders accomplished what King had hoped it would. Attitudes were mollified on both sides. Impressed by Hayes and Doyle, Rockefeller promised to use his influence to try to improve conditions in Colorado. As a result of their face-to-face discussion, the union leaders changed their opinion of Rockefeller. Hayes came away from the meeting convinced that they had misjudged him and that the severe public criticism of him was unjustified. He saw a chance for compromise and was pleased that Rockefeller had extended the invitation to discuss the Colorado matter. To King's delight, Mother Jones also professed that she no longer held Rockefeller responsible for what had happened in the coalfields of southern Colorado. After spending time getting to know him, she came to believe that Rockefeller did not know what "those hirelings out there were doing."[14]

However, by meeting with the union leaders and Mother Jones, Rockefeller had further alienated Osgood and his allies among the Colorado mine owners, who viewed the talks and any hint of compromise with hostility.[15] What angered them most was Rockefeller's opening statement before the Commission on Industrial Relations in January, in which he noted that CF&I was taking steps to initiate a plan of representation for its employees and that he looked forward to working with the Seth Low Commission, which President Wilson had appointed the previous month as part of his truce plan. Rockefeller had concluded that changes needed to be made in the operation of the company. "I frankly confess," he admitted, "that I felt there was something fundamentally wrong in a condition of affairs which rendered possible the loss of human lives, engendered hatred and bitterness, and brought suffering and privation upon hundreds of human beings. Without seeking to apportion blame, I determined that in so far as lay within my power I would seek means of avoiding the possibility of similar conflicts arising elsewhere, or in the same industry in the future."[16]

Osgood and Brown, joined by sixty-nine other coal operators, denounced the appointment of the Seth Low Commission on the grounds that two of the three members were virtually UMWA appointees and that Low, president of the NCF and known for his favorable opinion of unions, might use the commission to advance the UMWA's cause. They rejected Low's offer to help the Colorado operators draw up a plan for a board of conciliation, as President Wilson had suggested.[17] In essence, Osgood and his cohorts told the Low commissioners to stay out of Colorado. The result of a new investigation, they warned, would only "raise new issues or revise those which have been settled by the termination of the strike." "[U]nder existing conditions," they rebuked the commissioners, "there is no way in which your commission can be of service to the coal mining industry in this state." There were no differences between them and their employees to be adjusted, they contended, but even if there were, "we would be loath to submit their adjustment to a commission a majority of which we believe to be strongly biased against us, or one which has in its membership an official or member of the United Mine Workers of America." Besides, they added, with the election of a law-and-order governor and other state officials, any differences that might arise in the future could be settled locally without the aid of an outside commission.[18]

Welborn, who had responded favorably to the appointment of the Seth Low Commission, was aware that he had angered Osgood and many of the other operators. Yet, he told Mackenzie King, he was glad he had responded as he did. Many operators had indicated to him "that they thought Osgood had made a mistake in drafting up the bitter sort of reply which he had sent to Seth Low." These same operators, at first offended by CF&I's response, had come to the realization that Rockefeller's "tack was a much better one" than Osgood's. Furthermore, Welborn told King, he was happy to be disassociated from Osgood and the other members of the Operators Association, which he admitted Osgood dominated. He indicated that he would be a counterforce to Osgood on this matter by using his influence to persuade the other operators to recognize and work with the Seth Low Commission.[19]

Welborn's break with Osgood and the Operators Association was limited, however, for he joined with the dissenting operators to request that the commissioners postpone their visit to Colorado until the autumn—a request

Low and his colleagues were willing to grant. Time was needed, Low told President Wilson, for everyone "to learn and apply the lessons which the recent past must have taught." The commissioners could wait, he added, for they had already secured the cooperation of the governor, CF&I officials, and several smaller operators, "and we believe that time will enlarge the area of cooperation, not only through the force of public opinion but also, as we hope, by the demonstrated usefulness of cooperation."[20]

The commissioners' patience was well-placed. As events turned out, their proposed trip to Colorado to encourage the operators to accept a conciliation plan became unnecessary. In mid-April Low reported to President Wilson the good news that the Colorado General Assembly had established an industrial commission and adopted a workmen's compensation law. "A good foundation" had been laid for industrial peace, "a condition desired by employers, workmen, and the people generally," Low assured the president, adding that "events are moving there precisely as we had hoped." Colorado, he believed, had become a leader among states in providing protection for workers and a means for mediation of industrial disputes. Pleased with the way the governor and legislature had dealt with the situation, Low delayed until late December the commission's visit to Colorado to report on the progress CF&I and the other companies had made in improving relations with their employees.[21]

Mackenzie King was well aware that Osgood was bitter over the appointment of the Seth Low Commission and angry about Rockefeller's changed attitude with regard to the Colorado situation. Secretary William Wilson reminded King of this shortly before he departed on his fact-finding trip to Colorado. Wilson expressed his appreciation of Rockefeller's newly expressed desire to do what he could to improve industrial relations in Colorado. He was happy about the new attitude, but he cautioned King about the problem Osgood posed. Osgood, Wilson stated, was the dominant influence in Colorado, and he still controlled many Colorado operators. He "had been through many fights with the Unions and had become bitter in his attitude towards labor generally." The Victor-American Fuel Company, Wilson added, "would have to be reckoned with in the future in Colorado."[22]

Although Rockefeller had planned to go to Colorado with King, the death of his mother forced him to delay his trip. Consequently, King, accompanied only by his secretary, Fred A. McGregor, departed for Colorado on

March 16, 1915, to survey the Rockefeller interests on his own. The time in the field alone was beneficial to him. His visit to every community in which CF&I had an interest, and his contacts with people at all levels inside and outside the company, enabled him to adjust his industrial relations plan to better suit the conditions he observed in the field. The trip also provided him with an opportunity to talk with managers, superintendents, and pit bosses about his plans. This was particularly true with respect to Welborn, with whom he established cordial relations and a mutual confidence. From this learning experience, he was also able to reach some conclusions about the conduct of the strike.[23]

King had arrived in Colorado with certain preconceived notions. He was inclined to blame both sides for the strike and its excesses. The CF&I officials in Denver, he was convinced, bore a great deal of the responsibility for the strike, and his conviction was strengthened by what he observed while visiting the camps. Although he severely criticized CF&I officials, he began his sojourn in Colorado with the belief that John Lawson was the central figure in the strike and the person most responsible for the extremes on the part of miners. His opinion of Lawson gradually changed during his stay. Eventually, King decided that the union leader did not fit the role of a villain. He assigned that role to Osgood.[24]

King's deeply held belief that character played a significant role in shaping society was a fundamental factor in forming his opinions about people. He believed good character was absolutely necessary for good leadership. Leaders with good character would work selflessly to rectify any wrongs inflicted on the people under their responsibility. In contrast, leaders with poor character caused social injustice and conflict. Those driven by egotism or who recognized no authority above their own will would abuse their power and fail in their responsibilities. They would be the source of the injustice that threatened the stability of a social democracy. These were his fundamental beliefs. During his stay in Colorado, King became convinced that Osgood, with his deeply flawed character, confirmed his theory of social conflict. Contrary to his earlier belief about Lawson, King concluded that Osgood had been the central figure in the strike.[25]

From the moment he arrived in Denver, King heard from all sides that Osgood was the person most responsible for the Colorado troubles. What he learned from people in whom he had absolute confidence corroborated in much more detail everything he had learned about Osgood before coming to Colorado. Henry Cohen and Horton Pope provided valuable information regarding the strike and Osgood's role during it. Cohen, a lawyer for the UMWA, told King that the present conflict was an uprising against the oppressive regime established by the major coal companies following the 1903–1904 strike. Pope, also a lawyer and a personal friend of most of the influential men in Denver, admitted to King that as counsel for Victor-American Fuel Company under Osgood, he had worked with Cass Herrington, counsel for CF&I, to manipulate the state's political affairs. They gained control of every position and situation in Huerfano and Las Animas counties for the companies. In those counties "they began with the county judge, the district attorney, the sheriffs and county officers, with the result that any man whom they wished to get rid of because he was an organizer [for the union] or for any other reason, they could readily free themselves of. They could get convictions where they wanted them, and exemptions from convictions where they wanted them."[26]

Pope had no doubts that Osgood had been the most influential person in directing the operator's strike policy. Pope described Osgood as "a complete reactionary, unrelenting and immovable." Osgood, he asserted, completely dominated David Brown and Jesse Welborn, the two other members of the operators committee, and in his opinion Welborn was too passive to free himself from once having worked under Osgood. Pope agreed with King that CF&I had to take the lead in establishing a new labor-management policy for the coal industry, which the other companies were bound to follow eventually, but he believed there was no chance of getting Welborn to adopt a new industrial plan as long as he was associated with Osgood. At the present, Pope explained, the other companies were opposed to CF&I's new course because it "was a departure from Mr. Osgood's point of view, and looked upon as a surrender to the enemy."[27]

Pope warned King that the situation in Colorado was still precarious. The labor people were wary. They wanted to see if Rockefeller's professions about changing industrial conditions would bring results. If actions instituting a more liberal approach to labor relations were forthcoming, Pope believed peace could be achieved. If, however, the reactionaries won, there would be revolution. As the single most powerful influence in the state, the action CF&I took would determine the future of capital in Colorado. Therefore, Pope stressed, Rockefeller must "clean up the affairs of his company" to prevent the "flames" from "bursting out afresh." In addition, the influence of Osgood and the reactionaries over the coal industry must be broken. He did not think either Welborn or Cass Herrington was up to the job.[28]

King, however, was not ready to advise that either Welborn or Herrington be dismissed or replaced. After talking with Pope, he visited both men and confronted them with the information he had gathered from Cohen and Pope. He talked first with Herrington, who verified some of the key points in Pope's statements and vowed to do whatever he could to advance Rockefeller's plans for the company. Like Pope, he warned of two major obstacles to bringing change and a new philosophy of labor relations. The first was CF&I's past association with the operators' policy committee, which, Herrington implied, Osgood dominated. Although in his opinion it would be difficult for CF&I to go it alone considering Osgood's influence over the majority of independent operators in the state, he agreed with King that the company must take its own course irrespective of the other companies. The second obstacle was Welborn, a product of the old school, with narrow, reactionary views. However, Herrington, unlike Pope, believed that by constantly pressuring him, Welborn could be brought around.[29] King was of the same opinion.

After supper with the Welborns on March 28, King began to apply the pressure Herrington had suggested earlier in the day. Although he took care not to allow the discussion to become controversial, King made it clear to Welborn that what was needed to provide the security necessary to enable employees to express their grievances without fear of reprisal was a permanent system that would allow representatives chosen by employees to meet with management to discuss existing grievances or ways to improve conditions in the camps and mines. King warned Welborn that if the workers were not allowed to organize in this way, it would be hopeless to try to combat the UMWA's organizational efforts. Although disappointed that Welborn seemed unwilling to embrace a dramatic course of action, King still believed he could be brought around. He "has the heart and the purpose, if he can surmount his training," King reflected, "but it is going to be very difficult and the best of schemes will not work out satisfactorily unless they are sympathetically administered."[30]

Through these interviews and those with Mother Jones and Governor Ammons, King had learned much about the coal companies' operations and the troubled labor relations in Colorado. He had also learned more about Osgood. The negative impression he had already formed of him was further strengthened by a near encounter with Osgood on March 25. On that occasion a companion pointed Osgood out to him at the Denver Club. King described the event in his diary:

> While we [King and Fred Herrington] were lunching together, Mr.
> Osgood was entertaining a party of ladies and gentlemen of the smart
> set, or as they call them here, the Sacred Thirty-six, at a table near by.

Herrington told me that the lady [Alma] who is Mr. Osgood's wife, and who is a fine appearing woman, is reported to have been his mistress for years, before their marriage, and yet it is from the people who belong to this group that one hears the denunciation of Mr. Rockefeller for having shaken hands with "Mother" Jones. If this is not characteristic of the hypocrisy to be found in high places, what is? The people who are loudest in their condemnation of Mr. R. for this action are, I believe with very few exceptions, the ones who most deserve criticism upon their lives. . . . This brings the solution of the labor problem back again to the question of character. How can it be expected that labor will show [the] respect to capital which it deserves when the representatives of the latter are of the type personified here. I may be wrong, but I could not help believing that the one who would in all probability be most insistent on relentless action in fighting the miners would be the woman who controlled Osgood. "Mother" Jones may influence the miners, but I venture to say this woman controls her husband.[31]

Apparently, King's antipathy toward Osgood was cast forever by this incident. But it was more than prudery that caused King to react the way he did to this story of Osgood's behavior; it was instead the manifestation of Osgood's poor character that stirred his anger. Osgood's personal life, King believed, illustrated "the universal truth" that men of poor character created social conflict.[32]

Perhaps King had the Osgoods in mind when he recorded his impressions of Mother Jones in his diary two days after he observed the couple at the Denver Club:

Her life illustrates the inevitable working out of moral law in the world, and should teach men who allow strikes to run on over a period of time, and the militia to be called in, to be careful of what they are doing. When I think of the 200 people that have been killed in this recent strike . . . and of the two years in which little children have lived in tent colonies with their daily thought concentrated in hate upon the militia and armed forces and brutal police as the symbols of capital, I shudder to think of what the American people may not reap when the sense of injustice and wrong seething in their hearts and beings breaks forth at some time during the manhood and womanhood of these lives, seeking the vengeance which they believe their natural right and which human nature, being what it is, will certainly demand at some time in some way. Revolution is never born in a day. A moment of time may be sufficient to bring it out of the secret unknown into the open. It is but the graphic expression of volcanic seethings which all injustice and oppression serves to feed.[33]

The "men who allow strikes to run on over a period of time" certainly included Osgood.[34] King was more explicit when he contrasted the attitudes of Mother Jones and Alma Osgood toward the miners in the two passages from his diary quoted here. But King's praise of Mother Jones's morality and her "true conception of the character of Christ" and his condemnation of Alma Osgood's hypocrisy perhaps had more to do with their attitude toward Rockefeller than with their concern, or lack thereof, for the miners. His anger at members of the "smart-set," which included Alma, following his lunch at the Denver Club was actually triggered by comments he had heard from Elsie Edgell a day or two earlier. Mrs. Edgell, the junior Rockefeller's sister-in-law, told King "she had met with a great deal of unpleasantness among people in some of the leading social circles here, who did not hesitate to condemn Mr. R. strongly before her, to ridicule him for his Sunday-school attitude for his meeting with 'Mother' Jones and the strike leaders." Elsie Edgell and her husband, Maurice, thought Osgood was "quite prepared to let Mr. R. suffer, that he himself might escape the censure which he deserves."[35]

A few days later, King pondered an invitation from Cass Herrington to attend a dinner party to meet "some of the influential people," with the purpose of explaining his work regarding Rockefeller's plans for Colorado. He speculated that the group would include those most critical of Rockefeller's meeting with Mother Jones and union leaders. While he perceived his role as one of helping them understand Rockefeller's position, he questioned whether they would ever see "that privilege is something for which the mass of men have only contempt, unless there is a very outstanding noblesse oblige." Although hesitant to accept the invitation, King recalled Horton Pope's advice to accept the "courtesies" extended to him privately but not to meet any of that group in public, particularly at the Denver Club, the "hotbed of conservative reactionaries." Therefore, on the basis that it was in Rockefeller's best interests, King accepted invitations to the homes of Rockefeller's severest critics, knowing full well that doing so would subject him to criticism from other quarters. "I feel that the larger purpose to be served will be more effectively met in the long run by my keeping their [critics] confidence and showing regard for their feelings and winning them to my point of view. One has to learn to work through the powers that be and to take the instruments that lie at hand, not always to be looking around for dramatic changes."[36]

The next evening, King walked into the lion's den. He attended a birthday dinner party given by Mrs. Lucius M. Cuthbert in honor of her brother, Crawford Hill, who along with his wife, Louise Sneed Hill, was a leader of the "smart-set," the Sacred Thirty-Six. Besides the Cuthberts and Hills, the guests included the Osgoods, Welborns, Edgells, and Popes, as well as Miss Charlotte Berger. Apparently, King's conversation with Osgood that evening was limited to reminiscences of Knebwerth Castle in England, which Osgood had rented at various times and where King had visited as a guest of Lord Strathcona. "We had a pleasant talk of the different rooms of the Castle," King recorded in his diary.

> He told me some of the happenings while he was there[,] all of which would go to show that he was a man self-indulgent, fond of display and pleasure. His remarks to me made him seem honest enough, but they all betrayed that his action was based on selfishness and policy. His remark that he did not drink when he was young because he thought his employers would think better of him [for not doing so], not because he had any scruples about it, is characteristic of much of his action, which is, I believe, begotten from policy rather than from conviction.[37]

That conversation was the second King had had with Osgood, for earlier in the day he had visited Osgood in his office. King admitted that he was more impressed with Osgood's personality than he had expected to be. Additionally, King observed, Osgood's presentation of the operators' side of the strike matter was logical and systematic, with only one or two vulnerable points once the premise of his argument—that the head of a large industry was the one to determine the conditions of work—was accepted. Osgood, King had been told by people who knew him well, was kind at heart, but he could not stand contradiction. He was agreeable and a "splendid fighter" as long as he had his own way, but he was domineering to the last degree.[38]

For over two hours during the meeting, King simply let Osgood give his and the operators' side of the story and explain the rationale for their actions. From King's account of the meeting, Osgood repeated what he had said publicly several times before. He defended the closed camps and towns as absolutely necessary to protect property and provide the services the miners needed. With miners more independent than men in any other profession, there was no need for organization in the coalmines, he professed. He also expressed his conviction that company men should be allowed to engage in political affairs by recounting how he had refused Governor Ammons's request to instruct the superintendents and pit bosses to refrain from interfering in politics or serving on state committees. "I told him I would do nothing of the kind, that I would not stultify myself by admitting that I had been doing what was wrong in this particular," King reported Osgood as saying. Ammons, Osgood continued, was a weak man who on more than one occasion had "cried, broke[n] down completely when the pressure was on." Osgood admitted that he had "said things that were unpleasant" to the governor "but had never once deceived him." The governor, he added, finally accepted what he told him about Lawson and the union men.[39]

Osgood lamented the difficulty of obtaining convictions in the "murder trials," where the evidence against hundreds of strikers was overwhelming. "If all of the men get off who have committed murder in the recent strike, as seems possible, human life will count for nothing when the next strike comes on," King reported Osgood as saying. Osgood also railed against the press, which published only what the public wanted to hear. King found this assertion one of the two major weak points in Osgood's argument. He believed there was an inconsistency in his charge that the press published articles hostile to the operators because that was what the people wanted while claiming at the same time that the people had sympathized with the operators throughout the entire strike. Furthermore, King rejected Osgood's contention that the operators could not meet with union leaders because the press would misconstrue their doing so as recognition of the union. "The idea that a man with his resources could not have informed the public in some way that they [operators] had met the Union men and had told them they could have no dealings with them is absurd," King stated, adding that the press had turned against the operators because they had declared that the public had no right to interfere in an issue that was between their workers and themselves.

King was interested in Osgood's announcement that several operators had recently formed a Welfare Association. The purpose of the organization, Osgood explained, was to bring together operators in a cooperative program to improve the welfare of their employees. He showed King several little books that contained information about conditions in the coal camps and assessments of the workers' social needs. One book gave statistics on the ages of schoolchildren, presence or absence of playgrounds, kinds of schools, and existence of halls for entertainment in the various camps surveyed. This information, Osgood explained, would be used as a guide for the association's welfare work. Finding the information "extremely interesting," King asked Osgood for a copy, which he believed would be useful to him for his own study of industrial relations.[40]

King considered Osgood's attitude during the interview a reflection "of a man who takes the old paternal attitude." He manifested splendid executive ability and a much larger personality in every way than Welborn did, King conceded, but he represented the old order that stood for the rights of property, "whether in men or materials." He could not accept represen-tation from beneath. "Everything," King concluded, "must be from above down." Horton Pope shared King's view of his former employer. Osgood, he remarked, was abusive to employees under him if they contradicted him in any way, and he would lose judgment and reason if "brooked in any particular."[41]

After a two-week hiatus during which he traveled to Toronto, King was back in Colorado by mid-April to continue his investigation and to press forward with his plans for a dramatic transformation of the way CF&I did business in the state. He went to work on Welborn to persuade him to accept King's recommendations for the company. King spoke "very frankly and plainly to him," letting him know that those King had talked with since coming to Colorado had formed two impressions of Welborn: that he was not his own master but was dominated by Osgood and that he failed or was unwilling to check on those to whom he delegated responsibility. King believed both impressions were true. He suspected that Welborn entrusted E. H. Weitzel, CF&I fuel manager, with management of the camps and that Weitzel, in turn, placed that management in the hands of the superin-tendents, who were left to do pretty much what they wished. With reports of superintendents and pit bosses brutally manhandling miners who com-plained of legitimate grievances, King concluded that the arbitrary exercise of power by the miners' immediate superiors was the real cause of the strike.[42]

Welborn was defensive during their conversation. He was reluctant to take "a bold stand" or to "declare himself for a radically different policy," King lamented in his diary. King insisted that Welborn take every oppor-tunity to show Osgood and the other operators, company managers, and superintendents that he, as president, was dictating CF&I policy "irrespec-tive of any of them." Even with Welborn's reluctance to change his policies, King did not give up on him. "Did I not believe that Welborn acted from honest motives, though from lack of experience of men, I would advise Mr. R. to change the whole outfit here. It is only because I believe that if helped and properly guided Welborn is strong enough to stand for the right thing, and I believe it better to give him his chance."[43]

King was particularly disturbed by Welborn's hesitancy to sever relations with Judge Jesse Northcutt. He had learned that the Operators Association, chaired by Osgood, had volunteered Northcutt as a "special prosecutor" to assist Frank West, assistant to the state attorney general, in the prosecution of John Lawson and other indicted miners. Northcutt was not only on the payrolls of the CF&I, Victor-American, and Rocky Mountain Fuel companies but was also on retainer from the Baldwin-Felts Agency. Just as disturbing to King was information he received indicating that the Operators Association had employed Baldwin-Felts detectives to collect evidence for Judge Northcutt against Lawson and the other miners on trial. This situation, King feared, would add to the perception that the trials had more to do with persecution than with justice. Warning that Rockefeller would be seen as seeking vengeance at Lawson's expense, King advised Welborn to instruct the state attorney general to replace Northcutt with someone not associated with CF&I and the other coal companies in these cases and to fire any Baldwin-Felts agents employed by CF&I. Welborn's hesitancy to act promptly on these instructions left King with the impression that Welborn still feared Osgood and did not want to defy him or do anything to displease the other operators. Only after further prodding did Welborn finally disassociate CF&I from Northcutt and the Baldwin-Felts Agency and eventually from the Operators Association as well.[44]

Welborn's public declaration that CF&I had no involvement in Lawson's prosecution came too late to repair the damage that had already been done. Northcutt's association with the proceedings against the miners, as well as the appointment of Judge Granby Hillyer—an attorney notorious for his support of the coal operators—strengthened the belief of both the miners and the public at large that CF&I was still a partner with Osgood and the other operators in their determination to see the indicted strikers go to jail or to the gallows. Horace Hawkins, the miners' attorney, advised King that the state attorney general's prosecution of miners was a major impediment to restoring peace in Colorado, particularly in John Lawson's case. To King's amazement, Hawkins told him that between 300 and 400 men were still under indictment on various charges of murder, arson, and assault. Although Hawkins and King agreed that it was too late to call off the Lawson trial, quashing the other indictments was one of labor's prime objectives. If the indictments were not dropped, Hawkins assured King, labor would hold Rockefeller responsible. When news reached King that Frank Walsh had ordered him, Rockefeller, Ivy Lee, and LaMont Bowers to appear before the Commission on Industrial Relations in Washington, he knew that Walsh intended to make Lawson's trial a focus of his attack on Rockefeller. The conviction of John Lawson for murder largely on the testimony of two Baldwin-Felts detectives employed by the Operators Association made it a certainty.[45]

As he prepared to return to the East for the hearings, King reflected on what he had learned in Colorado. Before arriving in the state, he had believed the UMWA leadership had initiated the strike and was responsible for most of the violence and disorder that had occurred. King had viewed John Lawson as a wild-eyed revolutionary whose angry attack on the Rockefellers' integrity during the New York hearings before the Commission on Industrial Relations proved, in King's estimation, that the entire union leadership was irresponsible. After his many conversations in Colorado, however, his perspective was greatly changed, not only with respect to Lawson and the union leadership in general but also about the causes and conduct of the strike. The words of Horace Hawkins stuck out: the miners were driven by despair. They had given up hope of securing justice from either the courts or the state government in their struggle against the oppressive regime established by the coal companies. The coal companies' domination of the mining camps and the coal counties was so complete that the miners, in desperation, had been compelled to take the law into their own hands. Thus, King concluded after talking with Hawkins and others, the coal companies had provoked much of the violence that occurred during the strike. "[P]erhaps more than any other factor, the mistaken policy of the corporations in fighting every honest cause that labor has had is responsible for this attitude on labor's part," King wrote in his diary. "It is only the story of privilege through all history," he continued. "Privilege is always blind and will never make way for justice save by some force which will overthrow it; that is why I hate Toryism with all my heart. . . . The maintenance of privilege against all sense of rights is Toryism."[46]

King also believed the operators had caused much of the labor strife by employing industrial spies and disreputable mine guards; and he lamented that the incidents of violence provoked by this practice, as well as the conviction of John Lawson, would undermine Rockefeller's credibility. "It is singular," he reminisced, "that during the last hours of our stay here we have really probed the bottom of the situation. I am convinced that this business of hiring detective agencies and allowing them to ferret out information is the wrong way to conduct industry. If men of character are obtained for the responsible positions and the truth is really desired all along the line, detective agencies will not be necessary."[47]

Placing "men of character" in responsible positions to ascertain the truth "all along the line" was one of the broad solutions King recommended for correcting the problems in Colorado. He recognized that at every level of the corporate hierarchy, the delegation of authority had removed all sense of responsibility and accountability. Not one owner or manager of the coal companies had sufficient respect or regard for the miners to seek the truth about their condition. Rockefeller had deferred to Welborn and Bowers about conditions in the coalfields and the attitude of the miners. Welborn, King had discovered, had depended on Osgood, Weitzel, and Baldwin-Felts detectives for information about the miners and conditions in the camps. Although Welborn and Weitzel had failed in their leadership, King, ironically, still supported their retention. He had confidence in their managerial skills and believed he could persuade them to accept his plans for changes in the company's operation.[48]

King knew that a great many changes had to be made and that it would not be easy. "The leaven is beginning to work," he noted in his diary, "but many old methods are so deep-rooted, and reactionary forces are so strong, it is going to take time to bring about change." Perhaps the most important adjustment, King concluded after conferring with Hawkins, was that of the attitudes of the coal company owners and managers. Their attitudes would have to change, Hawkins told King, to gain confidence among the miners that conditions would improve. An attitude like Osgood's, who believed the operators were so superior to the miners that they had no need to consult them, was conducive only to hatred and conflict. By way of contrast, Hawkins praised Welborn for articulating a new attitude in a statement recently published in the *Denver Post*. Although Welborn's statement expressed a new openness, King believed it was still too paternalistic.[49]

King left Colorado satisfied that he had found the root causes of the strike. He also believed he had devised a plan to prevent a strike from happening again. He had begun to resolve the two major problems that had to be overcome before his proposed "industrial constitution" could be implemented: to convert company officials—managers, superintendents, pit bosses, and others—to a new way of thinking and to convince employees that they had a voice in their own working and living conditions and an obligation to exercise that right.[50] His most immediate task, however, was to get Welborn solidly in his camp. King had to wait until after the end of the Commission on Industrial Relations hearings in May to accomplish that task.

NOTES

1. James Weinstein, *The Corporate Ideal in the Liberal State, 1900–1918* (Boston: Beacon, 1968), 185–186, 190.

2. Ibid., 188–189; Walsh quotations in Joseph A. McCartin, *Labor's Great War: The Struggle for Industrial Democracy and the Origins of Modern Labor Relations, 1912–1921* (Chapel Hill: University of North Carolina Press, 1997), 27.

3. Weinstein, *Corporate Ideal*, 190–191, quoting from Commission on Industrial Relations, *Final Report and Testimony*. The *Final Report* was popularly called the "Walsh Report."

4. John Lawson and Ed Doyle gave Walsh a copy of an intercepted telegram from Rockefeller to Welborn dated April 30, 1914, in which Rockefeller recommended that the Denver officials publicize CF&I's claim that the company had voluntarily granted all of the strikers' demands except recognition of the union. Welborn's verification of the telegram's authenticity opened the way for Walsh to demand copies of all correspondence between Denver and New York (McGovern and Guttridge, *Coalfield War*, 315).

5. John Fitch, "What Rockefeller Knew and What He Did," *The Survey* 34 (August 21, 1915): 471 (first quote): Fitch, "Split in Policy between Rockefellers and Their Colorado Operators," ibid., 33 (January 2, 1915): 342 (second quote).

6. Osgood's testimony, CIR/FR 7: 6429.

7. Ibid., 6448.

8. Ibid., 6438–6439.

9. Ibid., 6440–6441.

10. King Diary, January 28, 1915, G2539, 186–187. Garretson, an official of the Order of Railway Conductors, was one of the three labor representatives on the Commission on Industrial Relations.

11. King quoted in Dawson, *King*, 238.

12. Ibid., 238–239; King Diary, January 28, 1915, G2539, 179–183; Fosdick, *John D. Rockefeller*, 155.

13. King Diary, January 28, 1915, G2539, 179–183.

14. Dawson, *King*, 238–239; Mother Jones quoted in McGovern and Guttridge, *Coalfield War*, 318.

15. King Diary, February 23, 1915, G2539, 212.

16. "Formal Statement Read by J. D. Rockefeller, Jr. before the U.S. Commission on Industrial Relations," in *The Survey* 33, no. 19 (February 6, 1915): 480, 524–526. Seth Low noted a change in Rockefeller's attitude, as a letter from Edward M. House to President Wilson indicated: "He [Low] has had several talks with young Rockefeller who has changed his views to this extent that he now no longer talks of what is 'consistent with the good of our stockholders'" (January 18, 1915, in PWW 32: 84).

17. In suggesting a board of conciliation, President Wilson had the Anthracite Strike Commission in mind. "I would very much appreciate a report from the commission on the question [of] whether these principles which have served to secure peace by agreement in Pennsylvania for twelve years in the anthracite coal industry are not now suitable and applicable to the conditions in Colorado, whether it would not be possible to obtain their acceptance there," he wrote to the Low commissioners (December 21, 1914, in PWW 31: 503–504).

18. Colorado Coal Mine Operators to Seth Low, January 30, 1915, in the *New York Times*, February 14, 1915.

19. King Diary, February 23, 1915, G2539, 212 (quotes), and March 15, 1915, G2539, 323.

20. Low, Mills, and Gilday to President Wilson, March 5, 1915, in PWW 35: 537–540; "Wilson Commission Postpones Trip Here," *Rocky Mountain News,* March 17, 1915.

21. Low to President Wilson, April 16, 1915, in PWW 32: 532–533.

22. Wilson quoted in King Diary, March 15, 1915, G2539, 321.

23. Dawson, *King,* 240–241; "Expert Arrives on Labor Probe," *Rocky Mountain News,* March 20, 1915.

24. Gitelman, *Legacy of the Ludlow Massacre,* 122.

25. The information in this paragraph is from ibid., 119–122. Gitelman argued that King's views on character were founded on broad religious premises—particularly a reverence for the teachings of Christ. What King meant by good character, Gitelman explained, was "the acceptance of a force in life superior to one's own will, a force that bound one to think of others and to rise above oneself through the disciplines of work and purification" (ibid., 121).

26. Ibid., 123; quote in King Diary, March 27, 1915, G2539, 430–431.

27. Pope quoted in King Diary, March 27, 1915, G2539, 436–437.

28. Pope quoted in ibid., G2539, 430, 436–437; Gitelman, *Legacy of the Ludlow Massacre,* 124–125.

29. King Diary, March 28, 1915, G2539, 452–453.

30. Ibid., G2539, 453–458, quote on 458.

31. King Diary, March 25, 1915, G2539, 408–409.

32. Gitelman, *Legacy of the Ludlow Massacre,* 119, 122.

33. King Diary, March 27, 1915, G2539, 448–449.

34. Gitelman stated that King probably had Osgood in mind when he wrote this passage (*Legacy of the Ludlow Massacre,* 119).

35. King Diary, March 24, 1915, G2539, 403.

36. Second quote in ibid., March 27, 1915, G2539, 426; first and third quotes in ibid., March 28, 1915, G2539, 450–451. Pope repeated what Fred Herrington had told King about Osgood's intimate relationship with Alma while he was still married to his first wife, Irene. After Irene secured a divorce, Osgood married Alma. Pope added that Alma Osgood had only been received in Denver society within the last year or two. Alma's acceptance by the Sacred Thirty-Six around 1913 or 1914, after being rejected by the same group over a decade earlier, was perhaps a result of her husband's stature in Denver society as the leader of the coal operators in the fight against the UMWA.

37. Ibid., March 29, 1915, G2539, 473–474.

38. Ibid., G2539, 463–464.

39. Information for this and the next three paragraphs in ibid., G2539, 463–474.

40. King was already pressing Welborn to reintroduce welfare work as a feature of his program to improve the CF&I camps. Some of Osgood's welfare and indus-

trial betterment ideas and policies found their way into King's industrial relations plan.

41. King Diary, March 29, 1915, G2539, 463–474.

42. Ibid., April 19, 1915, G2539, 502; Gitelman, *Legacy of the Ludlow Massacre,* 134–135.

43. King Diary, April 19, 1915, G2539, 510.

44. Ibid., May 10, 1915, G2539, 655; Gitelman, *Legacy of the Ludlow Massacre,* 130, 142.

45. King Diary, April 25, 1915, G2539, 577–578; Gitelman, *Legacy of the Ludlow Massacre,* 139–141.

46. King Diary, April 25, 1915, G2539, 575.

47. Ibid., May 10, 1915, G2539, 656.

48. Gitelman, *Legacy of the Ludlow Massacre,* 133–135, 143.

49. Quote in King Diary, April 19, 1915, G2539, 500, and April 25, 1915, G2539, 580; Gitelman, *Legacy of the Ludlow Massacre,* 139.

50. Dawson, *King,* 240.

The Rockefeller Plan

The Commission on Industrial Relations hearings in Washington, D.C., in May 1915 were everything Mackenzie King had feared they would be. Frank Walsh, chair of the commission, used the proceedings to launch an aggressive attack against John D. Rockefeller Jr. and the Colorado Fuel and Iron (CF&I) operations in Colorado. Walsh set out to prove that the Rockefellers, both senior and junior, were not only responsible for the Colorado strike of 1913–1914 and the Ludlow tragedy but were also, through their insensitivity and irresponsible actions, a major source of all of the nation's industrial ills. Walsh also intended during the hearings to use the Rockefellers' vehement opposition to unionism, which he argued had resulted in industrial feudalism in Colorado, to expose antiunion sentiments among American employers more broadly. By doing this, he hoped to advance the cause of moderate unionism and social reform.[1]

As King had suspected he would, Walsh began his interrogation of Rockefeller by bringing up the trial and conviction of John Lawson on the charge of murder. King had predicted that one of Walsh's major goals in holding the hearings was to convince the public that the Rockefeller interests had brought about an unjust verdict, which, Walsh hoped to show, should be overturned. Indeed, Walsh quickly made this point as he confronted Rockefeller. Noting CF&I's involvement in the prosecution of the case, particularly the role of Baldwin-Felts agents in gathering evidence and testifying against Lawson and the close association between the company and some of the jurors who convicted him, Walsh suggested that a new trial was in order. He asked Rockefeller if he would intercede on Lawson's behalf. The answer was no. Following King's advice, the New York financier stated that he could not comment publicly on criminal proceedings that were still before the courts. The best he could do, he added, was to use his influence to remove any officer or person associated with CF&I who attempted to interfere with the course of justice in Colorado. Rejected in his bid to secure aid for Lawson, Walsh resumed a blistering attack on Rockefeller that lasted more than two days.[2]

As the hearings progressed, King worried that Walsh might succeed in portraying him and Rockefeller as thoroughly anti-labor, thus jeopardizing his chance to bring industrial peace to Colorado. Although he did not believe Lawson's conviction was a miscarriage of justice, he remembered Horace Hawkins's admonition that the prosecution of the strikers was an impediment to gaining labor's support in King's attempt to reconcile labor and management. Also troubling to King was Walsh's vigorous attempt to convey the impression that the Rockefellers controlled events in Colorado and had directed the 1913–1914 strike. Printed correspondence between Rockefeller in New York and Jesse Welborn and LaMont Bowers in Denver, to which Walsh frequently referred during the hearings, added credibility to the impression, or at least Walsh thought so. "The record of the Washington hearing of the commission," he stated on June 1, 1915, "is remarkable, to my mind, chiefly because every major indictment brought against Rockefeller, father and son . . . by the bitterest of agitators has been proven [to have come] out of the lips of John D. Rockefeller, Jr., . . . but above all the commission has proved the absolute responsibility of John D. Rockefeller, Jr., himself, for everything that happened in Colorado."[3]

Walsh was wrong when he stated that the commission had found the younger Rockefeller completely responsible for the tragic events in

343

Colorado. Only he and a minority of the commissioners had come to that conclusion. Further, the majority did not accept all the conclusions of the *Final Report* prepared by Basil Manly for the commission staff, the central thesis of which was its strong advocacy for industrial democracy. "Political freedom," the report stated, "can exist only where there is industrial freedom; political democracy only where there is industrial democracy." With the Colorado situation clearly in mind, the report noted that where communities were owned or controlled by single individuals or corporations and employees were unorganized, "industrial feudalism is the rule rather than the exception."[4] George West's *Report on the Colorado Strike*, also prepared for the commission, offered an even more stinging indictment against the Colorado coal companies:

> The Colorado strike was a revolt by whole communities against arbitrary economic, political and social domination by the Colorado Fuel & Iron Company and the smaller coal mining companies that followed its lead. This domination has been carried to such an extreme that two entire counties of southern Colorado for years have been deprived of popular government, while large groups of their citizens have been stripped of their liberties, robbed of portions of their earnings, subjected to ruthless persecution and abuse, and reduced to a state of economic and political serfdom. Not only the government of these counties, but [that] of the state, has been brought under this domination and forced or induced to do the companies' bidding, and the same companies have even flouted the will of the people of the nation as expressed by the President of the United States.[5]

The findings of West and Manly reflected the views of Chairman Walsh and Commissioners John B. Lennon, James O'Connell, and Austin B. Garretson, the commission representatives most sympathetic to labor. The rest of the commissioners, however, in two dissenting opinions, refused to endorse the *Final Report*. Commissioners Harris Weinstock, Richard H. Aishton, and S. Thruston Ballard, representing the employers, complained that the staff's alleged findings of fact as stated in the Manly and West reports were "so manifestly partisan and unfair that we cannot give them our indorsement" [sic].[6] Perhaps angered more by Walsh's brutal prosecutorial method in questioning John D. Rockefeller Jr. during the commission hearings than by the findings related in the *Final Report*, Commissioners John Commons and Mrs. Florence J. ("Daisy") Harriman were unable to agree with the document because its findings were "directed to making a few individuals scapegoats when what is needed is serious attention to the system that produces the demand for scapegoats, and, with it, the breakdown of labor legislation in this country."[7]

To many observers, the division within the commission, which found Walsh and "his" *Final Report* in the minority, greatly reduced the importance of the commission's work. Although hearings across the nation exposed the violence and social disruption that existed during the early twentieth century, the commission as a body, according to Howard Gitelman, left "little imprint on the future development of American labor policies or practices, whether public or private."[8] This view, however, does not take into account the importance of the national debate over the meaning of "industrial democracy" that Walsh and the commissioners provoked. The controversy surrounding the investigation brought attention to the issue of workers' rights and, as Walsh intended, placed the concept of industrial democracy on the national political agenda. Undoubtedly, the hearings and the *Final Report* improved the public image of conservative and moderate trade unions as well as labor's relative position in the corporate world.[9] Unionism, Walsh believed, was essential to the development of industrial democracy. Only with the establishment of industrial democracy, he emphasized, could the nation's labor problems be solved.[10]

Furthermore, notwithstanding their disagreements with the *Final Report*, the dissenters joined with Walsh and the pro-labor commissioners in recommending that the U.S. Congress enact laws to correct the industrial problems plaguing the nation. These recommendations included laws to ensure minimum wages and hours of work, including a six-day week in industry, and the unrestricted right of laborers to organize and belong to unions. Further recommendations called for equal pay for women, a child labor law, and a national mediation commission with power to recommend solutions to labor disputes. Along with the *Final Report*, these recommendations established a rationale and an outline for the labor legislation of the New Deal of 1933–1938. Like the members of the Commission on Industrial Relations, the drafters of the New Deal legislation sought to help working people while stabilizing and strengthening the corporate system.[11]

Although Walsh won the support of labor organizations and most of the left-leaning media, many other observers criticized him for failing to forge a consensus within the commission. John Fitch of *The Survey*, for example, faulted Walsh for preferring to use the commission to engage in a sensational prosecution of John D. Rockefeller Jr. rather than as a body to shape social and industrial reform. In fact, he believed Walsh had failed to make a convincing case against the Rockefellers. In a well-reasoned article entitled, "What Rockefeller Knew and What He Did," Fitch contended that the evidence submitted at the hearings did not support Walsh's claim that Rockefeller had actively controlled affairs in Colorado during the strike. Fitch's argument was based on what he called two kinds of responsibility: the responsibility of potential control and the responsibility of action. According to Fitch's argument, Rockefeller Jr. was not in direct control of events in Colorado because he did not will them to happen. He did not issue orders to officials in Denver directing the affairs of the strike. What the evidence proved, however, was that both Rockefellers had failed to exercise the responsibilities of corporate ownership. In particular, the son failed in the responsibility of action, as Fitch explained:

> Where was Mr. Rockefeller when, in the early days of the strike, the papers were telling day after day of machine-guns in the hands of deputy sheriffs, of attacks and counter attacks, of men and boys being killed? Granting as we must that the executive officials told him only of the violence of the strikers, he could have read in the papers that civil war was on foot. Whether the cause was just or not, people were dying for it. Was it not a time for the man whose word would have meant action or dismissal, to take up his responsibility, to take command and find out in person, from unbiased and disinterested sources[,] what lay back of it all, and then to act?[12]

The junior Rockefeller could have done "great and statesman-like things," Fitch concluded, had he taken up "the responsibility which was so clearly his whether he accepted it or not. By failing to find out for himself [what was happening in Colorado], he merely evaded this responsibility; by backing up his men without finding out, he weighted it [responsibility] down the more heavily." The Rockefellers, Fitch stressed, could have directed the course of events in Colorado had they exercised their power of ownership. They could have changed the policies of the executives in Denver "had they willed to do so."[13]

Fitch believed there was a more fundamental question involved in the Colorado affair than Rockefeller's responsibility. The hearings, he thought, revealed a breakdown in the economic structure of democracy caused by a separation between corporate owners and managers. This breakdown was a result of absentee capitalism. "The service that has been rendered by the inquiry into the Colorado strike," Fitch stated, "is the insight it has given us into the methods of absentee capitalism." This valuable insight, Fitch hoped, would not be lost by "a narrow, senseless and even vicious interpretation of it that does not go further than individual responsibility and individual guilt." The problem was much larger than Rockefeller himself. But, Fitch concluded with the young Rockefeller in mind, "[n]o platitudinous expression of good intent can cloud this bald revelation of its [absentee capitalism's] abuse of power, its shirking of responsibility, its disregard of the human right of the workers."[14]

Mackenzie King was well aware that the charge of absentee capitalism, with all its abuses, characterized Rockefeller's ownership of CF&I. The lesson of the Washington hearings was not lost on him. Therefore, along with bringing about a transformation of industrial relations between management and labor, King set out to reclaim the power of ownership for his employer. If he had his way, Rockefeller would become an active director of the corporation rather than an indifferent absentee owner.

During his excruciating ordeal on the witness stand, Rockefeller, coached by Mackenzie King, seized the opportunity to announce a new plan for labor-management relations. In doing so, he set in motion the implementation of the Industrial Representation Plan. The haunting memory of the events at Ludlow over a year before had finally changed the New York financier's heart. Had it not been for the commission hearings, Daisy Harriman opined, Rockefeller "might never have gotten close to the terrible drama for which, because he was Capital, he was in the last analysis responsible." Many years later, Rockefeller confessed that the Colorado strike "was one of the most important things that ever happened to the Rockefeller family."[15] The commission hearings and King's reports on the situation in Colorado convinced him that CF&I's outdated policies and practices were a major source of the industrial unrest in the southern Colorado coalfield. Realizing this, he endorsed King's Industrial Representation Plan as the way to solve CF&I's labor-management problems without recognizing the United Mine Workers of America (UMWA). Also on King's advice, Rockefeller instructed the officials in Denver to chart an independent course for the company. The combination of these two factors substantially reduced John Osgood's influence over the coal industry in Colorado and ultimately led to the signing of contracts with the UMWA in many of the state's mines.

Following the close of the hearings in Washington, King, Rockefeller, Welborn, and Starr Murphy returned to New York to take up the issue of how to address the problems King had uncovered during his visit to Colorado. Of primary concern was their involvement with the Operators Association, of which Osgood was president. Both Rockefeller and King pressed Welborn to sever all connections with the association and to chart an independent course for CF&I. King told Welborn that Osgood had organized the association to retain his influence over the coal industry in Colorado and that it was of no value to CF&I. Furthermore, King and Rockefeller argued, a continued relationship would put the company in a position of being compromised by Osgood and his supporters. Welborn rejected such a course of action but gave no real reason for retaining membership in the organization, except that he believed it was good to keep on friendly terms with competitors. Greatly disappointed, King concluded that Welborn was still reluctant to stand up to Osgood. "He did not like me telling him that the people regarded him as still under the influence of Osgood," King observed in his diary. Still, Welborn would not budge until Rockefeller told him that Osgood had recently come to New York with an offer to organize a syndicate to buy out the Rockefeller holdings in CF&I. Welborn was surprised by that revelation. His surprise turned to anger when it was suggested that, all along, Osgood's leadership of the operators' policy committee and conduct of the strike might have been part of a plan to take over CF&I. It was intimated that Osgood had counted on Rockefeller turning away from Colorado with disgust, thus creating the opportunity for a takeover of the company. The news that Osgood had made the proposition to Rockefeller worked "its effect," King noted. Believing Osgood had betrayed him, Welborn announced the next day that he would resign from the Operators Association.[16]

With Welborn now in agreement, the stage was set for Rockefeller, accompanied by King, to go to Colorado to present the Industrial Representation Plan, better known as the "Rockefeller Plan." On the eve of their departure, they learned that Osgood and the operators still in his camp had begun a rear-guard action against Rockefeller by misrepresenting him and denouncing his plans for CF&I. There was trouble on other fronts as well. With Governor George Carlson verbally attacking the UMWA, the operators launching a new antiunion publication and demanding the prosecution of indicted miners, and the union trying to have some mine operators and owners—including Osgood, Rockefeller, and Welborn—indicted on charges of criminal conspiracy, King worried that the emotionally charged atmosphere in Colorado would undermine his and Rockefeller's efforts to put CF&I on a new footing. At the least, the situation made Rockefeller's planned trip to Colorado a risky one.[17]

Rockefeller was determined to make the trip anyway. He and King had reached out to John White, William Green, and John Mitchell in an effort to gain union support for the Rockefeller Plan and to end the anti-Rockefeller agitation instigated by union supporters in Colorado. White and Green praised the statement Rockefeller had read at the beginning of his testimony before the Commission on Industrial Relations in May that sounded a note of conciliation and change for the coal industry in Colorado. They believed it was absolutely necessary to bring an end to the hatred and bitterness caused by the strike; to accomplish this, they stressed, it was imperative that Rockefeller visit the camps and talk to the miners to learn the truth about the situation. They also suggested that CF&I enter into a contract with its employees that stated the terms and conditions of employment and the ways grievances were to be handled. Any agreement, they believed, should also contain a clause stating that the company would not discriminate against employees because of union membership.[18] In response, King made the best case he could to Mitchell that CF&I was serious about charting a new course and was determined to cut all ties with Osgood and the other coal companies. He stressed that CF&I had welcomed the appointment of the Seth Low Commission while most other coal companies had not. By taking an independent course on this and other matters, he and Rockefeller hoped to improve working conditions and relations between the company and its employees. King was convinced that their charted course of action was the best way to achieve industrial peace.[19]

Believing they had secured the approval of the UMWA's White and Green for employee representation, King and Rockefeller set off for Colorado to sell the plan to CF&I managers and employees. From all accounts, Rockefeller's two-week tour of the company's coal camps and mines was a success. Without a hint of hostility from the miners and union sympathizers, Rockefeller and King were received everywhere with warm cordiality. At every stop, Rockefeller conversed with mine superintendents and miners and anyone else he met. He visited schools and clubhouses and asked women in the camps about the adequacy of the company stores. He swung a pick at a coal seam underground at the Frederick mine in Valdez and danced with the superintendent's wife and all the miners' wives at the Cameron camp. The last occasion was so special to him that he ordered construction of a dance pavilion for the community. But the "red-letter day" of his life was the day he addressed a joint meeting of officers and employee representatives of the company about the proposed Rockefeller Plan. He knew that the task of persuading those officials and employees had already been accomplished.[20] His tour ended on this note of optimism.

On the issues of the trials of indicted former strikers and John Lawson's conviction, however, Rockefeller met with far less success. There was speculation in the press that Rockefeller had asked Governor Carlson to dismiss the cases against the indicted strikers when the two men met on October 4. It was reported that Welborn now favored dropping the cases still pending

William Lyon Mackenzie King (center) *with Archie Dennison* (left) *and John D. Rockefeller Jr.* (right) *on inspection tour of CF&I properties, fall 1915. Courtesy, Library and Archives, Canada / C-29350, Ottawa, Ontario.*

for over 400 former strikers and that he supported a new trial or amnesty for Lawson. How hard Rockefeller pressed for suppression of these cases is not known, but the mere mention in the press that he had raised the subject with the governor excited Horace Hawkins, who organized a group of individuals to meet with Governor Carlson two nights later. Governor Carlson had already been visited by prominent state and national figures and had received hundreds of telegrams, letters, and telephone calls conveying the message that there could be no peace in Colorado as long as the miners were prosecuted in the courts.[21]

During the meeting, Governor Carlson listened patiently for hours to the group's pleas for dismissal of the strike cases. Carlson told them he would have to talk to several other people before he made a decision. A few hours later he informed Hawkins that he had decided to let the prosecutions proceed. He had talked to General Chase and a few coal barons, presumably including John Osgood or his representative, and they had all objected to dropping the cases. But Chase and the operators did not have the last word with respect to Lawson. Hawkins's disappointment turned to joy later in the day when he was summoned to the Colorado Supreme Court to hear the announcement that the justices had ordered Lawson's release on bond. Former U.S. senator Thomas Patterson and Verner Z. Reed, a wealthy Denver capitalist and metal mine operator, co-signed the $35,000 bail bond that freed Lawson, who was released on October 9—the day Rockefeller returned to New York.[22]

Rockefeller had outlined the plans for employee representation to CF&I officials and workers' representatives in Pueblo on October 2, 1915. Shortly thereafter, officials and employees of CF&I voted to accept the Rockefeller Plan. The plan was generous to the miners, even though it denied them the right to have their own union. In some respects, it gave them more than they had asked for when they had gone out on strike. The plan provided for the election of 2 men to represent the miners at each mine, or 1 for every 150 men, to meet annually with an equal number of company officials. The representatives would also represent the miners at the quarterly meetings of their respective districts and would serve on the four joint committees in each of the five districts: Industrial Cooperation and Conciliation; Safety and Accidents; Sanitation, Health, and Housing; and Recreation and Education. At any of the joint meetings, the representatives were empowered to introduce topics for consideration, bring up complaints, and consider changes recommended by company officials. A grievance procedure was also established. Appeals could be carried all the way to the company president and, if necessary, to the Colorado Industrial Commission.[23]

The second part of the plan was a constitution that amounted to a bill of rights, which committed the company to observe federal and state mining and labor laws, post its wage scale and work rules, refrain from discriminating against employees on the basis of union or non-union membership, give employees warning prior to dismissal from the company, permit employees to shop wherever they pleased, allow employees to select a check-weighman, and permit employees to press grievances themselves or through their elected representatives. The hours of work were set at eight hours a day for underground workers and nine hours for outside work. The company reserved for itself the exclusive rights to hire or fire employees, manage company property, and supervise work.[24]

The Rockefeller Plan also included a section on social and industrial betterment that featured many aspects of the initiatives and policies Richard Corwin had pursued as head of the Sociological Department from 1901, when it was established, to 1907, when LaMont Bowers, chair of CF&I's board of directors, severely curtailed its functions. Thus, Corwin's Sociological Department became the precursor of this section of the Rockefeller Plan. As Corwin had when he introduced industrial betterment in 1901, Mackenzie King in 1915 based this section of the plan on the settlement house model, with which, as a former resident of Hull House in 1896, he was familiar. This section of the plan called for the creation of worker-management committees for each of the coal camps to consider issues of safety, sanitation, health, housing, recreation, and education. The company also embarked on a large-scale program of camp improvements that included repairing and building new houses for workers, providing adequate water supplies and electricity, and building bath and clubhouses.[25] Although CF&I miners enjoyed improvements in their welfare, medical care, housing, recreation, and education, many of them as well as union critics of the plan argued that the company had granted the improvements in the spirit of the old paternalistic system. Moreover, the plan failed to relieve many of the miners' ordinary grievances. What Mackenzie King had believed was the strength of his plan proved to be a weakness, for the workers, still fearful of dismissal, did not make widespread use of the procedure for presenting grievances.[26]

Although the Rockefeller Plan was not revolutionary, its adoption marked the first acceptance of the principle of employee representation by a major American corporation.[27] In the short run, these "gifts" from management and the procedure for collective bargaining, however illusionary, undercut the UMWA, as King and Rockefeller had intended. In the long run, however, the Rockefeller Plan could not survive as a substitute for an independent union. Although King and Rockefeller continued to deny it, both opponents and supporters of the plan saw it as a means of preventing unionization. Organized labor described the plan as a pseudo-union, a tool by which the company pretended to grant concessions through the illusion of collective bargaining. Agreeing with this assessment, George West argued that the plan contained "none of the principles of effectual collective bargaining" and was instead "a hypocritical pretense of granting what is in reality withheld." It was not devised for the benefit of workers, according to West, "but for the purpose of ameliorating or removing the unfavorable criticism of Mr. Rockefeller which had arisen throughout the country following his rejection of President Wilson's plan of settlement."[28]

While UMWA officials and many labor leaders opposed the Industrial Representation Plan, Samuel Gompers, president of the American Federation of Labor, opined that it might be a blessing for organized labor. "The miners employed by the Colorado Fuel and Iron Company, of which Mr. Rockefeller is the head," he told reporters, "have been whipped by means of atrocious brutality and hunger into submission, back to the mines. And these miners have been formed into a union by Mr. Rockefeller's benevolent altruism. But he has organized them, and for that at any rate labor is truly grateful, for when men come together to discuss, even in the most cursory way, their rights and their interests and their welfare, there is afforded a splendid field for development and opportunity."[29]

John Lawson spoke even more optimistically than Gompers had about the future of unionism in Colorado when he arrived in Denver following his release from jail. "Colorado miners did not lose the strike," Lawson told the large crowd that had gathered to greet him. He continued: "It has been a victory for the things for which we contended. It has awakened the nation to the need of granting labor just compensation and decent working conditions. The Rockefeller Plan will not work as well with Rockefeller back in New York as it would if he remained here. What will the same old bunch of C. F. & I. Officials do when he goes away?" Asked by a reporter about recognition of the union, Lawson replied: "The Rockefeller Plan is recognition in part in that it recognizes many of our demands. I know they are going to recognize the union some time and this plan will prepare the way. Because of it, there will be less of a shock when union recognition does come."[30] Over the next few years, Lawson was instrumental in helping union recognition come to pass, albeit on a limited and temporary basis.

After postponing their investigative trip to Colorado until the situation there had settled down, the members of the Seth Low Commission finally departed on December 23, 1915, to ascertain the state of relations between miners and operators throughout the state. In addition, the commissioners told President Wilson they would review the operations of the newly established Colorado Industrial Commission and collect information that would allow them to form an impression of CF&I's Rockefeller Plan.[31] During their three-week tour of the state's coalfields, the commissioners received cooperation from the UMWA officials and all the operators they contacted, including John Osgood and others who had previously opposed the appointment of the commission. In their final report to President Wilson, submitted on February 23, 1916, the commissioners indicated that relations between operators and miners appeared generally harmonious and that most of the operators were prepared to "let bygones be bygones." They also found little evidence of discrimination against union members and predicted that the distrust of the operators that still lingered among many miners would dissipate with time.[32]

The commissioners credited three things for bringing about the greatly improved situation in the Colorado coalfields: increased public concern for workers' welfare, the passage of labor-related legislation by the Colorado General Assembly, and CF&I's adoption of the Rockefeller Plan. In terms of legislation, the commissioners specifically listed the laws (1) creating an industrial commission with compulsory power to investigate and mediate labor disputes, (2) establishing workmen's compensation, and (3) permitting the formation of mutual insurance companies to provide funds to underwrite workmen's compensation. In the commissioners' opinion, this legislation had greatly improved working conditions for the miners and diminished the operators' arbitrary control.[33]

The Seth Low Commission called the creation of the Colorado Industrial Commission, with its compulsory power to investigate and mediate labor disputes, and CF&I's adoption of the Rockefeller Plan the two most important results of the 1913–1914 strike. Of the two, the commissioners regarded the Rockefeller Plan, which they analyzed in detail, as the most important factor in bringing about the relative calm they found during their tour of the mines and camps in southern Colorado. With its provision for regulating relations between the company and its employees by means of a contract, the plan, in the words of the commissioners, would "exert [a] far-reaching influence on the industrial developments of the future." It was "practically" a certainty, they predicted, that the other large Colorado operators would "move along corresponding lines" if the plan worked successfully.[34]

Although the other coal companies followed "the developments under this [CF&I's representation] plan with undisguised interest," officials at

Victor-American and Rocky Mountain Fuel were not ready to "move along corresponding lines." They continued to refuse to adopt any plan for employee representation, and the relationship between management and workers remained as it had been: a contract between the employer and employees as individuals. There was no disposition on the part of the companies to establish boards of conciliation on which both miners and managers were represented, and the procedure for resolution of grievances remained little changed. According to that procedure, the superintendent at each mine set aside a specific time to hear complaints from employees, who had the right to take their grievances to the superintendent if they felt the pit boss or foreman did not redress or give them proper consideration.[35] Under this procedure, few complaints were registered.

The failure of Victor-American and Rocky Mountain Fuel to embrace the concept of employee representation did not deter Low and his fellow commissioners from expressing satisfaction with the progress made in achieving industrial peace in Colorado. Convinced that Colorado had established adequate machinery to deal with future labor disputes, Low asked President Wilson to disband the commission, which the president did after expressing appreciation for its "most gratifying" report. Undoubtedly, the president felt a sense of satisfaction that his administration had helped end one of the most violent labor conflicts in the nation's history. He concluded, as the commissioners did, that the miners' rebellion of 1913–1914 had not been entirely in vain.[36]

Although John Osgood certainly noticed the changing opinion in Colorado as recorded in the Seth Low Commission's report, he seemed reluctant to change his policies. Yet he cast an anxious eye on what CF&I was doing in terms of labor relations. He and other operators had complained to the Seth Low Commission that the Rockefeller Plan would open the door to the unionization of all CF&I mines. He observed that several smaller operators were already signing union contracts. As local UMWA organizations were reestablished across the southern Colorado coalfield throughout 1916, Osgood felt increasingly vulnerable to the union threat, one that in his increasingly isolated position he would have to face virtually alone. The breakup of the old alliance with CF&I had undermined his influence among the coal operators. He had neither the resources nor the will to introduce his own employee representation plan for Victor-American to combat the UMWA. When the economic situation turned sour and competition for workers became critical, he did what was in his best interest at the time, as he always had done. In this case, it was signing a contract with the UMWA.[37]

Those who judged Osgood as inflexible in his approach to labor relations overlooked his pragmatism when economic circumstances dictated a change of policy. Such was the case in the spring of 1917. With the flow of immigrants shut off by the war in Europe, companies were forced to scramble for workers. Although far short of what the workers wanted, CF&I's Representation Plan gave that company an advantage in the recruitment war. As a result, the Victor-American and Rocky Mountain Fuel companies were forced to consider new recruitment methods. In May 1917, Edward Doyle reported that Rocky Mountain Fuel was about to initiate an industrial plan similar to Rockefeller's CF&I plan. Many observers were surprised when the company offered the position of grievance officer to John Lawson, at a salary to be determined by Lawson himself. Lawson declined the offer, however, after the company rejected his recommendation that it sign a contract with the UMWA. Instead, he accepted the position of recruitment officer with Victor-American at a monthly salary of $150 and expenses because the company had signed a contract with the union.[38]

Lawson's acceptance of Osgood's offer surprised many, but the turn of fortune for both had driven the once bitter enemies together. A few weeks earlier, in April 1917, the Colorado Supreme Court had reversed Lawson's conviction for murder, a conviction Osgood had played a leading role in obtaining. After more than two years, Lawson was finally cleared of any crime committed during the tumultuous days of 1914, as were over 400 other strikers whose cases were either overturned or never brought to trial. Although exonerated of the crime of murder, Lawson stood disgraced in the eyes of the union's national officials. Both he and Ed Doyle were cast aside as union officers when officials in Indianapolis reorganized District 15. Lawson's acceptance of the position of employment agent for the Victor-American Company formally marked his complete severance from the union, although he still remained a hero among the miners. Osgood's hiring him was a shrewd move on his part. Among other things, it demonstrated how seriously he intended to compete with CF&I and Rocky Mountain Fuel for labor.[39]

The news that Osgood had signed a contract with the UMWA, according to a contemporary account, "came as an unbelievable surprise to those familiar with the industrial history of Colorado."[40] Yet it should have been anticipated, for Osgood's economic fortunes had declined as a result of the labor troubles over the past few years. In a letter addressed to all Colorado coal operators, Osgood observed:

Following the calling off of the strike of 1913–1914, which, with your assistance, we had successfully resisted, the Colorado Fuel and Iron company . . . withdrew from all association and co-operation with the other operators who had loyally joined with them in resisting the unreasonable demands of the United Mine Workers of America, and without any consultation with them, put in effect a plan which, if not an invitation, opened the door to the unrestricted activities of the organizers of the United Mine Workers of America in their mines, a very large number, if not a majority of their employes [sic] now being members of the union.

CF&I's action, Osgood contended, had forced most other operators in the state to open their mines "to agitators and organizers, so that in some cases practically all of their men" were now members of the union.[41]

Osgood stressed that CF&I's independent course of action brought about the dissolution of the Operators Association and left the other operators powerless in the struggle against the UMWA. The national union leaders, he noted, "were not slow in recognizing the opportunity offered to them" by the divisions among the operators and the shortage of labor as a result of the war in Europe. With their financial condition greatly improved and with no serious difficulties in any other coal mining areas, the national union leaders had begun a "vigorous campaign" to unionize all the mines in Colorado, New Mexico, and Utah. "We all know," he warned, "that if their efforts are resisted a strike will be called at the most favorable opportunity, and [a]s in past strikes, acts of violence against life and property will be committed." Under these conditions, Osgood believed the operators could not resist such a strike "without great danger to life and property and a serious financial loss." Therefore, after long and careful consideration, he had concluded that it was in the "best interest of our business, our employes [sic] and the public to negotiate a contract with the United Mines Workers of America and thus prevent to the best of our ability a strike which would be disastrous to all concerned."[42] It was obvious that Osgood had another reason to sign the contract: with the shortage of labor, he hoped he could draw dissatisfied miners from non-union mines, particularly CF&I, to his own.

The terms of the contract maintained the fiction of an open shop, although Osgood agreed that the company would collect union dues from workers who agreed to the deduction from their pay, as was done with all other company charges. The company retained the absolute right to employ whomever it wanted without regard to union membership and to discharge employees for a reasonable cause. Any grievances that could not be resolved between the employees and their representatives and company officials would be submitted to an independent arbitrator.[43]

To some contemporaries, Osgood's action helped undermine CF&I's Industrial Representation Plan. One CF&I miner stated:

> I'll tell you what I think killed the [Rockefeller] plan in this district. We were getting along very well for the first two years. But in 1917 the Victor-American Fuel Company, which has two mines near here, signed an agreement with the United Mine Workers. The men here immediately began to ignore the representation plan. They thought that they also could get a contract. If our next-door neighbors can get a contract, they argued, why can't we? With the signing of the contract by the other company there came at the same time a number of union organizers into this district. They constantly advised the men against co-operating with the plan.[44]

Other views were offered as well. In the opinion of one miners' representative, Osgood had taken a far more economical approach than CF&I had in dealing with his employees. "I have often remarked to my friends," he commented, "that [CF&I] was very foolish to try to have the representation plan when the men don't want it. It must cost the company a lot of money to administer it. It would cost them less to have a union contract and they wouldn't have to concede as much to the men as they do under the plan." Another representative said that the workers grumbled but "won't bring grievances to the representatives. They want a union contract and won't be satisfied until they get one."[45]

Osgood had faced reality and blinked. No more would he proclaim, as he had before the Foster Congressional Committee in 1914, that he would close his mines and quit the industry before signing a contract with the UMWA. Frank Walsh and Mackenzie King had changed the dynamics of the Colorado coalfields. Although Rockefeller Jr. would never acknowledge any responsibility for the Ludlow Massacre, Walsh's exposure of his failed leadership stirred his conscience and awakened in him a new sense of corporate responsibility. King showed him a way—the Rockefeller Plan—to assume that responsibility. With CF&I's adoption of the plan, John D. Rockefeller Jr. replaced Osgood as the most dominant voice in Colorado's coal industry. Had Rockefeller by his independent course of action not shattered the coal operators' solidarity—something the union had failed to do through its repeated strikes—and had World War I not shut off the supply of immigrant labor to the coalfields, Osgood might have maintained his leadership, or at least his influence, over the industry in Colorado. Had the old conditions prevailed and the economic situation remained good, there is little doubt that he would have continued his fight against the UMWA. But this was not to be. After 1917, Osgood found sanctuary in his New York residence and office far from Colorado and the "agitators" and "anarchists" with whom he had been forced to make peace.

NOTES

1. Dawson, *King*, 237–238; Weinstein, *Corporate Ideal in the Liberal State*, 188–189; McCartin, *Labor's Great War*, 28–29.

2. McGovern and Guttridge, *Coalfield War*, 327–328; Gitelman, *Legacy of the Ludlow Massacre*, 145.

3. Walsh quoted in Fitch, "What Rockefeller Knew," 461.

4. U.S. Congress, Senate, *Final Report of the Commission on Industrial Relations, Including the Report of Basil M. Manly and the Individual Reports and Statements of the Several Commissioners*, 64th Cong., 1st sess., 1916, reprinted from Doc. 415, 17–18; hereafter cited as *Final Report*.

5. West, *Report on the Colorado Strike*, 15.

6. Commissioners Weinstock, Aishton, and Ballard Report, in *Final Report*, 1: 233.

7. Commissioners Commons and Harriman Report, in ibid., 171.

8. Gitelman, *Legacy of the Ludlow Massacre*, 161.

9. The Walsh Commission investigation exposed many of the evils of absentee capitalism and many of the injustices under which labor suffered at the time. It also gave trade unionism a status it had hitherto not been accorded in the United States (Dawson, *King*, 237–238, citing Selig Perlman, *A History of Trade Unionism in the United States* [1922], 228.

10. McCartin, *Labor's Great War*, 13, 27, 29–30.

11. Weinstein, *Corporate Ideal in the Liberal State*, 211–212.

12. Fitch, "What Rockefeller Knew," 461–472, extract on 472.

13. Ibid., 461 (last quote), 472.

14. Ibid., 472.

15. Adams, *Age of Industrial Violence*, 168 (first quote); Fosdick, *John D. Rockefeller*, 167(second quote).

16. King Diary, May 26 to June 4, 1915, G2539, 690–691; Gitelman, *Legacy of the Ludlow Massacre*, 154–155.

17. Gitelman, *Legacy of the Ludlow Massacre*, 157–158, 163, 178.

18. King did not tell the union leaders that their suggestions were completely in line with his thinking and his plans for a new system of industrial relations. A CF&I contract with its employees, the very heart of the Industrial Relations Plan, was the nucleus of what became known as a company union.

19. Gitelman, *Legacy of the Ludlow Massacre*, 169–175.

20. Ibid., 181–182; Fosdick, *John D. Rockefeller*, 161–162; McGovern and Guttridge, *Coalfield War*, 333–334.

21. Beshoar, *Out of the Depths*, 333.

22. Ibid., 334; McGovern and Guttridge, *Coalfield War*, 337–338.

23. Gitelman, *Legacy of the Ludlow Massacre*, 190–191; McGovern and Guttridge, *Coalfield War*, 335; Brandes, *American Welfare Capitalism*, 125; "Mr. Rockefeller in Colorado," *Outlook* 111 (October 13, 1915): 345–346.

24. Gitelman, *Legacy of the Ludlow Massacre*, 191; Fosdick, *John D. Rockefeller*, 163.

25. Weed, "Sociological Department," 281; "Rockefeller Plan," *The Survey*, 75.

26. McGovern, "Colorado Strike," 438.

27. Brandes, *American Welfare Capitalism*, 126.

28. West, *Report on the Colorado Strike*, 156–157. McGovern and Guttridge stated that the plan was "paternalism's latest and most pernicious guise" (*Coalfield War*, 336).

29. Gompers quoted in *New York Times*, October 5, 1915, in Gitelman, *Legacy of the Ludlow Massacre*, 192.

30. Lawson quoted in Beshoar, *Out of the Depths*, 336.

31. Low to President Wilson, December 8, 1915, in PWW 35: 317.

32. *Labor Difficulties in the Coal Fields of Colorado*, 1–16.

33. Ibid.

34. Ibid., 3–9.

35. Ibid., 3.

36. Ibid., 15; President Wilson to Low, March 3, 1916, in PWW 36: 245; Boemeke, "Wilson Administration," 229.

37. Osgood's letter in *Denver Post*, March 31, 1917.

38. Doyle to Mr. and Mrs. Lee Champion, May 18, 1917, Doyle Papers, Box 1, FF 4.

39. McGovern and Guttridge, *Coalfield War*, 338–340, 343.

40. Quote in Benjamin M. Selekman and Mary Van Kleeck, *Employees' Representation in Coal Mines: A Study of the Industrial Representation Plan of the Colorado Fuel and Iron Company* (New York: Russell Sage Foundation, 1924), 281.

41. Osgood's letter in *Denver Post*, March 31, 1917.

42. Ibid.

43. Fox, *United We Stand*, 179.

44. Miner quoted in ibid., 196.

45. Ibid.

Epilogue

Two men in Colorado could have prevented the 1913–1914 Colorado coal strike or ended it before it had run its tragic course: John Osgood and LaMont Bowers. Few, if any, were fiercer opponents of organized labor and collective bargaining than these two men. These powerful coal executives were totally inflexible and uncompromising in their archaic view of labor relations during the period leading up to and during the strike. What was needed to prevent the strike or, once it had begun, to end it was for them—together or individually—to agree to a meeting between the leading operators and union officials to discuss the miners' grievances or, once the strike was under way, to agree to arbitration by a board of conciliation. They rejected both courses of action. Instead of providing enlightened leadership that could have prevented the tragic Colorado labor conflict, Osgood and Bowers remained bound by the reactionary policies of the past.

The two men had a preponderance of influence in separate areas: Bowers over Colorado Fuel and Iron (CF&I) and Osgood over the Colorado coal operators. Although he did not directly conduct the operators' strike policy, Bowers decisively shaped attitudes about the Colorado situation in CF&I's Denver and New York offices.[1] Jesse Welborn, dominated from all sides, deferred to him throughout the strike, and John D. Rockefeller Jr. trusted him absolutely and accepted without question his convictions concerning the Colorado situation until late summer 1914. Bowers's influence was such that he could have altered the course of events had he thought it best for the company's interests.

Osgood was the predominant leader of the coal executives who determined the strike policy in 1913–1914. He directed the operators' policy committee, which established the strategy and determined the means for combating the union during the strike. Under Osgood's leadership, in 1913 the Colorado coal operators "set in motion" what John Reed described as "their powerful machine for breaking strikes—a merciless engine refined by thirty years of successful industrial struggle."[2] As the evidence collected by Mackenzie King indicates, Osgood dominated Welborn just as Bowers had. Osgood stood firm in his conviction that the operators should avoid any action that might be construed as recognition of the union. Had he been willing to meet with union leaders to discuss the miners' grievances in September 1913 or had he been willing to accept arbitration after the strike had begun, the history of the Colorado coalfield labor dispute would have been far different. In all probability, it would not have resulted in the Ludlow Massacre and the tragic events that followed.

Although it took longer than the operators anticipated, the strikebreaking tactics succeeded once again, and the United Mine Workers of America (UMWA) was dealt a severe blow. The miners had little to show for their desperate struggle against the coal companies. Yet the strike, more precisely the Ludlow Massacre, changed the dynamics of the southern Colorado coalfield. It exposed the oppressive political, economic, and social system the coal barons had imposed upon the miners. Although it would take years to dismantle the system, the coal companies never regained the control over southern Colorado they had enjoyed before the strike. What happened at Ludlow would prevent the coal operators from returning to the status quo ante. In this respect, the strikers' sacrifices were not made in vain.

"Once a union man, always a union man" was the sentiment of most miners long after the events of 1913–1914. This was John Lawson's sentiment as well, even though he had been cast aside from union leadership. With his union card still in his pocket, he spoke from a platform before thousands of men, women, and children of scores of nationalities who had gathered on the Ludlow field on April 20, 1917, to celebrate the UMWA's purchase of forty acres where the tent colony had been located. Special trains had carried hundreds of people from Trinidad and other southern Colorado towns to Ludlow, and automobiles and rigs lined the roads leading to the site of the former tent city. People were greeted by an array of bands. Five thousand men, women, and children marched in a parade from Tollerburg to the site, each wearing a red bandanna—the strikers' emblem—and many carrying tiny American flags. The Ludlow flag, scorched and tattered from the battle waged exactly three years earlier, waved in the breeze at the head of the line. Thousands of people lined the road to cheer the marchers as they proceeded to the site of the ceremony to honor the "martyrs for unionism."[3]

At the conclusion of the speeches, most of them in Italian, Slavic, Spanish, or Greek, Lawson dropped flowers into the Black Hole as the band played and the crowd sang "Nearer My God to Thee." Lawson then turned to Ed Doyle, who had also participated in the ceremony, and, according to Barron Beshoar's reconstruction of their conversation, said:

> "See those shadows, Ed. Those same shadows were here three years ago today. They stabbed at the colony. They foretold the tragedy of that day."
>
> Doyle nodded soberly.
>
> "It was a tragedy the like of which we won't see again," Doyle said. "Death is gone from these hills now."
>
> Lawson let his eyes wander along the ragged line of foothills where the mines were located before he replied:
>
> "Death is always present in the coal districts, Ed. It will strike many times, perhaps in a different way and in different circumstances, but it will always be present."
>
> "I know what you mean," Doyle said. "A rock fall and a man dead."
>
> "Yes," Lawson replied. "Hundreds, perhaps thousands, will die here yet for King Coal."[4]

Exactly seven days later, less than three miles from where Lawson and Doyle had been standing the week before, the Victor-American Hastings mine blew up. On hearing the news, Lawson, now an employee of the company, rushed to the scene, where he was put in charge of the rescue party. Arriving at the mine, he reported that it was the worst explosion Colorado had experienced. All he and his party of rescuers found in the mine were the badly mutilated and burned bodies of 121 miners. As the bodies were brought up and placed in the machine shop, Lawson made the rounds of the camp, consoling everyone he met. He stayed on for the funerals and worked several more days to help clean up the mine. Victor-American officials who had come to despise him during the strike thanked him for his compassion and help. The officials' new attitude toward Lawson was not lost on a Denver newspaper reporter: "To those who witnessed the frightful scenes in Ludlow, just three miles from here, and then can see the present attitude of the mine owners and labor leaders toward each other, the contrast is striking. It means but one thing—everlasting industrial peace in the southern coal camps."[5]

Ed Doyle had a different view of the comparison between events at Ludlow and the Hastings explosion. "The Hasting's [sic] explosion is but the same old story of 'cut down expense,'" he wrote to Mr. and Mrs. Lee Champion. "Your splendid letter . . . giving expression to your feelings about the Hastings horror . . . brought clearly to my mind another letter which I received from Mr. Champion at the time so many gave up their lives at Ludlow and I thought if only the world could see the connection between these two disasters as clearly as you folks do the miners would not be long in securing the protection they are entitled to as human beings."[6]

Although the Ludlow episode was not repeated, everlasting industrial peace did not prevail in the southern Colorado coalfield.[7] Coal companies continued to ignore the law, particularly in the area of mine safety, and to cut wages during periods of economic hard times. Miners continued to go out on strike to protest pay cuts and other grievances. The most serious strikes occurred in 1921 and 1927, the latter called by the radical Industrial Workers of the World. Both strikes resulted in the proclamation of martial law and the calling out of the National Guard to restore order. As in previous strikes, the coal companies forced the strikers back to work without granting them significant concessions.

Through the success of its Industrial Representation Plan, which had brought some improvements in the areas of welfare, medical care, housing, recreation, and education, CF&I had been able to keep the UMWA at bay. The union had largely abandoned the field during the early 1920s. By the end of the decade and the beginning of the next, however, circumstances made it difficult for the company to continue its fight against the union. This was particularly true as a result of UMWA's success in obtaining contracts with a number of Colorado coal companies. The union's greatest achievement was with the Rocky Mountain Fuel Company. In 1928, after the Colorado Industrial Commission declared that many of the miners' demands were justified and that the coal industry was at fault for not providing a system of collective bargaining, Josephine Roche, principal owner of Rocky Mountain Fuel, signed a contract with the UMWA. John Lawson, now vice president of the company, wrote the union contract that gave the employees independent rights in determining their working and living conditions.[8]

By signing the contract and increasing the miners' salaries, Roche's company was able to attract the most skilled workers. As a consequence, the company's coal production increased, enabling it to survive during the bad economic times of the early 1930s. CF&I was less fortunate. In 1931 the company was placed in federal receivership. In 1933, after the majority of the miners voted in favor of an independent union, CF&I abandoned the Industrial Representation Plan and signed a collective-bargaining agreement with the UMWA.[9]

Mackenzie King's endeavor to get John D. Rockefeller Jr. more involved in the management of CF&I had succeeded.[10] After a successful tour of the company's properties in 1915, Rockefeller, accompanied by his wife and King and his wife, was back in southern Colorado in May 1918 to assess the company's progress in improving the miners' working and living conditions. On May 28, the first day of the tour, Mrs. Rockefeller urged them to visit the site of the former tent colony at Ludlow. When they arrived, they found a towering granite monument shrouded by a large silk American flag. Later in the day, King learned that UMWA officials planned to dedicate the monument on Memorial Day to commemorate those who had perished in the Ludlow Massacre.

The following day, King told Rockefeller that he should participate in the dedication ceremonies by addressing the crowd. At breakfast the next morning, which was the day of the ceremony, Rockefeller announced that he had concluded that it was right for him to go to Ludlow and that he would speak to the audience if given an opportunity to do so. Everyone in the party agreed with the decision, including Mrs. Rockefeller, who stated that she would accompany her husband. King contacted the union officials and helped Rockefeller prepare his remarks.

Although he learned that some union officials were opposed to his appearance at the ceremony, Rockefeller was still determined to go. He wanted to express his respect for the memory of those who had died four years ago during the unfortunate "disruption," as he now called it, and extend his sympathy to surviving relatives and friends of those who had

Ludlow Monument. Courtesy, author.

perished. He did not intend to talk about the past and would not apportion blame for the tragedy, although he would admit that mistakes had been
made. He wanted to assure the audience that everyone must work together

to prevent such tragic events from occurring again and express his hope that a new era had dawned in which capital and labor would cooperate in furthering the cause of liberty.

Despite the opposition of CF&I company officials, the Rockefellers and the Kings, accompanied by a driver, set out for Ludlow, where the ceremony had already begun. At the site, nearly 3,000 people were picnicking, visiting with friends, and listening to speakers who praised the miners and their families in various languages for the sacrifices they had endured during the great strike. More than one speaker congratulated the people for raising $12,000 from subscriptions ranging from 5 cents to $1 to build the monument, which was unveiled by Mary Petrucci, whose three children were among those who died in the Black Hole only a few feet away on that terrible day four years earlier. The unveiling of the twenty-foot monument with life-sized figures of a miner, a woman, and a child was the final act commemorating the "martyrs" of the Ludlow Massacre and the miners in their struggle against industrial feudalism.

Upon their arrival, the Rockefeller party parked on the road near the speakers' stand. While the Rockefellers remained in the car, King approached the stand and introduced himself to Frank Hayes, UMWA president. Former president John White and vice president William Green soon joined Hayes. King conveyed Rockefeller's wish to speak, but Hayes indicated that he and the other union officials were apprehensive about the reaction of those in the audience. They could not guarantee Rockefeller's safety and were reluctant to have him speak. Accepting this explanation, King invited Hayes and his colleagues to accompany him back to the car to greet Rockefeller. The union leaders refused. King returned to the car alone, and the party departed.

Whether Rockefeller went to Ludlow in an attempt to expiate his responsibility for the Ludlow Massacre or as a means to convince the miners that he was a champion of a new enlightened industrial relations policy is uncertain. From the evidence at hand, however, it seems the latter was his motive. He never accepted responsibility for the Ludlow Massacre or any of the other violence that occurred during the 1913–1914 strike. By not being allowed to speak at Ludlow, he achieved neither exoneration for his past deeds nor admiration for adopting a new industrial policy. Yet his visit to Ludlow on Memorial Day 1918 marked the final chapter in the story of the great strike and the Coalfield War of 1913–1914.

Osgood never regained his influence over the Colorado coal industry or the status he had enjoyed before the 1913–1914 strike. From all indications, his relations with many fellow operators and former allies turned acrimonious following the strike. An account of a verbal battle between Osgood and David Brown of the Rocky Mountain Fuel Company, reported in the *Denver Post* on April 7, 1915, captured the strained relations between the two former allies in the struggle against the UMWA. The incident occurred at the Denver Club and, according to the paper, was "still a topic of conversation among members of . . . one of this city's most exclusive organizations." The argument, the report continued,

> arose over acquisition of the Pennical mine by Osgood's company, a deal originally declined by Brown. Brown was much grieved to think he had allowed a good thing to escape, and in language that fairly reeked with disdain accused Osgood of having double-crossed him. Osgood's retort was just as vitriolic and for several moments the atmosphere of the sedate club was electrically charged. The lights were dimmed by blue hues of profanity and recriminations which poured from the lips of these two leaders of the coal industry. No casualties were reported and no ambulance was summoned.[11]

Osgood's confrontation with Brown was reminiscent of his earlier encounters with John Jerome over business matters. Jerome's and Mackenzie King's observations are the best extant accounts of Osgood's personality and character. They portray an ambitious man who was extremely self-confident, overbearing, and ruthless in pursuit of his interests. He was domineering and extremely dogmatic, and he became greatly agitated when opposed or confronted with a contrary point of view. His business success, Jerome charged, came at the expense of his closest associates, whose lives were ruined or severely harmed through his financial maneuvers. King believed Osgood, with his deeply flawed character, was the main source of the labor troubles that had plagued the coal industry in Colorado. With his intractable reactionary views, King concluded, Osgood could never have provided the leadership necessary to change the dynamics of the state's coalfields.

Osgood was dead by the time Rocky Mountain Fuel and CF&I, the two companies with which he had partnered to fight the UMWA, came to terms with the union. Osgood had spearheaded the struggle against the UMWA in Colorado, but that struggle effectively ended in 1917 when he signed a contract with the union. Although the contract lasted only three years, his company, the Victor-American Fuel Company, escaped the worst of the labor troubles that affected CF&I in 1919 and 1921. Residing mostly in New

York City and Europe, Osgood spent very little time in Colorado during the last decade of his life. Although he remained the principal owner of Victor-American, he turned operation of the company over to officials in Denver. But in August 1924, for reasons not entirely clear, he made a hurried trip to Denver to announce the resignations from the company of W. H. Huff, president; G. F. Bartlett, vice president and chair of the board of directors; and S. I. Heyn, secretary. Osgood announced that he would take over all three positions and actively manage the company's affairs. The change in personnel, he said, "meant only his giving to the business a closer personal consideration."[12]

With his resumption of complete control over the Victor-American Fuel Company, Osgood moved back to Colorado and reopened his country home at Redstone. The once thriving village and estate, the site of his ideological dream, now sat shuttered and virtually deserted. During 1925, Osgood and his third wife, Lucille, expended a considerable amount of money in an attempt to restore Redstone to its former glory. Workers were brought in and repairs were made. Activity returned to the village and estate. But time was too short for Osgood. Declining health forced him to resign as president of his company in late December. A few days later, on January 4, 1926, Osgood died of abdominal cancer at home in his beloved Cleveholm.

At the time of his death, Osgood was almost a forgotten man. His days of power and influence had ended. He was remembered at his funeral as a "benefactor to the underling," a man whose "idealism, amounting to a religion, forbade the existence of poverty and ugliness, where they could be replaced by him with a fair wage, provision for the widow of a deceased employe [sic], a garden spot with a vine-covered cottage. That to him was virtue."[13] But to union members, Osgood was a tyrannical villain. He was indeed an enigmatic man.

NOTES

1. McGovern and Guttridge, *Coalfield War,* 148.

2. John Reed, "The Colorado War," *Metropolitan* (July 1914): 13.

3. The description of the event is from Beshoar, *Out of the Depths,* 356–357.

4. Ibid., 357.

5. Reporter quoted in ibid., 359.

6. Doyle to Mr. and Mrs. Lee Champion, May 18, 1917, Doyle Papers, Box 1, FF 4.

7. The closest event to Ludlow was the so-called Columbine Massacre, which occurred on November 21, 1927, at the Rocky Mountain Fuel Company's Columbine

mine in the northern Colorado coalfield. On that date, state police killed 6 strikers and injured dozens more when they fired into a crowd of 400–500 strikers protesting the company's reopening of the mine.

8. McGovern and Guttridge, *Coalfield War*, 344.

9. Ibid., 342. For all practical purposes, the 1935 Wagner Act outlawed company unions, the heart of Rockefeller's Industrial Representation Plan.

10. Information for this section is from Gitelman, *Legacy of the Ludlow Massacre*, 241–245; Martelle, *Blood Passion*, 211–212; "Rockefeller, Jr., Attends Ludlow Shaft Unveiling," *Rocky Mountain News*, May 31, 1918.

11. *Denver Post*, April 7, 1915.

12. Osgood quoted in *Rocky Mountain News*, January 5, 1926.

13. *Denver Post*, January 7, 1926.

Bibliography

MANUSCRIPTS AND ARCHIVAL SOURCES

Colorado Historical Society, Denver, Colorado
    Colorado Fuel and Iron Company Papers
    John Lathrop Jerome Papers
    Jesse Floyd Welborn Papers
Colorado State Archives, Denver, Colorado
    Elias Ammons Papers
    James H. Peabody Papers
Denver Public Library, Western History Collection, Denver, Colorado
    Edward S. Doyle Papers
    Frank E. Gove, "Letter to the Newspaper Editors from the Legal Adviser of the Victor-American Fuel Company," September 27, 1913, MS

John R. Lawson Papers
John C. Osgood, "History of the Coal Strike in Colorado, 1913–1914," MS
Jesse F. Welborn, "Statement Regarding the Colorado Coal Strike, 1913–1914," MS
Las Animas County Courthouse, Trinidad, Colorado
District Court Cases
Library and Archives, Canada, Ottawa, Ontario
William Lyon Mackenzie King Diaries
Rockefeller Family Archives, Rockefeller Archive Center, Pocantico Hills, New York
IIC. Office of the Messrs. Rockefeller. Colorado Fuel & Iron Company Papers
University of Colorado at Boulder, Western Historical Collections, Boulder
Colorado State Federation of Labor Papers, *Proceedings of the Special Convention of the Colorado State Federation of Labor*, Denver, December 16, 1913
Link, Arthur S., ed. *The Papers of Woodrow Wilson*. Vols. 28–33. Princeton, N.J.: Princeton University Press, 1978

U.S. GOVERNMENT DOCUMENTS

U.S. Congress. *Congressional Record*. "The Strike in Colorado: Letter of Hon. Thomas M. Patterson." Washington, D.C.: Government Printing Office, June 12, 1914.
U.S. Congress, House. *Brief for the Striking Miners: Conditions in the Coal Mines of Colorado, Hearings before a Subcommittee of the Committee on Mines and Mining.* 63rd Cong., 2nd sess., 1914, pursuant to H. Res. 387.
———. Committee on Mines and Mining, *Report on the Colorado Strike Investigation*, made under H. Res. 387. 63rd Cong., 3rd sess., 1915, Doc. 1630.
———. *Brief of the Coal Mining Operators: Conditions in the Coal Mines of Colorado, Hearings before a Subcommittee of the Committee on Mines and Mining.* 63rd Cong., 2nd sess., 1914, pursuant to H. Res. 387.
———. *Conditions in the Coal Mines of Colorado, Hearings before a Subcommittee of the Committee on Mines and Mining.* 2 vols. 63rd Cong., 2nd sess., 1914, pursuant to H. Res. 387.
———. "Report of the Colorado Coal Commission on the Labor Difficulties in the Coal Fields of Colorado during the Years 1914 and 1915." In *Labor Difficulties in the Coal Fields of Colorado.* 64th Cong., 1st sess., 1916, Doc. 859.
———. *Report on the Colorado Strike Investigation.* In *Massacre at Ludlow: Four Reports.* Ed. Leon Stein and Philip Taft. New York: Arno and the *New York Times*, 1971.
U.S. Congress, Senate. *Final Report of the Commission on Industrial Relations, Including the Report of Basil M. Manly and the Individual Reports and Statements of the Several Commissioners.* 64th Cong., 1st sess., 1916, reprinted from Doc. 415.
———. *Industrial Relations: Final Report and Testimony Submitted to Congress by the Commission on Industrial Relations, Created by the Act of August 23, 1912.* 64th Cong., 1st sess., 1916, Doc. 415, 7–9.
West, George P. United States Commission on Industrial Relations. *Report on the Colorado Strike.* Washington, D.C.: U.S. Commission on Industrial Relations, 1915.

Wright, Carroll D. *A Report on Labor Disturbances in the State of Colorado, from 1880 to 1904, Inclusive, with Correspondence Relating Thereto.* Washington, D.C.: Government Printing Office, 1905.

COLORADO PUBLIC DOCUMENTS

Colorado Bureau of Labor Statistics. *Eighth Biennial Report of the Bureau of Labor Statistics of the State of Colorado, 1901–1902.* Denver: Smith-Brooks, 1902.

———. *Ninth Biennial Report of the Bureau of Labor Statistics of the State of Colorado, 1903–1904.* Denver: Smith-Brooks, 1904.

———. *Twelfth Biennial Report of the Bureau of Labor Statistics of the State of Colorado, 1909–1910.* Denver: Smith-Brooks, 1911.

———. *Thirteenth Biennial Report of the Bureau of Labor Statistics of the State of Colorado, 1911–1912.* Denver: Smith-Brooks, 1913.

———. *Fourteenth Biennial Report of the Bureau of Labor Statistics of the State of Colorado, 1913–1914.* Denver: Smith-Brooks, 1914.

Osgood, John C. *Statement before the House Committee on Mines and Mining.* Denver, February 16, 1903.

COMPANY REPORTS AND PUBLICATIONS

Coal Mine Managers. *Facts Concerning the Struggle in Colorado for Industrial Freedom.* Series I and II. Denver, 1914.

Colorado Fuel and Iron. *Annual Report of the Sociological Department of the CF&I for 1901–1902.* Denver, 1902.

———. *Annual Report of the Sociological Department of the CF&I for 1902–1903.* Denver, 1903.

———. *Annual Report of the Sociological Department of the CF&I for 1904–1905.* Denver, 1905.

———. *Camp and Plant (1901–1904).*

———. *Second Annual Report of the Colorado Fuel and Iron Company for the Year Ending June 30, 1894.* Denver, 1894.

NEWSPAPERS

Denver Daily News
Denver Express
Denver Post
Denver Republican
Denver Times
New York Times
Pueblo Chieftain
Pueblo Courier

Pueblo Labor Advocate
Pueblo Star-Journal
Rocky Mountain News
Trinidad Chronicle-News
Trinidad Daily News

ARTICLES AND CHAPTERS IN BOOKS

Allen, James B. "The Company-Owned Mining Town in the West: Exploitation or Benevolent Paternalism?" In *Reflections of Western Historians*. Ed. John A. Carroll. Tucson, Ariz.: University of Arizona Press, 1976, 177–197.

Ammons, Elias M. "The Colorado Strike." *North American Review* 200 (July 1914): 35–44.

Atkinson, Henry A. "Why the Miners Struck." *Harper's Weekly* 58 (May 23, 1914): 9–11.

Bowden, Witt. "New Developments in the Colorado Strike Situation." *The Survey* 31, no. 20 (February 14, 1914): 613–615.

———. "Two Alternatives in the Settlement of the Colorado Coal Strike." *The Survey* 31, no. 12 (December 20, 1913): 320–322.

"The Cause of the Colorado Strike." *Coal Age* 5, no. 26 (June 27, 1914): 1058.

"Collective Bargaining and Colorado." *The Survey* 33, no. 16 (January 16, 1915): 426–430.

"Colorado Editors Confer on Coal Strike." *The Survey* 31, no. 10 (December 6, 1913): 232.

Creel, George. "Poisoners of Public Opinion." *Harper's Weekly* 59 (November 14, 1914): 465–466.

Davis, W. T. "The Strike War in Colorado. I—The Story of the War. II—The Conditions in the Strike Region." *Outlook* 107 (May 9, 1914): 67–73.

Eastman, Max. "Class War in Colorado." *The Masses* 5 (June 1914): 5–9.

Fishback, Price V. "The Miner's Work Environment: Safety and Company Towns in the Early 1900s." In *The United Mine Workers of America: A Model of Industrial Solidarity?* Ed. John H.M. Laslett. University Park: Pennsylvania State University Press, 1996, 201–223.

Fitch, John A. "Law and Order: The Issue in Colorado." *The Survey* 33, no. 10 (December 5, 1914): 241–258.

———. "More Light on Colorado at the Last Industrial Hearing." *The Survey* 34, no. 10 (June 5, 1915): 212, 230, 232–235.

———. "Split in Policy between Rockefellers and Their Colorado Operators." *The Survey* 33, no. 14 (January 2, 1915): 350–352, 389.

———. "The Steel Industry and the People in Colorado." *The Survey* 27, no. 18 (February 3, 1913): 1706–1720.

———. "What Rockefeller Knew and What He Did." *The Survey* 34, no. 21 (August 21, 1915): 461–472.

————. "When Peace Comes to Colorado." *The Survey* 32, no. 8 (May 16, 1914): 205–206.

"Formal Statement Read by J. D. Rockefeller, Jr. before the U. S. Commission on Industrial Relations." *The Survey* 33, no. 19 (February 6, 1915): 480, 524–526.

Fuller, Leon W. "Colorado's Revolt against Capitalism." *Mississippi Valley Historical Review* 21, issue 3 (December 1934): 343–360.

Hoffman, F. L. "Problems of Labor and Life in Anthracite Coal Mining," *Engineering and Mining Journal* 74 (December 20, 1902): 811–812.

Lewis, Lawrence. "How One Corporation Helped Its Employees." *Engineering and Mining Journal* 83, no. 26 (June 29, 1907): 1233–1238.

Long, Priscilla. "The 1913–1914 Colorado Fuel and Iron Strike, with Reflections on the Causes of Coal-Strike Violence." In *The United Mine Workers of America: A Model of Industrial Solidarity?* Ed. John H.M. Laslett. University Park: Pennsylvania State University Press, 1996, 345–370.

————. "The Voice of the Gun: Colorado's Great Coalfield War of 1913–1914." *Labor's Heritage* 1, no. 4 (October 1989): 4–23.

Margolis, Eric. "Western Coal Mining as a Way of Life: An Oral History of the Colorado Coal Miners to 1914." *Journal of the West* 24, no. 3 (July 1985): 1–115.

McGregor, [no first name given]. "The Way Rockefeller Looks at It." *Harper's Weekly* 58 (May 23, 1914): 12–13.

"Mr. Rockefeller in Colorado." *Outlook* 111 (October 13, 1915): 345–346.

Mulnix, Michael William. "The Story of Cleveholm Manor." Redstone, Colo.: Morrison's Nostalgia Shop Antiques, n.d.

Porter, Eugene O. "The Colorado Coal Strike of 1913—an Interpretation." *The Historian* 12 (Autumn 1949): 3–27.

"President's Colorado Committee Unwelcome." *The Survey* 33 (February 27, 1915): 571–572.

Reed, John. "The Colorado War." *Metropolitan* (July 1914): 11–16, 66–72.

"The Rockefeller Plan." *The Survey* 35, no. 3 (October 16, 1915): 72–75.

Scamehorn, H. Lee. "John C. Osgood and the Western Steel Industry." *Arizona and the West* 15 (Summer 1973): 133–148.

"Southern Colorado Coal Strike." *Outlook* 106 (January 3, 1914): 24–26.

"Statement of Colorado Operators." *Coal Age* 5, no. 19 (May 9, 1914): 775–776.

Strong, Josiah. "What Social Service Means: A Clearing House of Experience in Social and Industrial Betterment." *Craftsman* 9 (February 1906): 620–633.

Suggs, George G., Jr. "The Colorado Coal Miners' Strike, 1903–1904: A Prelude to Ludlow?" *Journal of the West* 12 (January 1973): 36–52.

Talbot, Elisha Hollingsworth. "Editorial Notes." *The Great West* 1, no. 3 (December 1896): 279–280.

Weed, Frank J. "The Sociological Department at the Colorado Fuel and Iron Company, 1901–1907: Scientific Paternalism and Industrial Control." *Journal of the History of the Behavioral Sciences* 41 (Summer 2005): 269–284.

BOOKS

Adams, Graham, Jr. *Age of Industrial Violence, 1910–15: The Activities and Findings of the United States Commission on Industrial Relations.* New York: Columbia University Press, 1966.

Allen, James B. *The Company Town in the American West.* Norman: University of Oklahoma Press, 1966.

Barton, Holly. *Cokedale, 1907–1947.* Trinidad, Colo.: Las Animas County Centennial-Bicentennial Committee, 1976.

Beshoar, Barron B. *Out of the Depths: The Story of John R. Lawson, a Labor Leader.* Denver: Golden Bell, 1942.

Brandes, Stuart. *American Welfare Capitalism, 1880–1940.* Chicago: University of Chicago Press, 1976.

Brody, David. *Workers in Industrial America: Essays on the Twentieth Century Struggle.* New York: Oxford University Press, 1980.

Clyne, Rick. *Coal People: Life in Southern Colorado's Company Towns, 1890–1930.* Denver: Colorado Historical Society, 1999.

Craig, James C. *The History of the Strike That Brought the Citizens' Alliance of Denver, Colorado into Existence.* Reprinted from *George's Weekly.* Denver, July 4, 1903.

Dawson, R. MacGregor. *William Lyon Mackenzie King: A Political Biography, 1874–1923.* Toronto: University of Toronto Press, 1958.

Eberhart, Perry. *Guide to the Colorado Ghost Towns and Mining Camps.* Chicago: Sage Books, 1974.

Fosdick, Raymond B. *John D. Rockefeller, Jr.: A Portrait.* New York: Harper & Row, 1956.

Fowler, Gene. *A Solo in Tom-Toms.* New York: Viking, 1946.

Fox, Maier B. *United We Stand: The United Mine Workers of America 1890–1990.* Washington, D.C.: United Mine Workers of America, 1990.

Gitelman, Howard M. *The Legacy of the Ludlow Massacre: A Chapter in American Industrial Relations.* Philadelphia: University of Pennsylvania Press, 1988.

Goodstein, Phil. *Denver from the Bottom Up.* Volume One: *From Sand Creek to Ludlow.* Denver: New Social Publications, 2003.

Green, Marguerite. *The National Civic Federation and the American Labor Movement.* Washington, D.C.: Catholic University of America, 1956.

Josephson, Matthew. *The Robber Barons.* New York: Harcourt Brace, 1934.

Keating, Edward. *The Gentleman from Colorado: A Memoir.* Denver: Sage Books, 1964.

Kelly, Marjorie. *The Divine Right of Capital: Dethroning the Corporate Aristocracy.* San Francisco: Berrett-Koehler, 2001.

Kenney, Norma. *The Hidden Place Redstone.* Carbondale, Colo.: Redstone Press, 1992.

Long, Priscilla. *Where the Sun Never Shines: A History of America's Bloody Coal Industry.* New York: Paragon House, 1989.

Martelle, Scott. *Blood Passion: The Ludlow Massacre and Class War in the American West.* New Brunswick, N.J.: Rutgers University Press, 2007.

McCartin, Joseph A. *Labor's Great War: The Struggle for Industrial Democracy and the Origins of Modern Labor Relations, 1912–1921*. Chapel Hill: University of North Carolina Press, 1997.

McGovern, George S., and Leonard F. Guttridge. *The Great Coalfield War*. Boston: Houghton Mifflin, 1972.

Meakin, Budgett. *Model Factories and Villages: Ideal Conditions of Labour and Housing*. London: T. F. Unwin, 1905.

Mechau, Vaughn. *Redstone on the Crystal*. Denver: Westerners Brand Book, 1948.

Nelson, Daniel. *Managers and Workers: Origins of the New Factory System in the United States 1880–1920*. Madison: University of Wisconsin Press, 1975.

Nelson, Jim. *Marble and Redstone: A Quick History*. Fort Collins, Colo.: FirstLight, 1968.

Papanikolas, Zeese. *Buried Unsung: Louis Tikas and the Ludlow Massacre*. Salt Lake City: University of Utah Press, 1982.

Parton, Mary Field, ed. *The Autobiography of Mother Jones*. Chicago: Charles H. Kerr, 1972.

Robbins, William G. *Colony and Empire: The Capitalist Transformation of the American West*. Lawrence: University of Kansas Press, 1994.

Rottenberg, Dan. *In the Kingdom of Coal: An American Family and the Rock That Changed the World*. New York: Routledge, 2003.

Ruland, Sylvia. *The Lion of Redstone*. Boulder: Johnson Books, 1981.

Sampson, Joanna. *Remember Ludlow*. Denver: Colorado Historical Society, 1999.

Scamehorn, H. Lee. *Mill and Mine: The CF&I in the Twentieth Century*. Lincoln: University of Nebraska Press, 1992.

———. *Pioneer Steelmaker in the West: The Colorado Fuel and Iron Company, 1872–1903*. Boulder: Pruett, 1976.

Selekman, Benjamin M., and Mary Van Kleeck. *Employees' Representation in Coal Mines: A Study of the Industrial Representation Plan of the Colorado Fuel and Iron Company*. New York: Russell Sage Foundation, 1924.

Suggs, George G., Jr. *Colorado's War on Militant Unionism: James H. Peabody and the Western Federation of Miners*. Detroit: Wayne State University Press, 1972.

Tolman, William H. *Social Engineering: A Record of Things Done by American Industrialists Employing Upwards of One and One-Half Million People*. New York: McGraw, 1909.

Tone, Andrea. *The Business of Benevolence: Industrial Paternalism in Progressive America*. Ithaca, N.Y.: Cornell University Press, 1997.

Weinstein, James. *The Corporate Ideal in the Liberal State, 1900–1918*. Boston: Beacon, 1968.

Whiteside, James. *Regulating Danger: The Struggle for Mine Safety in the Rocky Mountain Coal Industry*. Lincoln: University of Nebraska Press, 1990.

Whittaker, Milo Lee. *Pathbreakers and Pioneers of the Pueblo Region*. Pueblo, Colo.: Franklin, 1917.

Wolff, David. *Industrializing the Rockies: Growth, Competition, and Turmoil in the Coalfields of Colorado and Wyoming, 1868–1914*. Boulder: University Press of Colorado, 2003.

Wright, Gwendolyn. *Building the Dream: A Social History of Housing in America*. New York: Pantheon Books, 1981.

THESES AND DISSERTATIONS

Andrews, Thomas G. "The Road to Ludlow: Work, Environment, and Industrialization in Southern Colorado, 1870–1915." Ph.D. diss., University of Wisconsin–Madison, 2003.

Boemeke, Manfred F. "The Wilson Administration, Organized Labor, and the Colorado Coal Strike, 1913–1914." Ph.D. diss., Princeton University, 1983.

Lonsdale, David L. "The Movement for an Eight-Hour Law in Colorado, 1893–1913." Ph.D. diss., University of Colorado–Boulder, 1963.

McClurg, Donald Joseph. "Labor Organization in the Coal Mines of Colorado, 1878–1933." Ph.D. diss., University of California at Los Angeles, 1959.

McGovern, George S. "The Colorado Coal Strike, 1913–1914." Ph.D. diss., Northwestern University, 1953.

Wilson, Howard K. "A Study of Paternalism in the Colorado Fuel and Iron Company under John C. Osgood: 1892–1903." M.A. thesis, University of Denver, 1967.

Index

CPSIA information can be obtained at www.ICGtesting.com

227368LV00003B/2/P

9 781607 321002